The

ISLAMIST CHALLENGE

in

ALGERIA

A Political History

The
ISLAMIST CHALLENGE
in
ALGERIA

A Political History

MICHAEL WILLIS

NEW YORK UNIVERSITY PRESS
Washington Square, New York

Published by Ithaca Press / Garnet Publishing Ltd (UK) in 1996

First published in the U.S.A. in 1997 by
NEW YORK UNIVERSITY PRESS
Washington Square
New York, N.Y. 10003

Printed in Lebanon

Library of Congress Cataloging-in-Publication Data
Willis, Michael.
    The Islamist Challenge in Algeria : a political history / Michael Willis.
        p.   cm.
    Originally published: Berkshire, U.K. : Ithaca Press. 1996.
    Based on the author's Ph.D. thesis.
    Includes bibliographical references (p.   ) and index.

    ISBN 0–8147–9328–2
    1. Algeria—Politics and government.
    2. Islam and politics—Algeria. I. Title.
DT295.5.W56 1997
965.05—dc21

                                                            97–2756
                                                               CIP

Contents

Acknowledgements

I have been fortunate enough to have received the help and advice of a large number of different people and organisations during the research and writing of both this book and the Ph.D. thesis on which it is based. All deserve thanks, but there are several to whom I am particularly grateful.

The idea for the project was originally given to me by Simon Fraser of the Foreign and Commonwealth Office whose prediction of the growing importance of Maghrebi and particularly Algerian Islamism has proved extremely prescient. The early backing I received from Christopher Clapham at Lancaster University was important in launching the project as well as instrumental in helping me to secure funding for the research. In this context I am thankful to the Economic and Social Research Council (ESRC) for granting me a three-year research studentship, without which research for this book would not have been possible.

In the course of gathering information and ideas for my research I am especially grateful to Hugh Roberts for his valuable time, advice and suggestions; to John Shipman and Azzam Tamimi for their advice on contacts; and to Avril Shields, Margaret Greenhalgh, Jim House and Delphine Tempé for help with provision of sources. The staff at both the Institut de Recherches et Etudes sur le Monde Arabe et Musulman (IREMAM) in Aix-en-Provence and at the Centre de Documentation National in Tunis are deserving of thanks for their help and patience.

The increasingly violent and uncertain climate in Algeria has produced an understandable reluctance on the part of many people connected with Algeria to speak openly about developments. I therefore owe a considerable debt of gratitude to those people who were willing to talk about their direct experiences and express their opinions to me, all of which have provided me with invaluable insights. Many people spoke to me under the necessary condition of anonymity but of those I am able to acknowledge explicitly I am particularly thankful to Abdelhamid Brahimi, Rachid Ghannoushi, Rabah Kebir, Abdallah Djaballah, Hussein Amin, Adel Hussein and Ibrahim El-Bayoumi Ghanem for their uniform helpfulness and courtesy. I hope that I have represented their views and statements fairly and accurately.

Other appreciations go to everyone at the Centre for Middle Eastern and Islamic Studies at Durham University, including Mustafa

Hogga, Anoush Ehteshami and Emma Murphy; Faisal Ajami for his invaluable help at a number of important points; and George Joffé and Suha Taji-Farouki for their valuable comments and corrections. Thanks also go to Lara Marlow, Essam Al-Frian and Robin Lamb.

Lastly, and most importantly, I thank firstly Tim Niblock, who supervised my original research, for his patience, encouragement and perseverance during the preparation of my Ph.D. thesis; and secondly my parents, Ann and Brian, for being willing to act as proofreaders for the final typescript and for giving their unwavering support to this project from start to finish.

Abbreviations

AIS   Armée Islamique du Salut (Islamic Salvation Army)

ANP   Armée Nationale Populaire (People's National Army)

APC   Assemblée Populaire Communale (Popular Communal Assembly)

APN   Assemblée Populaire et Nationale (National Popular Assembly)

APW   Assemblée Populaire de Wilaya (Popular *Wilaya* Assembly)

AUMA   Association d'Ulama Musulman Algérien (Association of Algerian Muslim Ulama)

BEC   Bureaux Executifs de Communaux (Executive Offices of the Communes)

BEN   Bureau Executif National (National Executive Office)

BEP   Bureau Executif Provisoire (Provisional Executive Bureau)

BEW   Bureaux Executifs de Wilaya (Executive Offices of the *Wilaya*)

CCN   Conseil Consultatif National (National Consultative Council)

FFS   Front des Forces Socialistes (Socialist Forces Front)

FIS   Front Islamique du Salut (Islamic Salvation Front)

FLN   Front de Libération Nationale (National Liberation Front)

GIA   Groupes Islamiques Armées (Armed Islamic Groups)

GPRA   Gouvernement Provisoire de la République Algérienne (Provisional Government of the Algerian Republic)

HAMAS   Harakat al-Mujtama al-Islamiyya (Movement of the Islamic Society)

HCE   Haut Comité d'Etat (High State Council)

LADH   Ligue Algérienne des Droits de l'Homme (Algerian Human Rights League)

MAIA   Mouvement Algérien Islamique Armée (Algerian Armed Islamic Movement) see also MIA

MAJD   Mouvement Algérien pour la Justice et le Développement (Algerian Movement for Justice and Development)

MDA   Mouvement pour la Démocratie en Algérie (Movement for Democracy in Algeria)

MIA   Mouvement Islamique Armée (Armed Islamic Movement) see also MAIA

MNI   Mouvement de la Nahda Islamique (Islamic Renaissance Movement)

PAGS   Parti de l'Avant-Garde Socialiste (Progressive Socialist Party)

PPA   Parti du Peuple Algérien (Algerian People's Party)

PNSD   Parti National pour la Solidarité et le Développement (National Party for Solidarity and Development)

PRA   Parti du Renouveau Algérien (Party of Algerian Renewal)

PSD   Parti Social-Démocrate (Social Democratic Party)

RCD   Rassemblement pour la Culture et la Démocratie (Rally for Culture and Democracy)

RPN   Rassemblement Patriotique National (National Patriotic Rally)

SIT   Syndicat Islamique du Travail (Islamic Labour Union)

UGTA   Union Générale des Travailleurs Algériens (General Union of Algerian Workers)

Glossary[1]

colons	European inhabitants of Algeria under colonial rule
fatwa	Official ruling on a point of Islamic law
hadj	Islamic pilgrimage to Mecca
hedjab	'Islamic' women's clothing
ijtihad	Independent reasoning or interpretation of the Quran and the Hadith
jihad	Struggle for Islam. Often implies 'holy war'
Mahdi	Awaited divinely guided figure, who will lead Muslims to Islamic righteousness
majlis shura	Consultative council
mujahidin	'Warriors for Islam'
rai	Popular Algerian fusion of traditional and modern music
sharia	Islamic law
shura	consultation
tariqa	Sufi brotherhood
umma	The Islamic nation
wilaya	Administrative departments (province)

---

1 No systematic form of transliteration has been followed throughout this book with regard to Arabic words. Instead, the most common or recognised spelling and form have been adopted. The use of French variations has frequently been preferred for reasons of wanting to stay consistent with most of the other main sources.

Introduction

There can be few countries in the world that have undergone as dramatic a series of upheavals and convulsions over the last decade as Algeria. Many states, notably those in Eastern Europe and the former Soviet Union, have experienced huge changes over this period but none, with the dismal exception of the former Yugoslavia, has witnessed the same levels of violence that have accompanied the changes that have occurred in Algeria. In less than ten years, Algeria has been transformed from what appeared from the outside to be one of the most stable, if politically austere, states in both Africa and the Arab world into a country feared by its neighbours as a source of huge instability – a state torn apart by political and armed conflict which had claimed over 50,000 lives by 1996.

Algeria's particular path to internal chaos was remarkable for its incorporation of an element largely unseen in the Arab world. From the late 1980s it had been the scene of a remarkable political experiment. Seemingly overnight from 1988 Algeria's rulers shifted the political basis of the country from being a classic one-party state to one which not only tolerated the formation of competing political parties but which allowed such parties to participate in some of the most genuinely unfettered elections for political office that the Arab world had ever witnessed. It was the forced closure of this political opening in 1992, barely three years after it had been created, that precipitated the violence that was to claim so many lives over the following four years.

At the centre of this whole political drama was a political force that had been brought dramatically to the fore during Algeria's startlingly rapid period of political change and whose presence was the foremost factor in explaining both the ending of the experiment with liberal politics and the violent conflict which followed it. The rise to prominence of a movement which had the religion of Islam as its core ideological base was not a development unique to Algeria. Most countries across the Muslim and Arab worlds had seen over recent decades the rise of movements which shared a common belief in the need to transform Muslim states and societies on the basis of a rereading of the sacred texts of Islam. This phenomenon of Islamic fundamentalism (as it became popularly known) or political Islam or Islamism (as most academic observers preferred to term it) attracted huge international attention by the 1980s as elements of this loosely linked movement came variously to assassinate the President of Egypt, dominate the politics of Lebanon and, most dramatically of all, establish an "Islamic Republic" on the back of a popular revolution in Iran.

Much was written about these and other events, often predicting the eventual domination of the entire Muslim world by Islamist movements. The various and varied Islamist groups, organisations and political parties that emerged in virtually every Muslim state were studied and analysed as the basis of future possible governments, particularly as Islamists became the main opposition force to many existing governments. The powerful and popular Islamist movements of Egypt, Syria, Lebanon and more latterly, the Israeli-occupied Palestinian territories, attracted particularly close scrutiny. Less attention was naturally drawn to those states where Islamist movements were less prominent and whose activities appeared to pose no immediate challenge to the ruling order. It was therefore somewhat ironic that it was one of these latter states, Algeria, that appeared to develop in almost a matter of months in the early 1990s the most visibly popular and vibrant Islamist movement anywhere in the Muslim world. Moreover, with the opening up of Algeria's hitherto closed political system this movement seemed to enjoy an almost unparalleled opportunity to exercise real political power through participation in elections.

The meteoric rise of Algeria's Islamists prompted a natural desire on the part of observers both within and outside Algeria to seek explanations for this development and its implications. The problem of the relative lack of literature dealing with Algeria's Islamists before their explosion onto the political scene in the late 1980s was compounded by the extremely rapid pace of events inside Algeria after this point. Chronicling contemporary developments became as important as searching for historically rooted explanations. Moreover, the rise of Islamism was just one, albeit increasingly central, part of the wider political changes sweeping Algeria at this time and which were equally deserving of attention. Political liberalisation had raised a huge number of important issues and unleashed a vast array of other political forces all of which had a bearing on developments. However, as the 1990s developed and as Algeria's dramatic series of events unfolded, the deficit of information on Algeria began to be made up through a fresh wave of academic studies, media reports and eventually full-length books.

This book aims to draw together these newly emerged sources, as well as others, into a single framework in the hope of constructing a more extended and comprehensive view of developments in Algeria. Whilst Algeria itself and France, as Algeria's former colonial master, has now produced a sizeable amount of literature on both recent developments and the Islamists, the English-speaking world is still in need of more, particularly book-length, studies on contemporary Algeria.

The chosen focus of this book is the Algerian Islamist movement itself. By concentrating on this theme I hope to provide not only an explanation of the origins and development of Islamism in Algeria, but I also aim to cast some light on the complex series of events that have befallen Algeria as a whole, particularly since the late 1980s, and in which the Islamists played an increasingly central and inextricable role. In this way the study focuses, as the title indicates, on the challenge Algerian Islamism has made to Algeria's rulers not just over recent years, but in an historical context as well. The attitude and response to Islamism by governments ranging from the French colonial administration through to those constituted after the abandonment of elections in 1992 is examined to provide an overall picture of the political role and impact of the movement.

The need to understand the roots and background of Algerian Islamism is behind the decision to adopt a specifically historical and chronological approach to the subject. Most existing studies, particularly in France, have concentrated on thematic issues. However, there remains a place and need for a more detailed historical chronology of events which can illustrate more developmental features as well as, hopefully, providing a factual source base for more theoretical and conceptual studies. The study is an explicitly *political* history since it concentrates on the political dynamics of the Islamist movement and its relationship with the Algerian state. The ideas, statements and platforms of Algeria's Islamists over time are examined, as are the social bases of support they have succeeded in attracting. However, a truly detailed and methodical study of the specifically intellectual and social aspects of the movement does not fall within the scope of this book. These aspects have been covered very ably by a number of other writers and academics.[1]

---

1 For more comprehensive treatments of intellectual and social aspects of Algerian Islamism see notably the works of Ali Merad, Abderrahim Lamchichi, Lahouari Addi, and Luis Martinez listed in the bibliography.

The book is divided into eight chronologically defined chapters. The opening chapter charts the origins and precursors of the Islamist movement as it emerged during the long period of French colonial rule. It looks at how the movement found its first modern institutional expression in the Association of Algerian Ulama and how this Association became increasingly involved in and contributed to the Algerian national struggle against France, culminating in the war for independence of 1954–62. Chapter Two studies how the movement fared in the new Algerian state and how it was substantially marginalised by the new leaders of Algeria through co-option and repression, particularly during Houari Boumedienne's thirteen-year presidency between 1965 and 1978. The third chapter examines developments in the decade following Boumedienne's death, how the movement began to grow in strength and influence whilst still being kept in check by the state. Chapters Four, Five and Six deal with the birth and legal life of the Front Islamique du Salut which became the main vehicle for Islamist activism and demands following the decision by the regime to politically liberalise after severe civil unrest and upheaval in October 1988. They detail how the creation and direction of the FIS was not unanimously endorsed by senior figures in the movement, but also show how and why the party became far and away the most popular and influential new political party in Algeria. The response of the regime to the FIS's emergence and success is considered and the extent to which this contributed to the remarkable advances the party made. The decision by certain elements within the Algerian regime to end the period of political liberalisation and thus forestall the accession of the FIS to national political power in 1992 is also explored and explained. The final two chapters concern themselves with the course of the Islamist movement following the formal dissolution of the FIS by the authorities in March 1992, how it reorganised itself, how elements of it entered into increasingly bloody armed struggle with the regime and how various parts of it attempted to solve the conflict either through dialogue with the authorities or through the pursuit of military victory. Internecine disputes and even conflicts within the movement during this period are also charted. Throughout the study four broad areas are routinely, if unsystematically, looked at in the context of the general history of the movement. The movement's ideology, bases of support and external influences are considered, as is the attitude and response to the movement of the various colonial and post-independence regimes that have governed Algeria.

Although the contents of the bibliography to this book hopefully speak for themselves, a further word about sources and information is necessary. A main aim of this book was to draw together most of the existing writings and sources on Algeria and its Islamist movement. A deliberately eclectic approach was adopted in the hope of synthesising a wide range of material in order to produce as comprehensive a study as possible. Nevertheless, it should be stated that particularly heavy use has been made of a number of secondary sources whose ideas and material (where not consistently acknowledged in either the text or notes) I would not want to take the credit for. This list includes most notably: all the works listed in the bibliography under Hugh Roberts; Abed Charef's *Algérie: Le Grand Dérapage* and François Burgat and William Dowell's *The Islamic Movement in North Africa*. I was also fortunate enough to consult a copy of Séverine Labat's recently published *Les Islamistes Algériens* shortly before the completion of this book.

A second point that needs to be made with regard to sources is the potentially awkward issues confronted when attempting to write about events that have occurred a relatively short time ago. This problem is particularly acute in Algeria's case since the increasing violence and political uncertainty within Algeria since 1992 has made the gathering of direct and reliable material very difficult. Not only are there the practical problems of gaining access to information, but, more importantly, there is the need to be aware that a bitter conflict of the sort that has raged inside Algeria since 1992 produces a desire on all sides to portray events in a manner that is most supportive of their particular viewpoint. Such a climate raises questions of "balance" and objectivity of anyone seeking to explain developments and the extent to which fair coverage is given to differing views and standpoints. Whilst I would not claim, nor wish, to give exactly equal attention and credence to every section of opinion on the debate, I have attempted to look at as wide a cross-section of views and writings as is feasible. Consequently, my bibliography includes both literature produced by the FIS in exile as well as Algerian newspapers notoriously hostile to the Islamist movement. My interviewees included both members of and sympathisers with the Islamist movement, alongside figures who are, by contrast, critical and profoundly wary of the movement's nature and agenda. The only "axes" I, personally, have to "grind" in relation to Algeria are, firstly, a desire to see the provision of the most accurate portrayal of events; and secondly, a wish for a just and peaceful solution to be found to the depressing cycle of violence and decline in which Algeria has become locked.

1

Origins: Resistance, Reformism and Nationalism, 1830–1962

Algeria as a state in the modern sense has only formally existed since it famously wrested independence from France in 1962. Under both the French and the Ottomans (whose rule had preceded that of France), however, the country had enjoyed a recognised geographic and administrative identity. Even before these periods of lengthy foreign domination, the huge area of the central Maghreb occupied by present-day Algeria had had a distinct and varied history. It was a history that was marked by the ebb and flow of many empires and kingdoms but one that, in common with most of the surrounding region, was dramatically and indelibly changed and influenced by the arrival of the religion of Islam.[1]

Insurrection and Resistance, 1830–1871

Background: Islam and Algeria
Islam first arrived in the part of North Africa now occupied by the modern state of Algeria in the second half of the seventh century. North Africa, like much of the Levant, Asia and eventually parts of southern Europe, became part of the remarkable series of conquests achieved by armies fanning out from the Arabian peninsula in this period. The new faith these Arab armies brought with them, Islam, founded on the powerful visions and teachings of the Prophet Muhammad, had effectively

---

1 A number of studies exist relating the early history of both Algeria and the Maghreb generally examining this history in far greater detail than can be given here. See for example Charles-André Julien, *History of North Africa: Tunisia, Algeria, Morocco* (London, Routledge and Kegan Paul, 1970); Jamil Abun-Nasr, *A History of the Maghreb in the Islamic Period* (Cambridge, Cambridge University Press, 1987).

established itself under Arab rule by about AD 710. The speed and depth of the acceptance of the new religion was underlined by the fact that although Arab rule was fiercely resisted by the indigenous, mainly Berber, population of north-west Africa, Islam became and remained the almost exclusively dominant religion of the region. The resistance to Arab rule, some of the fiercest encountered by Arab armies, did, however, partly explain the subsequent embracing by the Berbers of the Kharijite schism of Islam as part of their rebellion against their more religiously orthodox Arab masters in the early part of the eighth century. The more ascetic and egalitarian doctrines of Kharijism provided an attractive, as well as dissident, rallying point for the rebellion. The Kharijite Berber kingdoms established in the wake of the rebellions, although lasting several centuries, were eventually to disappear and Kharijite practices persisted only in small peripheral communities. Nevertheless, it is argued that these and other historical developments were to give Maghrebi Islam an importantly heterodox complexion even after the orthodox Maliki school of Islamic jurisprudence came to predominate in the region.

The most visible indications of this heterodoxy could be seen in the emergence, persistence and importance of various manifestations of what was broadly termed "popular Islam" in the region. This "popular Islam", which did not explicitly dissent from orthodox Islam, ranged from the variety of Sufi brotherhoods and orders (*tariqas*) present in the Maghreb through to the more unorthodox marabouts or "living saints". The Sufis, with their emphasis on the more mystic expressions and experiences of Islam, and maraboutism, which involved veneration of the lives and deeds of certain individual Muslims supposedly blessed with divine grace (*baraka*), together gave a less scripturalist and orthodox dimension and hue to Islam in the Maghreb. More tangibly, the Sufi tariqas, in particular, through their series of informal structures and networks, acted as mediators between localised Maghrebi society and the succession of different rulers the region witnessed over the centuries. Such a role for the Sufi brotherhoods was another more peculiar feature of Maghrebi Islam, Sufism elsewhere in the Muslim world playing a far more quietist and less activist part in society. In times of particular popular grievance with the ruling order, the tariqas and the other elements of "popular Islam" actually supplied the organisational basis and leadership of resistance to the authorities. The most prominent latter example of this came with the revolts that occurred under the reign of the Ottoman

Turks (who had dominated the central Maghreb region since the early sixteenth century) during the opening decades of the nineteenth century and which were in reaction to increasing tax burdens being imposed on the local populations by the Ottoman administration.

The maraboutist and Sufi-led revolts against the Ottomans were soon to be eclipsed by events of far greater significance. The arrival of nearly forty thousand French troops on the coast of Algeria in June 1830 signalled the beginning of an incursion into Algerian history as dramatic and far-reaching in its impact as the arrival of the Muslim Arab conquerors nearly 1,100 years earlier. The effect of the French presence in Algeria was to be direct, through the processes of colonisation and imperial rule, and near absolute over the next 130 years, leaving a legacy that was to be still deceptively pervasive even after Algeria had achieved its independence.

Resistance and capitulation on the part of the native Algerian population both played their parts in early reactions to the French take-over of various parts of Algeria, but it was the tariqas that once again organised and led the most significant opposition to the French in the early years of their presence in Algeria. However, whilst the revolts against the Ottomans had been against fellow Muslims, the significance of the resistance against the French was that it pitted Muslim against non-believer.

Abd al-Qadir's revolt

At the forefront of the resistance to the French was the movement led by Amir Abd al-Qadir. A member of the important Qadiriyya Sufi order which had played a leading role in the revolts against the Ottomans, Abd al-Qadir led a revolt that lasted for fifteen years from his election as Amir of the tribes of the western province of Oran in 1832 to his final defeat by and capitulation to the French in 1847. His revolt was significant for three reasons. Firstly, it was far and away the most successful campaign of resistance to the French. Secondly, Abd al-Qadir founded and ran an independent native Algerian state, for several years ruling over a substantial part of the territory covered by modern Algeria. Thirdly, and most important of all, Abd al-Qadir conducted his war against the French and organised his nascent state under the banner of Islam, explicitly stressing throughout the *religious* motivations for his struggle against the French and for the establishment of his independent state.

The importance of Islam in the struggle against the French was almost inevitable since it was difficult to conceive of any other framework in which resistance to the Christian invader could be so effectively mobilised. Nevertheless, it was certainly the case that Abd al-Qadir specifically emphasised Islam in his campaign. Abd al-Qadir's specific use of the term "Amir" derived from the fuller title *Amir al-Muminin* (Commander of the Believers), was indicative of the Islamic context in which he both clothed and conducted his struggle and was used in preference to other less religious titles he could have assumed. His use also of the term *jihad* to characterise his campaign against the French was clearly much more than the expedient rallying cry of previous conflicts. This was underlined by his requesting of *fatwas* from the ulama at Fez in 1837 on a number of issues relating to the conflict. In the state he briefly presided over, set up following a temporary truce with the French in 1837, the application of *sharia* law became an important part of Abd al-Qadir's rule there; the Amir believing that every Muslim within the areas he controlled should be subject to its prescriptions. Hence alcohol, tobacco and gambling were prohibited and prostitution and homosexuality suppressed. Similarly, soldiers in his army were obliged to be as devoted as their commander was in performing the set of five daily prayers of the devout Muslim.

The period of peace with the French lasted just two brief years before conflict was once more resumed in 1839, this time resulting in the final defeat of Abd al-Qadir and his forces in 1847 and the end of what might be termed the first independent Algerian state.

The precise nature of the campaign and fledgling political entity has been argued over by historians of this period of Algeria's history; points of issue concerning the extent to which the Amir was a proto-Algerian nationalist, a genuine religious zealot or simply a traditional opportunist who sought to use religious symbols and language to establish some form of political hegemony over Algeria's varied and divided population. Whilst opportunism undoubtedly played its part, there can be no mistaking the genuinely *religious* nature and intent of much of Abd al-Qadir's period of influence. Islam and freedom from French domination became essentially inseparable notions for most Algerians during this time. The exigencies of politics frequently pushed Abd al-Qadir into compromises and expediencies that were not necessarily strictly related to Islam and the sharia but such actions could often be seen as serving the greater goal of preserving his fiefdom and with it the unhindered practice of Islam within it.[2]

Other revolts and movements, 1845–1871

Abd al-Qadir, whilst the most prominent, was not the only element of resistance to the French that leaned heavily on Islam for its inspiration and orientation. Whilst active opposition in Algeria's large towns was mainly aimed at defending the established Ottoman-constructed social and political order, resistance in the country's smaller towns and rural areas invariably took on a much more religious form. From the 1840s a number of revolts occurred that were led by individuals who claimed religious inspiration. In 1845 a serious insurrection developed in the Dahra mountains led by a young charismatic figure, Bou Maza or the "Goat Man", who proclaimed himself to be the Mahdi come to lead and deliver Algeria's Muslims at the apocalypse. A number of smaller successor movements, invariably Mahdist in inspiration, sprung up in the wake of this uprising which was finally crushed in 1847. The most notable of these was that led by Bu Ziyan who claimed to have had visions from the Prophet Muhammad telling him that he was the Mahdi and who enjoyed considerable support in Ziban, Aurès and Hodna before his eventual defeat in 1849. The last significant uprising against the French in this period took place in 1871. Sparked by economic hardship and famine, and encouraged by the defeat of the French Second Empire in Europe, the revolt once again was spearheaded by religious elements – this time the important Rahmaniyya Sufi Brotherhood whose support had been solicited by the revolt's leader, Muhammad al-Hajj al-Muqrani. Some historians have viewed the assumption by al-Muqrani of the title of *Amir al-Mujahidin* (leader of the holy warriors) and his proclamation of jihad as pure personal opportunism, but there is little doubt that

---

2   Critics of Abd al-Qadir's portrayal as an exclusively Islamic leader point to, for example, his willingness to cede Muslim-held land to the French as part of the truce he signed at Tafna with them and which allowed him to form his "state". This was seen as theologically inconsistent with the jihad he had proclaimed against the French. Similarly his continued use of non-Islamic courts and legal officials to administer secular law, alongside Islamic judges or *qadis,* in the areas he controlled was likewise seen as incompatible with his stated intent of creating a state founded on *sharia* law.

the widespread support the revolt attracted was the result of al-Muqrani's ability to use the mobilising power of Islam. However, despite this significant popular support, the rebellion suffered the fate of all those before it. It was crushed in such a significantly brutal fashion that it ensured that such resistance would not be seen in Algeria again for another generation.

These later revolts differed from that headed by Abd al-Qadir in that they laid claim to the concept of Mahdism in Islam, whereas al-Qadir, although charismatic, had never attempted to portray himself in this way. Nevertheless, all these rebellions shared the common characteristics of being both intensely traditional and Algerian in origin and inspiration. The Islam that they expressed and sought to defend in the face of the French imperial onslaught was very much the popular Islam that had come to dominate and characterise Algeria over the centuries. Abd al-Qadir had emerged from the traditional rural strongholds of the Sufi brotherhoods and marabouts in the west of the country. The messianism and millenialism of the various Mahdist revolts reflected the even more mystic trends present in the remote and peripheral mountain and semi-desert area in which they predominantly occurred.

Although these movements spearheaded indigenous resistance to the French and, moreover, drew on Islam for their legitimacy and core ideology, it was not these traditional elements that became the true fore-fathers and founders of Algeria's Islamist movement. It was developments in twentieth-century Algeria that produced new elements in Algerian Islam that provided the real starting-point in the history and development of Algerian Islamism.

Reformism and Nationalism, 1871–1962

Capitulation and co-optation

The decades following the crushing of the revolt of 1871 were primarily characterised by a push by France to make Algeria something more than just another imperial possession. The pursuit of the policy of *Algérie française* involved much more than a facilitation of greater European immigration and landowning (both of which doubled in the 1870s). It signalled an intention to transform Algeria into a quite different society: socially, politically and economically. As part of this process Algeria became increasingly assimilated administratively, in the closing decades of the nineteenth century, to metropolitan France.

The implications of this for Algerian Islam were mixed. The defeat of the revolt of 1871 and the ruthless pace of colonisation, together with the parallel destruction of Algerians' own institutions and social order in its wake, left Algeria's Muslims demoralised, leaderless, confused and incapable of organising any political, religious, cultural – let alone military – resistance to the enforced transformation of their society. For most the only option was acquiescence and co-operation. The French for their part, though, still feared the mobilising power of Islam and sought a two-pronged approach to what settlers, colonial administrators and metropolitan politicians alike viewed as the main potential threat to colonial authority in Algeria. Firstly, as an integral and natural part of the policy of assimilation with France, the practice and teaching of Islam were curtailed: many Quranic schools were closed and religious festivals and pilgrimages were monitored and controlled. More importantly, the whole of the education system, as John Entelis points out, became "designed to submerge the Arab–Muslim identity".[3] This policy of suppression of Islam and its manifestations dovetailed with the second part of the approach to the perceived "threat" of Islam: official control of religion by the colonial state. Perhaps recognising that Islam could not be eradicated, at least in the short run, France decided to emasculate it by creating and maintaining its own Muslim clergy which it trained in its own "Muslim" colleges and through whom it felt it could control the teaching and observance of Islam in the mosques.

However, whilst such a policy worked in the mosques of the urban centres of Algeria, control of Islam and Islamic observance in the rural areas was more problematic. Indeed the tightening control of the colonial authorities on the religious establishment (which invariably saw no alternative to co-operation) in the towns and cities could well explain the growth in membership at the end of the nineteenth century of the Sufi brotherhoods which attracted the support of Muslims alienated by the collaboration of the urban imams with the French. The colonial administration was not unaware of this development. Although it could not exercise the same authority over the Sufi tariqas and rural marabouts

---

3   John P. Entelis, *Algeria: The Revolution Institutionalized* (Boulder, Colorado, Westview, 1986), p. 33.

as it could over the urban religious establishment, it was able to "tame" the former through a combination of stick and carrot policies operated by its rural administrators. Interestingly, John Ruedy argues that such co-optation of rural Islam, which ironically of course had provided the backbone of resistance to the French earlier in the nineteenth century, was facilitated by the growth in popularity and membership of these organisations. This influx of support, he argues, diluted the orthodoxy of the brotherhoods in particular and led to "eclecticism, superstition and charlatanism", making them more susceptible to the overtures of the colonial authorities.[4] He concludes on this development:

> Historical process combined with colonial policy to produce the irony that, in the twentieth century, the colony depended for much of its religious support upon the movement that had been the principal mobiliser of resistance to its implantation in the nineteenth.[5]

The advent of reformism

The capitulation of both establishment and rural "popular" Islam to the assaults of the French colonial authorities marked something of a water-shed for the role of Islam in modern Algerian politics. Maraboutism and the tariqas subsequently ceased to be the leading forces in resisting French domination and asserting Algeria's Muslim identity. The reason for this was not only the emasculating effect of co-optation by the colonial state. Far more importantly, in terms of the history of Islam and politics in Algeria, these more traditional forms of Islam were eclipsed by new Islamic ideas and movements which gained ground in Algeria after the turn of the century.

It was the ideas of the *salafiya* movement of thinkers, writers and activists that came to have a profound effect on Islamic thought and organisation in both Algeria and the Maghreb generally during the early years and decades of the twentieth century. Emerging in Egypt towards the end of the nineteenth century the new movement was essentially an intellectual response to the challenge of European superiority. In common with the Maghreb, Egypt had similarly largely succumbed to

---

4   John Ruedy, *Modern Algeria: The Origins and Development of a Nation* (Indianapolis, Indiana University Press, 1992), p. 102.
5   *Ibid.*

the domination of a European colonial power – in its case Britain. The movement stressed the need to return to the pure, original religious practices of the first Muslims or forefathers (*salafiya*) as being the appropriate and best response not only to Western domination but to the general sense of moral and civilisational decline and inferiority which many in the Muslim world had begun to perceive. The doctrine of salafiya argued that the problems and failures of the Muslim world were not a function of the Muslim religion itself but rather its corruption through dilution and blending with other ideas and values which had led to backwardness and superstition. More importantly, perhaps, for Muslims demoralised and confused by the technological superiority of the Europeans, salafiya stressed that Islam was not opposed to scientific and technical progress. Indeed, Islam should not be afraid to borrow selectively from Western ideas to enhance itself and hasten the inevitable recovery and pre-eminence of Islam once it had rediscovered its true roots in the Quran and Sunnah. In essence this new set of ideas represented a development on previous Islamic thought in that, whilst it stressed a return to the practices and principles of the earliest Muslims, it stressed the importance of progress and renewal rather than just a preservation of some existing or previous order.

The ideas of the salafiya movement were brought to the Maghreb by both native Maghrebis who had travelled, worked or studied in the Arab East and by some of the thinkers and activists of the original movement itself. The Egyptian Muhammad Abduh, one of the central figures in the whole salafiya movement visited Tunisia in 1884 and returned again nearly twenty years later in 1903, this time also travelling on to Algeria itself. His stay in Algeria in 1903 came to be viewed as an important starting-point and inspiration for what has been termed the "reformist" movement in Algeria which based itself on the teachings of the salafis like Abduh – salafiyism stressing the need for the "reform" and renewal of Islam. Some writers have stressed that many of the ideas that Abduh brought with him echoed traditions and ideas already present in Algeria and that the impact of his visit should therefore not be over-stressed,[6] but there can be little doubting the symbolic and exemplary effect of his visit on many of the Algerians he came into contact with.

6   It has been argued, for example, that Algeria had confronted the central issue of Western non-Muslim domination of Muslims earlier than other parts of the Muslim world. This was due to the fact that Algeria, unlike much of the Arab East which had significant native non-Muslim minorities, had an almost exclusively

Ben Badis and the Association of Algerian Ulama

Among the people that Muhammad Abduh met during his brief stay in Algeria was a young Algerian named Abdelhamid Ben Badis. From a respected Constantine family with a long tradition of political and religious leadership, Ben Badis became, over the next forty years, the leading and most influential exponent of the type of reformist ideas expressed by Abduh. Ben Badis emerged as the most prominent figure amongst small groups of Algerians who were attracted to reformism and had begun to meet in the universities from the 1890s. Many of these individuals, who had come into contact with reformist ideas through time spent living and studying outside Algeria in the Arab East and Tunisia (Ben Badis himself studied at the Islamic University in Tunis), became increasingly active and organised in and around Constantine by the 1920s.[7] Newspapers were established, notably *Shihab* (The Meteor) in 1925, which served as forums for debate on Islam and the ideas of reformism as well as a means of spreading the reformist message – often relaying the views of leading reformists such as Muhammad Abduh published in foreign journals. It was through writing in these journals that Ben Badis, who had become a full-time preacher and teacher, swiftly established himself as the movement's leading thinker and visionary. From the outset he promoted the idea of some form of more formal organisation for what was still a fairly disparate and largely unorganised group of intellectuals. This, he argued, would enable the movement to harmonise their efforts and doctrine in a much more effective fashion. His efforts finally resulted, after nearly six years of theological debate in the pages of *Shihab* and the other journals of the movement, in the formal founding of the Association of Algerian Ulama (often known by its French acronym – AUMA) in May 1931, which succeeded in attracting the support and membership of the majority of the country's reformists. [8]

Muslim native population which had brought the religious dimensions of the confrontation with the West much more readily to the fore. See Fawzia Bariun, *Malik Bennabi: His Life and Theory of Civilization*, (Kuala Lumpur, Budaya Ilmu Sdn, 1993), pp. 41–2.

7 Although also under French domination, Tunisia's status as a protectorate meant that there was far less official control over religious education than in Algeria and thus far more scope for the teaching and propagation of reformist ideas.

8 Ali Merad advances several possible reasons as to why Ben Badis was particularly convinced of the need to create a formal association. Besides the references in the Quran to the *Hizb Allah* (party of God) he suggests that Ben Badis may have

In its founding articles the Association described itself as "an association for moral education" and gave as one of its primary aims the fight against the "social scourges" of "alcoholism, gambling, idleness [and] ignorance". It also declared its intention "to open . . . centres, circles and elementary schools"[9] and indeed, these activities formed the centre piece of the Association's work over the next two decades and attracted the involvement of growing numbers of Algerians. Although the Association itself remained numerically fairly small and elitist (the question of restrictive membership had been one of the main impediments to the founding of an Association before 1931[10]) the expansion of the movement's educational establishments, in particular, brought many more people into contact with the ideas of the reformists. The Association's clubs and intellectual circles grew and spread in a similar fashion, and by 1934 the Association had some form of presence in virtually every urban centre of note in the country.

The type of people attracted to the AUMA and its various activities appears to have varied greatly. Ali Merad, the principal biographer of Ben Badis and documentor of his reformist movement, found that the Association's following differed in nature from place to place in Algeria and was frequently determined by factors peculiar to the individual area – such as family politics and the nature of the person who had originally introduced the reformist message.[11] There was also a geographical dimension to the movement's support. It enjoyed a presence across the country, but was strongest in eastern Algeria, in and around Constantine, the home of Ben Badis and most of the senior figures in the Association, and was correspondingly weakest in the western areas of Algeria. Merad also concluded that reformism did appear to particularly attract certain sectors

---

been influenced by the formation of similar organisations in Tunisia (where he had studied) and Egypt (where many other reformists had studied). It is also possible he was impressed by the efficacy of the Catholic Church in Algeria and by the formation and function of European-style political parties and associations. Ali Merad, *Le Reformisme Musulman en Algérie de 1925 à 1940* (Paris, Moulton & Co., 1967), pp. 120–4.

9 *Statuts de l'Association des Oulémas d'Algérie* (5 Mai 1931) reproduced in Claude Collot and Jean-Robert Henry, *Le Mouvement National Algérien: Textes 1912–1954* (Paris, L'Harmattan, 1978), pp. 44–7.

10 The debate over membership centred around fears for the doctrinal purity of the movement if maraboutist elements joined the Association.

11 Merad, *Le Reformisme Musulman*, p. 206.

of the population more than others. Petit bourgeoisie intellectuals and tradesmen formed, according to him, "the principal support – material and moral – of the reformist cause".[12] This support was attributed to the relative openness of such people to new ideas and the progressive image that the Association projected. This contrasted with the superstitious and backward image of the more traditional forms of Islam which these mobile and mainly urbanite sectors of the population were already little attracted to. The clubs and intellectual circles established by the Association became, in the view of one writer, the "gathering places of the Algerian-educated classes".[13]

The schools and other educational establishments set up by the reformists were also popular with sections of Algeria's petit bourgeoisie and traders. Not only did they provide an alternative to the archaic traditional schools which were the fall-back for those unable to gain access to the limited places in the more prestigious French-run schools, but they also provided a means of opting out of the French-administered education system altogether. The Islamic *madrases*' emphasis on the Arabic language and on religious instruction pleased conservative Muslims concerned by the cultural emphases of the French-administrated schools, many of whom contributed financially to their maintenance. More importantly, the religious schools were also attractive to many Algerians for the simple reason that they represented some form of cultural and educational bulwark to the march of *Algérie française*.

The assault on popular Islam

A major feature of reformist Islam was its emphasis on doctrinal ortho-doxy strictly based on Islamic scripture. This approach deviated from and contrasted markedly with the strong elements of mysticism and doctrinal eclecticism found within the traditional Algerian Islam of the marabouts and the Sufi brotherhoods. For Ben Badis and his reformers in the AUMA, these more indigenous religious phenomena were ana-thema and, in their view, blocked the way for Algerian Islam to become vibrant and progressive again. Consequently, Ben Badis and his followers launched a concerted campaign across Algeria to combat and discredit

---

12 *Ibid.*
13 Entelis, *Algeria: The Revolution Institutionalized*, p. 44.

maraboutism and mysticism. Arguing that these practices and traditions were alien to Islam, primarily because of their emphasis on intermediaries between God and Man and led to decadence and superstition, the reformists shifted the focus of Islamic leadership away from the marabouts and tariqas and towards their own organisation and agenda. This drive had significant success in some areas and often resulted in the "conversion" of marabouts to the reformist cause. However, it was in areas such as the western region of Algeria, where maraboutism and Sufism had always been strongest, that the Association of Algerian Ulama made least headway.

One of the implications of the advances reformist Islam had made against popular Islam was that Algerians' perceptions of themselves as Muslims took on a far broader and more *national* perspective. By its very nature traditional Algerian Islam with its emphasis on holy men and living saints had been highly parochial in nature. Reformism, facilitated by its nationwide network of schools and clubs and established dogma, had a much wider and more uniform impact.

This further contribution towards the creation of a more genuinely national Algerian identity for Algerians, in addition to that provided by the Association's emphasis in its schools on the country's Arabic and Islamic heritage, undoubtedly helps explain its burgeoning popularity in the 1930s. However, it also shifted the reformists further towards addressing the whole issue of French colonial rule.

The reformists and French colonial rule

The Association of Algerian Ulama had made clear in its founding articles in 1931 that it was an association concerned with "moral education" and thus would confine its attentions and activities to the cultural and educational fields. The eschewal of the field of politics was not just simply implied, it was explicit. The founding statutes stated unambiguously that "all political discussion" and "all intervention into political questions" was "rigorously forbidden".[14] The new Association was to be one exclusively taken up with the task of propagating the reformist message and returning Algerian society to the true path of scriptural Islam.

---

14 *Statuts de l'Association des Oulémas d'Algérie* (5 Mai 1931) reproduced in Collot and Henry, *Le Mouvement National Algérien*, pp. 44–7.

This apolitical stance goes some way to explaining the co-operative and even "loyalist" position the reformist Ulama took towards colonial power in the years following the AUMA's creation. As early as the mid-1920s Ben Badis had argued on the pages of the reformist newspapers for good relations to be established with the French. He even argued that rule by France was beneficial for Algeria: a weak nation like Algeria needing to be taken "under the protective wing" of a strong state such as France. At the same time Ben Badis quite clearly saw the reformists' role as being to provide a mediating role between the colonial authorities and the Algerian people: "to explain to the government the aspirations of the Algerian people; to plead for their rights favourably and in all sincerity".[15]

However, the Association's expressed goal of re-establishing "true" Islamic beliefs and practices, which Ben Badis and the other leaders of the Association did not see as necessarily incompatible with French colonial rule, inevitably clashed with the stated goals of the French. The reformists' emphasis on the reassertion of Arabic language and culture as well as the Islamic religion ran counter to French efforts to slowly eradicate the Arab–Muslim identity of Algeria's pre-colonial population. Tolerance characterised official attitudes towards reformist Islam in its early years, the colonial administration seeing little threat from this relatively small and explicitly apolitical movement.[16] However, this attitude began to shift in the 1930s. On 16 February 1933 an official circular by the Secretary-General of the Algiers prefecture gave voice to the growing concern within the colonial administration:

> Most heads of orders and saintly families venerated by the natives are sincerely converted to our domination and see themselves threatened by a grouping which, by an active and skilful propaganda, recruits new adherents daily . . . It is not possible to tolerate a propaganda which, under the mask of Islamic culture and religious form, hides a pernicious orientation . . .

---

15 *Al Muntaqid* (forerunner to *Shihab*), quoted in Merad, *Le Réformisme Musulman*, p. 392.

16 Official tolerance of Ben Badis was also partly due to French respect for his influential father, Mustafa, on whom Napoleon III had bestowed the Legion of Honour. The influence and wealth of Ben Badis's father and family in Constantine also facilitated Ben Badis's extensive studies abroad and contributed to the successful establishment of the various schools and educational establishments set up by Ben Badis.

> Hence I ask you to survey with most careful attention meetings and lectures organised by the Association of Muslim Scholars presided over by Ben Badis . . . [17]

The reference made in the circular to the "threat" felt by "heads of orders and saintly families . . . converted to our domination" indicates that the reformists' campaign against popular Islam also had political implications. The French were sensitive to assaults on the allies that they had so successfully tamed and co-opted since the turn of the century. The reformists' critique of popular Islam had been overtly religious in nature, but the French were aware of the linkage that much of their anti-maraboutist and Sufi propaganda suggested. Not only was there the obvious implied accusation that the administration was fostering heretical and impure forms of Islam, but more importantly and politically, there was an increasing tendency to point to the representatives of popular Islam's collaboration with the colonial authorities as an indication of their degeneracy.

This implied criticism of French colonial rule, whilst not articulated by those at the head of the Association, indicated to the French the willingness of the Association to tap into popular resentment of the French in order to enlarge their appeal. The early months of 1933 consequently saw a series of measures taken by the authorities which were aimed at curtailing the Association's influence. Foremost of these was the Michels Decree in March which sought to prevent all but officially sanctioned imams from preaching in the mosques of Algiers – thus attempting to deny Ben Badis and his followers an important outlet for their views.[18] Such measures provoked significant protests from the movement and its followers. Further measures in 1934, notably restrictions on and closures of the reformists' press and newspapers, led to more protests with demonstrations in Tlemcen and Constantine in May attracting estimated crowds of 5,000 and 10,000 respectively.

---

17   Ernest Gellner, 'The unknown Apollo of Biskra: the social base of Algerian puritanism' in *Muslim Society*, (Cambridge, Cambridge University Press, 1981), p. 167.

18   The main cause of this particular measure against the reformist ulama was said to have been the inflammatory preaching of one of the senior figures in the Association, Tayyib Uqbi, who had become renowned for his verbal assaults on maraboutism.

Fears that such demonstrations of the reformists' popular support could provoke the authorities into expanding their offensive against the movement and through that potentially destroy it, prompted efforts from some of the ulama to avert this threat. Taking the opportunity of the appointment of a new, less combative French governor in 1936, Tayyib Uqbi, a senior member of the AUMA, forged a deal with the authorities which amounted to a truce being agreed between the two sides. Under this the administration agreed to cease its attacks against the reformists. In return Uqbi – who, it should be noted, had always been a firm advocate of apoliticism for the Association – agreed to tone down the political content of the Association's propaganda.[19] A further concession won by the French was the dismissal, from the post of Secretary-General of the Association, of Lamine Lamoudi, a figure who had been a strong promoter of the Association, co-ordinating their activities with other native Algerian groups. Official interest in securing this last point was indication of the growing concern that the various organised manifestations of indigenous opinion in Algeria would come together to form some form of common front against the colonial administration. Indeed, it was this issue of co-operation with other Algerian organisations that came increasingly to preoccupy the Association of Algerian Ulama from the mid-1930s onwards.

The Association of Algerian Ulama and the opposition movements

Besides the birth of the Association of Algerian Ulama, the 1930s had also witnessed the emergence of a range of other indigenous Algerian associations that concerned themselves more explicitly with Algeria's political situation. As explored earlier, the decades following the crushing of the revolt of 1871 had witnessed a concerted assault on the identity and structure of the Muslim population of Algeria, depriving them, through political, economical and educational domination, of their leadership and consciousness as a community. The years following the First World War, however, had seen (in common with large parts of

---

19   Tayyib Uqbi had declared in the 1920s: "Since the beginning of the World War I have shunned politics, and I will continue to shun it until the Day of Resurrection." *Shihab*, 31.12.25, quoted in Merad, *Le Reformisme Musulman*, p. 126.

the colonised world at this time) the growth, or perhaps resurgence, of organised Algerian Muslim opinion. Declining economic conditions in the 1930s, combined with hostility aroused by the triumphalism of French celebrations marking the centenary of French colonial rule in 1930 resulted in these movements achieving greater attention and popular support.

Despite its official shunning of political activity, the Association of Algerian Ulama participated in the first significant act of co-ordination between these groups which took the form of the convening of a Muslim Congress in Algiers in June 1936. Encouraged by the accession of a left-wing government in metropolitan France, the Association joined with the Féderation des Elus Indigènes (an increasingly influential organisation of mainly middle-class Algerians) and the Algerian Communist Party in drawing up a programme of demands set out in a political charter. These demands essentially constituted an appeal for political and economic equality with the European *colon* population of Algeria to be achieved by the formal integration of Algeria into France. The aim was to abolish the existing ambiguous arrangements and replace them with a unified system which would give the same set of rights to *colons*, native Muslims and metropolitan Frenchmen alike, thus ending the effective second-class "citizenship" that the second of these groups experienced.

The support of the Association for this agenda was curious, not only in the unlikely partners it gave them in the shape of the irreligious communists, but also in the essentially integrative vision of the Congress's political charter. Whilst demands such as the separation of Muslim worship from state control and the ability of Algerians to retain their status as Muslims even after receiving French citizenship were in tune with the Association's views, total integration did not appear to be so. In early 1936, prior to the Congress, Ferhat Abbas, the leading advocate of this policy of assimilation and senior figure in the Féderation des Elus Indigènes had written an article in his own journal *Entente* which explicitly denied the existence of Algeria as a distinct nation and nationality. He claimed that he had "examined history" and found no evidence to support such an idea.[20] Such a position fitted in well with and reinforced his argument for full integration with France: the idea of a separate Algerian nation and identity clearly providing a natural obstacle to integration

---

20   Entelis, *Algeria: The Revolution Institutionalized*, p. 38.

with France. For the reformist Ulama, though, this view was anathema. Their cultural and religious agenda quite clearly and unashamedly stood for all those elements that marked Algeria's native population out from the European and French population: Arabic culture, Arabic language and, most importantly, Islam. In *Shihab* Ben Badis unequivocally rebutted Abbas's denial of the existence of an Algerian identity:

> History has taught us that the Muslim people of Algeria . . . have their history, illustrated by noble deeds; they have their religious unity and their language; they have their culture, they have their customs . . . The Muslim community is not France; it cannot be France, it does not want to be France. Its population is very far from France in its language, its life and its religion; it does not want to incorporate itself in France. It possesses its fatherland whose frontiers are fixed, and this is the Algerian fatherland.[21]

That this rebuttal did not create an obstacle for either the AUMA's participation in the Muslim Congress of 1936 or for their adherence to the resulting political charter is unusual, although it can be speculated that the Association's support was temporary and tactical: making use of the broad front of the Congress to advance their own agenda and aims. Indeed, when a delegation from the 1936 Congress travelled to Paris to present their charter, Ben Badis, accompanied by a sixteen member delegation from the AUMA, also presented their own separate set of demands. These included calls for recognition of Arabic as an official language and for allocations from the public purse to be made to Muslim associations for the upkeep of mosques.

Support from the Association for efforts aimed at co-ordinating native Algerian opinion continued despite the evident ideological differences they had with groups such as the Algerian Communist Party and individuals such as Ferhat Abbas. The main reason for this was the attitude of the French administration. Not only did Paris appear to buckle under adverse pressure from the *colons* over the granting of any of the demands of the Muslim Congress, but official attempts at suppressing the Association resumed again in the late 1930s. Although the authorities had considered proscribing the organisation in July 1937 and had been dissuaded from this by the prefect in Constantine (who presumably felt

---

21 *Ibid.*, p. 44.

his city stood in the front line of any potential backlash – an indication of the perceived strength of the Association there[22]), they introduced a series of measures aimed at curtailing its activities. Members were arrested, premises searched, individual associations placed under official control and a ban placed on the opening of any unauthorised schools. It was these measures (particularly the last, which threatened the very core of the Association's work) together with the authorities' failure to move on any of the demands of 1936 (particularly the refusal to retain Muslim personal status for those few Algerians granted French citizenship) that finally pushed the Ulama and the reformist movement into political opposition to French colonial rule. Calling the law against the schools (introduced in March 1938) "the darkest day in the history of Islam in Algeria" Ben Badis effectively signalled the end of his long-standing policy of co-operation with the authorities, when he called on the Féderation des Elus Indigènes to cease all collaboration with the governing authorities in 1938.[23]

Changes and developments, 1940–1954

Two events occurred over the end of the decade that changed the landscape for the reformists. The first was the outbreak of the Second World War in Europe in September 1939 which led to the dramatic fall of metropolitan France to the Germans eight months later in May 1940. The second, and more immediately important, event was the death of Abdelhamid Ben Badis in April 1940.

The involvement of France, the colonial power, in a major war appeared to open up the potential options for both the AUMA and Algerians generally. For the Association, Ben Badis had officially declared neutrality towards the conflict, stating that it was a conflict that did not concern Muslims. However, he was reported to have told another senior figure in the Association that if Italy were to join the conflict then he himself would not hesitate to lead an insurrection against the French. Both these stances, the official and the private, were a final tangible

---

22 Ali Merad had remarked: "By 1931, the province of Constantine as a whole had been won over to reformism." Merad, *Le Reformisme Musulman*, p. 141.

23 Charles-Robert Ageron, *Histoire de L'Algérie Contemporaine* (Paris, Press Universitaires de France, 1979), vol. 2, p. 347.

indication of the AUMA's break with its policy of co-operation with the colonial authorities. A year before the outbreak of the war, Tayyib Uqbi had officially resigned from the Association in protest over its refusal to send a message confirming the Association's loyalty to France as events in Europe took an ominous turn in September 1938. The departure of Uqbi, the foremost and most strident defender of the principle of apoliticism signalled that the reformists were now committed to the political aim of securing, at the very least, a loosening of the French grip on Algeria.

Despite raised hopes the war did not initially bring much benefit to the movement. Many of its senior leaders were interned in 1939-40 over suspicions of a potential willingness to collaborate with the Axis powers and were generally not released until after the arrival of British and American troops following the North African landings of 1942-3. Ironically, the administration set up by the metropolitan Vichy government between 1940 and 1943 opted not to release them, although the hated March 1938 decree on the establishment of schools was abolished. The emergence of the Free French under General de Gaulle led to some hopes of change but it soon became clear that the prevailing attitude in liberated France was for an effective *status quo ante bellum* in Algeria.

The death of Ben Badis, although not unexpected, was an unmistakable milestone in the history of Algerian reformism. The loss of the man who had not only been the Association of Algerian Ulama's founder but also its guiding spirit, was clearly likely to affect the future course of the movement. However, although Ali Merad judged that reformist Islam failed to break any new ideological ground in the wake of Ben Badis's death (the doctrine of the Association having been synonymous with that of its founder),[24] the AUMA made significant organisational progress in the 1940s following the release of its leaders.

At the end of the 1930s the Association ran something in excess of one hundred institutions (schools, intellectual circles, clubs) across the country and in the view of the prefect of Constantine could count on no more than 1,800 actual members – a fact that was used to justify easing repression of the Association since it was no longer seen as a threat. However, the Association subsequently saw a rapid rise in the number of its institutions which multiplied to several hundred by the end of the 1940s. Much of this growth was the result of the work of Ben Badis's

---

24 Merad, *Le Reformisme Musulman*, pp. 213–4.

successor as leader of the AUMA, Bachir Ibrahimi. Although lacking his predecessor's charisma and vision Ibrahimi worked hard at raising funds for the movement and at building and expanding its institutional structures and supported organisations. Particular emphasis was placed on the Association's educational work – the 1940s witnessing the establishment of the movement's first important upper school: the Ben Badis Institute. The academic programmes of the schools were standardised and teachers working in them were able to move from one part of the country to another within the system. This, following in the wake of the reorganisation of the Association itself in 1937 when a central bureau and departmental committees were created, led one historian of the movement to speak of it becoming "bureaucratised" in this period.[25]

Politically, the Association lent continued support to those groups campaigning for greater rights for native Algerians and retained only the demand for separation of religion from the control of the colonial state as the centre piece of its own agenda. The AUMA participated in the formation of the Amis du Manifeste et de la Liberté (AML) in 1944 which sought to create another broad front for all the various Algerian parties and groupings. The leadership of the AUMA still favoured the general position of Ferhat Abbas, which in the face of French and *colon* intransigence had shifted from assimilation to federation of France and Algeria. However, there was a growing popularity in the movement for the far more radical agenda being propounded by figures such as Messali Hadj who also supported the AML. Arguing for full independence for Algeria, Hadj and his Parti du Peuple Algérien (PPA) articulated an unambiguously nationalist platform that became increasingly popular as time and French intransigence wore on.

Despite a temporary rift with the PPA following large-scale violent unrest at Setif in May 1945, which had largely been the work of Messali Hadj's supporters and which resulted in the deaths of several thousand Muslims and the arrest of Bachir Ibrahimi, the Association grew closer to the PPA and the nationalist cause from the late 1940s into the early 1950s. There were two main reasons for this, in addition to the ongoing reluctance of the French administration to make any concessions to the Muslim population. Firstly, the growing strength of nationalism and

---

25 Allan Christelow, 'Ritual, culture and politics of Islamic reformism in Algeria' in *Middle Eastern Studies*, vol. 23, no. 3, (July 1987) pp. 264–5.

desire for independence in the neighbouring Maghrebi states of Tunisia and Morocco in this period impressed the pan-Arab and pan-Muslim sensibilities that formed part of the ideology of reformist Islam. The consequent involvement of senior members of Algeria's AUMA in region-wide organisations – Bachir Ibrahimi, for example, becoming president of the Comité d'Unité et d'Action Nord Africain in 1952 – further helped convince many inside the Association of the efficacy and importance of forming common fronts with other groupings. A second impetus towards unity with the nationalists was the rise to prominence within the Association of Algerian Ulama of younger more radical figures who did not share the older leadership's reticence over political activism. This stance was shared with most of the Association's younger supporters in the schools and clubs. Prominent among these new figures were Tewfik Madani and Larbi Tebessi, the latter becoming official leader of the Association inside Algeria following Ibrahimi's self-imposed exile from Algeria in 1951 resulting from charges of misuse of funds being brought against him. It was with Tebessi's assent that supporters of the Association began seizing back control of the mosques from officially appointed imams, beginning in the reformists' heartland of Constantine in 1952.

The War of Independence, 1954–1962

On 1 November 1954 a series of attacks launched against institutions and members of the colonial administration marked what was subsequently acknowledged as the start of the armed struggle by native Algerians against French rule and for independence. This seemingly inevitable development was generally welcomed by the AUMA with Bachir Ibrahimi and those leaders around him endorsing the rebel programme shortly after the initial insurrection. The Association's general assembly convened in January 1955 and published a manifesto in which it denounced colonialism, declared that the only route to a peaceful solution would be through recognition of the Algerian nation with its own government and institutions, and stated that the authorities should negotiate a truce with the leaders of the revolt.

This backing for the nationalist insurrection was, however, soon to be put under strain as the conflict grew and became more brutal on both sides and as gaps began to appear between the positions of Ibrahimi abroad and some of the younger more nationalistic leadership inside

Algeria. Use of terror by the FLN (Front de Libération Nationale), the nationalist grouping that launched the struggle, led Ibrahimi to retract his initial endorsement and move to an official position of neither supporting nor opposing the uprising. In contrast, Tewfik Madani, in line with his more radical and nationalist views, vigorously defended the armed campaign. It was thus of little surprise, in the face of a deepening of the conflict and significant efforts on the part of the FLN to unite all of Algeria's native organisations under its banner, that Madani announced his formal adherence to the FLN in Cairo in April 1956. Joined in his declaration by Ferhat Abbas, these adherences gave to the FLN the hegemony they wished and effectively rang the death-knell for the independence of both the Association of Algerian Ulama and the various parties that had existed around Abbas. By absorbing the other two major trends that had existed alongside nationalism within native Algerian opinion from the 1920s the nationalists of the FLN became increasingly *the* exclusive embodiment of Algerian Muslim opinion after 1956. Virtually all of the AUMA's former supporters gradually adhered to the armed struggle of the FLN. The Front frequently used them to set up its own religious apparatus which resulted in the Association of Algerian Ulama formally ceasing to exist after 1957.

The subsummation of the Islamic reformist movement into the FLN provided the latter with the means of imbuing their struggle with religious legitimacy, clearly an important goal for them and one that demonstrated the impact of the AUMA on Algeria. From the initial attacks of November 1954 the rebels had assumed the Islamically inspired title of *mujahidin* – "fighters of the faith". Moreover, the FLN proclaimed as one of its aims on the eve of the revolt: "The restoration of the sovereign, democratic and social Algerian state within the framework of Islamic principles."[26] Once the struggle matured from the early sporadic revolts and guerrilla attacks, Islam continued to provide a symbolic underpinning for the war. Jihad was frequently referred to and the importance of the observance of Ramadan was emphasised by many military commanders, evoking echoes of Abd al-Qadir's moral prescriptions for his troops in their fight against the French over a century earlier. Islam too was used to coerce the less fervent in the struggle through threats couched in religious terms. Jean-Claude Vatin characterises these

---

26   Ruedy, *Modern Algeria*, p. 159.

developments as the reintroduction of Islam, by the leaders of the revolt, as a "strategic weapon" to rally Algeria's Muslims to the nationalist cause.[27] Nevertheless, it should not be ignored that many of the prominent leaders and top military commanders in the struggle had devout religious backgrounds or legitimacy.[28] Tewfik Madani and Taalbi Tayeb, another former member of the Association, sat on the FLN's parliamentary body, the CNRA (Conseil National de la Révolution Algérienne), following their joining of the party. More importantly, Madani was named as one of the members of the GPRA (Gouvernement Provisoire de la République Algérienne), the FLN's "government-in-waiting", which was announced in September 1958 in Cairo.[29]

Organisationally, the AUMA provided significant support to the FLN's cause. The continued expansion of the Association's education network – the number of schools it administered doubling from 90 in 1947 to 181 by 1954, with its *madrases* alone providing an education for 40,000 pupils – provided important logistical bases for the rebels. Together with the reformist-run mosques they also provided useful collection points for funds and centres for the spread of information and the nationalist message. Sermons during the month of Ramadan, in 1956 in particular, helped to stoke patriotic fervour and popular support for the struggle. This contribution of the Association to the rebellion was acknowledged by the French who shut down the group's newspaper, *El Bacair*, in April 1956 and progressively closed down its institutions and seized its assets, sending some of its members to prison camps. By 1957 the Association ceased to have any real institutional manifestation in the country.

---

27   Jean-Claude Vatin, 'Religious resistance and state power in Algeria' in Alexander S. Cudsi and Ali E. Hillal Dessouki (eds.), *Islam and Power* (London, Croom Helm, 1981), p. 146.

28   For examples of some of the military commanders who came from religious backgrounds see Alistair Horne, *A Savage War of Peace: Algeria 1954–62* (London, Papermac, 1987), p. 131.

29   Madani was named Minister of Cultural Affairs in the GPRA.

Conclusions

The eventual victory in 1962 of the Algerian nationalists in their war against the French colonial state and the final achievement of full political independence clearly opened a whole new chapter in both Algerian history and the role of Islam and Islamism in it. However, it also closed a chapter: that of the role of Islam in the colonial period.

Changes and developments 1830–1962: from popular to reformist Islam

The period of French domination of Algeria witnessed the rise of movements that explicitly based themselves on the Islamic religion and which made significant incursions into the field of politics and whose impact there was considerable.

These movements, however, appeared to fall into two distinct camps that were divided not only by their ideology, origins and social and geographic bases, but also by time. The nineteenth century was dominated by groups and movements that had their roots firmly in the institutions and expressions of what has been broadly termed as "popular Islam" – that which manifested itself through marabouts, Sufi orders and the more mystical expressions of Islam that had come to predominate in Algeria. Its nature and role has been succinctly summed up by Allan Christelow who has said it could be defined as "ecstatic in style, predominantly rural in social foundations, and, historically, as a major factor in resistance to the French colonial invasion up until the 1880s and as strongly tinged with collaborationism from the First World War onward".[30]

The effective crushing by the French of these movements and the resistance they organised and articulated by the 1880s created a vacuum into which eventually another movement stepped, one which although similarly basing itself on Islam differed significantly from earlier movements. The reformist movement that achieved eventual institutional expression through the Association of Algerian Ulama was distinct from those of Abd al-Qadir, Bou Maza and the various Mahdist movements that had risen against the French in the mid-nineteenth century. It

---

30 Allan Christelow, 'Algerian Islam in a time of transition', *Maghreb Review*, vol. 8, no. 5-6, (1983), p. 124.

grounded itself theologically in scripturalist interpretations of Islam, rather than ones based on entrenched local traditions and mysticism and drew its inspiration from foreign thinkers and movements. It also emerged in and appealed to a different section of Algerian society. Reformist Islam's open hostility to the manifestations of these more traditional expressions of Islam further underlined these differences.

The reasons for the shift from popular to reformist Islam and its success can be explained by reference to these fundamental distinctions between the two forms. Whilst popular Islam played an important role in mobilising resistance against the French in the nineteenth century, its roots were still essentially and overwhelmingly Maghrebi and Algerian. The rise of Islamic reformism in the twentieth century, in contrast, reflected ideas and movements whose origins stretched wider and beyond North Africa and was part of what John Entelis, for example, describes as "the broader awakening of Arab–Muslim consciousness that was taking place among the peoples of the Middle East and North Africa during the inter-war period".[31] The 1920s, the decade which witnessed the first real growth and spread of reformist ideas in Algeria, was also the period which saw the founding of the Muslim Brotherhood by Hassan al-Banna in Egypt. Although far more influential throughout the Muslim world than Ben Badis and his followers, and differing in some important ways from the movement in Algeria, the Egyptian Muslim Brotherhood shared several characteristics with the Association of Algerian Ulama: notably its emphasis on such things as doctrinal purity, Arabic–Islamic education and moral social behaviour. Both also operated in the important context of European colonial rule.

A second major feature of the shift from popular to reformist Islam was the change in the type of people involved in Islamic activism. As explained earlier, when looking at the revolts of the nineteenth century, "Islamic" resistance to the French (according to a useful typology by John Ruedy) could be separated into three basic types determined largely by geography: the defence of the old deyical establishment in the larger towns and cities; the Sufi-inspired movements of the plains and small towns of the interior (of which Abd al-Qadir's was an example) and Mahdist uprisings of the more remote areas of the mountains and the

---

31   Entelis, *Algeria: The Revolution Institutionalized*, p. 42.

Sahara.[32] It was quite clearly these last two that had a greater impact overall and, moreover, had a greater and more recognisable "Islamic" content than the resistance in the towns and cities which was arguably more about the maintenance and protection of the dominant social and political order.

The rise of reformist Islam in the twentieth century was, in contrast, largely an urban-based phenomenon. Hugh Roberts explains the assault conducted by Ben Badis and his followers on the doctrinal impurity, backwardness and collaborationism of the marabouts as representing a clash between "urban, literate, bourgeois society" and the "massively illiterate rural population".[33] The victory and subsequent "hegemony" established by the former over the latter was a new and important development. This eclipsing of the old rural religious order has been explained through reference to the rapid changes that occurred in Algeria's economic and social geography from the closing decades of the nineteenth century. French colonial policy, with its large-scale appropriations of Algerian-owned land and its centralising of administrative controls in Algeria's towns and cities, contributed, along with inherent demographic trends, to the growth in importance of Algeria's urban areas. The more cosmopolitan nature of towns and particularly cities (such as Constantine) exposed Muslim inhabitants not only to ideas emanating from the Arab East, such as reformism, but also to European and Western ideas that also contributed to the rise of reformism. Ali Merad argues that whilst the specifically religious aspects of Islamic reformism might not have been particularly attractive to some Algerians, the movement's philosophical utilisation of Western concepts of modernisation and individualism appealed especially to the young. Such a stance contrasted starkly with the perceived backwardness and ideological stagnation of the marabouts and the other representatives of popular Islam. Nevertheless, Merad observes that the great debate between reformism and "maraboutism" in reality left the vast majority of ordinary Algerians unmoved. It could therefore be concluded that it was the qualities of reformism itself that attracted people rather than its perceived advantages over popular Islam.[34]

---

32 Ruedy, *Modern Algeria*, p. 67.
33 Hugh Roberts, 'Radical Islamism and the dilemma of Algerian nationalism: the embattled Arians of Algiers', *Third World Quarterly*, vol. 10, no. 2 (April 1988), p. 561.
34 Merad, *Le Reformisme Musulman*, pp. 207–8 and p. 435.

The latter was neither ideologically, organisationally nor demographically ready to form the basis of a vibrant and influential Islamic movement in the twentieth century. That role could only seriously be provided by a more urban, progressive and organised vehicle such as that provided by Islamic reformism and Ben Badis's Association of Algerian Ulama. As much as reformism appealed to "urban, literate, bourgeois society", it also drew ideas and skills from it. The involvement of the urban bourgeoisie, with their awareness of modern ideas of mobilisation, organisation and propaganda (which were of growing importance in Europe in the interwar years) meant that the Islamic movement became more cohesive, more orthodox and was able to spread effectively its ideas and recruit support from the other sections of society.

In addition to its bourgeois following, significant support for the reformist movement in the 1920s also came from that part of the Algerian upper middle class which felt itself excluded from social and political advance within the French colonial state. Whilst some other members of the upper middle class had opted for "Frenchification", culturally and educationally, in order to achieve such an advance, this group had not and instead opted for what Jean-Claude Vatin terms the "counter-code or counter-strategy" of reformist Islam which stressed the importance of an Arabic and Islamic culture and identity.[35]

It is important, however, not to overstate the divide between popular and reformist Islam. Although different in many ways, both were essentially expressions of the same set of fundamental religious beliefs. The salafi reformism of Ben Badis and the AUMA certainly did not represent some completely new variant of Islam. In neighbouring Morocco there were clear continuities between popular and reformist Islam with Sufism being historically present in both expressions and with both Sufism and reformism drawing their leadership from essentially the same urban elite. However, whilst the divide between the two was more complete in Algeria, for a number of reasons, the overall integrity of Algerian Islam should be appreciated.[36]

---

35 Vatin, 'Religious Resistance and State Power', pp. 142–4.
36 The differences between the Moroccan and Algerian cases were severalfold. Firstly, the various expressions of popular Islam were more deeply rooted in Moroccan society as a whole and thus were more likely to have influence upon other ideas, such as reformism, that arrived in Morocco. Importantly, it was in the part of Algeria that bordered Morocco, the western Oran region, which

Reformism and nationalism

It was the formation of a cultural "counter-code" that registered as reformist Islam's greatest impact on Algeria during the colonial period, an impact that ironically far outweighed any advances the reformists may have made in their central field of religious education. It is universally acknowledged that the AUMA made a specific and vital contribution to Algerian nationalism (and thus Algerian independence) through its defining and forging of an Algerian national identity and consciousness that was much more accessible and understandable to the mass of ordinary Muslims than the more complex and essentially foreign ideas of liberalism and socialism articulated by the likes of Messali Hadj and Ferhat Abbas. The Association of Algerian Ulama's motto "Islam is my religion, Arabic is my language, Algeria is my country" succinctly indicated those things that made Algeria's Muslims distinct from their European Christian rulers. The particular importance of Islam here should not be underestimated. It could be argued that a nationalist consciousness could have been formed on the basis of either or both of the other two parts of the motto: language and territory. All three elements are almost organically linked (Arabic, for example, being the language of the Quran), but Islam played the role of an overarching ideology which had the advantage over other

---

provided the starting point for both the rebellions against the Ottomans and Abd al-Qadir's revolt, both of which were led and organised by the Sufi tariqas and, moreover, were largely rural, rather than urban, in origin. In contrast, the Association of Algerian Ulama emerged and found their main source of support and strength in *eastern* Algeria around Constantine where popular Islam had traditionally been weaker and where more orthodox forms of Islam had a stronger presence. Correspondingly, the movement was least influential in the western areas of the country where marabouts and several of the tariqas resisted its incursion. It was notable also that Ben Badis and most of the other senior founding figures of the AUMA came from what Abun-Nasr has described as "comfortable *urban* surroundings (italics added)". A second difference with the Moroccan experience was the relative absence of elements of Sufism and popular Islam in the Algerian reformist movement compared to that in Morocco. There had been an extended debate within the AUMA during the early 1930s over whether the Association should retain a highly selective membership in order to prevent infiltration by maraboutist elements. Both Moroccan and Algerian reformism came from the same eastern Arab sources and were both hostile to many of the manifestations of popular Islam, but the Algerian reformists were far less qualified in their antipathy than their Moroccan counterparts. For a full examination of the Moroccan case see Henry Munson, *Religion and Power in Morocco* (New Haven and London, Yale University Press, 1993), pp. 81–114.

ideologies, such as Marxism and liberalism, in being truly a religion and more importantly in being pre-colonial and near indigenous in origin. As Rachid Tlemcani asserts: "It was the only cultural current able to challenge colonial ideology which was aimed at the moral conquest of the native population from the beginning."[37] That the French had made at times quite concerted efforts to undermine, co-opt and ultimately destroy Algerian Islam undoubtedly heightened the importance of it in the minds of many Algerians as something that stood against French domination.

The role of the French and of French policy did, ironically, contribute significantly towards the impact made by reformist Islam. The nature of the policy pursued by the colonial authorities boosted and raised the profile of the AUMA. The failure, for example, of the French to culturally assimilate a significant part of Algerian youth prevented the rise of a French-educated and more European-style opposition movement. Even when those Muslim Algerians who had received a French education, such as Ferhat Abbas and his liberal assimilationists, tried to represent Algerian aspirations and interests, the refusal of the French to make any concessions to them undermined them and their agenda and opened the way for the reformists. As Entelis points out:

> The discrediting of indigenous secular movements by the colonial power allowed Islam to arise as the only legitimate and popular ideological rallying cry around which all Algerians could unify.[38]

More fundamentally, Entelis goes on to argue that the simple fact of the French presence and their policy was more crucial to an understanding of the rise of an Algerian national consciousness based around Islam than the specifics of the reformist ulama and their programme:

> There can be no doubt that, however profound the Islamic identity at the individual or community level remained, it was the disruptive nature of French colonial policy that ultimately provoked the aggressive reassertion of an indigenous Algerian identity with strong ties to native Islamic culture.[39]

---

37   Rachid Tlemcani, *State and Revolution in Algeria* (London, Zed, 1987), pp. 51–2.
38   Entelis, *Algeria: The Revolution Institutionalized*, p. 42.
39   *Ibid.*, p. 76.

The incorporation of Islamic symbols and themes, alongside more modern ones, into the programmes and propaganda of overt nationalists such as Messali Hadj and the PPA was a clear recognition of the important role Islam had come to play in Algerian Muslim organisations by the 1930s. Their coexistence there with more clearly Marxist-influenced elements may have been due to a genuine belief in the compatibility and importance of Islamic and socialist ideas or perhaps to Messali Hadj's, involvement, for example, in the Sufi brotherhoods in his youth. The more likely reason for the inclusion of Islamic values and symbols in the nationalists' agenda, though, was the evident support they had enjoyed when used by Ben Badis and the AUMA. The first major nationalist unrest at Setif in May 1945, for example, saw the use of Islamic symbols and rallying cries by the rebels who spoke of jihad and, interestingly, raised the green and white banner of Abd al-Qadir. The reformists had clearly won the argument, in the minds of the Algerian people, with the assimilationists over the issue in the 1930s of the existence of the Algerian nation and people. Ben Badis's rebuttal of Ferhat Abbas's article in 1936 had, according to Abun Nasr, "a deep impact on the political consciousness of the Algerian Muslims".[40] Some historians have gone so far as to suggest that "nationalism proper" had been born with the founding of the Association of Algerian Ulama in 1931.[41]

The reformist agenda

The Association of Algerian Ulama's increasing involvement in and eventual formal absorption by essentially political questions and movements clearly confused identification of the organisation's central goals and ideology. Ali Merad speaks of the movement's "progressive slide towards areas certainly far from its primary vocation".[42] This slide was the result of the steady growth in importance of the issue of the exact status of Algeria and its indigenous population *vis-à-vis* France. The incursion of this overwhelmingly *political* question into the considerations and activities of the AUMA, which had unambiguously declared at its birth its intention

---

40   Abun-Nasr, *A History of the Maghreb*, p. 335.
41   Charles-Robert Ageron, *Modern Algeria: A History from 1830 to the Present* (London, Hurst & Co.,1991), p. 94.
42   Merad, *Le Reformisme Musulman*, p. 433.

to avoid politics, was substantially the result of a growing number of its own, predominantly younger, supporters becoming involved in the issue. More important still were the political implications and impact the Association's essentially *cultural* agenda (with its emphasis on Islam and Arabic) and work had had on the whole issue of Algeria's national identity.

Nevertheless, the ease with which the politicians of the FLN, in particular, were able to subordinate the organisation to its control has led to suggestions that this indicated that the Association had retained its essentially religious and cultural character. It had, for example, made no rival bid for the political leadership of the nationalist movement. Even if such leadership had been desired, the Association would have been unable to achieve it. Alistair Horne, the foremost Anglo-Saxon historian of the Algerian independence struggle, attributes the political eclipse of the AUMA during the war as being the result of its leadership's fundamental unsuitability to political activism because "tied up in their theological coils, they failed to find pragmatic applications for their doctrines".[43] Abdelhamid Ben Badis had himself addressed issues of a political character in his writings, in *Shihab*, in particular, but these did not contain many tangible proposals for a future Islamic political order (preferring to stick largely to broad principles and a critique of the existing order).[44] The death of Ben Badis in 1940 deprived the AUMA not only of its leader but of any more detailed thoughts and ideas he might have produced in response to developments in the political field. It was an area he had only just begun to venture into at the time of his death, and one which was to come to overshadow so much of the Association's activities in the following two decades.

If, then, the reformists of the AUMA succeeded in fundamentally retaining their original religious character and agenda, what advances did they make in this, their chosen field during this period? The reality was that only fairly limited progress had been achieved in the Association's central stated objective of spreading the reformist message and reviving scripturally based belief and behaviour amongst Algeria's Muslim population. Ali Merad believes that the popularity of the movement in the

---

43   Horne, *A Savage War of Peace*, p. 38.
44   For a detailed analysis of Ben Badis's writings on politics and political issues see Ali Merad, *Ibn Badis: Commentateur du Coran* (Paris, Librarie Orientaliste Paul Geuthner, 1977), pp. 202–17.

1930s, which surpassed that of all other native movements in the interwar period, was due not to its religious agenda but to its presentation of a range of principles (such as cultural renewal and distinctiveness, and social progress) that could find support even amongst those "still indifferent to religious propaganda".[45] For young Algerians in particular, who might otherwise have been put off by the severity of some of the Association's moral prescriptions (alcohol, tobacco, dancing, music and sport being "rigorously condemned"[46]), "the reformist movement of Ben Badis represented more of a source of political enthusiasm and cultural emotion than a school of moral and religious discipline."[47]

The failure of the reformists to inculcate a significant section of the Algerian population with their specific ideas and values was counterbalanced by the obvious success that had been achieved in making Algerians considerably more aware and appreciative of Islam generally – as indicated by the nationalists' use of religious symbols and language. However, it was also argued that through its ferocious assault on the traditional expressions of Algerian Islam, the Association actually served to *weaken* the implantation and observance of Islam in the country. By attacking, on religious grounds, the most deep-rooted forms of Islam in Algeria it perhaps deprived many areas of an Islamic tradition that might be essential to the survival of the religion in the face of future non-religious challenges. The rapid progress that secular forms of nationalism made both during the war of liberation and afterwards were perhaps in part facilitated by this aspect of the reformists' agenda.

---

45 Merad, *Le Reformisme Musulman*, p. 435.
46 Horne, *A Savage War of Peace*, p. 38.
47 Merad, *Le Reformisme Musulman*, p. 209.

2

Islam in the New State, 1962–1978

Ben Bella's Reign, 1962–1965

Independence

The final achievement of independence in June 1962 shifted the whole focus of Algerian activity and attention away from the all-consuming struggle against the French and towards the construction and consolidation of their new state. Fracturing inevitably occurred in the institutional front and hegemony that the FLN had been able to forge during the nearly eight years of the war of liberation as different ideological, regional, personal and factional interests engaged in a struggle for pre-eminence. However, whilst liberals, Marxists, internal and external army commanders, the wilaya commanders, the imprisoned leaders and Berber-based factions entered the political and occasionally armed competition for influence, an independent and identifiable lobby arguing for a specifically Islamically based Algeria was notably absent. The Islamic current, so robustly represented by the Association of Algerian Ulama in the two decades preceding the war of liberation, had been sidelined during the struggle, its absorption by the FLN, in contrast to other groupings that joined the front, having deprived it of its independent voice and agenda.

As has been shown (see Chapter One) the religious and cultural nature of the AUMA meant it presented no serious challenge to the organised, specifically political, elements within the FLN. Moreover, the formal adherence of the majority of the members of the Association from 1956, together with France's resultant dissolution and break-up of the Association's institutional base of schools and clubs, effectively ended the AUMA's existence as a distinct and independent entity. The death and dispersal of many of its senior figures during the war further accelerated this process, leaving the tendency as a whole in no real position to assert itself following independence.

Yet as had been the case in the run-up and during the war, it was the AUMA's *ideological* rather than institutional contribution to the Algerian political scene that was its most important achievement in the period following independence. The presence of powerful competing ideas inside the FLN ensured that a specifically Islamic state, based upon sharia law, was never likely to be achieved. Such a demand had been made by Tewfik Madani and other former members of the AUMA during debates in the various organs of the FLN during the war, but these debates had proved inconclusive.[1] Nevertheless, Islam and Islamic symbols were still clearly present in the debate and formulation of the new state. In the initial power struggles between the various factions and leaders of the FLN in the wake of independence, reformist Islam was regularly invoked by all the main contenders to bolster the legitimacy of their claims to power. This both recognised and reinforced the ideological primacy of Islamic reformism in both the foundations of the new state and in the popular perceptions of ordinary Algerians.

The adoption of the AUMA's slogan "Islam is my religion, Arabic is my language and Algeria is my country" as independent Algeria's national slogan was tangible recognition of the contribution reformist Islam had made to the national struggle. It was notable that it was specifically *reformist* Islam, rather than just Islam generally or the traditional Islam of the marabouts and Sufi brotherhoods, that was accorded this recognition. The detailing in Algeria's first post-independence Constitution that Islam was to be the religion of state and that the country's President must be a Muslim was further evidence of this significant ideological influence. It overrode the strong liberal, Marxist and nationalist strains within the FLN that were naturally inclined towards more secular forms of state and constitution.[2]

Any attempt on the part of reformist Islam, to play a more tangible and active role in both the formulation and governing of the new Algerian state was, however, precluded. Tewfik Madani was given a minor ministerial position (that responsible for *habous* or religious trusts) in the post-independence governments but he remained the sole and increasingly

---

1   The issue of an Islamic state had been debated notably at the meeting of the CNRA (the FLN's parliament in exile) in Cairo in August 1957 where Tewfik and his supporters had clashed with elements demanding a European-style liberal parliamentary regime.

2   Ernest Gellner argues that support for a formally secular independent state declined when it became clear, following the flight of the virtual entirety of Algeria's European inhabitants at independence, that independent Algeria's non-Muslim population was likely to be negligible in size. Gellner, 'The unknown Apollo of Biskra', pp. 167–8.

pliant representative of the former AUMA in the new regime. This effective exclusion from influence was attributable to two main factors, in addition to the explained weakness of the movement in 1962. Firstly, the desire of the FLN during wartime to subordinate religion and the AUMA to the party's control persisted into the designs and structures of the new state. Religion and all groups or tendencies referring to or basing themselves on Islamic principles were effectively co-opted and controlled by the authorities of the new state. This desire on the part of the FLN to dominate nearly all aspects of Algerian life, including religion, after independence was partly due to the thinly disguised ambition of several of the major figures in the party who strove to control the FLN and through it the new state itself. However there were other, ideological, reasons for this tendency which explain the second major constraint on the ulama in the period after independence.

"Muslim socialism"

The reformist ideology of the AUMA, whilst prevailing over other expressions of Islam in independent Algeria, was challenged by another, secular, ideology which threatened to hold sway in the counsels of the leadership of the new state. The ideology of socialism in its various doctrinal forms had first become prominent in Algeria in the interwar period, finding particular manifestation in the work, ideas and organisations of Messali Hadj. During the war of independence itself, a remarkable consensus emerged amongst the FLN and its constituent elements that independent Algeria should be socialist. This was a conviction common to most other nationalist movements in the decolonising world of the 1940s, 1950s and 1960s; socialism being viewed as the most appropriate means of achieving social and economic progress.

An outspoken advocate of Algeria's adoption of socialism was Ahmed Ben Bella, the senior FLN figure who triumphed in the power struggle against other FLN leaders and who duly became independent Algeria's first President. Three months before the official proclamation of Algerian independence, the future President unambiguously declared that "Algeria will have a socialist government."[3] However, whilst he pressed ahead

---

3 *Agence France-Presse* despatch, 1.4.62, quoted by Raymond Vallin, 'Muslim socialism in Algeria' in I. William Zartman, *Man, State and Society in the Contemporary Maghrib* (London, Pall Mall Press, 1973), p. 50.

with what he saw as a "socialist" programme, largely involving the take-over of land, businesses and property abandoned by the departed *colons* (which in many ways made socialist-style nationalisation unavoidable) the more fundamental question of state ideology needed to be addressed. Although Ben Bella's government initially adopted no coherently recognisable or defined socialist ideology, many of the basic tenets of socialism as practised in other countries, particularly the inherent secularism and atheism of more Marxist ideas, appeared to clash with the influential religious ideology of reformist Islam.

Ben Bella was aware of this potential clash and how potentially damaging it could be to popular support for and perceptions of his new government. Reformist Islam had made a considerable contribution to the popular and psychological foundations of the new state. Ben Bella had himself appealed to Islamic sentiments and symbols to aid his victory in the leadership struggle. Consequently, he set about trying to "merge" the ideology of socialism with that of Islam. Undoubtedly building on Gamal Abdul Nasser's concept of "socialism in Islam" in Egypt, Ben Bella constantly pushed the concept of "Islamic socialism" and the compatibility of Islam and socialism. To elaborate on this theme Ben Bella made particular use of the official press as well as Tewfik Madani, who, as a minister, proclaimed in January 1963 that "Islam is a socialist religion, it is a religion of equity."[4] More formally, the Algiers Charter of 1964, which aimed to clarify the organisation and make-up of the new state, declared socialism to be totally consistent with the nation's Arabo-Islamic heritage.[5]

The rise of Islamic opposition and criticism: 1962–1965

Ben Bella's efforts to create his vision of a socialist Algeria were continually hampered over the next few years by an awareness on the part of the new

---

4 Vallin, 'Muslim socialism in Algeria', p. 51.
5 Ben Bella was, however, careful not to equate Marxism (with its explicitly atheistic philosophy) with Islam. In an interview in January 1965 he stated: "We adopt the Marxist economic analysis because we believe it is the only one valid for the economic development of our country; but we do not espouse the Marxist ideology because we Algerians are Muslims and Arabs." Interview with Ahmed Ben Bella, *Révolution et Travail*, 20.1.65, quoted in David and Marina Ottaway, *Algeria: The Politics of a Socialist Revolution* (Berkeley and Los Angeles, University of California Press, 1970), p. 181.

President that many Algerians were far from convinced of his equation of his socialist programme with Islam. Despite the institutional decline of the AUMA, attachment to the Islamic values of the Association remained strong in many quarters, including amongst some senior figures within the leadership of the FLN and the army. Criticism of his removal of several religious figures from the government during the first year of his presidency was voiced both outside and, undoubtedly, within the regime. This prompted Ben Bella to introduce a series of measures aimed at placating this criticism. The government made the Ramadan fast and the charity offering that ended it national duties in January 1963. Later that year the government reversed its liberalisation of the sale and consumption of alcohol. Alcohol had been banned under the wartime wilaya administration of the FLN, but Ben Bella had considered the ban unnecessary following independence. Government decrees of 28 December 1963 forbade Muslims to drink alcohol, closed down cafés and raised taxes on alcohol.

Such measures did not succeed in stemming religiously based unease at Ben Bella's rule. The government's expanding nationalisation drive, in particular, provoked opposition, as Raymond Vallin comments:

> Islamic socialism also caused concern among religious people and prominent personalities known for their religious zeal, who considered it imprudent, if not sacrilegious to erase thirteen centuries of consensus on religious property and fall into an arbitrary collectivism whose origins were foreign to Algeria and to Islam.[6]

This concern proved not to be purely passive. As Peter R. Knauss adds: "Ben Bella appeared to be veering leftward and this provoked Muslim traditionalists to come out of hiding."[7] Some of the first of these "traditionalists" to make their opinions known were former members of the Association of Algerian Ulama itself. Whilst most of the Association had been co-opted and neutralised by the FLN, there were still those figures who were able and willing to voice their unhappiness at the course independent Algeria was taking. Prominent among these was Bachir Ibrahimi, the former head of the Association, who had, in contrast to

---

6   Vallin, 'Muslim socialism in Algeria', p. 56.
7   Peter R. Knauss, *The Persistence of Patriarchy: Class, Gender and Ideology in Twentieth Century Algeria* (New York, Praeger, 1987), p. 105.

most of the rest of the Association, kept his distance from the FLN during the liberation struggle (see Chapter One) and thus felt free to use formal platforms to criticise the government's direction. In the FLN party congress of April 1964, which was boycotted by a number of sections of the party which Ben Bella had also succeeded in alienating, Ibrahimi made a clear appeal, reflecting unease at the growing opposition to the government throughout Algeria. During the vigorous debate over the relationship between Islam and socialism that took place at the congress, he declared:

> The hour is grave. Our country is sliding nearer and nearer to hopeless civil war, an unprecedented moral crisis and insurmountable economic difficulties. Those governing us do not seem to realise that what our people aspire to above all is unity, peace and prosperity and that the theories on which their actions should be founded are to be found not in foreign doctrines but in our Arab–Islamic roots.[8]

The former president of the AUMA's message was well received across many sections of Algerian society but inevitably not by the government itself. Ibrahimi was put under house arrest by the President who, ironically, had personally welcomed him back from exile less than two years earlier.

Once again the government felt obliged to show some sign of concession to conservative religious opinion. In September 1964, the President replaced the leftist editor of the influential journal *Révolution Africaine* with an appointee who began to put greater emphasis on Algeria's Islamic nature and who drew attention to the government's programme of rural mosque-building.[9] Later that autumn, with opposition to his regime and policies still mounting from all quarters, Ben Bella pushed several overt Marxists out of the government and in education "Arabised" the first year of primary school and made religious training compulsory.

Many Algerians were still highly sceptical of the real significance of these changes, having regarded the references to Islam in the Algiers Charter of 1964 (which in truth were eleventh hour additions) as largely

---

8   Arslan Humbaraci, *Algeria: A Revolution that Failed* (London, Pall Mall Press, 1966) p. 237.

9   Across Algeria, Ben Bella's government made an undertaking to restore 170 mosques and to construct 187 new ones.

cosmetic. This scepticism was undoubtedly reinforced by a renewed drive on the part of the regime to promote socialist values using both the officially controlled media and its allies in the socialist labour unions (such as the UGTA which had launched virulent attacks against Ibrahimi's views). More importantly, the remaining religious figures in the government, mainly old AUMA figures, were finally purged in December 1964. However, the importance of the AUMA and their views remained amongst the Algerian population and when Bachir Ibrahimi died in May 1965, his funeral was heavily attended, a fact interpreted by many as "a veiled demonstration by the more conservative elements against Ben Bella's socialist policies".[10]

The emergence of Al Qiyam

Islamically-oriented opposition to the regime also took a more organised form during the opening years of Algerian independence. The Al Qiyam (Values) association made its first real impact in Algeria by holding a meeting in January 1964 in Algiers which was attended by several thousand people.[11] Ostensibly gathering to protest at the continuing influence of French culture in independent Algeria and to demand that the government take more steps to promote Arabic and respect for Islamic values, the association became a focus for both popular protest against the regime and for independent Islamic criticism of the direction of government policy.

Using public meetings and its own journals, such as *Humanisme Musulman*, Al Qiyam promoted, in much the same fashion as the Association of Algerian Ulama had done in the interwar period, their analysis and cure for the ills of Algerian society. Containing several former members of the AUMA, the new association consciously presented itself as the inheritor of Abdelhamid Ben Badis and his movement. Philosophically,

---

10   Ottaway and Ottaway, *Algeria: The Politics of a Socialist Revolution*, p. 47n. There are no available figures for the actual attendance at the funeral, but the Ottaways speak of "an enormous crowd".

11   Estimates vary on the numbers attending. David and Marina Ottaway speak of 3,000 (*ibid.*, p. 179); Raymond Vallin of 3,000–4,000 (Vallin, 'Muslim socialism in Algeria', p. 56) and Hugh Roberts states that "up to 5,000" attended the association's various meetings during this period (Roberts, 'Radical Islamism', p. 564).

the president of the association, Hachemi Tijani, Secretary-General of the University of Algiers, affirmed in an interview in 1964 that he identified with the views of the main pillars of the Islamic reformist movement such as Jamal al-Afghani and Muhammad Abduh (the latter having had, as has been shown, a substantial influence on Ben Badis and the leaders of the AUMA).

Hachemi Tijani also specifically identified with more recent writers, thinkers and activists, such as Hassan al-Banna and Sayyid Qutb, who took a far more radical view of the need and means of reintroducing Islamic values back into Muslim societies. Qutb, for example, a senior member of the Egyptian Muslim Brotherhood, comprehensively rejected the conviction of reformist Islam that Western technology and ideas could be used selectively to promote Islam and combat Western influence and dominance. Instead, as he outlined in his book *Signposts*, Qutb argued that Muslim societies had become so polluted by Western and non-Islamic influences that nothing short of a "revolution" to drive out such alien influences could succeed in restoring them to the point at which they could again be seen as truly "Islamic" societies.[12] Such radicalism was indeed reflected in both the publications and occasionally the activities of Al Qiyam, members of the association distributing tracts by al-Banna and Qutb as well as other radical Islamist thinkers such as the Pakistani Abu al-Ala Maududi. All non-Islamic influences, ancient and modern, were anathematised by the association. Members of Al Qiyam were involved in an attack on statues in a Roman theatre in Guelma and, more seriously, *Humanisme Musulman* declared, for example, in 1965 that:

> All political parties, all regimes and all leaders which do not base themselves on Islam are decreed illegal and dangerous. A communist party, a secular party, a Marxist party, a nationalist party (the latter putting in question the unity of the Muslim world) cannot exist in the land of Islam.[13]

---

12 For a fuller explanation of the ideas and work of Sayyid Qutb see Gilles Kepel, *The Prophet and Pharaoh: Muslim Extremism in Egypt* (London, Al Saqi, 1985), pp. 43–59.

13 *Humanisme Musulman* ,August 1965. Translation from Roberts, 'Radical Islamism', pp. 563–4.

The actual impact made by Al Qiyam is difficult to assess. Peter Knauss characterises the association as an "organisation of teachers, businessmen, salaried workers, and imams" and it is certainly true that it had a fairly distinguished and middle-class membership profile.[14] It even had a number of sympathisers within and close to the regime including Mohammed Khider, one of the "historic chiefs" of the revolutionary FLN, who often spoke in support of the objectives of the association and who attended the January 1964 meeting.[15] Many contemporary observers, however, believed that the conservative and morally severe nature of the association's vocabulary and agenda would not only limit its appeal to the progressive minded but also laid it open to ridicule from the government and socialist press.[16] Al Qiyam's reliance on French to promote their ideas (the French-language edition of *Humanisme Musulman*, for example, outsold its Arabic edition) was also seen as undermining the association's demand for greater use of Arabic.[17]

The influence of the association was, however, certainly greater than these observers estimated. Many, particularly young, Algerians may well have been put off by the anti-modernism of Al-Qiyam, but many more shared the unease of the association at the direction of Ben Bella's government. Far from undermining its position, Al-Qiyam, by publishing in French, was clearly aiming to achieve a wider audience for its ideas.

More fundamentally, the activities and ideas of Al Qiyam put further pressure on Ben Bella's increasingly isolated and beleaguered regime, which although never directly challenging the state, served to undermine the legitimacy of those in government. The concern with which the regime viewed the activities of Al Qiyam was demonstrated by the eviction of the association's president, Tijani, from his post at the University of Algiers in 1964. The rise of the association was also a symptom as well as a cause of Algeria's growing problems at this time. For Hugh Roberts the emergence of the association was evidence of the regime's loss of control of the important "religious sphere" of Algerian politics and life, Ben

---

14   Knauss, *The Persistence of Patriarchy*, p.104.
15   There were several known sympathisers of Al Qiyam and its agenda within Ben Bella's cabinet and close to the President himself, such as Ali Mahsas, Safi Boudissa and Mohammed Seghir Nekkache.
16   See Vallin, 'Muslim socialism in Algeria', p. 56.
17   See Ottaway and Ottaway, *Algeria: The Politics of a Socialist Revolution*, pp. 45–6.

Bella being unable to find a single senior religious figure to condemn Al Qiyam on religious grounds.[18]

Boumedienne's coup

Al Qiyam and the body of opinion it represented was just one of the sections of Algerian society that became increasingly hostile to Ben Bella during the first years of independence. Lack of any coherent progress in the area of economy, constant political manoeuvring and shifting of alliances and government personnel, and the doctrinaire policies he seemed intent on pursuing, gradually deprived the President of any true allies outside his close personal circle and elements of the far left. Such isolation meant that when the army, which had become increasingly and fatally alienated from the government, finally ousted Ben Bella in a bloodless coup on 19 June 1965, there was virtually no public protest or resistance.

The leader of the coup and the new President was Colonel Houari Boumedienne, the vice-president and the commander of the army. Boumedienne's opposition to Ben Bella had became increasingly open in the closing stages of the latter's period of rule and a large part of his critique of the regime and its policies had been couched in religious terms. The new President, who had attended both an Islamic school and the Ben Badis Institute in Constantine, used many of the arguments articulated by the regime's religious opponents from both the dissident elements of the old AUMA and even Al Qiyam to attack Ben Bella's policies. His stress on the importance of Algeria's Islamic roots won him significant support amongst the religious opposition which had organised significant public demonstrations in the months preceding the coup. Ben Bella's downfall was explicitly welcomed by many in the Islamic opposition, a group of whom sent an official communiqué proclaiming their solidarity and support for the new "Council of the Revolution" and thus becoming the first group to come out publicly in favour of the coup.

The remnants of the AUMA were mistaken in believing that Boumedienne and the army acted primarily to defend the place of reformist Islamic values in Algeria. Despite his religious background and

---

18   Roberts, 'Radical Islamism', p. 564.

the support many in the army had given to the Islamists' critique of Ben Bella's rule, Boumedienne had been aware of the extra popularity and support he could gain by "playing the religious card". He did not hesitate to use it in his growing struggle against Ben Bella; a feud which had its origins more in personal and political rivalry than in attachment to Islam. As David and Marina Ottaway comment, "Boumedienne's opposition to Ben Bella's policies was veiled behind a pseudo-religious argument over the compatibility of Marxist socialism."[19] Boumedienne's stress on the importance of Algeria's Arab and Islamic past and identity and his support for the Islamic criticism of the influence of foreign ideas reflected more a nationalism on the part of himself and the army (whose leadership had received favourably Ibrahimi's statement at the 1964 Congress) than anything more clearly religious. Their criticism of the principles of the 1964 Algiers Charter was based more on their dislike of the principles' foreign origins than any unhappiness at their lack of basis in the Quran and Hadith.[20]

The Boumedienne Era: 1965–1978

Boumedienne and the Islamic opposition, 1965–1971: incorporation and repression

Given Boumedienne's opportunistic use of Islam it was not surprising that once again the Islamic tendency in its various shades found itself largely excluded from the centres of power in the new regime. However, aware of the damage the tendency had been able to inflict on Ben Bella, Boumedienne's new government sought to handle this exclusion with more deftness than its predecessor. The new strategy for dealing with the Islamic "movement" that Boumedienne adopted from 1965 has been characterised by Hugh Roberts as having two main elements. Towards Al Qiyam, in particular, the new government pursued a strategy "combining

---

19 Ottaway and Ottaway, *Algeria: The Politics of a Socialist Revolution*, p. 179.
20 Boumedienne and the army's hostility to Marxism was also due to a concern that Ben Bella's strengthening links with the Algerian Communist Party and the UGTA would give the President the allies he needed to oust Boumedienne and the other army commanders.

the suppression of the association with the selective incorporation of its programme".[21]

The "selective incorporation" of Al Qiyam's agenda was arguably the more important part of the strategy, since it appeared to succeed in presenting an Islamic image for the government whilst not appearing, as the Ben Bella government had done, to be making just token and cosmetic concessions. From the outset Boumedienne's new government took care to put the regime on a broader footing by including many of the elements and interests that Ben Bella had excluded and which had hastened his downfall. A practical example was the appointment of Bachir Ibrahimi's son, Ahmed Taleb, to be a director of national education. More subliminally, this policy involved a more meticulously built-up Islamic image for the regime, which culminated in the autumn of 1970 with the announcement by the Minister of Religious Affairs, Mouloud Kassim, of a major campaign on the part of the state against the "degradation of morals" in Algeria. Publicised through a significant three-month campaign in the media involving interviews and round table discussions, the campaign skilfully wove together nationalist and Islamic concerns in arguing that the social evils of "alcoholism", "semi-nudity" in dress and the break-up of families were directly attributable to the West and its pernicious values.[22]

In tandem with this "selective incorporation" of the Islamic agenda, the authorities also embarked on a progressive repression of the institutional manifestations of the Islamist movement. A prefectoral decree in September 1966 ordered the dissolution of Al Qiyam in the *wilaya* (region) of Algiers and three and a half years later a ministerial decree banned the association throughout Algeria. The timing of both moves was prompted by specific events, namely the sending of protest letters to Nasser following his execution of Sayyid Qutb in 1966 and continued attacks against "improperly dressed" women on the streets in 1970. However, this repression was clearly part of a general plan on the part of the regime to neutralise Islamic opposition to the regime.

The policies of repression and incorporation were usefully combined in the crushing of social unrest that occurred in Mostaganem in eastern

---

21 Roberts, 'Radical Islamism', p. 564.
22 *El Moudjahid*, 29.9.70 and 25.12.70, quoted in Bernard Cubertafond, *La République Algérienne Démocratique et Populaire* (Limoges, Presses Universitaires de France, 1979), pp. 88–9.

Algeria in 1968. Led by the Alouia Sufi brotherhood, these disturbances presented the government with the opportunity to move against religious-led opposition whilst being able to clothe its repression in Islamic garb. The government press and officials rejuvenated the original rhetoric of Ben Badis and the Islamic reformists of the 1920s and 1930s by railing against the "mysticism", "obscurantism" and "neo-paganism" of the Sufi brotherhoods and the marabouts, thus appearing to align themselves with the heritage of Ben Badis and the AUMA.[23]

The reassertion of the state

The period 1965–71 was marked by the government's success in controlling the growth of a sizeable opposition movement based on Islam. The use of the twin-pronged strategy of repression and incorporation had meant that far from bowing to the demands of the Islamist lobby, the government had effectively "de-fanged" organisations like Al Qiyam by undercutting their agenda and then moving to break them up.

Other factors besides this central strategy helped Boumedienne's regime achieve this. The new President's "opportunistic remobilisation of nationalist fervour", in the view of Hugh Roberts, was useful in staving off the growth of Islamically based opposition.[24] This was particularly the case with Algeria's successful "riding out" of the psychological storm which hit the Arab world generally following the Arab states' catastrophic and comprehensive defeat by Israel in the Six Day War of June 1967. For many states, particularly in the eastern Arab world, the defeat presaged a significant growth in Islamic opposition groups within states as the abrupt breaking of the ideological spell of Nasser's Arab nationalism left many Arabs believing that it was the secular nature of their regimes, which had turned their back on Islam, that was largely to blame for the rout on the battlefield. Boumedienne, however, maintained and even rallied support for his regime by roundly criticising Nasser's capitulation to the Israelis. In this he was clearly helped by still fresh memories of the Algerian revolution which gave the Algerian regime far greater popular

---

23 Vatin, 'Religious resistance and state power', p. 136; Vatin; 'Popular puritanism versus state reformism: Islam in Algeria', in James P. Piscatori, *Islam in the Political Process* (Cambridge, Cambridge University Press, 1983), p. 116.
24 Roberts, 'Radical Islamism', pp. 562–5.

legitimacy than the regimes of the Arab East that had come to power largely through coups, colonial patronage or quasi-dynastic succession. Boumedienne built on this legacy through nationalisations and the building-up of local government in the late 1960s, which undoubtedly added to his popularity and legitimacy in the public's eye.

Boumedienne was also infinitely more skilful than his predecessor in handling religious opinion towards his still essentially secular political, social and economic programme. Much greater effort and care was taken to marry and merge leftist and socialist concepts and policies to Islam. For example, the government showed more sophistication in arguing that the doctrine of selective use of Westernisation and progress inherent in the reformist Islamic thinking of Afghani, Abduh and of course, Ben Badis, was essentially the same as that found in socialist ideas of modernisation. Both employed the central idea of the transformation of society through progressive thinking derived from doctrine. Generally, this approach appeared to be successful in so much as it did not provoke any high profiled rebuttal of the sort given by Bachir Ibrahimi in April 1964, but it did not always go unchallenged. In 1968, for example, Boumedienne and his Health Minister were forced to back down when their plans to introduce birth control were met with a united front of opposition from religious and traditionalist opinion. There were clearly some policies that could not be sold, at least not yet, by the regime and the government was wise enough not to try and press ahead with such a policy and thus risk provoking opposition to the regime.

By 1970 Boumedienne and his government had recovered the new state of Algeria from the situation of crisis that Ben Bella had enmeshed it in so soon after independence. Islamic opposition to the regime, expressed both through specific organisations such as Al Qiyam as well as more generally through public unrest, had posed a genuine threat to the government in 1964-5 but, through careful handling, the threat had virtually disappeared over the following five years. As Hugh Roberts comments:

> In this context, the Al Qiyam agitation was a false dawn, reflecting not a crisis of Algerian nationalism but merely the temporary breakdown of the state–society relationship, as a consequence of the incoherence of the Ben Bella regime.[25]

25   *Ibid.*, p. 565.

The *Révolution Socialiste* and the rekindling of Islamism

The period 1970-71 witnessed a number of developments which helped stimulate Islamist sentiment once again. For Hugh Roberts this period was marked by the embarkation by the Boumedienne regime, after a successful period of control of Islamic activism, "upon a course of action which made the revival of Islamist agitation not only possible but inevitable". This course of action on the part of the regime, he argues, had two elements: a generalised leftward shift in government economic policy after 1970 and the continued push for the "Arabisation" of Algeria's educational and administrative systems.[26]

Both of these elements formed part of a new political initiative that the President launched in November 1971. Employing unusually Marxian rhetoric, Boumedienne had declared the need to "radically change the social relations and the ownership of the means of production" and to achieve this he declared the beginning of "the second stage of the Algerian revolution from this point".[27] In this way the *Révolution Socialiste,* which embodied Boumedienne's policy for the 1970s, was launched. Composed of three constituent planned "revolutions", in the fields of industry, culture and agriculture, the *Révolution Socialiste* contributed to the reinvigoration of an Islamist tendency in Algeria through the workings and effects of at least two of these component "revolutions".

The Agrarian Revolution

The *Révolution Agraire* or Agrarian Revolution was the most comprehensive and most genuinely "revolutionary" element of the *Révolution Socialiste.* Essentially it involved the nationalisation of many of Algeria's large estates which were then turned into collectives and which by 1974 had also necessitated the takeover by the state of the wholesaling of agricultural produce. Over and above the specific economic and social successes and failures of this policy, the effect it had on the Muslim landowners from whom the land was expropriated and the wholesalers whose trade was nationalised was substantial. What was significant was that much of the opposition to this policy was expressed in religious terms, even by those not necessarily materially affected by the changes.

---

26   *Ibid.,* p. 566.
27   Quoted in Tlemcani, *State and Revolution in Algeria,* p. 125.

Quranic endorsement of the concept and legitimacy of private ownership formed the basis of much of this criticism of this policy. As various members of the AUMA had done under Ben Bella, many Islamic leaders, including Sheikh Noureddine, formerly a senior member of the AUMA, came out against Boumedienne's policy. Abdellatif Soltani, another former member of the AUMA, questioned the validity of prayers said on nationalised land and the Government felt compelled to call in civil and religious leaders alike to defend its policy. In 1972 the President himself felt obliged to declare that "It should be specified that no religious text prevents application of the Agrarian Revolution."[28]

The relationship this debate had to the Islamist movement is interesting. It is clear that many Islamists opposed the nationalisations for the scriptural reasons given above. However, it appears that the Agrarian Revolution did receive support from those elements of the Islamist movement which came from poorer and peasant backgrounds and who clearly stood to benefit from the reforms. There was also an element of opportunist self-interest amongst those Islamists and ulama who opposed the land nationalisations. A form of alliance emerged between the landowners and the ulama (particularly the older ulama) whereby the ulama would act as the ideological spokesmen for the landowners through attacking the nationalisations on religious grounds. In return, the landowners agreed to help finance the construction of a significant number of mosques as well as fund various religious and cultural organisations.[29] The Agrarian revolution also benefited the Islamist movement in another, indirect, way by concentrating official attention on the rural areas and away from the urban areas where, as will be shown, the Islamists began to build up their support and organisation in the mid-1970s.

---

28 François Burgat and William Dowell, *The Islamic Movement in North Africa* (Austin, Center for Middle Eastern Studies, University of Texas 1993), p. 255.

29 This alliance between the private sector and the Islamist movement was a fairly long-standing one that had been established during the time of the AUMA (see Chapter One). Allan Christelow argues that it was government nationalisations in the period after independence that undermined the private sector, thus depriving the Islamists of one of their main social and financial bases of support and explaining their relative weakness in the 1960s and 1970s. Christelow, 'Ritual, culture and politics', p. 268.

The "Révolution Culturelle" and the impact of Arabisation

The *Révolution Culturelle*, with its essentially nationalistic aim of establishing a distinct cultural identity for Algerians in place of the overwhelmingly French one that 130 years of colonial rule had imprinted on the country, primarily influenced the growth of the Islamist movement through its core objective of securing the linguistic "Arabisation" of Algeria. Algeria's programme of Arabisation had actually begun as early as 1964 with Ben Bella's Arabisation of primary education and introduction of compulsory religious instruction. It was under President Boumedienne, however, that Arabisation became a real priority for the Algerian government.[30]

Arabisation aimed to make modern literary Arabic the national language of Algeria through the important state-controlled channels of education and the state administration. Arabisation proceeded quite rapidly through the education system but it advanced at a far slower pace through Algeria's large state administration. The net result of this was that the education system was turning out far more Arabic-speaking students or "Arabisants" than could be absorbed by the administrative sector, which in many places was largely still Francophone. There were also few jobs for Arabic-only speakers in the state sector and the large corporations. The corporations, in particular, preferred students fluent in French or other European languages to deal with their mainly Western clients and suppliers.

The implications of this problem for the government and for the potential revival of Islamist agitation and sentiment were severalfold. Two particular groups suffered from the lack of employment opportunities for Arabic-educated students. A high proportion of Arabisants came from poor, originally rural, families which had migrated in large numbers to Algeria's large towns and cities over the past few decades. Not only, then, did this increasingly frustrated group become a significant source of agitation in urban areas, but moreover, in coming from the rural hinterland they retained much of the religious conservatism of those areas (which had largely been left untouched by the modernist ideas of the post-independence governments) and thus were more likely to be sympathetic to Islamic

---

30 For a fuller discussion of the Arabisation question see Rachida Yacine, 'The impact of French colonial heritage on language policies in independent North Africa' in George Joffé, *North Africa: Nation, State and Region* (London, Routledge, 1993), pp. 228–9.

activism and ideas. The fact that it tended to be poorer, more rural Algerians that became Arabisants, whilst the wealthy, more urban groups stayed largely Francophone (through choice), also meant that the social and economic cleavages between the two groups widened as the language preferences of both met with differing success in the job market, thus enhancing already present social tensions.

The second group that appeared to be adversely affected by the Arabisation policy and who consequently presented a potential threat to the government came from a different social background to that of the rural migrants and the possible challenge they represented was different to that of the mass unrest that the new urban poor represented. A significant proportion of "Arabised" students, particularly from wealthier and better-educated backgrounds, chose to study Arabic and Islamic law and literature at university rather than follow more Francophone-based courses in science and technology. This, however, did not do much more to improve their job opportunities over the poor Arabisant school-leavers. The potential danger that this posed for the regime was that it created a significant number of well-educated but unemployed graduates whose intellectual training and political awareness could help mobilise opposition.

It was therefore almost inevitable that both frustrated groups would find themselves identifying with opposition to the government which identified itself with Islamic values, since not only were both groups far more aware, through their education, of Arabo-Muslim ideas and concepts, but both believed that it was the persistence of secular and French influences that was responsible for their frustration. A return to the sort of Islamic, Arabised order advocated by most Islamist critics of the government would clearly be in their interests. Indeed, Jean-Claude Vatin indicates that calls for greater Islamisation of Algeria, which clearly grew amongst Arabisants in the 1970s, were linked to calls for Arabisation "as a mere device for gaining access to those jobs more or less monopolised by their French-speaking co-religionists".[31] A further possible reason for the growth of an Islamist sentiment amongst the Arabisants was the influence of Arabic teachers brought in from outside of Algeria to compensate for the lack of suitably qualified native teachers. These teachers frequently brought with them the sort of Islamist ideas that were increasingly influential in the eastern Arab world in the late 1960s and 1970s.

---

31   Vatin: 'Popular puritanism versus state reformism', p. 100.

The link between Arabisation and Islamism is, however, not entirely straightforward. Whilst it appears that Islamist-type movements in the universities in the late 1960s largely recruited from amongst students of Arabic and Islamic studies who felt bypassed by the educational system, Rachid Benaissa, an Islamic activist at that time, maintains that most of the students attending the mosques and involved in Islamic groups were Francophone. The sermons in the mosques were delivered in French and it was not until later that Arabic students came to both the mosques and the organisations. More generally, Benaissa points out that the Arabic press in Algeria at this time "was more violently anti-Islamic than the Francophone".[32]

By the mid-1970s, though, Arabisation and Islamism were increasingly closely linked. The years 1974, 1975 and 1976, for example, all witnessed violent clashes between Arabophone and Francophone students at Constantine University over whether Algeria should adopt a traditional Islamic or modern secular legal system.

Arabisation was not the only element of the *Révolution Culturelle* that served to bolster the Islamist movement. The regime's emphasis on the religious aspects of the Arabo-Muslim identity of Algerians, whilst reinforcing the state's control over the religious sphere, also increased awareness of Islam and Islamic themes, thus preparing more fertile ground for the Islamist message. This was certainly true of the Campaign Against the Degradation of Morals of 1970 which, as has been shown, articulated many of the religious and moral themes of the Islamist agenda.

This was equally the case with the launch of the government-backed review *Al Asala* in March 1971, a publication which sought to put the government's point of view across with regard to religion. Employing several former members of the AUMA, the review propounded the ideas of Ben Badis and his followers, referring extensively to all the major figures in the movement including figures such as Bachir Ibrahimi who had not been an enthusiastic supporter of either the liberation struggle

---

32 Quoted in Burgat and Dowell, *The Islamist Movement in North Africa*, p. 257. The reason for the relatively late arrival of Arabophone students to the Islamic organisations at this time may, of course, have been due to the fact that the Arabisation of education was still in its infancy and its effect on the education system as a whole was only just beginning to be felt. However, this does not detract from the fact that there already was an Islamist tendency and movement in existence which Arabisation served to feed rather than create.

or secular nationalism. Such coverage and personnel employed suggested that *Al Asala* enjoyed a degree of autonomy from state control. However, whilst the themes in the review were unambiguously supportive of Islamic reformism and the Islamic agenda, Luc-Willy Deheuvels who conducted a comprehensive study of the publication, concluded that *Al Asala* failed to provide a pole or personality around which Islamists could unite. The experience of the liberation struggle and the dominating personality of Houari Boumedienne, he observed, had totally changed the landscape and deprived the AUMA of its previous prestige and influence.[33]

The issue of Islamist sympathisers within the regime itself is an important one. As seen earlier, Al Qiyam had a number of sympathisers within Ben Bella's government and although Boumedienne kept a much tighter and more personal grip on Islamist activity outside the institutions of the state, this internal Islamic opinion remained. Their presence, particularly that of former members of the AUMA, was tolerated by the regime in return for help in providing religious legitimacy for the regime. Certain sections of the administration, notably those dealing with culture, religion and education (the traditional areas of concern of the Islamic reformists) contained significant numbers of personnel supportive of the broader Islamic agenda. In this context, the *Révolution Culturelle*, particularly its central plank of Arabisation, was largely the work of these elements.

It would be mistaken to say that there was real collusion between these figures within the administration and the more radical elements of groups, but it was certainly the case that individuals such as Mouloud Kassim and his successor at the Ministry of Religious Affairs, Abderahman Chibane, discreetly encouraged both the Arabisants and the Islamists. The supporting ideological link between the two Islamic parties was evident. The writers of *Al Asala*, for example, although never attempting criticism of the existing regime, provided "an anchor" for the Islamist current, in the view of François Burgat, through their exposition of religious ideas.[34]

---

33 Luc-Willy Deheuvels, *Islam et Pensée Contemporaine en Algérie: La Revue 'Al-Asala' 1971–1981* (Paris, Editions du CNRS, 1991), pp. 273–4.
34 Burgat and Dowell, *The Islamist Movement in North Africa*, p. 254.

Government reaction and the National Charter

By 1976 the regime appeared to show the first signs of being aware of the gradual swell of Islamic opposition it was building up against itself. One strand of the Islamically based criticism of the government was its lack of consultation with the people, enshrined in the Islamic concept of shura. This criticism had first been raised by Bachir Ibrahimi when he had voiced his more general concern over the direction of the Ben Bella government in April 1964 and called for a "return to the principles of consultation so dear to the Prophet".[35] In 1974 tracts had appeared in Algiers bearing essentially the same message. Indeed it appeared that a growing number of Algerians were increasingly restive not only at the doctrinaire attitude of the government but also at the prolonged period of unconstitutionality that had been operating since the coup of 1965.

In apparent concession to this opinion Boumediennc held both a constitutional referendum and a presidential "election" (in practice also a referendum). The new National Charter of 1976, which the constitutional referendum "endorsed", gave Islam the status of state religion. It was a change that came in the wake of other concessions that had been made to the Islamic "lobby" earlier in the year. In March the government had outlawed gambling and in August 1976 Friday had replaced Sunday as the official weekly holiday. Religious festivals were also declared official holidays with government backing being given to their full observance.

These concessions were more gloss than content. References to Islam were largely brief and perfunctory, with socialism instead providing the explicit ideological heart of the whole document. The brief sub-section of the Charter that dealt with religion was entitled "Islam and the socialist Revolution" and was contained within the larger section headed "Building the socialist society". Furthermore, the new Charter went on to directly refute one of the core tenets of the Islamist and reformist movement when it stated:

> The decline of the Muslim world is not attributed to purely moral causes . . . There is only one way for the Muslim world to regenerate itself: it must go beyond reformism and advance towards social Revolution.[36]

---

35 Humbaraci, *Algeria: A Revolution that Failed*, p. 237.
36 *National Charter: Democratic and Popular Algerian Republic* (Algerian Ministry of Culture and Information, 1976), pp. 18–19.

This "social revolution" clearly aimed to surpass and indeed absorb Islamic reformism and religion generally within the ideology of the state. Almost to demonstrate this stance, Boumedienne, in a reshuffle of his government in early 1977, reduced the Ministry of Religious Affairs to a sub-section of the presidency itself.

The revolutionary drive and rhetoric produced added problems for the government not only because it attracted the usual Islamic criticism of being too attached to secular and Marxist doctrines (such accusations increased when the regime developed closer relations with the communists of the PAGS party) but also for more subliminal reasons. Hugh Roberts argues that Boumedienne's fostering of a revolutionary, millenialist mentality and spirit among young Algerians in particular, encouraging them to mobilise against elements within the regime itself who resisted this "revolution" "legitimised a radically critical attitude among the younger generation towards the existing bases of authority in the society".[37]

Contrary to their design, some of the apparent concessions the regime made served to boost Islamist opinion in the country. The apparently symbolic and insubstantive recognition in the National Charter of Islam as the religion of state gave the Islamists a potential new platform for their views. They could now appeal to the Charter itself to press openly for their agenda of Arabisation, Islamisation and application of the sharia since Islam was now officially endorsed as the religion of state.

The Islamist movement, 1970–1978

Atomisation: the new groups

The exact shape, form and strength of the Islamist "movement" in the 1970s was difficult to assess. The government's banning of Al Qiyam in March 1970 meant that organised focus for Islamic opinion and opposition to the regime subsequently became much more disparate and more covert. The official proscription of Al Qiyam removed only the organised manifestations of the grouping, leaving a still significant number of activists committed to continuing to promote their agenda. From the late 1960s these activists appeared to have regrouped over the following few years in a

---

37   Roberts, 'Radical Islamism', pp. 569–70.

series of successor organisations such as Ansar Allah (which was broken up by the authorities) and then Dawa wa Tabligh.[38]

The forcibly atomised nature of the movement from the late 1960s led also to the emergence of other trends within the Islamist opposition which established groups for themselves in various parts of Algerian society. Several were inspired by and enjoyed close links with the rapidly growing and influential Islamist movements of the Arab East, particularly those of Egypt. A group of young Algerians led by a secondary school teacher, Mahfoud Nahnah, who had begun to organise themselves during Ben Bella's presidency, had strong doctrinal and personal ties with the Egyptian Muslim Brotherhood.[39] Similarly, in 1974-75 tracts began to appear on the streets of Algeria's cities by a group calling itself Takfir wa Hijra, the same name as that given to a radical Egyptian faction. The similarities in the extremist messages these tracts bore to the ideology of the Egyptian grouping suggested clear inspirational and possibly organisational links between the two namesakes.

Malek Bennabi and the "Jazara"

Another, more intellectual, mainly student group began to meet from the mid-1960s, in the Central Faculty of the University of Algiers. Their patron was the leading Islamic intellectual Malek Bennabi, a prolific writer and individualistic thinker, who had spent most of his adult life abroad, mainly in France and Egypt, but had returned to Algeria following independence. Bennabi had not been formally involved with the Association of Ulama but this had more to do with his intellectual differences with the Association than with his lengthy absences from Algeria. Although applauding the main thrust of the reformists' campaign to revive Islam in Algeria, Bennabi believed that they and the intellectual forefathers of the wider reformist or salafiya movement, such as Afghani and Muhammad Abduh, were only superficially correct in the analysis and cure for the perceived decline of Muslim society. Bennabi shared with the reformists

---

38 This clandestine organisation appeared to draw its influence from the Jama'at Tabligh, an Islamic grouping that emerged in the Indian subcontinent during the 1920s. In Algeria the grouping remained small and negligible in influence due to its strict attachment to the principle of apoliticism.

39 Mahfoud Nahnah's contacts with the Muslim Brotherhood and their ideas were apparently established through Egyptian professors he encountered during his time at Algiers University.

their concern with this decline but he believed Abduh, for example, had placed too much emphasis on the simple teaching and dogma of the Islamic faith, whilst neglecting "the effectiveness and the social impulse of that faith",[40] the deeper understanding and transformation, which Bennabi believed was more crucial to the renaissance of the Muslim world.

Bennabi's writings had been particularly influential in Algeria in the 1940s when even the AUMA's newspaper, Al-Basair, had acknowledged the "great effect on the youth whatever their political tendency or cultural orientation" his ideas had.[41] Bennabi nevertheless remained apart from the Association, and was critical of its steady drift in the 1930s and 1940s towards involvement with party politicians. He had been particularly critical of the AUMA's decision to travel to Paris with other representatives of the Muslim Congress in 1936 (see Chapter One) and had even gone to see Abdelhamid Ben Badis and the other leaders of the Association in an effort to dissuade them from going. His antipathy was due both to his fierce opposition to the assimilationist views of Ferhat Abbas – which he felt the AUMA were appearing to support – and to his hostility towards involvement in politics.[42] On his return to Algeria in 1963 he criticised the Islamic reformists whose writings he characterised as being "by and large nothing more than a polemic against maraboutism and colonialism" which did nothing to address Algeria's problems or suggest solutions to them.[43] His intellectual standing led Bennabi to be appointed Director of Higher Studies in the Ministry of Education in 1964 where he became an important public advocate for the government's Arabisation programme. His appointment survived Boumedienne's coup but he was finally dismissed in 1967, possibly because of his perceived association with Al Qiyam.

It was student disciples of Bennabi who established themselves in the University of Algiers from the late 1960s. There, with Bennabi's

---

40   Malek Bennabi, *Wijhat al 'Alam al Islami* (Cairo, 1959) quoted in Bariun, p. 151.

41   Quoted in Allan Christelow, 'An Islamic humanist in the 20th Century: Malik Bennabi, *Maghreb Review*, vol. 17, nos. 1–2, (1992), p. 76.

42   Staunch belief in apoliticism was a position Bennabi shared with the arch-defender of that principle within the AUMA – Tayyib Uqbi. Significantly, both had met in the 1930s had become good friends and Bennabi was said to believe at one stage that Uqbi was more entitled to the leadership of the Association than Ben Badis.

43   Malek Bennabi, *Perspectives Algériennes* quoted in Christelow, 'An Islamic humanist', p. 79.

encouragement, the group undertook to establish a mosque in the faculty in 1968 and five years later they set up their own *majlis shura* (consultative council). Despite their small, secretive and elitist nature, this predominantly Francophone group also published a review, *Que sais-je de l'Islam*, in which their cerebral discussions on Bennabi's key themes of civilisation and the compatibility of Islam and science were aired. Bennabi's interest in the subject of science undoubtedly helped explain the predominance of science students in his discussion groups. However, their presence was equally explained by the fact that French was the predominant language of both Bennabi's writings and of the science courses in the university. The Francophone orientation of Bennabi and his followers attracted the antipathy of other, invariably Arabophone, Islamist groups on the campuses which were also critical of Bennabi's expressed differences with Ben Badis and other respected salafist thinkers and activists. Sceptism of salafiyism and the work of modern salafist-influenced groups such as the Muslim Brothers in Egypt, separated Bennabi and his followers from most other Islamist groups which drew their inspiration overwhelmingly from these sources. This apparent rejection of the tutelage of ideas from the Arab East led to Bennabi's group earning for itself over time the sobriquet of the Jazara or "Algerianists".[44]

The universities

Bennabi and his followers formed part of a general trend amongst Islamists in the 1960s and 1970s of organising themselves in the universities. An indication of this development came with the wearing of the *hedjab* by women students. The first examples of this began to appear on the Algerian campuses in 1967, although this practice was for several years largely restricted to small groups such as those around Bennabi. Although these developments indicated that the universities were becoming the new repositories of Islamist sentiment in Algeria, these groups were neither very extensive nor particularly strong over the next few years. Not only was

---

44 Despite Bennabi's time spent abroad, his disciples' association with a more specifically Algerian orientation was due both to Bennabi's originality as a thinker (rather than an advocate of existing, invariably foreign, ideas) and to Bennabi's use of explicitly Algerian terms of historical reference in preference to more general Islamic ones used by other groups and thinkers. For a much fuller treatment of Bennabi's life, work and ideas see Christelow, 'An Islamic humanist'; and Bariun, *Malik Bennabi*.

the movement largely confined to certain faculties in certain universities but its quite considerable efforts at proselytism appeared to meet with little success, fellow students possibly being put off by the dogmatism of its stance and propaganda.[45]

The Islamist organisations in the universities also had to contend with the far stronger leftist movements which dominated the campuses in the late 1960s and 1970s. Part of the reason for the growth of Islamist student organisations in the late 1960s had been government toleration and reliance on them to combat leftist influence in the universities at this time. However, with the advent of the *Révolution Socialiste* after the turn of the decade, Boumedienne appeared to reverse this policy as he recognised the leftists as potential ideological allies in the struggle to introduce his more radical and socialist policies. Consequently, Islamist support waned and declined back to its original base of small scattered groups of activists. Those Islamists who did remain were largely driven out, silenced and excluded from the campuses by the ascendant, largely Marxist, left. As a persecuted minority in the early 1970s the Islamists retreated from the campuses and increasingly focused their activities in the mosques themselves, retaining a low profile except for the occasional contribution to the Arabisation debate. Arabisation, though, did signal something of a reassertion of the Islamist movement in the universities with increasing clashes between Arabophone and Francophone students from 1974. As already shown, Arabic had become increasingly associated with Islamism whilst leftist students were largely Francophone and secularist. This resurgence was further boosted by another switch in government policy, which in 1976 reverted once more to using the Islamists against what the regime perceived to be an overly strong leftist element on the campuses.

The mosques

The forced retreat from activism in the universities and the refocusing of their activities in the country's mosques gave the various Islamist groups a much more secure base to work from and one which they worked to

---

45 It is interesting to note that the hedjab that began to appear on the university campuses was not the traditional white veil or *haik* of Algerian women, but was instead the semi-chador of the Arab East, thus illustrating the penetration of Islamist ideas and practices from outside Algeria.

expand. One of the main features of their work in the 1970s became the construction of mosques. Able to secure official recognition as associations for each project, the Islamists not only worked to convert large numbers of buildings into mosques and build new purpose-built places of prayer. More fundamentally they sought to carve out their own independent institutional framework free from the control of the state. This was particularly achieved through securing non-governmental funding (often from local merchants) for projects which enabled them to establish so-called "free" mosques outside of state control.[46] By 1976-7 many of the various "discussion circles" established by the different groups had managed to escape the watchful eye and control of the Ministry of Religious Affairs and had relocated themselves in the mosques.

The growth in the numbers of mosques, both free and otherwise, also provided centres of contact between the various Islamist groupings. The Islamist "movement" in the early 1970s was a fairly atomised affair with individual associations running their own preaching and teaching activities largely in isolation from each other. According to Abdallah Djaballah, the leader of a grouping in eastern Algeria which was active in the construction of mosques and opening of prayer rooms in Annaba and Constantine, he and his group had contacts with the Jazara in the universities but there was little overall co-ordination during this early period.[47] However, most of the "Sheikhs" of these different associations, including Djaballah, began to meet informally from the mid-1970s in the private mosque of Abdelhamid Chentli in Constantine which, together with the eastern region as a whole, remained the centre of Islamist activity in Algeria.[48]

Themes and Aspects

The unexpected death of Houari Boumedienne in December 1978 effectively marked the end of the first chapter of Algeria's independent history.

---

46 These projects are the essential focus of Ahmed Rouadjia's book, *Les Frères et la Mosquée: Enquête sur la Mouvement Islamiste en Algérie* (Paris, Karthala, 1990).

47 Author's interview with Abdallah Djaballah, London, 7.10.94.

48 Djaballah states that Islamist activity as a whole was restricted to the east and central (Algiers) region of the country during this period. Author's interview with Djaballah, 7.10.94.

Ben Bella had been the first President of Algeria, but it had been his successor's personality and policies that had dominated this early formative period. It was also the first time in several centuries in which Algeria's Muslims were able to conduct their own affairs. What then can be concluded about the role of Islam and Islamic sentiment during these years?

Islam and the state

The new rulers of independent Algeria, both Ben Bella and Boumedienne and their supporters, clearly realised the value and importance of Islam, not just through its contribution to the independence struggle but also through its potential contribution to the construction of the independent Algerian state. The Islamic reformism of the Association of Algerian Ulama had been absorbed by both the Algerian people during the war and in the view of one commentator more or less became "the political language" of the new state.[49] Its use by the various competitors for power in the period 1962–5 provided evidence of this. The state, under both Ben Bella and Boumedienne, tried to incorporate this reformism into the state itself: its policies, its propaganda and its internal battles. This creation of the idea of what was widely termed "state reformism" became a perceived source of legitimacy for those both in power and for those aspiring to it.

Those in power were primarily concerned with both retaining power and in advancing their own political, social and economic agendas. As has been shown in the case of both Ben Bella and Boumedienne, these agendas frequently had little to do with anything recognisably Islamic but owed more to essentially secular and particularly socialist-style programmes and ideas. Through these programmes, notably Boumedienne's "social revolution" of the 1970s, the politicians hoped to mould and transform what at independence was still a fairly divided and fragmented society. As John Entelis points out, Islam's role in this was to be fairly limited: "A secular state with an Islamic cultural component would thus be the manner in which a nationalist synthesis would be achieved."[50]

This "nationalisation" of Islam, though, did not go unchallenged. The view of the political leadership that "Islam was to serve as an identity-forming instrument, not as a legal code by which to order state and

---

49 Vatin, 'Religious resistance and state power', pp. 133–4.
50 Entelis, *Algeria: The Revolution Institutionalized*, p. 81.

society" profoundly contradicted much traditional and reformist Islamic thinking and teaching in Algeria.[51] Official attitudes towards religion prompted the formation of many of the Islamist groups in the 1970s. Abdallah Djaballah, in particular, was motivated by how widespread ignorance of Islam was and how the government appeared happy to exclude it from Algerian social life and even made jokes about those who attended the mosques. This clash between religious opinion and political authority, seen throughout the post-independence period, in many ways reflected a tradition in Algerian politics and society that stretched back well before independence. It could be seen in the nineteenth-century revolts against both the Ottomans and the French and in the key, if initially reluctant, role the AUMA played in the run up to the war of liberation.

The view that Islam and Islamist activism was a means of articulating more generalised opposition to the government, is an interesting and important one. In this context it seems important to judge how far Islamist groups and opinion in the 1960s and 1970s were promoting a clearly "Islamic" agenda and to what extent they were an expression and vehicle for wider grievances against the state. During Ben Bella's period of power, it would seem that whilst the criticisms of his regime voiced by Sheikh Ibrahimi and Al Qiyam were essentially Islamic in nature, they reflected the growing crisis in the regime generally. Without this crisis it seems unlikely that such criticism would have received the attention it did. Under Boumedienne, the new President's broadening of the base of the regime and his use of nationalism dispelled the crisis that had built up under his predecessor and thus cut away much of the ground swell of public unrest that Al Qiyam had briefly ridden on. It is instructive to note that the two issues that brought the Islamist movement to the fore in the 1970s, Arabisation and the Agrarian Revolution, both had their origins in socio-economic as much as religious grievances.

It was also important to note, however, that although the Islamist movement had found its strength and voice in alliance with wider issues and grievances, it still retained and developed its own ideology and agenda over this period.

---

51 *Ibid.*

Ideology and agenda

The achievement of independence by Algeria in 1962 clearly changed the context in which Algeria's Islamic movement operated. The colonial European threat to Islamic identity, culture and practice was removed but the imperative of returning Algerians to the teachings of pure scripturally based Islam remained for the supporters and members of the old AUMA. As has been seen, a section of this grouping was effectively co-opted into the state apparatus by the post-independence governments, particularly that of Boumedienne, and worked to contribute an Islamic element to the Algerian state. The section that remained outside this official framework, however, became increasingly radical in their outlook both towards the state and society in general.

This was evident from a fairly early stage of Algeria's independence. Despite explicitly claiming to be the inheritors of the legacy and ideals of Ben Badis's AUMA, Al Qiyam was a clearly more radical organisation. The association's hostility towards non-Islamic ideas and organisations illustrated earlier displayed, as Jean-Claude Vatin and Jean Leca rightly argue, "a fanatical fundamentalism, quite foreign to the thought of the founder of the Association of Ulama".[52] This hostility and radicalism was present not only in the writings and the propaganda of the organisation's leaders – which called for the closure of shops at times of prayer, the exclusion of non-Muslims from public service and particularly the restriction of female emancipation – but was also carried through to the actions of some of its members.[53] Not only were members of Al Qiyam responsible for continued harassment of "immodestly" dressed women on Algeria's streets, but threats were also issued to owners of bars selling alcohol in the capital. Such actions did not stop with the final dissolution of the organisation in 1970 and were continued by its former members and successor organisation into the following decade.

---

52 Jean Leca and Jean-Claude Vatin, *L'Algérie Politique: Institutions et Regime* (Paris, Presses de la Foundation Nationale des Sciences Politiques, 1975), p. 308.

53 The role of women in independent Algeria became an important theme of much Islamist discourse after independence. Bachir Ibrahimi had complained about the participation of young women in tennis skirts at the independence celebrations, Al Qiyam had called for a restriction on women's employment as a solution for male unemployment and Abdellatif Soltani in his 1974 diatribe attacked the presence of women in offices and the military.

The other element of this growth in radicalism, besides that addressing the perceived moral and social decline in independent Algeria, was an increasing hostility to the Algerian state itself. Official repression and alienation from the apparatus of the state contributed to this antagonism but it was a fundamental antipathy towards the perceived ideology of the new state, particularly its socialism, that underpinned much of this stance. In 1974 one of the former leaders of Al Qiyam, Abdellatif Soltani, launched a bitter attack on the regime in the form of an article. Published from exile in Morocco, the article attacked Boumedienne's socialist policies as "destructive principles imported from abroad".[54] He equated socialism with heresy and argued that it was responsible for many social vices such as alcoholism through its support of the planting of vineyards. Elsewhere Dawa wa Tabligh, one of the successor organisations to Al Qiyam, called in its literature for the abolition of socialist regimes in all Muslim countries. More generally, a view increasingly propagated privately in the schools and mosques loyal to the Islamists was that the victory of Islam against the French in 1962 had been "confiscated at independence by a coalition of communists and atheists".[55]

The near total ideological breach with the whole foundation of the Algerian state that this last view implies has certain echoes of the ideas of Sayyid Qutb in Egypt. However, despite the Qutb-inspired calls for the overthrow of the regime and the installation of an Islamic state through force of arms in the tracts distributed by Algerian Takfir wa Hijra in the mid-1970s, there appeared to be no real evidence of Islamist opposition to the Algerian government adopting a violent course of action. Dawa wa Tabligh were reported to have been responsible for the death of a policeman in Algiers in January 1971 and one Islamist was caught and convicted of sabotaging telegraph poles in opposition to the National Charter of 1976. Even though this last figure was the influential Mahfoud Nahnah, his was not a serious offence and these remained isolated or unsubstantiated incidents.

Explanations for these shifts were severalfold. Much of the radicalism had to do with the movement's political and institutional alienation from the Algerian regime, official repression, in particular, providing a natural

---

54 Mohammed Harbi, *L'Islamisme dans tous ses Etats* (Paris, Arcantere, 1991), pp. 135–9.
55 Rouadjia, *Les Frères et la Mosquée*, p. 147.

dynamic towards more radical positions. The movement's greater concentration on more specifically moral issues (such as those relating to women) and away from more egalitarian issues once utilised by the AUMA, has been seen as the result of the increasing monopolisation of egalitarian themes by the regime's socialist rhetoric and policies. A second reason for the movement's radicalisation was undoubtedly the influx of more extremist ideas from other parts of the Muslim world, especially Egypt, which came in with far greater ease following the achievement of Algerian independence and notably, as has been shown, with the teachers brought in for the Arabisation programmes. The death of Malek Bennabi in 1973 deprived Algerian Islamism of probably its most profound indigenous thinker since Abdelhamid Ben Badis and led to the country's Islamists looking even more towards the wider Muslim world for guidance. Writings by thinkers such as Hassan al-Banna and Maududi, as well as Ben Badis, became the staple intellectual diet of most of the Islamist students in the universities in the 1970s. Links with other Muslim countries were further cemented by growing financial as well as ideological ties. Saudi Arabia became an increasingly important source of funds for Algeria's Islamists by the 1970s. Islamist leaders made frequent trips to the Kingdom to exploit Saudi fears of the perceived atheistic tendencies of the Algerian regime which were fuelled by the latter's close relations to the godless Soviet Union.

Conclusion

In the context of events both inside Algeria and the development of the Islamist movement across the Muslim world as a whole, Algeria's Islamists remained strictly peripheral during this period. Despite enjoying a brief broader platform with Al Qiyam in the first few years of independence their influence from 1965 remained very limited. Inside the regime the few minor ministries that contained Islamist sympathisers and co-opted former members of the AUMA saw only slight advances of the Islamist agenda. Outside the institutions of the state, the fragmented and largely covert Islamist movement only really made itself felt through pockets of unrest and activism on the university campuses. Numerically, the movement remained a small-scale affair, a reflection of a more general decline in religious observance and awareness in the 1960s and 1970s that also spoke of the Islamists' failure to publicise their agenda. In 1964 Raymond Vallin wrote of "a feeling of decline in popular religion . . . Beneath the respect paid to it lies a good deal of indifference. People no longer pray in public, the pious are ridiculed, and the faithful are becoming rare, less than 1% from personal observations in Algiers."[56] This appeared particularly true of Algeria's younger population where secular and nationalist ideas were more prevalent. A survey of students in 1968 showed that only 17% of those questioned identified the term "Arabo-Islamism" with "a state governed according to the rules of Islam" whilst 81% identified it with "the affirmation of the Algerian national personality".[57] Boumedienne's state-building policies – his grand industrial and economic projects, the active and prestigious role he forged for Algeria in international and particularly third world politics – were clearly the main preoccupations for both Algerians and observers of the country in the 1960s and 1970s.

Similarly, whilst the 1970s witnessed the growth of significant and muscular Islamist movements in countries such as Syria, Egypt and Iran and indeed most other Middle Eastern states, Algeria appeared to be resistant to this trend. It was totally justified for one writer in 1980 to describe Algeria as marching in "the rearguard" of the international Islamist movement and thus seek to write a piece seeking to explore the subliminal reasons why Algeria had *not* developed such a movement in this period.[58]

---

56 Vallin, 'Muslim Socialism in Algeria", p. 57.

57 Leca and Vatin, *L'Algérie Politique*, p. 307.

58 Peter von Sivers, 'National integration and traditional rural organisation in Algeria 1970–80: background for Islamic traditionalism?' in Said Amir Arjomand: *From Nationalism to Revolutionary Islam* (London, Macmillan, 1984). The main reasons that von Sivers identifies as being behind this absence include the exposure through prolonged colonial rule to European ideas, low levels of Arabic literacy, the proletarianising of parts of the rural population under the French, the small size of the traditional urban class, and the rigour of state control and planning.

3

The Rise of Islamism, 1979–1988

From Boumedienne to Chadli

The fairly small-scale and largely clandestine nature of the Islamist "movement" in the late 1970s meant that the Islamists' reaction to the sudden death of President Boumedienne in December 1978 was neither widely canvassed nor considered amongst the main concerns of Algeria, as it sought to assimilate the fact that the dominant and shaping force of its post-independence history was now gone. Most attention focused on the succession to Boumedienne, which was resolved without any overt signs of a power struggle with the formal election of Colonel Chadli Benjedid as President in February 1979.

Although Chadli Benjedid's assumption of the presidency initially indicated continuity rather than any real break with the policies and approaches of his predecessor, this did not imply that Boumedienne's death would have no, particularly longer-term, impact on Algeria's Islamists. Nor did it indicate that the late President's largely successful containment of any Islamist "challenge" in the thirteen years of his rule would be continued by the new President. Chadli Benjedid, although a respected figure, had been a compromise choice pushed forward by the Algerian military in preference to the two main contenders for the office. The long-standing military commander of the Oran region, the new President lacked his predecessor's charisma, intellect and vision; qualities that had enabled Boumedienne to establish control and unity over Algeria's traditionally fractious society and polity and which had succeeded in preventing the emergence of any serious challenge to either him or the Algerian state.

For Algeria's Islamists, the departure of the figure who had espoused so much that was anathema to them and, moreover, had so successfully suppressed and silenced their organisations, was a welcome development. With a strengthening and expanding (if still relatively small-scale) institutional base in the country's mosques and universities, the various groups and associations that made up this still fairly nebulous "movement" believed this growth was likely to continue and accelerate under the new regime.

Several actions by Chadli's government during its opening years served to encourage the hopes of the Islamists. High-profile political opponents of Boumedienne were released from prison (most notably Ahmed Ben Bella) and, more significantly, several figures seen as sympathetic to the Islamists' agenda were appointed to the government. Abderahman Chibane, a figure who despite his closeness to the regime had attracted the deference of many Islamists outside the administration, was promoted in July 1980 to Minister for Religious Affairs – a portfolio existing in its own right again after four years under the direct control of the presidency. Figures committed to Arabisation took over the Ministries of Information and Culture and of Primary and Secondary Education in Chadli's first government, thus boosting this part of the Islamists' agenda and, more importantly, bolstering a proven constituency of support. Evidence of this was seen in the renewed vigour with which Arabisant and Islamist students began to press their frequently interwoven agendas. Arabisant high school and university students held a long strike in the winter of 1979-80 as part of a more general campaign to draw official attention to the failings of the Arabisation programme – specifically the continued failure of most Arabisants to make progress in the job market. In the universities Islamist students also began to adopt a far higher profile.

The growth of Islamist activism: 1979–1982

Having contracted under pressure from the student left in the early 1970s, the Islamists had begun to expand once again from the middle of the decade their presence and activities on the university campuses (see Chapter Two). Clashes with leftist students continued into the 1980s and also began to occur against the increasingly vocal and organised Berber student groups on the campuses. This latter group had also been encouraged by President Chadli's liberalising gestures and they saw the Arabisation programmes as a threat to their own language, culture and job prospects (most Berber students were also accomplished Francophones). Violence against groups allied to the regime itself also became a feature of Islamist activism in this period. In May 1981 violent Islamist disruption of several meetings organised by the leftist-led official youth movement (the UNJA) to commemorate the "Day of the Student" led to thirty people being badly injured at one meeting. Islamist willingness to attack symbols and allies of the regime was also reflected that month in attacks by students on public buildings, especially university and prefecture buildings, in cities across Algeria including Abbès, Algiers, Annaba and Bedjaima.[1]

The new-found self-confidence of the Islamist students was not limited to sporadic violence against other students but also began to exhibit itself in more concrete and co-ordinated ways. In December 1979 students took over a large lecture room at the Institute of Law in Algiers and converted it into a mosque. The success of this move, which was not resisted by the university authorities, appeared to encourage the campus militants generally who increasingly sought to make their ideas and presence felt in more and more areas of campus life. Overt and unsolicited recruitment, involving speeches and pamphlet distributions, by Islamists in university and college classes became increasingly commonplace. Bolder still, was the forcing of sexual segregation in the classes.

By 1982 the influence of Islamist students on university campuses had become considerable and could even be said to dominate certain faculties in certain universities. One non-Islamist student in Oran commented as follows on the influence of the Islamists at her university:

> They have created an environment at the university where it is dangerous to be politically involved. Those who speak out risk being silenced by force. They have gained implicit control of the student ambience.[2]

The early years of the Chadli presidency also saw the growth of Islamist activism in other areas. In 1979, an organisation calling itself the Group for Defence Against the Illicit was formed under the leadership of a Mustapha Bouyali. An FLN veteran of the liberation struggle, Bouyali had been disillusioned by what he saw as the failure to establish an Islamic

---

1   In April 1982 the FLN headquarters in Oran and vehicles of party officials had also come under attack from rioting *lycée* students, who although essentially protesting about examination failures were also believed to have been involved with Islamist groups.

2   Knauss, *The Persistence of Patriarchy*, p. 119.

state at independence. He was further dismayed by the socialist emphasis of the 1976 National Charter and used sermons at the El-Achour mosque in the Mitidja to campaign for a return to Islamic values in social and political life. Collecting together a number of still fairly autonomous groups based in the mosques of Algiers, Bouyali's organisation sought initially to put pressure on the government to amend its policies. However, following his failure to persuade other Islamist groups and leaders to participate in a protest march on 1 May 1981 to demand the implementation of the sharia, Bouyali began to contemplate the use of force to establish an Islamic state and from mid-1981 he and his supporters started to collect and stockpile weapons. A network of clandestine cells was established across the country which Bouyali had divided into various operational regions in probable conscious imitation of the original wilaya system of the FLN. The martial orientation of the organisation was confirmed by its metamorphosis into the Mouvement Algérien Islamique Armé (MAIA) when it merged with other smaller groups in July 1982.[3]

Confronting the regime: November–December 1982

Throughout the period 1979–82 the Chadli regime had practised a fairly tolerant approach to the clearly growing Islamist tendency. The reasons for such an approach were probably linked to the presence of Islamist sympathies amongst some of the senior personnel in the government but more likely were the result of wider policy considerations and needs on the part of the regime. Initially, Chadli, like his predecessor Boumedienne quietly encouraged the Islamists in order to stifle leftist agitation on the campuses.[4] For Chadli, the Islamists could also be used to combat two further threats to his regime: the newly assertive Berberist movement and leftist opponents within the regime itself. This second grouping consisted particularly of those disciples and supporters of Boumedienne's more

---

3 Each cell of the MAIA was headed by an Emir who provided the ideological input for the group as well as being the sole point of contact with other cells. Not all the cells were concerned with armed action, some were of a more political or religious orientation.

4 It has been suggested that ministerial level intervention had been behind the failure of the university authorities to evict the Islamist students who had occupied the classroom in the Institute of Law in Algiers in 1979. Whether this intervention was on the part of a sympathetic individual or part of wider government policy is uncertain.

radical socialist policies who were suspicious and hostile towards the economically liberalising reforms that Chadli had begun to introduce in this period.

The regime had still maintained a watchful eye over the Islamist movement during this period, particularly those parts of it which tried to make too obvious a challenge to the authorities. The government intervened in Sidi Bel Abbès in 1981 following an aggressive campaign by Islamists there under the leadership of Othman Mohammed who had sought to take over all the town's mosques from officially appointed imams. Significant disturbances, involving at least a thousand people, following intervention by the local authorities, finally prompted the government to clamp down and dismantle the group. Official attention was also attracted to the activities of Mustapha Bouyali and his followers. The security services had noted Bouyali's rhetorical forays into the area of politics in the occasional sermons he had given at the El-Achour mosque and they monitored his and his supporters' activities. It was during this surveillance that a confrontation occurred between Bouyali's group and the police in April 1982 which resulted in Bouyali's brother, Mokhtar, being shot – an incident that undoubtedly prompted Bouyali to transform his organisation into the more covert and organised MAIA.

These moves against the Islamist movement still remained exceptions to the general policy of tolerance operated by the Chadli regime. This approach, however, came under increasing strain throughout 1982 and was finally cast aside in November 1982 following a further outbreak of violence in the universities, which had resulted for the first time in the death of a student. The fatal stabbing of Kamel Amzel, a leftist, during disturbances following elections to residence hall committees on the Ben Aknoun campus of Algiers University on 2 November led to a significant clamp down by the authorities. Nearly 400 Islamist supporters were arrested in attempts to quell the unrest.

The crackdown did not, however, dampen the Islamist unrest. In reaction to the arrests, Islamists organised a prayer meeting at a university building in the centre of Algiers on 12 November. The meeting attracted several thousand people (estimates vary considerably[5]) and disrupted traffic

---

5   5,000 is a figure most frequently quoted (e.g. Burgat and Dowell, *The Islamist Movement in North Africa*, p. 263) but attendances as large as 100,000 are recorded (Entelis, *Algeria: The Revolution Institutionalized* p.87)

in that area of the city for several hours as it overflowed into the streets. Such a significant display of public support for the Islamists was a further clear indication of the growing self-confidence of the movement and, moreover, represented a clear challenge to the Government. This challenge manifested itself not just in the size of the meeting and its defiance of the threat of a further official clampdown but, more importantly, was directly articulated by the issuing of a written set of demands by the organisers of the meeting. This fourteen-point document, besides calling for the release of the arrested activists, contained most of the traditional demands and rhetoric of the Islamist movement. They included demands for increases in religious and Arabic education, greater legal status for the sharia, an end to the mixing of the sexes in schools and offices and more general railing against the incursion of Western and colonial influences in Algerian society.[6]

The regime reacted to this challenge by making further large-scale arrests, taking into custody the three leaders of the demonstration who had been the signatories of the list of demands. All three figures were well-established figures in Algeria's Islamist movement. Two, Abdellatif Soltani and Ahmed Sahnoun, were ageing well-respected Sheikhs, who had been members of Ben Badis's original AUMA and had continued to be active and independent through the 1960s and 1970s – Soltani having been the author of the uncompromising attack on Boumedienne's socialism from exile in Morocco in 1974 (see Chapter Two). The third figure, Abassi Madani, was younger but had been involved in Al Qiyam as well as the group around Malek Bennabi. He had spent a significant part of the 1970s studying for a Ph.D. in Britain, but had returned at the end of the decade to teach the sociology of education at university in Algiers, where he played a significant role in the organisation and mobilisation of the Islamist students.

The regime also chose this time to strike against Bouyali's MAIA. The grouping had become increasingly active in the wake of the events of early November and had mounted operations to steal equipment and explosives. Following the discovery of several caches of arms and explosives by the authorities, twenty-three members of the organisation were arrested in mid-December 1982. This move by the authorities forestalled alleged

---

6 For the full text of the document see M. Al-Ahnaf, Bernard Botiveau and Frank Frégosi, *L'Algérie par ses Islamistes* (Paris, Karthala, 1991), pp. 45–8.

plans by the MAIA to launch a series of attacks against various official targets. Scheduled for December, these plans had included the assassination of the Prime Minister, the kidnapping of the FLN's number two figure, Chérif Messadia, and attacks against the headquarters of various organisations (such as the official women's organisation) and certain public monuments in the capital.

The firm-handedness with which the regime had dealt with the Islamist movement in late 1982 was, however, curiously not matched by its subsequent actions. Despite the large-scale arrests, no Islamists were brought to trial during the seventeen months following the unrest. When proceedings finally did take place, in September 1984, twelve of the nineteen defendants on trial for acts of violence were acquitted. One was sentenced to eight years' imprisonment for the manslaughter of Kamel Amzel, and the remainder received sentences ranging from one to five years. The apparent leniency of these sentences and the intervening delays appeared to be at odds with the original tough approach of the authorities.

The reason for this leniency was the continuing unease within the Government over the apparent strength and size of the Islamist movement which appeared to be undiminished by the repression of late 1982. A dramatic demonstration of the enduring support enjoyed by the movement occurred with the funeral of Abdellatif Soltani in April 1984 – the ageing Sheikh having died whilst still under the house arrest he had been sentenced to following his arrest in 1982. Attended by a crowd of mourners tens of thousands strong (estimates again vary[7]) the funeral was another testimony to the mobilising powers of the Islamists. The Government's decision to postpone trials of Islamists arrested in 1982 from May 1984 (the month after Soltani's funeral) to the following September was clearly due to concerns that the trials might provoke Islamist unrest. The release of the other two leaders of the November 1982 demonstration, Abassi Madani and Ahmed Sahnoun, on the original trial date in May 1984 was a further indication of official willingness to appease the Islamists.

---

7   Al-Ahnaf, Botiveau and Frégosi quote the number attending as 20,000 (*ibid.*, p. 310); Roberts cites a figure of 25,000 ('Radical Islamism', p. 579); Entelis uses 100,000 (*Algeria: The Revolution Institutionalized*, p. 87).

Government co-optation and concessions, 1982–1986

The government policy of combining repression of Islamism's militant edges with conciliatory gestures to avoid provoking the wider movement also encompassed measures aimed at undercutting the bases of Islamist support and sentiment within the country. Primarily this involved the state in efforts, similar to those adopted by Boumedienne, directed at incorporating religious activity and life into the institutional framework of the state as well as including selective elements of the Islamist agenda in government policy.

Chadli Benjedid had, as has been shown, already made several apparent concessions (albeit for different reasons) to the Islamists in the early years of his presidency, through appointing sympathetic government ministers and by continuing with the Arabisation programmes. Such initiatives were continued and intensified in the aftermath of the disturbances of late 1982. Levels of government funding to Quranic educational establishments (the construction of which the government had begun itself to fund) were rapidly increased as was recruitment of young imams to serve in the mosques. Many of them were trained in four new training centres for imams that the regime established. In October 1984 the government opened the Emir Abdelkader University of Islamic Sciences in Constantine which became the largest mosque–university complex in North Africa.

These institutional moves represented not just a desire on the part of the regime to portray itself as a supporter of Islam. More importantly, they were attempts to halt the growth in the number of "free" or independent mosques staffed by imams who had not been appointed by the state and which, as has been shown, had been an important feature of Islamist institutional expansion since the 1970s. The issue of Islamist activity and control of mosques had become one of increasing concern to President Chadli. Fear of Islamist influence even prompted him in 1985 to ask his Prime Minister, Abdelhamid Brahimi, one of the few members of the government who still regularly attended the mosque, to do so no longer.[8] As a consequence of these concerns, new rules covering the mosques were introduced, requiring all imams to possess a degree from an appropriate

---

8   Chadli's fears were perhaps prompted by the fact that Brahimi was the son of Mubarak Mili, one of the senior figures in Abdelhamid Ben Badis's Association of Algerian Ulama.

(government-supervised) religious institute, and sole authority for the assignment of Muslim clergy to positions countrywide was vested in the Ministry for Religious Affairs. The end of official tolerance of the existence of independent Islamist imams, which had effectively operated since the beginning of the 1970s, was signalled in a speech given by the President in November 1986. In announcing the introduction of measures requiring the construction of new mosques to be subject to official approval, Chadli had declared that: "We cannot leave the mosque at the mercy of certain pernicious elements who will use it for destructive purposes."[9]

There were also continued attempts to dominate and direct the discourse, as well as the institutional manifestations, of Islam in the country. There was increased use of religious references and language by government officials and ministers in their speeches, which often sought to portray the regime and its leaders as upholders and protectors of Islam. In one speech the Minister of Religious Affairs, Abderahman Chibane, praised President Chadli for striving to "re-establish the hierarchy of values by placing faith in Allah above any other allegiance".[10] The government made use of the media to achieve its twin aims of gaining control of the Islamic discourse as well as persuading the populace that it was not (as the Islamists claimed) forgetting the country's Islamic character and heritage. Television programmes on Fridays became almost exclusively devoted to religious themes and substantial media coverage was given to Sheikh Mohammed Ghazali, a cleric and former member of the Egyptian Muslim Brotherhood and new head of the Islamic University of Constantine, who spoke out against more radical interpretations of Islam claiming Islam to be a religion of "humanism and progress". Significantly, almost exactly the same words were used to describe Islam in the new Algerian Constitution which was approved in January 1986.

The regime also made various concessions to Islamist sentiment and opinion, the most important of which being the new Family Code passed and introduced in 1984. The Code, described by John Ruedy as "a blend of Islamic and traditional Algerian notions" included many stipulations, such as those defining and restricting women's rights to marriage, divorce and work, that were in line with Islamist social values but which

---

9   *El Moudjahid*, 12.11.86.
10   Entelis, *Algeria: The Revolution Institutionalized*, p. 88.

were, not surprisingly, anathema to large numbers of Algerian women.[11] The strength and effectiveness of organised women's opposition had helped prevent the introduction of a similar (although, ironically, more moderate) Family Code three years earlier in 1981.[12] The successful introduction, though, of the 1984 Code was attributed to the growth in the influence of the Islamists in the intervening period. The increased use of violence and intimidation by Islamists (as witnessed in the universities) explained the failure of the women's movement to successfully re-mobilise against the new code.

Desire to undermine the Islamists' appeal was not the only reason for these official concessions. As in the 1960s and 1970s there existed elements within the regime itself that shared many of the views, if not the increased radicalism, of the Islamist movement. Chadli Benjedid's appointment of Abderahman Chibane as Minister of Religious Affairs had been popular with Islamists outside the regime and the presence of officials from the Ministry at the funeral of Abdellatif Soltani in April 1984 was evidence of the sympathy with the Islamist cause. Such sympathies were not confined to individual ministries or officials. The Algerian legislative assembly – the APN (Assemblée Populaire et Nationale) – although consisting solely of FLN deputies, produced far more restrictive proposals for women's personal status following debates over the Family Code than had been expected by the President. This indicated the strength of Islamic and traditionalist views in the Assembly.

Fragmentation, co-operation and conflict: the Islamist movement, 1979–1982

Despite the impact that Algeria's Islamists had made on the political scene between 1979 and 1982 and the alarm this had caused within the regime, the Islamist "movement", such as it was, remained as fragmented as it had been in the 1970s. The contacts that had been established between the various groups from the mid-1970s were, however, retained

---

11 Ruedy, *Modern Algeria*, p. 243. Specifically the Code made women the wards of their family until marriage; prohibited Muslim women from marrying non-Muslims; made divorce "almost totally a male prerogative" (Ruedy) and made a woman's right to work outside the home subject to the approval of her guardian.

12 For a fuller account of the debate and struggle over the 1981 Family Code see Knauss, *The Persistence of Patriarchy*, pp. 125–40

and even expanded, two mosques in particular becoming centres for increased co-ordination and co-operation. The Bait al-Arqam mosque became the base for the work and preaching of both Abdellatif Soltani and Ahmed Sahnoun and hosted numerous conferences, lectures and discussions from 1976-77. The Ben Achour mosque also became an important focus for Islamist activity and co-operation, providing the forum for what one contemporary Islamist leader described as "the first important meeting" between representatives of all of Algeria's major Islamist tendencies and groups in early 1979.[13] However, despite the supposed intent of this gathering to forge some form of unity between the various factions, the range of views (and undoubtedly personalities) frustrated any move towards greater co-operation.

Relationships between the groups were frequently marked by rivalry and animosity, despite the fact that most of the groups and their leaders were familiar with each other. Demonstrations of apparent Islamist strength and unity, such as the 12 November meeting in 1982, frequently obscured divisions and hostility between different factions. The decision to call the November rally, the idea of Abassi Madani, had been strongly contested by the Jazara, whose Majlis Shura had rejected the move. Furthermore, the Jazara's leaders, Mohammed Said and Thabet Aouel Mohammed, had called on Islamists not to participate in the planned meeting. This loss of support from the Jazara, which was still centred in the universities led, it is argued, Abassi to solicit the participation of Soltani and Sahnoun in the show of force in order to add weight to its significance and resulting charter of demands. Despite the evident success of the move, the Jazara proceeded to try and block attempts by Abassi Madani to speak at mosques in the immediate aftermath of the rally, before he was arrested by the authorities.

On another front, the Jazara were equally opposed to those Islamists led by Mahfoud Nahnah whose pan-Islamic ideas and contacts were in conflict with their nationalist, Algerianist beliefs and who was consequently accused of being controlled by foreign powers. The university campuses became a particular field of competition between the two groups, especially from the end of 1982, as Nahnah sought to use the universities as

---

13 Doudi Mohammed Abdelhadi quoted in Burgat and Dowell, *The Islamist Movement in North Africa*, pp. 261–2. Abdelhadi had preached at both Bait al-Arqam and Ben Achour mosques.

a base to present himself as the premier figure in the Islamist movement in the absence of the imprisoned Sahnoun, Soltani and Madani.[14] The failure of the leadership of the Jazara to prevent the rally of November 1982 – which had resulted in many of its members being arrested – prompted it over the next two years to structure and organise itself properly in order to exert more influence and to combat the influence of Nahnah.

The relationship between Mustapha Bouyali and his supporters and the rest of the Islamist movement was interesting. The leader of the MAIA's involvement in the Ben Achour mosque from the late 1970s indicated that he had contacts with most of the other major figures and factions in the movement and indeed it appeared that he constantly sought the support and blessing of other Islamist leaders. However, he was unable to gain such endorsement. His plan to stage a combined march by Islamists on 1 May 1981 was rejected by nearly all the senior Islamist figures he consulted. When he began to make plans for a campaign of violence it appeared that several senior figures actually sought to stop him from embarking on such a course of action. It is alleged that in 1981 Abassi Madani used sermons to appeal for people not to involve themselves with Bouyali's campaign, a message that led on one occasion (in Sidi Bel Abbès at a mosque controlled by Othman Mohammed) to him being attacked and harangued by some of his listeners.[15] It has also been alleged, in this case by one of Bouyali's lieutenants, Ahmed Merah, that Mahfoud Nahnah, who had received Bouyali on several occasions despite being the main opponents of Bouyali's plans for a march, had maintained contacts with Bouyali in order to gain intelligence about the MAIA which he then passed on to the authorities.

These divergences and conflicts underlined the continually divided and fractious nature of the Islamist movement in the 1980s. Differences

---

14 Nahnah had not been arrested along with the other Islamist figures since although he had agreed to draw up the document unveiled at the rally on 12 November (by virtue of his superior command of Arabic) he had not attended the rally itself. His absence together with his recent early release from prison (following his conviction in 1976 – see Chapter Two) by President Chadli marked the starting point of speculation amongst other Islamists about Nahnah's relationship with the regime and the importance of his own personal ambitions.

15 It was furthermore alleged that Abassi reported this incident to the authorities, thus precipitating the clampdown on the organisation referred to earlier.

over ideology and leadership continued to plague relationships between the various groups and factions, only partially overcome during times of perceived crisis such as November 1982. Rivalries and splits even emerged within groups. Abdallah Djaballah's significant organisation in the east of the country which had grown out of the mosque associations of the 1970s, became riven with internal conflict, resulting in most of the senior figures quitting the organisation in the mid- and late 1980s. Abassi Madani, who was intentionally not attached to any particular grouping, made particular efforts in the early part of the decade to unite and foster co-operation between the disparate factions of the Islamist movement but, with the exception of 1982, he made little headway.[16]

Bouyali's campaign, 1983–1987

The move against the MAIA by the government in December 1982 – which was consolidated by further arrests in January 1983 and the break-up of the command cell of the organisation – did not, however, signal the end of Mustapha Bouyali's plans for armed insurrection against the state. He himself evaded the authorities and fled abroad (it is thought to either Iran or Libya) returning covertly to Algeria at the end of 1984. Re-establishing contacts with many of his old supporters (92 of whom had been released by the authorities in May 1984) Bouyali formally reconstituted the MAIA at a secret meeting in February 1985 and began plan once more for a campaign of armed insurgency.

The first evidence of these plans and the re-emergence of the MAIA came in August 1985 when the group mounted two significant operations. The first took the form of an armed robbery at a factory near Algiers on 21 August, in which the large works' payroll was stolen. The second, six days later, was an attack against a police barracks in the southern town of Soumma, in which arms and ammunition were taken and a police cadet killed. That these operations were something more than simple acts of criminal banditry and were aimed at securing financial

---

16   Although a member of Al Qiyam in the 1960s Abassi Madani claimed that he had "no confidence" in the notion of Islamic organisations and thus preferred to work independently. Author's interview with Rachid Ghannoushi, leader of the Tunisian Islamist movement, London, 18.4.95.

and logistic supplies for an armed jihad was indicated by the painting of the phrase "Allah the Avenger is with us" across the gate of the barracks at Soumma following the attack there.

In response to these events the government dispatched a significant force to the Atlas mountains, where the group appeared to be based, with the intention of swiftly crushing the group. However, Bouyali and his followers proved difficult to track down and even when there were sightings, the MAIA, despite its small size, proved capable of inflicting disproportionate losses on the pursuing government forces. Rejecting official attempts to establish channels of communication, the group continued its campaign against targets it considered to be anathema to Islam with "un-Islamic" buildings such as girls' schools, libraries, restaurants and cinemas being attacked. Bouyali himself continued to avoid capture and continued to make regular public appearances at mosques in the region. Aided by his expert knowledge of the mountainous region, gained as an FLN guerrilla in the War of Independence, as well as by noticeable support from the local population, Bouyali managed to avoid being tracked down by the authorities until early 1987 when he was finally killed in an ambush by the security services.

The fall of Mustapha Bouyali represented the end of the MAIA's sixteen month campaign of armed resistance. Nearly all those members of his group who had not been killed during the course of the campaign were put on trial by the authorities in July 1987. Compared to the relative leniency of the sentencing of those Islamists arrested in 1982, the sentences delivered on Bouyali's companions this time were far more severe. Reflecting an improved official confidence in the face of the Islamist challenge as well as a desire to deal harshly with this first serious attempt at armed insurrection by the movement, the courts acquitted just 15 of the 202 defendants with 5 members of the group receiving the death penalty.

Support for Islamism, 1979–1988

The 1980s witnessed a clear increase in the confidence and activism of Algeria's Islamists, but the degree of popular support the movement actually enjoyed remained unclear. The absence of any institutional unity in the movement made any attempt at calculation of support difficult. Of the main individual groups, one observer estimated that, at most, the

Muslim Brothers' support was roughly 20,000 strong across the country.[17] The trials of Mustapha Bouyali's MAIA gave a more concrete indication of his following, the 202 defendants in the trials of 1987 reflecting, in the view of one Algerian newspaper, an activist base of around 600 during the decade.[18]

For the movement generally, the, albeit imprecise, figures for attendance at both the 12 November rally in Algiers in 1982 and the funeral of Abdellatif Soltani eighteen months later indicated five-figure levels of active popular support for Islamism. However, Hugh Roberts has observed that the significance of this level of support is reduced when it is remembered that Al Qiyam's public gatherings in the 1960s had been able to attract similar crowds to those gathered in November 1982. Similarly, attendance at Soltani's funeral, although more substantial, was comparable to that at Messali Hadj's interment ten years earlier – both men being figures largely disapproved of by the authorities.[19] It would therefore be fair to assume that the core support for the movement had not really increased over the whole period, although it is probably true that support in the 1980s was up on the level it had declined to during the previous decade.

Nevertheless, the influence the movement appeared to have over Algerian society generally clearly increased in the 1980s. This was most noticeable in the areas of dress and public social behaviour, with many more Algerians adopting Islamic dress and observing Islamic mores than had been the case in the 1960s and 1970s.

Estimating the level of support for the Islamist movement in the 1980s remained difficult, but identifying the sections of Algerian society that aligned themselves with the movement became easier as it became more open and assertive in this period. It appeared that the movement

---

17 Mohammed Boudiaf, quoted in Knauss, *The Persistence of Patriarchy*, p. 121. Boudiaf had been one of the senior figures in the FLN during the war of liberation but had been in exile since 1963. He was later to return to Algeria to become President in 1992 (see Chapters Six and Seven).

18 *Algérie Actualité*, 23.2.93.

19 Hugh Roberts, 'From radical mission to equivocal ambition: the expansion and manipulation of Algerian Islamism, 1979–1992' in Martin E. Marty and R. Scott Appleby, *The Fundamentalism Project, Volume 4: Accounting for Fundamentalisms: The Dynamic Character of Movements* (Chicago, University of Chicago Press, 1994), p. 446.

attracted an extremely wide and heterogeneous cross-section of the Algerian population. Students continued to provide the most organised and visible manifestation of Islamism, but the rally held at Algiers University in November 1982 also attracted significant numbers of workers, minor government functionaries and tradesmen. The involvement of these groups has been explained in economic terms, liberalising economic reforms introduced by the government having increased unemployment in the 1980s, thus threatening the livelihoods of these sections of the population as well as the job prospects of students.[20] However, whilst this probably had an impact, Islamism also appeared to have a robust following amongst elements of the bourgeoisie who provided, in the view of one commentator, the main source of support for the movement outside the universities.[21]

There also appeared to be no particular geographic base for the movement. Virtually all of the activism that was witnessed between 1979 and 1982 was centred in urban Algeria, but Mustapha Bouyali's campaign of the mid-1980s was based in and around the foothills of the Atlas mountains away from Algeria's major cities.[22] Bouyali's continued ability to evade capture by the authorities was in large part due to the support he and his group enjoyed locally in the small towns and villages of the region. Larbaa, the town in which Bouyali was finally cornered by the security services, has been described as one "notorious for its Islamist sympathies"[23]. Furthermore, another observer writing in the 1980s argued that support for the Muslim Brothers was actually stronger in the villages and small towns of Algeria than in its cities.[24]

The trial of Bouyali's associates provided further evidence of the heterogeneous nature of Islamist support. Amongst the 202 defendants, there were workers (49), agricultural labourers (29), technicians (4), tradesmen (22), teachers (12), students (8), artisans (5), functionaries

---

20 See for example Vatin, 'Popular puritanism versus state reformism', pp. 108–9.
21 François Burgat, *L'Islamisme au Maghreb: La Voix du Sud* (Paris, Karthala, 1988), p. 169.
22 Initial units of the MAIA were to be found in Algiers, Oran, Sétif and Skikda but its real strength was to be found in the Sahel and the Mitidja region.
23 Roberts, 'Radical Islamism', p. 581. Roberts attributes this Islamist sympathy, common to other towns in the region, to social dislocation caused by migration from the hill villages thus enhancing the appeal of the Islamist message and its certainties.
24 Knauss, *The Persistence of Patriarchy*, p. 123.

(7), several professionals as well as a number (13) of unemployed.[25] This wide cross-section of backgrounds also indicated that even the radical stance adopted by Bouyali had no greater apparent appeal to one section of Algerian society over another.

One minor qualification to this overall conclusion that the Islamist movement did not seem to markedly attract particular areas of Algerian society was that age appeared to become a feature of Islamist support in the 1980s. Details of the backgrounds of the MAIA defendants give no real indication of their ages, but it was a noted fact that specifically *young* men became increasingly involved in Islamist activism in this period. This was not just confined to the universities. As Richard Parker observed in 1983:

> . . . in Boumedienne's time, mosque attendance was like church attendance in Moscow – the old, the infirm and the idle made up the congregation. This has changed in the last five years – there is a marked increase in the number of young men congregating at mosques.[26]

The involvement of particularly young men in Islamist activism, like the involvement of students, was a notable feature to be found in Islamist movements elsewhere in the Muslim world. Increased feelings of confusion and alienation in societies which have experienced rapid change have been advanced as an explanation for this phenomenon – these having led the young to take refuge in the cultural and religious certainties of the Islamists' message.[27] In Algeria it was undoubtedly the declining economic and employment prospects of the 1980s that predominantly pushed young men towards supporting groups, such as the Islamists, who were highly critical of the ruling order. It was also true that Islamist groups deliberately targeted this section of the population, mounting aggressive recruitment drives outside Islamist-controlled mosques.

---

25 Analysis by Mohammed Harbi in *Jeune Afrique Plus*, September–October 1990.
26 Parker, *North Africa: Regional Tensions and Strategic Concerns* (New York, Praeger, 1984), pp. 97–8.
27 See for example Knauss, *The Persistence of Patriarchy*, p. 123.

Ideology and agenda

The rather fragmentary nature of the Islamist movement during this period makes an effective analysis of the ideology and agenda of the movement, as a whole, rather difficult. Nevertheless, the various tracts, speeches, publications and activities of the different groups provided some good indications of the ideas and inclinations of Algeria's Islamists.[28]

Much of the apparent agenda of the Islamists into the 1980s seemed to share a large part of that espoused by earlier Islamist organisations such as Al Qiyam and Ben Badis's Association of Algerian Ulama. Certain social, cultural and educational demands remained a central feature of Islamist campaigns and discourse. The list of demands drawn up by Abassi Madani, Abdellatif Soltani and Ahmed Sahnoun at the time of the mass meeting of 12 November 1982 contained many of the traditional Islamist demands of the AUMA and Al Qiyam and, moreover, reflected the three leaders' past membership of these organisations. In education, demands for greater Quranic instruction and the ending of co-education and, indeed, of all education for women after the age of 12, were regular features in Islamic propaganda and speeches. In other fields calls for more attention to Islamic themes and issues in the media were frequently heard as were the perennial concerns about women's social behaviour and dress.

There were some detectable innovations in the ideology and agenda of the Islamists. There was a widening, in some sections of the movement, of the focus and attention of Islamist activism and thought from concentration on specific religious issues and individual policies of the government (such as those identified above) to a wider analysis of the whole nature of government and the state itself. This development, beginning in the late 1970s, in the independent mosques, was described by one activist who witnessed the change in sermons and discussions:

> These were no longer lessons dealing with how to pray or perform a fast and all that. No, these were lessons at a high level in which we explained, or we searched for a method by which we could live in an Islamic state . . . And we also touched on the problems which

---

28 For most of this period the movement lacked a newspaper of its own of the sort published by Islamist groups in other countries, although in the period of relative political liberalism under Chadli, before the clampdown of late 1982, a number of Islamist publications began to appear.

the Algerian nation was confronting. We spoke about everything. Of all the situations, the economy, of all the aspects of life.[29]

Such new emphasis, as indicated, did not simply refer to the adoption of a more critical attitude towards the government. As Al Qiyam had done in the 1960s and Soltani in the 1970s, Islamists in the 1980s continued to attack the regime's espousal of socialism, branding President Chadli "red" or "pink" and condemning alleged corruption in high places.[30] However, by the late 1970s, Islamists had become increasing critical of the institution of the state itself, arguing that the existing political structures led to glorification of the state rather than Islam and had thus disrupted the unity of the wider Muslim *umma*. Furthermore, Islamists began to propose an, albeit very unformulated, alternative to the existing Algerian state. The welter of tracts and leaflets produced and distributed by the Islamists during the unrest in November 1982 frequently called for the creation of an "Islamic" republic and the abrogation of the National Charter of 1976 and its replacement, as a constitution, with the Quran.

This shift has been explained as being largely the result of the rise of younger militants in the movement who were not only more radical but more intellectually oriented than the older generation of Islamists such as Soltani, who, one commentator argues was "partially marginalized" by this new influx.[31] This influx, of new ideas and leaders, was in turn largely the result of the continuing and growing influence of foreign Islamist thought and movements in Algeria.[32] This growth in foreign influence was greatly assisted by the emergence of more and more Arabophones in the Islamist movement – the products of the Arabisation programmes

---

29 Doudi Mohammed Abdelhadi quoted in Burgat and Dowell, *The Islamist Movement in North Africa*, p. 261.
30 Entelis, *Algeria: The Revolution Institutionalized*, p. 85.
31 Burgat and Dowell, *The Islamist Movement in North Africa*, p. 259.
32 Foreign Islamist thought, it ought to be stressed was itself far from homogeneous in nature and not all of it was radical in its ideology. The Egyptian Islamist movement, which had a particularly important ideological influence on Algerian Islamism, was divided by the 1970s between followers of the more radical and revolutionary ideas of Sayyid Qutb and the more mainstream Muslim Brotherhood who officially renounced violence. Given the hostility of Algerian Islamists to the Algerian regime and the use of violence by Mustapha Bouyali, John Entelis has observed that Algerian Islamism in the 1980s was "more radical socially and politically" than the Muslim Brotherhood. Entelis, *Algeria: The Revolution Institutionalized*, p. 85.

of the 1970s – who were clearly drawn to the Arabic texts of Islamist writers from elsewhere in the Arab world.

Despite this general observation of overall continuity with a more radical and politicised edge, the segmented nature of the Islamist movement in the 1980s ensured that there was no uniform ideology. Whilst many groups were influenced by foreign ideas, groups such as the Jazara, even though they were numerically much smaller than groups such as the Muslim Brothers, still adhered to an essentially *Algerian* Islamist viewpoint. More importantly, whilst violence became an increasingly common aspect of Islamist activism, particularly in the universities,[33] Mustapha Bouyali's belief in the necessity and efficacy of armed struggle to install an Islamic state by force was clearly one that was not shared by most of the wider Islamist movement, as indicated by Abassi Madani and Mahfoud Nahnah's opposition to his efforts.[34] The reality was that the Islamist movement collectively possessed no coherent programme. Even individual groups invariably lacked anything approaching a comprehensive platform. For all the rhetoric about an Islamic state, no real alternative to the status quo was produced by Islamists in this period. This was a reflection of the fact that, unlike most other Islamist movements elsewhere in the Muslim world during this time, the Algerian Islamist movement lacked any real intellectual figure of standing, thus further explaining the reliance on and appeal of foreign ideas.[35]

External influences

The issue of the impact of developments abroad upon the Islamist

---

33 There had been other incidents of Islamist involvement in violence in this period, notably serious clashes that occurred when the authorities tried to use police to re-establish control over an Islamist-occupied mosque in the town of Laghouat in September 1981, as well as continued sporadic attacks on "improperly" dressed women and establishments selling alcohol. Hugh Roberts offers a more detailed explanation of the Islamists' increasing use of violence in this period. Roberts, 'Radical Islamism', pp. 577–8.

34 François Burgat asserts that Bouyali's use of armed violence was something that the rest of the Islamist movement in Algeria "were far from adopting". Burgat and Dowell, *The Islamist Movement in North Africa*, p. 268.

35 Such a lack of intellectual leadership was apparently even acknowledged by Bouyali himself, who had stated that he was willing to step aside for a more learned figure to lead his group. *Ibid.*, p. 265.

movement in Algeria assumed a new importance from the late 1970s at the same time as Islamism itself began to attract greater attention from observers both within and beyond the Muslim world.

Iran

The main explanation for both the increase in and importance of Islamism was the revolution that took place in Iran in 1978-79. The particularly remarkable and unique feature of the Iranian revolution, which toppled what had appeared to be one of the developing world's most muscular regimes, was the clear presence and, indeed, pre-eminence of Islamist ideas and language in both the revolution's leadership and in its appeals to the Iranian people who participated in their millions in the mass demonstrations which finally ousted the regime of the Shah. Furthermore, it was the subsequent assertion of this already dominant Islamist strain of the revolution in the period after the fall of the Shah which resulted in the actual founding of an "Islamic Republic" in Iran.

These developments had obvious implications for Islamist movements across the rest of the Muslim world as these groups realised that the overthrow of a ruling regime and the establishment of a society run according to Islamic principles was possible. This was no less the case for Algeria's Islamists. One of the main implications of the events in Iran was that they caused an intellectual break with the essential conservatism that had been a feature of the movement since the time of Ben Badis. The popular and revolutionary nature of the Islamist movement in Iran helped also to divest Algeria's Islamists of the label of reactionaries.

This development helped explain the shift to the much more radical stance towards the state that the Islamist movement in Algeria adopted from the late 1970s. As has been shown, the prime movers behind this change were new younger members of the movement and it certainly appears that the Iranian revolution had a particular impact on Algeria's youth. An illuminating anecdote bearing this out was told by a Western Ambassador who related the story of an English teacher he knew who, in the early 1980s, asked her class of young students to write an essay about the country in the world that they most admired. Over 70% of the class chose to write about Iran.

This was not to say that older members of the Islamist movement were not impressed by the example set by Iran's Islamists. In debates over unifying the Algerian movement, Abdellatif Soltani had used the example of the revolution in Iran to argue the case against the establishment of a formal Islamist political party in Algeria, pointing out that Ayatollah Khomeini had not had the backing of an organised religious party when he had toppled one of the mightiest dictatorships in the Muslim world.

Paradoxically, the Iranian revolution also appeared to have an impact on another prominent older Algerian who had hitherto had no involvement at all with the Islamist movement. The apparent conversion to the ideas of Ayatollah Khomeini by Algeria's first President, Ahmed Ben Bella, was a particularly surprising development given his unpopularity with the Islamists during his brief period in power between 1962 and 1965. His founding of the Movement for Democracy in Algeria (MDA) in 1984 and his launching, from voluntary exile in Switzerland, of a newspaper *Al Badil*, was aimed at uniting Algeria's various Islamist groups under a single banner. However, despite the historical weight and influence that Ben Bella wielded, Algeria's Islamists chose to ignore these overtures which they viewed as the product of simple opportunism from someone whom they still regarded as an unrepentant socialist.

Ben Bella's enthusiasm with the Iranian revolution was, however, prompted as much by excitement at the success of popular revolution in a Third World country as by interest in the theological ideas of Ayatollah Khomeini. The parallels with Algeria's own popular revolution twenty years earlier were clear and indeed were picked up by the Algerian regime itself, which initially appeared to share Ben Bella's interest in and enthusiasm with developments in Iran. The government portrayed Iran's revolution as being a successor to its own and even organised large-scale seminars across the country to discuss and publicise the parallels with Algeria's own experience of which it wished to remind the people. Official enthusiasm with Iran and its revolution, however, lasted only a few brief years before the Algerian government began to have increasing reservations about the potentially adverse effects of Iran's revolution. Not only did it become, along with the rest of the world, more and more aware of the specifically Islamist orientation of the new regime in Iran, but was clearly alarmed by the new republic's talk of "exporting" its revolution to other Muslim states. A number of measures were therefore taken from the early 1980s to combat Iran's possibly damaging influence. Many of the measures listed earlier which were aimed at combating Algeria's own Islamists, such as the recruitment of Sheikh Mohammed Ghazali and the adoption of the initial Family Code of 1981, were widely seen as being equally aimed at counteracting Iran's influence.

Government concern inevitably came to focus on the possibility of links between Algeria's Islamists and the Tehran regime, particularly as domestic Islamist activity clearly grew in the years following the Iranian revolution. In the wake of the events of late 1982, President Chadli blamed the disturbances on small groups inspired and paid by foreigners and during the same period the authorities published photos of suspects believed to have been involved in Islamist violence, who were described in the press as supporters of Ayatollah Khomeini. However, besides the clear inspiration the Iranian revolution and its aftermath gave to Algeria's Islamists, evidence of more direct and tangible Iranian involvement in the activities of the movement was hard to find and it seemed that the fears of the government were largely unfounded. As one observer remarked in 1984, emphasising the important fact that the specifically Shi'ite nature of the Iranian revolution limited its applicability to non-Shi'ite countries:

> . . . while Khomeini may provide an inspiring example . . . Shi'i missionaries from Iran do not appear to be active in Sunni Algeria, and it is doubtful that they would have a following if they did.[36]

The theological divide between the two branches of Islam did in the end present a largely insurmountable barrier to the full translation of the Iranian revolution to a country such as Algeria. As one contemporary Islamist activist – later to become a senior figure in the Algerian movement – subsequently remarked:

> The Iranian Revolution increased the zeal of the zealots – its victory had a special glamour. At that time we did not distinguish between Sunni and Shi'a; we saw the revolution merely as a victory for Islamists. But as time passed and as the sectarian nature of the revolution began to emerge, we realised that there were differences between us . . . The glow of the Iranian revolution waned and few, at most perhaps 100, considered that religious or political solutions lay in Shi'ism.[37]

---

36 Parker, *North Africa*, p. 100.
37 Interview with Rabah Kebir, FCO unclassified document.

Nevertheless, there did appear to be evidence to suggest, if not comprehensive links with the Algerian movement, then periodic instances of co-operation and co-ordination with individual groups. Mustapha Bouyali is believed to have spent time in both Libya and the Islamic Republic during the period 1983-84 before returning to Algeria to begin his campaign of armed insurrection. Furthermore, a statement reputedly put out by Bouyali's group in April 1986 appeared to indicate that the MAIA allied itself with the "Party of Allah" of Iran and that six out of the seven leaders of the grouping named by the statement had spent time in the Party of Allah's training camps in Iran and Lebanon.[38] Apart from this, though, the only other evidence of Iranian involvement was that the Iranian Embassy in Algiers appeared at times to be a rallying point for some Islamists during the early 1980s.

Other influences

Ideological influence and example, rather than direct involvement and co-operation, appeared also to be the main contribution made by other external Islamist influences to Algeria's Islamist movement in this period. Such influence and example was most obviously demonstrated by the appearance of various forms of dress, behaviour and demands among Algeria's Islamists which quite clearly had their origins elsewhere. A particular example of this was the growth in the early 1980s in the number of petitions made to authorities running public buildings and factories, requesting that some provision be made for a place of prayer.[39] Provision of this kind had been common in the countries of the Levant but was, until the demands by what were evidently Islamist sympathisers, noticeably absent in the Maghreb. More established aspects of Islamist activity in Algeria, such as attacks on establishments selling alcohol and upon women deemed to be "immodestly" dressed, which continued in this period, also duplicated practices first witnessed outside Algeria.

One foreign country which became a central preoccupation for Algeria's Islamists during the 1980s was Afghanistan. The conflict there between the Soviet army and the native Muslim mujahidin had a huge

---

38 For more details of this see Amir Taheri, *Holy Terror: The Inside Story of Islamic Terrorism* (London, Hutchinson, 1987), pp. 181–2.

39 Besides the demand for "mosque space" these petitions often also included demands that alcohol be prohibited in canteens and that certain imams be given free access to the establishment's facilities.

symbolic appeal since not only did the Afghan resistance proclaim their Islamist credentials but their struggle against domination by foreign non-Muslims had unmistakable echoes of Algeria's own liberation struggle. Islamist organisations in Algeria collected funds for the war in Afghanistan – one group requesting its members to contribute half their salaries – and several hundred ardent volunteers were dispatched to join the mujahidin. It was the gradual return of many of these volunteers in the second half of the 1980s that had a significant impact on Algeria's domestic Islamist movement. Militant and extremist ideas were brought back, engendered not only by involvement in armed conflict but also by the hothouse atmosphere of the conflict which had drawn militant zealots from across the Muslim world. A tangible indication of the influence of the conflict in Afghanistan on Algeria's Islamists could be seen in the growth in the use of Afghan-style dress in Islamist areas in the late 1980s, which initially provoked amusement from other Algerians but later unease as the radical nature of these influences became more clear. Prior to the return of the Afghans and their imported forms of dress the use by Algerian Islamist women of the black chador dress-form of the Arabian peninsula increased notably in the 1980s from its first rare appearances on the university campuses in the 1960s, as did other forms of dress from the Arab East.

One of the main reasons for the increasing influence of ideas and examples from elsewhere in the Muslim world in this period was the discovery and growing use by Islamists across the Middle East of the audio cassette. By recording and producing multiple copies of sermons delivered by prominent Islamist preachers, ideas could be circulated very rapidly throughout the Islamist movement both at home and abroad. The circulation of these cassettes, usually brought back by those going on pilgrimage, was not simply limited to the "religiously active". Algeria's Islamists increasingly encouraged their dissemination amongst the general population as well so that the ideas of preachers from as far away as Egypt, Kuwait and Syria could reach as wide an audience as possible.

Ironically, the Algerian state itself assisted in the spreading of Islamist ideas. The media coverage given to Sheikh Mohammed Ghazali in Algeria, whilst undermining support for more radical forms of Islamism, helped, in many observers' views, to actually underpin Islamism generally. The large audiences the Egyptian preacher was able to attract encouraged Algeria's Islamists who welcomed such a significant platform for religious ideas and also the fact that it helped legitimise debate on Algeria's Islamic nature and future.[40] In a similar fashion the substantial and laudatory attention the regime initially drew to the Iranian revolution undoubtedly served to publicise Iranian Islamism but, more significantly, focused the attention of Algeria's young on the possibilities of mobilisation against an entrenched but unpopular regime. By seeking to draw attention to the parallels between the Algerian and Iranian revolutions, Algeria's rulers overlooked the possibility that many ordinary Algerians might derive a rather different lesson from the parallel from that which the regime had intended.

Beyond these issues, though, the role external factors played in the development of Algeria's Islamist movement in this period was limited. Indeed, Algeria's movement seemed to be more autonomous than similar movements in other countries. Compared to the Islamist groupings in, for example, Egypt and Tunisia, the Algerian movement did not appear to receive significant funding from outside and even its Muslim Brothers did not appear to have as close an organisational connection with the original Muslim Brotherhood in Egypt as did their namesakes in Syria, Sudan and Jordan. Whilst the ideological contribution of external influences to the Algerian Islamist movement was substantial and even arguably predominant, the nature, make-up and strength of Algerian Islamism was very much determined by domestic factors and events. The rise in Islamic activism that occurred in Algeria from the end of the 1970s had more to do with the death of President Boumedienne in 1978 than with the Iranian revolution. The precise coincidence (December 1978) of Boumedienne's death with the effective collapse of the Shah's regime in Iran made the disentangling of the relative influence of domestic and external factors all the more difficult.

The Algerian regime in the 1980s: crisis and decline

The domestic factors and events that had such a determining influence on the development of Algeria's Islamist movement took the form in the 1980s of a growing and profound series of fundamental difficulties that the Algerian regime encountered and which clearly aided and facilitated the re-emergence of a more robust manifestation of Islamism.

---

40   Although close to President Chadli Benjedid, who clearly benefited from the respected cleric's backing, Ghazali was also known to have good relations with Abassi Madani during his time in Algeria, thus underlining the links with Algerian Islamists.

The abrupt departure of President Houari Boumedienne, the dominant figure in independent Algerian history, from the helm of the Algerian state in December 1978 was clearly a very significant event. Many of the problems the Algerian government faced politically from the late 1970s (it should not be forgotten that this period was marked by feminist, leftist, Berberist as well as Islamist activity and unrest) were as much due to the new regime under Chadli Benjedid lacking the legitimacy and the charismatic leadership that the Boumedienne regime had enjoyed as to the new regime's initially less repressive attitude towards dissent. The unexpected death of Boumedienne and the consequent demise of his only semi-implemented plans for Algeria's social, political and economic development threw Algeria into confusion and opened the way for a growth in the appeal of Islamism. In the view of Hugh Roberts, this "eleventh hour collapse" of Boumedienne's ambitious nationalist project embodied in the *Révolution Socialiste* (see Chapter Two) left many, particularly young, Algerians politically "orphaned". Having been inspired and mobilised by Boumedienne's "vision of the just society" they found themselves deprived of a guiding influence and vision when the President so unexpectedly died. Many such people subsequently found themselves drawn towards the group in society which did appear to offer a similar "vision of a just society". Ironically, this group consisted of Boumedienne's old adversaries in the Islamist movement who, in turn, were heartened by the removal from the political scene of the figure who had all but eliminated them in the late 1960s and early 1970s.[41]

Boumedienne's departure also heralded the beginning of a period of increasing popular disillusionment with and alienation from the government and regime. For many Algerians Boumedienne's charisma and comprehensive vision for Algerian society had encouraged them to continue their at least tacit support for his government and for the time being, until his national "project" was completed, persuaded them to overlook the many social, economic and political shortcomings of the Algerian state. The accession to power of Chadli Benjedid, who had neither the charisma nor vision of his predecessor meant that these popular grievances were increasingly brought into the open.

---

41   Roberts, 'Radical Islamism', pp. 575–6.

The political field: the absence of consent

The continued lack of opportunity for political expression outside the strict confines of the officially ruling FLN resulted by the late 1970s and early 1980s in a series of significant demonstrations of popular dissatisfaction and frustration with the regime. The mobilisation of Algeria's Islamists, which reached its height in late 1982, formed only one element of this broader display of public unhappiness with the regime. The women's movement that had successfully blocked the implementation of the Family Code of 1981 was another, very different, symptom of this tendency. Vocal and well-organised, if numerically relatively small, this movement represented an assertion of the view that Algerian women should be allowed to play a more equal and active role in what had become, even since independence, a more male-dominated and run society and polity. However, as has been seen, as the 1980s progressed the influence of this movement was significantly curtailed through the rise and strength of the Islamist movement, as much as by official antipathy.[42]

A third force that began to assert itself in this period and which even rivalled at times the strength and impact of the Islamists, was that of Berberism. Based in the mountainous Kabyle region fifty miles east of Algiers, this movement, as its name suggested, sought to defend and promote the distinct cultural and linguistic identity of the Kabyle Berbers. Although present beforehand, the Berberist movement came dramatically to the fore in 1980 when the central Kabyle town of Tizi Ouzou became the centre of a mounting series of demonstrations and strikes, culminating in a general strike against the government in March and April. The specific cause of this upsurge of unrest, which developed into rioting and battles with the security police that the regime dispatched to Tizi Ouzou, was the government's attempt to reduce the already limited avenues for the expression of Berber culture in Kabylia. The more genera context and corollary of this move was the Algerian regime's continued push to Arabise linguistically most areas of Algerian life – a process had been accelerated since 1979. Not only did this programme threaten the usage and survival of the Kabyle Berber language, *tamazigh*, but it also menaced

---

42   For more details on Algeria's feminist and women's movement(s) see Knauss, *The Persistence of Patriarchy*; and Bouthenia Cheriet, 'Islamism and feminism: Algeria's "rites of passage" to democracy' in John P. Entelis and Phillip C. Naylor, *State and Society in Algeria* (Boulder, Colorado, Westview, 1992).

the advantages in education and employment that many Kabyles enjoyed through being traditionally accomplished Francophones.[43] The government eventually succeeded in quelling the unrest in Kabylia through a combination of repression and largely symbolic concessions, but it proved incapable of eliminating the underlying resentment felt by the population of Kabylia. Throughout the 1980s the events of 1980, which became subsequently known in Kabylia as the "Berber Spring" (in conscious evocation of the Prague Spring of 1968), were marked by demonstrations and rallies in Tizi Ouzou, indicating a spirit of continued resistance towards the government in Algiers.[44]

Although representing three very different and often conflicting sets of agendas and demands these three main poles of protest – Islamist, feminist and Berberist – were symptomatic of the more general alienation and frustration most ordinary Algerians felt towards those who ruled over them. There was an increasing perception that the country was being ruled by an exclusive and self-interested clique which had no intention of allowing other groups access to the decision-making process – as had been indicated by the crushing of, particularly Berberist and Islamist, dissent in the early 1980s, which had signalled the end of Chadli's brief and modest experiment with political tolerance. This perception was enhanced by the growing influence Algeria's military leaders appeared to have in the government. Following independence, the Algerian army had assumed a central place in the new state through the influence it had been able to wield through its head, Houari Boumedienne, who had successfully backed Ahmed Ben Bella for the presidency before taking power himself in 1965. The influence of the army's senior figures had, however, been limited (along with every other force in Algeria) during the 1960s and 1970s by Boumedienne's comprehensive personal grip

---

43 The prevalence of and proficiency at the French language amongst Algeria's Kabyle Berbers was due to French colonial policies which had built a disproportionate number of schools and education establishments in the Kabyle as part of an attempt to divide the Kabyle Berbers from the Arab population.

44 For a fuller treatment of the whole issue of Berberism, the Kabyle and their role in Algeria see Hugh Roberts, 'The unforeseen development of the Kabyle question in contemporary Algeria', *Government and Opposition* vol. 17, no. 3, (Summer 1982); Salem Mezhoud: 'Glasnost the Algerian way: the role of Berber nationalists in political reform' in George Joffé, *North Africa: Nation, State and Region* (London, Routledge, 1993).

on Algerian political life. Boumedienne's death and the accession of Chadli Benjedid (who was drawn from the military) to the presidency had consequently signalled an inevitably increased role for the military in Algerian politics. This influence was not immediately apparent but became more so as Chadli began from the mid-1980s to rely increasingly on only a small number of senior military figures for advice.[45]

As a prominent part of the expression of generalised disillusion-ment with the regime, Algeria's Islamists clearly benefited from this overall and popular trend. Aspects of the Islamist discourse and agenda often reflected popular concerns about the political monopoly exercised by the regime through the FLN, particularly the regular references made to the concepts of justice, egalitarianism and the rule of law. In the view of many Algerians, the whole idea of the rule of law (which, it should not be forgotten, played an important role in traditional Muslim society) had been put to one side by the post-independence regime in its drive towards the implementation of its revolutionary ideology. This absence of the rule of law, together with the evident corruption, nepotism and abuse of power which became inevitable features of a closed political system such as Algeria's, produced an increasing popular resentment against the regime (particularly since the passing of Boumedienne, under whom such vices grew but were largely tolerated). Such resentment found an echo and a possible solution in the Islamist talk of a return to the rule of law.[46]

The economic field: inequality and decline

The regime was also gradually losing the confidence of the populace in its handling of the economy. Boumedienne's ambitious programme of heavy industrialisation had not produced the promised economic and social dividends for Algeria. Chadli Benjedid's accession to power saw a gradual shift in economic policy away from the rigid central planning that had characterised Boumedienne's policy. From the early 1980s attempts were made to break up and decentralise the huge industrial units constructed in the 1960s and 1970s, in an effort to combat rising

---

45 Abdelhamid Brahimi, Algeria's Prime Minister between 1984 and 1988, claimed that following his "re-election" as President in 1984, Chadli, who had previously consulted widely on policy, came to rely almost exclusively on General Larbi Belkheir, who became his Cabinet Secretary.

46 Roberts, 'Radical Islamism', p. 586.

inefficiency and falling productivity. As the decade progressed, the pace of these changes was accelerated and more thoroughgoing reforms were introduced: prices began to be deregulated, foreign investment was encouraged and incentives were given to Algeria's small but growing private economic sector.

Chadli's progressive abandonment of his predecessor's economic project in favour of a more liberalised economy, however, inevitably led to the loss of jobs from overmanned, inefficient state industries. These redundancies boosted Algeria's already serious unemployment problem which was further fed by the country's consistently high birth rate – during 1980–84 alone the population grew from 18.3 million to 21.6 million.[47] Between 1982 and 1984 the number of unemployed in Algeria grew by 200,000, the majority of this increase coming not from workers laid-off from the state-owned enterprises but from young Algerians entering the job market. By 1986 it was estimated that nearly 75% of Algerians aged between 16 and 25 were without work.[48] Chadli's liberalisation also led to greater economic inequalities within Algeria which contrasted badly in the public perception with Boumedienne's clear commitment, whatever his other failings, to social and economic egalitarianism.

The social and economic tensions and inequities produced by Chadli's reform programme were seen – at least in theory – by the regime as short-term adverse effects which could be cushioned by the revenues from Algeria's substantial oil and gas exports until the overall beneficial effects of the programme could be felt. However, the inherent flaws in this strategy became dramatically apparent with the collapse of the international oil price that occurred in 1985-86. The impact that this development had on the management of Algeria's economy can hardly be overemphasised. Within the space of a year the revenues Algeria received from its oil and gas exports fell by a colossal 40%, depriving the state of close to $5 billion worth of anticipated income. The impact of this loss was substantial for virtually all of the world's oil-producing states, but the particular predicament it posed for Algeria concerned the country's national debt. Since the 1970s Algeria's leaders had consistently relied on oil and gas sales not only to support projects such

---

47   Mahfoud Benoune, *The Making of Contemporary Algeria: 1830–1987* (Cambridge, Cambridge University Press, 1988), p. 286.

48   *Jeune Afrique* 26.11.86 and 3.12.86

as Boumedienne's massive programme of rapid heavy industrialisation but also as a base to support further borrowing for these projects. Algeria consequently accumulated a significant international debt which was further swollen by the increasing proportion of the country's foodstuffs requirement that had to bought abroad following the neglect of the Algeria's agricultural sector during Boumedienne's industrialisation drive.[49] It was assumed by Algeria's leaders, particularly following the rises in the international oil price in 1973-74 and 1979-80, that oil and gas revenues would remain sufficient to fund this large but still manageable debt. The oil price collapse of the mid-1980s served to massively inflate the size of Algeria's debt from a significant $14.8 billion in 1984 to $24.6 billion by 1987. The percentage of the country's foreign earnings needed to service the debt grew in a similarly dramatic fashion climbing from 33% to 54% over the same period.[50]

The implications of these developments for Algeria's domestic economy were grave. Oil and gas sales made up roughly 95% of the country's total exports, thus limiting the government's options in terms of finding alternative sources of hard currency with which to service Algeria's debts. Instead, imports and the state budget were cut back severely, leading to shortages and increasing inflation and unemployment as the government struggled to deal with the massive crisis that had overtaken it. The social and political implications resulting from these events were also clearly serious, as the majority of the Algerians experienced a significant fall in their already declining living standards. Thus a massive and wholly tangible dimension was added to the more abstract political grievances of the Algerian populace – the one compounding the other as Algerians were further reminded of the complete absence of any institutional mechanism or channel designed or able to express popular concern or distress at their worsening economic position.

---

49 This decline in agricultural self-sufficiency was demonstrated by the fact that Algeria had been able to produce 93% of its domestic food requirements in 1963, a year after independence, but by 1984 this figure had fallen to just 40%. *The Middle East*, July 1987.

50 Ruedy, *Modern Algeria*, p. 246. For a fuller discussion of Algeria's debt crisis and economic problems in the 1980s see also Karen Pfeifer, 'Economic liberalization in the 1980s: Algeria in comparative perspective' in John P. Entelis and Phillip C. Naylor, *State and Society in Algeria* (Boulder, Colorado, Westview, 1992).

The economic crisis clearly boosted support for the Islamists. This was not only because social and economic problems fuelled disillusionment and anger at the regime. It was also the case that Chadli Benjedid's economic policies, even more so than Boumedienne's, were associated with Western influence and ideas – traditionally identified by the Islamists as being at the root of many of Algeria's troubles. Thus the failure of these policies and the resultant economic crisis appeared to confirm the arguments and accusations of the Islamists. Furthermore, as economic and social hardship hit a growing number of Algerians with increasing severity many more people than before began to fall back on their religious faith as a means of both refuge from and protest at the failures of modernity. Such people were welcomed with open arms by the Islamists who had established in many deprived areas "charitable" associations centred on mosques, providing rudimentary health and welfare provisions for the poor.

The FLN: the decline in legitimacy and the challenge of Islamism

Algeria was not alone in experiencing a swell of alienation and dissatisfaction with the failed economic, social and political promises of the regime: many other countries in the Middle East experienced similar popular shifts in the 1970s and 1980s. What marked Algeria out from other countries in this regard were the implications this shift in popular perceptions had for Algeria in the context of its revolutionary origins as a state. When the FLN came to power in 1962 at the end of the bloody eight-year struggle against the French it arguably enjoyed greater popular support and legitimacy than any other comparable regime in the region, having proven itself beyond question as the champion of Algeria's Muslim population. The subsequent manifest failure of the FLN and the regime to produce political, social and especially economic progress for ordinary Algerians crushed the expectations of the Algerian population which had suffered the war of independence and hoped for so much in its aftermath. It provoked a degree of disillusionment not experienced by the populations of other states in the region whose regimes had been established by coup or dynastic succession.

The break of confidence with the post-independence regime led many Algerians to look around for some true successor to the spirit and ideals of the original revolutionary FLN. For a growing number, Algeria's Islamist movement showed itself to be the suitable inheritor of the revolutionary and truly authentic mantle of the Algerian national identity. This inheritance came not only from the involvement of Ben Badis's Association of Algerian Ulama in laying the ideological groundwork and allying with the FLN in the independence struggle, but also stemmed from other more concrete continuities with the war of independence. Chief amongst these continuities was that of personnel. Senior figures in the Islamist movement of the 1980s, such as Abassi Madani and Mustapha Bouyali, participated in the war as part of the FLN. Abassi had actually been a member of the small original grouping of the FLN which had launched assaults against symbols and institutions of French rule on All Saints Day in November 1954 formally heralding the opening of the war of independence. This early involvement, together with the eight years he spent in prison following capture by the French, gave Abassi Madani a degree of personal legitimacy that he was subsequently able to invest in the Islamist movement as one of its senior figures. It similarly lent great credence to the Islamist charge that Algeria's post-independence regime had perverted the true nature of the Algerian revolution.

There was also a certain apparent continuity between the outlook and behaviour of the historic revolutionary FLN and the Islamists of later years. The total adherence to their aims that Islamist groups began to demand from their followers, the methods they used and the absolute conviction with which they conducted their mission "all vividly recall the behaviour of the wartime FLN" in the view of Hugh Roberts.[51] Through employing the same methods and language that the revolutionary party had originally used, Islamism had also come to represent a form of competition to the vision and hegemony of the FLN. Houari Boumedienne had successfully fended off this ideological challenge during his presidency by constructing a radical vision for Algeria. However, the death of both Boumedienne and his ideological vision meant that the more pragmatic and managerial Algerian regime under Chadli Benjedid encountered mounting difficulties in dealing with the sort of specifically ideological questions thrown up by the Islamists.

---

51   Roberts, 'Radical Islamism' p. 580.

Conclusions

A number of significantly new developments were witnessed in the Islamist movement during the decade that followed Boumedienne's death.

Firstly, and most importantly, the Islamist movement was far more active and assertive during this period than it had been at any time in Algeria's history – both before and since independence. Whilst lacking the central focus of a single unified organisation such as the Association of Ulama and Al Qiyam, which had existed in previous decades, Islamism was by the 1980s much more of a movement than a vague tendency tipped by a vocal pressure group, as had arguably formerly been the case. Although this movement was numerically no stronger than it had been in the 1960s and remained fragmented between an array of groups and tendencies, a significant degree of co-ordination operated at an informal rather than institutional level. That tens of thousands of people turned out for Abdellatif Soltani's funeral in April 1984 – despite it occurring just the day after he died and there having been no mention of the Sheihk's death in the media – was evidence of the strength and extent of informal links between Algeria's Islamists. The greater influence the Islamists appeared able to exert in this period was borne out by both the wider popular conformity to Islamist ideals of social dress and behaviour and by the regime's increased incorporation of Islamist demands and language into its own programme.

Such activism, at its height during the years 1979–82, was notable not just for its raised profile (compared to the clandestinity of the 1970s) and its significant influence in various parts of Algerian society (particularly the universities) but also for its substantially more radical and militant character. The almost habitual use of violence by Islamists in pursuing their aims in the late 1970s and early 1980s represented a break with the tactics of previous periods and also reflected the movement's increasingly fundamentally hostile attitude towards the regime and the state itself. This was a development from the stance of the Islamists in the 1960s and 1970s who had begun to voice their antipathy towards the state but who had directed most of their rhetorical fire against the ideology of socialism and specific state policies. The petition of demands presented by Abassi, Soltani and Sahnoun in November 1982 was of great significance, since it set out for the first time a platform for the Islamist movement and thus issued a direct challenge to the state. In response, the state offered nothing of any substance that was new in terms of methods of controlling and eliminating the Islamists. The old approach of combining repression with concession and co-option was continued with mixed effectiveness.[52]

Discussion as to why there should have been an upsurge in Islamist activity during this period revolves around two broad suggested factors: that it was the result of the influence of elements and events outside Algeria, and that it was the product of particular developments within Algeria itself. Both the timing of the emergence and many of the characteristics of Algeria's Islamist groups had clear and unmistakable parallels with similar groups and developments elsewhere in the Muslim and Arab world. However, it seems fairly apparent that whilst external factors, such as the Iranian revolution, gave shape and direction to Algeria's Islamist movement, the support it enjoyed and many of its expressions were overwhelmingly the result of changes in the country's internal political, social and economic climate both before, but particularly after, the death of Houari Boumedienne. It was his departure that provided something of a psychological as well as a political and economic watershed in Algeria's post-independence history.

The watershed represented by the death of Boumedienne and the accession of Chadli had important implications for Algeria's Islamists other than those associated with a strengthening of Islamist sentiment and support against the state. The changes of the 1980s brought to the fore other political forces which, although also challenging the authority of the Algerian state, were implacably opposed to the Islamists and their agenda. The two other movements of popular protest that had emerged in the early 1980s, the Berberist and women's movements, championed issues and causes that placed them directly at odds with the Islamists. They challenged two of the long-established pillars of the Islamist agenda in Algeria: support for Arabisation and a belief in a restricted and defined

---

52   Hugh Roberts argues that although Chadli Benjedid consciously copied the largely successful twin-pronged strategy of repression and co-option of the Islamist tendency employed by Boumediene in the 1960s and 1970s, he embarked on measures of co-option and incorporation of religion *before* the activists of the Islamist movement had been properly suppressed. In contrast, Boumediene had effectively crushed organisations such as Al Qiyam before he launched, for example, the "Campaign Against the Degradation of Morals". Roberts thus argues that Chadli's approach left Islamist morale and support intact. Roberts, 'Radical Islamism', p. 579.

role for Algerian women. The Berberist movement's hostility to Arabisation pitched it against the programme's staunchest advocates and defenders, the Islamists, whose agitation had largely prompted the speeding-up of Arabisation by the government. From the late 1970s and early 1980s Berberist and Islamist students fought periodic battles on the country's campuses over Arabisation. In the same way, Algerian feminists' success in heading off a more restrictive Family Code in 1981 resulted in a concerted campaign by the Islamists to secure the introduction of a similar Code three years later which was facilitated in part by intimidation of the smaller and less muscular women's movement.

The significance for Algeria's Islamists of the rise of both these movements was that there emerged a pole in Algerian society and politics that was opposed to the regime but whose vision for Algerian society was juxtaposed to that demanded by the Islamists. The fact that this pole called for the establishment of an explicitly secular state modelled largely on the arrangements to be found in most Western states clearly set it fundamentally against the Islamist goal of an Islamic state. In this way an important part of Algerian opinion had declared itself to be in total opposition to the Islamists and their agenda irrespective of the stance of the regime itself. Whilst the women's movement was largely confined to the small, if potentially influential, intellectual classes of urban Algeria, the Berberist movement had a substantial popular and geographical base in the Kabyle region. The Islamist movement had thus, by the 1980s, attracted the opposition of two important parts of Algerian society.

4

The Emergence of the FIS, 1988–1990

As Algeria entered the late 1980s it appeared that the regime had effectively solved its Islamist "problem". What notable agitation it had experienced in 1982-83 had not resurfaced as the decade progressed; the one exception of Bouyali's campaign having been small-scale and geographically confined. In contrast to most other Muslim countries in this period, notably its immediate neighbour, Tunisia, Algeria did not see Islamist activism and membership of Islamist groups increase in the mid to late 1980s. However, by the turn of the decade Algeria was widely acknowledged as having one of the largest and potentially most influential Islamist movements in the entire Muslim world. The reasons for this rapid and unexpected development lay in the chain of events that resulted from the dramatic crisis that gripped Algeria in the closing months of 1988.

The riots of October 1988

The protests, demonstrations and severe rioting that swept across most of Algeria's major cities in the first two weeks of October 1988 constituted a crisis unprecedented in Algeria's independent history. On 5 October crowds several thousand strong swept through the centre of Algiers attacking shops and public buildings in an explosion of rage and destruction that was eventually to cost an estimated $20 million. Within the next two days Oran, Mostaganem Annaba and most other urban areas were experiencing similar unrest. Unable to re-establish calm using the regular forces of order, the regime sent the army onto the streets on 6 October and proclaimed a curfew. The brutality with which the military attempted to quell the unrest by firing on protesters and rioters alike further deepened the crisis. An eventual death toll of 150 was acknowledged by the government, but most other estimates cited a figure at least three times as large.[1]

---

1 As shocking to the general public as well as damaging to the regime was the evidence that emerged of the use of punitive torture by the security forces against those

The exact origins of this immense conflagration were subsequently the subject of intense debate. Many in Algeria believed that initial incidents that paved the way for the later chaos were deliberately orchestrated by certain groups, particularly rival factions within the regime itself.[2] However, whether the sparking of the near uprising of October 1988 could be attributed to a specific event or conspiracy was not the central issue. The vastly more important issue was the sheer extent of the popular feeling and anger unleashed that month which went far beyond anything that could have been organised or directed by any one group or faction. As George Joffé observed: "Whatever the cause, the riots rapidly became a vehicle for expressing the intense frustration and alienation of a predominantly youthful population against a regime which appeared to have abandoned them."[3]

The mass unrest of early October 1988 had not come out of nowhere. The preceding two years had seen a steady rise in incidents reflecting popular discontent and unrest and across Algeria. In 1985 riots had occurred in the Algiers Casbah and in the autumn of 1986 a series of strikes, protests and demonstrations by students across the country had culminated in serious unrest in Constantine and Setif in November. The following year indicated that discontent was not limited to students and the young as industrial disputes and strikes steadily increased in number. By the summer of 1988 industrial strikes had become endemic and it was as the prospect of a general strike strengthened in the autumn that the explosion of October finally occurred.

The reasons behind this huge swell of popular rage were easily identified. The economic crisis into which Algeria had been plunged

---

they arrested. This revelation was of particular significance in Algeria since the use of terror by the French during the liberation struggle had been a major rallying point for the nationalist cause. Its use by the Algerian regime itself was thus seen as a terrible betrayal of one of the leitmotifs of the independence struggle.

2　There were allegations that leftist elements, particularly within the UGTA, the officially tolerated former Algerian Communist Party – the Parti de l'Avant Garde Socialiste (PAGS) – and even the FLN itself, provoked the unrest as a means of sabotaging Chadli's programme of liberalising economic reforms. Conversely, it was also argued by some that it had been Chadli and his government themselves who had helped organise the disturbances as a smoke screen against their opponents. For an example and details of this latter assertion see Mahfoud Benoune, 'Algeria's façade of democracy', *Middle East Report* (March-April 1990).

3　George Joffé, 'Algeria: The Failure of Dialogue' in *The Middle East and North Africa 1995*, p. 6.

with the collapse in the oil price of 1985-86 (see Chapter Three) had continued to deepen throughout the second half of the decade. There had been no real recovery in the international oil price and the country's international debt had continued to mount. Government efforts to cut spending as part of continuing efforts to contain the crisis had led to mounting misery for the vast majority of the population. Wages were frozen whilst prices soared – cuts in government subsidies leading to increases in food prices of 40% between January and October 1988 alone.[4] Shortages in even basic commodities became commonplace. Unemployment levels rocketed to over a quarter of the workforce as lay-offs occurred and more people continued to enter the jobs market. These developments hit Algeria's young disproportionately hard. They became the main victims of unemployment as the Algerian economy managed to create only half the number of jobs needed for school and college leavers. The size of the youth unemployment problem was compounded by Algeria's pyramid-shaped demographic profile. A consistently high birth rate of over 3% had created by the late 1980s a situation in which 60% of the population were under the age of 20. It was therefore not surprising that the majority of those who came out onto the streets in October 1988 came from the vast and growing pool of idle and discontented youth. Added to this backdrop of economic injury was the perceived insult to most ordinary Algerians of the sight of a significant minority of the population who through speculation in the new liberal economy or old-fashioned embezzlement seemed able to insulate themselves from this crisis. It was these developments that really underlay and explained the eruption of October 1988. The events of the opening week of that month can clearly be seen as the culmination of more than three years of worsening hardship and hardening resentment.

The extent to which the riots and demonstrations, once underway, sought to express anything more overtly political than simple social and economic rage and despair was also the subject of great debate. It did seem clear that much of the protesters and demonstrators anger was directed at manifestations of the regime. Offices of the FLN were physically attacked and at least two government ministries were destroyed during the first

---

4   Lynette Rummel, 'Privatization and Democratization in Algeria' in John P. Entelis and Phillip C. Naylor, *State and Society in Algeria* (Boulder, Colorado, Westview, 1992), p.58.

day of the unrest in Algiers. However, the size and manifestly hetero-geneous nature of the protests indicated that they were not subject to the control of any particular grouping – the unrest appearing to be a straightforward explosion of protest against the regime and its policies.

There was, however, considerable attention paid in the foreign media to the role that Algeria's Islamists had played in the unrest. There was significant speculation as to whether the events of October constituted some form of an Islamically inspired uprising. Islamists had been prom-inent in many of the marches and demonstrations and at stages in the turmoil they appeared to have established control of several districts of the capital. Most informed commentators were, however, united in asserting that the mainly foreign theories advanced concerning Islamists' role in precipitating the unrest were some way from the truth. Islamist activity and sloganeering had been a significant feature of the protests and demonstrations but, crucially, had only appeared several days after the start of the unrest. This testified to the reality that Islamism had had no part in inspiring the demonstrators and rioters and that the Islamists were merely riding the popular bandwagon.

Algeria's Islamists had, in fact, been largely taken by surprise by the events and took some days to formulate their response to these clearly portentous developments. The fragmented nature of the movement meant that, as had been the case in the early 1980s, any "Islamist" response was unlikely to be either unanimous or unified.[5] As many of the senior Islamist figures hesitated over their response in the early days of the crisis, Ahmed Sahnoun and Abassi Madani met and decided that they should arrange a peaceful march for Friday 7 October, both to make their presence felt and to test official attitudes towards the movement. Attended by an estimated 6–8,000 Islamist supporters, the march, which took

---

5   There was some speculation as to the organised involvement of Islamists in earlier incidents of popular unrest. The disturbances of November 1986 took place in Constantine and Setif in eastern Algeria – the part of the country that had long been the focus of Islamist activism. They had involved *lycée* students who were ostensibly protesting at plans to introduce compulsory courses in religion and politics. It is thought that the changes were seen by Islamists as an official attempt to impose its own viewpoint to counter Islamist (and other dissident) ideas. However, it appeared that most students were more concerned with the prospect of being set another academic hurdle to overcome. Nevertheless, the authorities blamed the disturbances on Islamists together with Berberists and Ben Bellists.

place in the Algiers quarter of Belcourt, attracted immediate attention as it became not only the first politically homogenous demonstration but, more importantly, became the first to be fired upon by the army which had been called on to the streets the previous day.[6]

The deaths of nearly fifty marchers convinced Ahmed Sahnoun that such a tactic should not be repeated by the Islamists, but the events of the day had brought to the fore another Islamist leader who took a very different line. Ali Belhadj, a young, fiery and increasingly popular preacher at the Al-Sunna mosque in Bab el-Oued had played a significant role both in organising and whipping up support for the march. Despite the death toll, the young preacher began to organise a second march to be held just three days later on 10 October. The plan met with vehement opposition from Ahmed Sahnoun, who together with the leader of the Jazara, Mohammed Said, tried to stop the march. However, they did not succeed in preventing it taking place and attracting, this time an estimated crowd of 20,000.

Once more the march resulted in bloodshed with over thirty people being shot dead by the army. However, despite this, these events came to have important and beneficial repercussions for the Islamists. Whether the Islamists were perceived to be leaders or opportunists by the mass of ordinary Algerians who took to the streets in October 1988 is uncertain. What does seem clear is that they were identified by the regime as playing a central role. This recognition might initially have resulted in greater repression being inflicted on Islamists on the streets, but it rapidly worked to the Islamists' ultimate advantage. Progressively realising that the situation on the streets was moving beyond that which could be controlled by a security clampdown, Algeria's leaders began to search for spokesmen for the largely "headless" revolt that they were witnessing, with whom they could strike some agreement to halt the violence. The high-profile role Islamists had come to play in developments with the marches they had organised and the mediatory role that Ali Belhadj had attempted to play when the security forces had attacked these and other demonstrations, suggested that the leaders of the Islamists could fulfil this role. The receipt by Chadli Benjedid of an open letter from Ahmed Sahnoun, containing a

---

6   It was alleged by a number of witnesses that the police had opened fire on the marchers only after having coming under fire themselves. This supported rumours that some participants in the Islamist march had been armed.

list of measures that the regime should take to end the crisis, reinforced this view.[7] Consequently, on 10 October Sahnoun, together with Ali Belhadj, Abassi Madani and Mahfoud Nahnah, was invited to see the President who would listen to their grievances. This was very significant. As François Burgat remarks:

> The choice was highly symbolic. The president had just admitted the Islamists were part of the group that would allow him to renew his contract with civil society.[8]

Political reform and the new constitution

On 10 October, shortly after the conclusion of his meeting with the Islamist leaders, President Chadli went on national television to announce the government's intention to introduce a number of political reforms which would seek to address the grievances that had given rise to the unrest. The exact substance of this intent remained unclear as the turmoil on the streets gradually subsided – through a combination of repression, official placation and sheer exhaustion – over the next few days. The first concrete steps Chadli took in the direction of political reform consisted of the sacking of several senior figures in the regime, particularly those associated with the excesses of the brutal security clampdown during the unrest. He also declared his intent to make a series of constitutional amendments to make, among other things, the government more responsible to the National Assembly. However, it soon became clear that Chadli intended to go much further than simple constitutional adjustments. Following his formal "re-election" (he was the sole candidate) as President at the end of December 1988, he set about drafting and introducing an entirely new Constitution which was formally endorsed by popular referendum in February 1989.

The new Constitution's most remarkable and important feature was its removal of the twenty-five-year-old party-political monopoly exercised by the FLN. This not only took the form of a formal separation of the ruling party from the state but, moreover, the Constitution accorded

---

7   Sahnoun's letter, whilst demanding the introduction of the sharia, also called for the lifting of the state of siege that had been imposed on 6 October, greater job creation and a more equal distribution of wealth.
8   Burgat & Dowell, *The Islamic Movement in North Africa*, p. 270.

Algerians the right to form "associations of a political character". The implications of this for Algerian political life were clear: Chadli appeared to be opening up the closed Algerian political system to other groups and forces who might wish to have a say.

The reasons behind this startlingly comprehensive shift in policy by the President, remarkable given that demands for political liberalisation of this type had not featured prominently in the unrest of October, are another source of great controversy.[9] It was believed in some quarters that the Chadli had been prompted by pressure from abroad, particularly from France, to open up Algeria's political system. However it seems certain that the main reason for the President's move was a desire to frustrate his opponents within the Algerian regime.

By the late 1980s the President had clearly lost much of the, albeit modest, popularity he had enjoyed both within and outside the regime during his first term. Internal opposition appears to have mounted along two, often overlapping, axes: political dissatisfaction with Chadli's rule and increasing dissent with his policies of economic liberalisation that had been pursued since 1980. On the political front Chadli's increasingly closed methods of policy making, relying on a small clique of military officers, had led several senior FLN figures, notably Mohammed Chérif Messadia, the FLN number two, and Ahmed Taleb Ibrahimi, the Foreign Minister, to look for an alternative candidate when Chadli's second term as President came to an end in late 1988. According to Abdelhamid Brahimi, Chadli's Prime Minister between 1984 and 1988, this possibility of not being reselected by the party led Chadli to instigate trouble in October 1988 at the end of his second term, thus provoking a national crisis which allowed him to achieve reselection by the FLN and the National Assembly through casting himself as a unifying and reforming figure.[10] The crisis also enabled the President to sack both Messadia and Ibrahimi as a convenient part of his efforts to demonstrate a break with the pre-October regime.

---

9 Lynette Rummel, however, argues that the more relatively more liberal political environment that had existed within Algeria since the death of Houari Boumedienne, together with changes outside the country had served to construct an important backdrop and basis for the events of October 1988. "Economic desperation may well have been a spark, but the conflagration was being fanned by the winds of political change." Rummel, 'Privatization and Democratization in Algeria', p. 60.

10 Author's interviews with Abdelhamid Brahimi, London, 19.12.94 and 6.9.95.

The President also faced considerable hostility towards his reforms from that section of the FLN and the bureaucracy that objected to the abandonment and dismantling of Boumedienne's socialist project either on ideological grounds or because of the threat it posed to their own administrative and financial power bases. From the mid-1980s onwards, as Chadli had accelerated his economic reform programme, the President and his pro-reform allies had fought an increasingly bitter rearguard action against these internal critics. It is therefore argued that Chadli seized the opportunity presented by the crisis of October 1988 (whether or not he deliberately provoked it) to open up the political system to provide competition for his enemies within the FLN and thus hamper or at least distract their efforts to oppose him. Chadli also hoped that such a move would have similar implications for critics of his political rule and in fact many of those who were opposed to Chadli's style of rule, such as Mohammed Chérif Messadia, were also prominent critics of his economic policy.

Chadli also sought to address the wider Algerian public through his reforms. Whatever the truth behind the various conspiracy theories concerning the instigation of the unrest of October 1988 and the internal intrigues within the regime, it had been ordinary Algerians who had expressed themselves most dramatically that month and whose mass presence on the streets had transformed the events into a national crisis. Such obviously deep-seated popular anger was clearly not going to be abated by the dismissal of a few ministers. It was true that specific demands for multi-party democracy were not prominently expressed during the disturbances, but Chadli was undoubtedly aware that political reform, or at least the promise of it, would hopefully serve to soothe the groundswell of popular anger. Whilst the new Constitution did not explicitly promise to improve the dire social and economic lot of most Algerians it did appear to be willing to provide them with new avenues – through being allowed to form "associations of a political character" – to express their discontent. It was also almost certainly the case that Chadli hoped to buy off and distract popular opposition to his policies and rule in much the same way he had done with internal critics within the regime. It was significant that not only did Chadli continue and even speed up his economic reform programme after 1988, he also strengthened his own position and personal powers as President in the new Constitution.

The Islamist response: the creation of the FIS

The moves towards political liberalisation had obvious potential implications for the Islamists. Boosted both in confidence and strength by their participation in the events of October and, more importantly, by the formal recognition the authorities had extended to them by inviting them to become interlocutors for the mass unrest, many Islamists believed that this opening up of the political system could work to their benefit.

The aftermath of the October crisis saw the creation of the first body that sought to bring all of the various Islamist groups and leaders together under one, albeit loose, institutional framework. The Rabitat Dawa (League of the Islamic Call) did not, however, primarily represent an attempt by Algeria's Islamists to create an organisation that would seek to take advantage of the regime's new liberalism. Its creation was a response to the events of October but it was aimed more at unifying the ranks of the movement that had become dangerously divided during the crisis. The swift reaction of Abassi Madani and particularly Ali Belhadj to events had created tensions between them and those leading Islamist figures who had hesitated to become involved. Ahmed Sahnoun became the driving force behind the creation of the Rabitat Dawa in an effort to prevent fissures appearing within the co-operating, if not formally unified, ranks of the Islamists.

It soon became apparent that, despite Sahnoun's efforts, the Rabitat would not be able to contain the tensions and dynamics that emerged in the Islamist movement in the wake of the October crisis. The effective entry of several of its senior figures into the realm of politics during that month had given rise to various hopes and beliefs that involvement in politics could be to the clear advantage of the movement – particularly if the significant popular and official attention and regard Islamists had attracted could be exploited. The important role Ali Belhadj, in particular, had played in the events of October – organising marches and mediating with the security forces – had led to the young and charismatic preacher and schoolteacher attracting a huge popular following amongst the mass of marginalised youth in the poor suburbs. Thoughts of making the most of this support were clearly encouraged by indications in early 1989 that the regime planned to open up the political system to other groups and political parties. The essentially apolitical nature of the Rabitat Dawa, which explicitly sought to work for the defence and propagation of Islamic values, meant that it was not an ideal vehicle for political mobilisation.

It therefore was concluded that a separate, specifically political, Islamist party needed to be formed to take best advantage of the rapidly expanding political landscape.

Accounts about the precise origins of the idea of an Islamist political party vary, but according to the newspaper subsequently published by the eventual party, the idea was originally that of Hachemi Sahnouni, official Imam of the Al-Sunna mosque. He shared his thoughts with Ali Belhadj, who frequently preached at Al-Sunna, who had himself been thinking along similar lines and who proposed putting the idea to the other senior members of the Rabitat. The first figure Sahnouni and Belhadj approached was Abassi Madani, to whom Belhadj had become increasingly close, following October. Welcoming the idea, Madani proposed that the new organisation be called the Front Islamique du Salut in conscious evocation of the Front element of the old FLN, of which he had been one of the earliest members.

The idea was less well received amongst other Islamist leaders. The concept of an Islamist party was a controversial one and one that had been rejected in the past. In the early 1980s Abdellatif Soltani had made clear his opposition to the formation of an Islamist political party, arguing that the whole idea was associated with factions and divisions. He believed that the informal movement of various groups served the movement's aims of education and propagation far better. Similarly, many of the senior figures in the Rabitat expressed their doubts when approached. Many held to the view that the central task of the movement had always been and should remain the gradual re-Islamisation of the Algerian state and society through preaching and education, rather than through politics. Other reservations were voiced. Mohammed Said of the Jazara argued that the movement should wait to see what other political developments occurred and what other parties appeared before committing itself in this manner. Abdallah Djaballah, though willing to attend meetings to discuss the project, similarly counselled patience, his procrastination like that of many of the others hiding an understandable reluctance to surrender control of groups and constituencies that had been carefully built up since the 1970s. Many Islamists shared Djaballah's fear that Chadli's supposed "opening" would prove to have little substance. Mahfoud Nahnah of the Muslim Brothers was more forthright in his rejection of the idea, claiming that there were already enough groups within the broader Islamist movement. He expressed his fear that such a party might be led by "kids" rather than the proper and appropriate leadership of religious scholars.[11]

This dissent, however, was not sufficient to crush the idea of an Islamist political party, which gained further impetus with the unveiling of the new Constitution on 5 February 1989. It was approved by national referendum on eighteen days later. On 18 February the formation of the Front Islamique du Salut was officially announced and the party held its founding meeting the following month. Abassi Madani was named president of the party – which rapidly became known by its French acronym, FIS – with Ali Belhadj as his recognised deputy. The new party attracted a wide array of senior Islamist clerics and figures, the majority of whom constituted the party's Majlis Shura, but Abassi and Belhadj remained the only two truly high-profile Islamist figures who participated in the launch of the party. There was some speculation as to whether, given their reservations, the other figures were formally invited to join the party. Mahfoud Nahnah and Ahmed Sahnoun did not attend meetings held in the run up to the launch of the party and Ahmed Sahnoun, when telephoned by a journalist soon after the founding of the FIS tersely replied: "They did not wait for us. We were not present."[12] Even Abdallah Djaballah, who had attended these meetings, appeared to portray the decision to form the party as a breakaway from the Islamist movement. When asked about his "decision" to not join the FIS Djaballah stated simply that "They left me."[13]

The absence of several senior Islamist figures (in addition to Sahnoun and Djaballah, neither Mohammed Said nor Mahfoud Nahnah had joined the party) meant that the FIS only represented a part of Algeria's Islamist movement and this had significant implications for the future development of the new party. The new party would be able to pursue a far more popular and political course than would have been the case with the involvement of figures such as Sahnoun, Djaballah and Nahnah. The more intellectual and specifically religious orientation of these three leaders was a likely handicap in the sort of multi-party competition for mass support that the new Algerian Constitution heralded. The assumption of the top two positions in the new party by Abassi Madani and Ali

---

11 Al-Ahnaf, Botiveau and Frégosi, *L'Algérie par ses Islamistes*, p. 31.
12 *Algérie Actualité*, 12.10.89.
13 Author's interview with Abdallah Djaballah, London, 7.10.94.

Belhadj, the two Islamist figures who had had the most experience of popular mobilisation for the Islamist cause (Belhadj in 1988 and Abassi in both 1988 and 1982) was a clear indication that the new party would pursue a more popular and political direction. It seems unlikely though that Sahnoun, Djaballah and Nahnah might have been, for the above reasons, *deliberately* excluded as some have suggested.[14] The three had already expressed reservations when originally canvassed and Abassi and Belhadj were unable to foresee the success that a popular-political strategy would later bring them. Nevertheless, it is probable that the new leaders of the FIS had been encouraged by their political experience and thus were willing to forge ahead with the project of the political party without the participation of other senior figures.

It was also the case that personal ambition and rivalry had at least some part to play on all sides. The swift rise of Ali Belhadj has provoked significant antipathy from more established leaders such as Sahnoun, Nahnah and Mohammed Said. Sahnoun and Said had been openly critical of Belhadj's unilateral decision to organise the second march by Islamists in October and both – Said publicly – had blamed Belhadj for the resultant deaths. There was also an undoubted element of jealousy and snobbery towards the young preacher. Mahfoud Nahnah's disdainfully expressed fear of an Islamist political party being run by "kids" was an unambiguous reference to the new-found prominence of Belhadj. Unlike most of the existing senior Islamist figures, Belhadj had not attended university, only teacher training college, and despite his growing popularity in the mosques, he had been accorded little respect by other senior figures before October 1988. It was therefore ironic that it was Belhadj's awareness of the sensibilities of ordinary uneducated Algerians that allowed the Islamist movement to tap such an important source of support.

Legal recognition for the FIS: September 1989

Despite the dissenting voices, the newly-formed FIS grew strongly in its first few months. However, the formation of a political party did not, of itself, guarantee meaningful participation in Algeria's emerging political system: several potential obstacles stood in the way of this aspiration. Firstly, the interpretation and application of the new Constitution had to

---

14   See Roberts, 'From Radical Mission', pp. 449–52.

be debated by the National Assembly (the APN: which, it should be noted, was still made up exclusively of FLN members) and made into law. More importantly for the Islamists of the FIS, was the likelihood that the law that emerged on permitting "associations of a political character" would ban a specifically Islamist political party such as the FIS. In both Egypt and neighbouring Tunisia, two countries that were also making attempts to liberalise their political systems in this period, steps had been taken to prevent the participation of an Islamist party in elections. In Tunisia this took the form of explicitly denying official recognition to the Islamist Nahda (Renaissance) Party because of its religious basis.

When the new law on political parties finally emerged from the National Assembly in July 1989, it appeared that the Algerian authorities had closely followed the example of their Tunisian neighbours. The new law banned "sectarian practice" and any party organised "on an exclusively confessional basis".[15] It therefore appeared highly unlikely that the FIS, on the basis of this legislation, would gain the official recognition that would allow it to participate in the series of multi-party elections for which the regime appeared to be opening the way. Nevertheless, the party, along with a growing number and diversity of other parties which had also emerged (or in some cases re-emerged) in this period, filed for official recognition as a legal political party. To the astonishment of virtually everyone outside the government leadership itself, which took the decision, the Front Islamique du Salut was formally endorsed and recognised by the authorities on 16 September 1989.

The reasons behind this decision appeared uncertain. Officially, Chadli Benjedid stated that to deny recognition to the FIS would be inconsistent with the regime's new commitment to multi-party democracy. He argued that recognition could not be extended to the Communists on the one hand whilst denying it to the Islamists on the other as "Democracy . . . cannot be selective." Furthermore, he acknowledged the legitimacy of a party based upon Islam, which was, after all, the religion of Algeria, and answered concerns about whether the Islamists would seek to abuse the democratic "opening" by pointing out that "The activities of the Islamist party are submitted to precise rules. If

---

15   Article 5, *Loi no. 89-11 du Juillet 1989. Relative aux Associations à Caractère Politique.* Reproduced in *Maghreb-Machrek,* no. 127 (Janvier–Mars 1990), pp. 200–5.

they respect them, we cannot forbid them."[16] The President was able sidestep the specific constitutional proscription of any party based on a "confessional basis" by emphasising that this phrase was prefixed by the word "exclusively" which appeared to allow a degree of flexibility.

It is possible that Chadli was genuinely committed to full democratisation and was averse to banning any political party, but other explanations seem more plausible.[17] The haste with which the President gave assent to the recognition of the FIS, without even waiting for the necessary modifications to the law on political associations to be made to allow a party based on religion to be endorsed, led many to believe that other reasons must have been behind the decision. It is likely that Chadli saw recognition of the FIS as a means of actually controlling and limiting Algeria's reinvigorated Islamist tendency, which one commentator had observed, as early as April 1989, had become "a crucial feature of the political scene since October".[18] Chadli was aware of the strength of the Islamists and took a gamble on including and working with them within the political system, in preference to the possibility of having to confront them on the streets if they were excluded from the system. As Chadli's Prime Minister, Mouloud Hamrouche was to explain six months later:

> If we had not taken the decision to legalise [the FIS] we would no longer be here. The FIS would have brought everyone onto the streets and formed alliances with former apparatchiks and young soldiers.[19]

By recognising the FIS Chadli sought to split the Islamist movement and isolate its radical elements from those willing to work within the system. Many Algerian ministers stressed to foreign diplomats that by bringing the Islamists out into the open it would also give a clearer indication of the actual strength and make-up of the movement. This

---

16 Burgat and Dowell, *The Islamic Movement in North Africa*, p. 274.
17 Abdelhamid Brahimi, a member of Chadli's cabinet between 1979 and 1988 and his Prime Minister since 1984, disputes that the President ever had any real belief in democracy stating: "I know Chadli very well and I know he has nothing to do with democracy." Author's interview, 6.9.95.
18 *Middle East Economic Digest (MEED)*, 14.4.89.
19 Pierre Dévoluy and Mireille Duteil, *La Poudrière Algérienne: Histoire Secrète d'une République sous Influence* (Paris, Calman-Lévy, 1994), p.118.

would allow the regime to understand and control it better and ultimately repress it if necessary. Official recognition of the Islamists' strength was emphasised for foreign consumption also because Chadli was aware of the unease with which Western countries, in particular, regarded Islamism. This he perhaps hoped would increase the West's willingness to support him, especially with respect to Algeria's huge international debt and the possible assistance and leniency they could offer.

The decision to legalise the FIS was, like the decision to open up the political system, also related to Chadli's relations with the old FLN. The President hoped to use the threat of the Islamists to curb opposition to him and his reforms in the FLN. Chadli believed that popular support for the FIS was sufficiently strong to deprive the FLN of victory in the multi-party elections he planned. Moreover, he thought it likely that support for the two parties would be fairly evenly balanced thus allowing him as President to dominate any future National Assembly since neither party would be able to wield a majority. The danger of any one party dominating would be further reduced by allowing large numbers of other parties to participate, which would splinter the vote even more and support the President's strategy of divide and rule. Indeed, there was significant evidence to suggest that the regime actually encouraged certain individuals to create new parties to achieve this end.[20]

The relative importance of these factors is impossible to gauge. However, Chadli Benjedid seemed intent on both holding onto the reins of power whilst reducing the power and influence of the old FLN, whether through a desire to protect his economic reforms, his own position or even his own vision of a democratised Algeria. Legalisation of the FIS thus appeared to serve these ends.

The FIS mobilised: 1989–1990

Having achieved official recognition, the FIS lost little time in organising itself and recruiting new supporters and members in preparation for

---

20 It was alleged that figures from the regime approached, among others, Said Saadi, a leading Berberist, and Abdelaziz Bouteflika, a former Foreign Minister, to form new parties. Bouteflika declined. However, Saadi, despite proceeding to launch a party – the Rassemblement pour la Culture et la Démocratie (RCD) – subsequently himself alleged that the head of Military Security had approached him with an offer of collaboration, stating that other parties had already agreed to co-operate.

forthcoming elections, the first of which were to be held for local government in June 1990. From the outset it became quite apparent that the new party was a highly organised and motivated affair. Full use was made of the network of some 9,000 mosques which Islamists had come to control, to co-ordinate activity and spread the party's message at the weekly Friday prayers and sermon. Within a month of its legalisation, the FIS had begun publishing its own paper, *El Mounqid*, which was directly distributed by activists. Leading FIS preachers were filmed and the footage distributed across Algeria and audio-visual equipment was frequently employed at the increasing number of rallies the party began to organise throughout the country.

It soon became clear that the FIS enjoyed a substantial level of support amongst the population. An estimated 10,000 supporters had been present at the official founding of the party in March 1989 and Ali Belhadj was able to attract 20,000 people to his Friday sermons at Al-Sunna in early 1989, totals which could only be added to by the FIS's subsequent higher profile and recruitment drives. Political campaigning and the mosque network were not the only means the FIS used to attract supporters. The party incorporated into itself and its activities the growing networks of medical clinics and social services that had been established by Islamists in Algeria's poorest urban areas during the 1980s, adding to and expanding their work.[21] The party's activists and doctors were also the first to arrive on the scene to provide relief to victims of an earthquake in a region to the west of Algiers in November 1989.

Despite indications of the Islamist party's following (*El Mounqid*, for example, was able to sell 100,000 copies of its first issue despite its high cover price of 5 Dinars) it was not until the FIS began to organise street demonstrations and rallies that the true extent of its support became more widely apparent. In December 1989 a rally called in response to one organised by Algerian women who were protesting against the Family Code of 1984, attracted over 100,000, people outnumbering the women's demonstration by several hundred to one. Several other rallies were held subsequently throughout Algeria. These shows of force culminated in a rally in Algiers on 20 April 1990 which journalists estimated drew

---

21 For more details on this see the interview with Rabia Bekkar, 'Taking up space in Tlemcen: the Islamist occupation of urban Algeria' in *Middle East Report* (November–December 1992).

an attendance of possibly 600–800 thousand marchers. The rally was conducted in complete silence and with great discipline, thus further enhancing the FIS's reputation for being highly organised.

The huge demonstrations of popular support, which were far in excess of anything the Islamist movement in Algeria had hitherto ever been able to attract, appeared to be a clear vindication of the decision to form the party. The FIS and its leaders thus became the most popular and influential Islamists in Algeria. Those Islamist leaders who had remained outside the party became increasingly marginalised and lacking in any real influence. Some other Islamists did form parties distinct from that of FIS, but these proved to be tiny affairs, usually dominated by quixotic individuals outside the Islamist mainstream, incapable of challenging the FIS.[22]

The Rabitat Dawa continued to exist but posed no threat to the increasing political hegemony the FIS exerted over Islamist activism. Abassi Madani actually participated with Sahnoun, Nahnah and Djaballah in the meeting that formally constituted a directorate for the organisation in October 1989. When questioned on the relationship between the Rabitat and the FIS, the leader of the FIS replied that: "The one complements the other and one will work for the other because Islam is all that matters." The other leading figures in the Rabitat were similarly anxious to reaffirm the independence and apolitical and exclusively religious nature of the organisation. Mahfoud Nahnah pointedly declared that: "The Rabitat will never be in the service of a tendency, an individual or a party. It will only be in the service of religion."[23]

The FIS and the Rabitat, nevertheless, co-operated and joined forces for the rally and march of December 1989. However, the influence of those leading figures who remained outside the new party waned as time progressed. This was demonstrated in the differences of opinion that

---

22 The most notable of these parties included the Al-Oumma party launched by Benyoucef Benkhedda, one time president of the GPRA during the liberation struggle who championed a nationalism based on Islam. Others included the Parti du Rassemblement Arabe Islamique (PRAI – which some alleged had been set up by Military Security) and even a party that laid claim to the name and ideology of Abdelhamid Ben Badis's Association of Algerian Ulama. For more details on these and other similar parties see Jean-Jacques Lavenue, *Algérie: La Démocratie Interdite* (Paris, L'Harmattan, 1992), pp. 74–5.

23 *Algérie Actualité*, 26.10.89.

emerged over the FIS's plans to hold its march of 20 April 1990 in direct conflict with one planned by the FLN. Persuaded by the FLN leadership that this would produce an unnecessary confrontation, Ahmed Sahnoun (who continued to be seen by many as the "patriarch" of the wider Islamist movement) together with Mahfoud Nahnah, urged the FIS's leaders to call off the march. Sahnoun went so far as to telephone Abassi Madani from the United Arab Emirates, where he was making a visit, but his pleas went unheeded. Abassi Madani explained that "We love Sheikh Sahnoun very much, but we also love justice. For us, it is justice that comes first!"[24] The patent failure of these attempts together with the huge triumph the march eventually constituted led to an inevitable decline in the status and influence of both Sahnoun and Nahnah, as both figures, along with Abdallah Djaballah, continued to haemorrhage supporters to the new party.

The response of the establishment: government and the FLN

The government: inaction and sympathy
The reaction and response of the political establishment to the rise of the FIS in this period was ambiguous. Gestures of antagonism were frequently more than matched with ones of tolerance and reconciliation. At times it appeared that elements within Algeria's ruling strata were actively encouraging and even aiding the new party.

The reason for these inconsistencies was the increasingly fragmented nature of the Algerian regime in the wake of the crisis of October 1988. The largely covert struggles that were waged inside the regime over Chadli's political position and economic policies were overlaid from 1989 by the institutional divisions that were introduced in the new Constitution – particularly those separating the FLN from the state and those carving a more independent role for the President.

Actual government policy in the year following the October crisis was notable for its increased emphasis on Islam and Islamic themes. The

---

24 *Algérie Actualité*, 26.4.90. It was also suggested, though, that despite his eventual enthusiasm for the march, Abassi Madani had had his own doubts about it, but feared it would go ahead without him and thus undermine his leadership.

new Constitution of February 1989, as well as omitting references to socialism, confirmed and stressed the Islamic character of the Algerian state. The National Charter was no longer identified as the highest authority in the state and the Higher Islamic Council was for the first time constitutionally recognised. It was also significant that the guarantees of female rights contained in the Constitution of 1976 were entirely absent in the 1989 version. In other areas too the regime was keen to display an Islamic orientation. Chadli Benjedid made a high-profile pilgrimage to Mecca in 1989, and in July of that year the 18th Congress of Islamic Thought was devoted to the revival of Islam.

Whether this renewed emphasis on Islam represented an attempt by the regime to improve its severely damaged sense of popular legitimacy in the wake of the unrest of October 1988, or whether it sought, as it had previously done, to "spike the guns" of the Islamists whose popularity and profile were clearly on the rise, is unclear. It seems, though, that whatever the intent behind the measures the effect was to boost the Islamists. The Law on Political Associations, for example, whilst containing the provisions against confessionally based parties, also obliged new parties to include in their aims "the protection and the consolidation of the social and cultural blooming of the nation within the framework of national Arab–Islamic values."[25] This, it was argued, not just further legitimised Islamist ideas and aspirations, but actually served to strengthen the FIS's hand against its non-Islamist and more secularist competitors – giving it a constitutional stick with which to beat them.

The reaction of the political authorities to the meteoric rise of FIS following its legalisation in September 1989 was characterised by inaction and even sympathy. The government failed to take any real steps to curb the mobilisation of the FIS even when it ventured into illegality through many of its activists' use of intimidation against members of other political parties and people seen as not conforming to Islamist notions of appropriate dress and social behaviour. At times the government appeared to be positively encouraging the FIS through allowing Islamist sermons to be broadcast over state television and by introducing legislation in February 1990 that allowed the FIS to establish its own

---

25   Article 3, *Loi no. 89-11 du Juillet 1989. Relative aux Associations à Caractère Politique.* Reproduced in *Maghreb-Machrek*, no. 127 (Janvier–Mars 1990), pp. 200–5.

trade union in competition with the official UGTA. In early 1990 Mouloud Hamrouche, appointed Prime Minister by Chadli in September 1989, officially denied any evidence of FIS involvement in a high-profile violent incident involving Islamists that had occurred in January of that year. By doing so he appeared to willingly abandon a possible propaganda tool the regime could have used against the FIS.[26]

The FLN divided

The reasons for this extraordinary policy of the regime – which signified a complete break with the policy of trying to contain the Islamist movement which had been pursued by all the governments in Algeria since independence – were to be found in the complex internal politics of the FLN. The aftermath of the October 1988 crisis witnessed the emergence of at least three different competitive tendencies within the historic party as it sought to come to terms with the huge political changes the crisis had engendered. Present before 1988 and often overlapping, these three tendencies struggled for influence in the dual and paradoxical arenas of the new electoral system – where it was technically just another political party – and within the regime itself where, despite its constitutional de-coupling from the state, its members dominated nearly all the government and the entirety of the National Assembly.

The first two of these tendencies or factions were delineated essentially by attitudes towards the President, Chadli Benjedid and more particularly his programme of liberalising economic reforms. As already explained, Chadli had been locked for some time in a struggle with elements within the FLN who were opposed to him and his reforms. The President, however, did not fight this conflict alone. He had gathered around him a core of supporters who were particularly committed to his economic reforms and who constituted an opposing faction within the FLN to those who sought to thwart the reforms.

The third main faction that became apparent was one that had been present much longer than these first two factions. The consistent presence since independence of Islamist-oriented figures within the Algerian regime

---

26 This violent incident, in which four people were killed, was an attack by a group of armed Islamists on a court house in Blida on 16 January. It was later acknowledged to have been the work of the small Shi'ite group Sunna Wa Sharia and therefore was probably not in fact linked to the FIS.

itself has already been explained. From 1988 this tendency became increasingly vocal, appearing to shake off its traditionally low profile and pushed far more openly for the FLN and the regime to adopt a more Islamist agenda. This became particularly apparent at the extraordinary conference that the FLN held at the end of November 1989 when a section of delegates made a robust call for the promotion of sharia law and for the first time since independence forced a discussion on the establishment of more single sex schools. A keynote speech by the influential former foreign minister, Ahmed Taleb Ibrahimi, long seen as being on the "Islamic" wing of the party, called for the reassertion of "Arabo-Islamic" values.[27] Besides the support of high-profile figures such as Ibrahimi, this tendency (often referred to using the French pun: *barbefelenes*) appeared to have a significant bloc of support in the party, one press agency estimating that close to 60 of the 200 FLN deputies in the APN "espoused the ideas of the Islamist party".[28] There were inevitable accusations that such a significant presence was evidence of the success of efforts by the FIS to infiltrate the former ruling party.[29] Whilst there may have been some degree of truth to this, the reality was that the Islamist tendency in the FLN had always been present and was only now beginning to really assert itself within the party. This reassertion was interpreted by many at the time as being part of an attempt to undermine the FIS by co-opting its agenda – the traditional strategy used by both Boumedienne in the 1960s and 1970s and by Chadli in the 1980s. However, it seems that this push by the *barbefelenes* was primarily a function of the new political environment both inside the FLN and in Algeria generally. This allowed the faction to press their agenda and quite possibly also helps to explain the concessions to Islamist sentiment made by the regime in 1988-89. From 1989 the significance of this group became their relationship with the other two warring factions in the FLN and their relationship with the FIS.

---

27 Ahmed Taleb Ibrahimi was, in fact, the son of Bachir Ibrahimi, the leader of the AUMA in the 1940s and 1950s
28 *L'Agence France Presse* quoted in *Jeune Afrique*, 7.5.90.
29 Such an accusation was made by the editor of the FLN journal *Révolution Africaine* who was consequently sacked from his job.

Chadli and the FIS

President Chadli Benjedid continued to feel under pressure from his opponents within the regime during 1989, despite the measures he had taken to distract and divide them. The October crisis had drawn several old-guard FLN figures, who were forceful critics of his rule and his economic programme, back into the political foreground and they reasserted themselves strongly in the party and at FLN congresses. In response to this continuing threat to himself and his policies, Chadli looked once again for a means of damaging his opponents and decided that the FIS would again be his tool for achieving this. It is this which explains the apparent tolerance and encouragement that was given to the Islamist party following its legalisation in September 1989. As before, Chadli believed that his interests would be best served by support for the FLN and the FIS being equally balanced, allowing him to dominate any future National Assembly. However, whereas in September 1989 Chadli had viewed the FIS as just a threat he could brandish at his enemies within the FLN, which would allow his allies to predominate, he increasingly appeared to think that a more active approach was needed. This took the form of not just smoothing the path for the FIS in the run-up to elections but also of seeking to sabotage the electoral prospects of the FLN. Furthermore, it seems that the President may actually have struck some manner of deal with the FIS to achieve this goal.

No concrete evidence exists of any formal agreement having been made between the FIS and the President, but there are strong circumstantial indications that this occurred. Chadli Benjedid met formally with Abassi Madani in January 1990 and it is suggested that some arrangement was achieved then.[30] The likely form of this arrangement is obviously uncertain but given the subsequent behaviour of the FIS it appears that Abassi Madani, in return for official tolerance, undertook to avoid criticism of the government's programme of liberalising economic reforms and to shift FIS anti-regime rhetoric and propaganda away from the person of the President and onto the FLN generally. It was clearly remarkable, for example, that a fifteen-point list of demands submitted by the FIS following the massive rally of 20 April 1990 should be headed

---

30 It was also rumoured that Chadli Benjedid and Abassi Madani had had a second, secret, meeting on the invitation of the Saudi King Fahd in January in Jeddah, Saudi Arabia, where a deal had been reached.

by an appeal for the continuation of the reform programme, rather than by any of the more traditional Islamist demands. It appeared equally strange that the leadership of the FIS were willing to forego targets such as the President and his economic reforms – both of which were increasingly unpopular – in their otherwise unabashedly populist push for votes in the run-up to the local elections of June 1990.[31]

In seeking to sabotage the electoral prospects of the FLN, Chadli and his allies sought not just to make sure that the former ruling party did not achieve a majority (which appears to have been a fear of the President during 1989) but also sought to shift the regime's unpopularity away from himself and his reforms and onto his opponents in the FLN. The re-entry of many of his sternest critics into the ruling circles of the party in 1988-89 provided Chadli with the opportunity of letting them take on the difficult task of defending the FLN and its record in government whilst distancing himself from the party. The President was noticeably absent from the campaign to support the party of which he was still a member.

There were also accusations that information damaging to the FLN was deliberately leaked and publicised. The most prominent example of all was the claim in March 1990 by the former Prime Minister, Abdelhamid Brahimi, that corrupt government officials had, over time, siphoned an estimated $26 billion worth of funds from the national coffers. This "revelation", which drew to near fever pitch the already powerful popular perception of the FLN regime of being one rotten with corruption and greed, inflicted further huge damage on the FLN and those who sought to defend its record. The FIS, in particular, immediately seized on the figure and vigorously publicised it and drew attention to the fact that the figure quoted by Brahimi was approximately equivalent to the country's crippling international debt – the supposed source of Algeria's economic woes. Brahimi, however, claimed that his statement did not represent a deliberate or sudden "revelation", but was a figure he had quoted in answer

---

31 January 1990 was the most likely date on which a deal could have struck between Abassi and Chadli, because not only was that the date of their official meeting but up until the beginning of that month, the FIS had criticised Chadli's reformist Prime Minister, Mouloud Hamrouche. Abassi Madani, for example, had lambasted Hamrouche for his "inability and his incompetence". Interview with Abassi Madani, *Algérie Actualité*, 4.1.90.

to a question put to him following a speech at Algiers University.[32] The prevalent accusation that the former Prime Minister had co-ordinated his remarks with Chadli and Hamrouche beforehand was also weakened by two further facts. Firstly, that Brahimi had been actually dismissed by Chadli in 1988 and secondly that he was fiercely criticised by Hamrouche following the supposed revelations. Nevertheless, it had provided a potent propaganda weapon for the FIS, which it used to great effect.

There were suspicions that although still a member of the FLN, the former Prime Minister was interested in seeing an FIS victory in the local elections. This was seen as being not only due to his growing rift with elements of the regime but also because he may have seen the FIS as being much closer to his own ideals. With Ahmed Taleb Ibrahimi, Abdelhamid Brahimi enjoyed the reputation of being one of the more high-profile members of the FLN's Islamic wing – sharing with the former Foreign Minister the religious prestige of being a son of one of the senior members of Abdelhamid Ben Badis's original AUMA. Clear recognition of this reputation came with approaches made to the former Prime Minister by the FIS itself at the end of 1989. Initially wary of such contact, Brahimi finally agreed to meet Abassi Madani in February 1990 and the FIS's motivations in seeking such a meeting rapidly became apparent. Although Brahimi made it clear that he was a member of the FLN and intended to remain so, this did not stop the leader of the FIS from subsequently making passing public suggestions that the former Prime Minister could reassume that office in a future FIS administration.

Brahimi's revelations induced another bout of infighting within the FLN over who was to blame for this alleged corruption, thus further weakening the party in the run-up to the local elections. Indeed, the multiple splits within the party had reduced it to a state of near catatonic inaction. As one Algerian newspaper commented as late as April 1990:

> Since October 1988 the FLN has walled itself in profound silence. It has rarely taken a position on anything and when it has it has been evasive. Towards the FIS, it has adopted an approach of extreme prudence.[33]

---

32 Author's interview with Abdelhamid Brahimi, London, 6.9.95.
33 *Algérie Actualité*, 26.4.90.

Mehri and the "new" FLN

A valiant attempt to rally the FLN was made by its new chief, Abdelhamid Mehri, who had sought to renew the party and present it as a new entity to the public. Increasingly disillusioned with the apparent willingness of his former ally, Chadli Benjedid, to abandon the party, Mehri fought hard in the months preceding the local elections to achieve a more robust front for the FLN. He called for a counter-march by the party on the same day, 20 April, that the FIS had planned to hold their own rally. However, in the face of enormous official pressure to avoid bloody confrontations on the streets, Mehri was forced to back down, bringing further humiliation and division on the former ruling party. [34] Even when the FLN was able to stage its own march later the following month the relatively large numbers of people it appeared to muster were, as François Burgat observed:

> . . . more a witness to the capacity of the old-style party to use the apparatus of the State and its means of persuasion than it was of any 'ideological' potential capable of actually leading a party to victory.[35]

Indeed, most of those Algerians attending the Algiers rally had been bussed in from the countryside. In other areas of the country and in contrast to the FIS, who seemed able to draw large numbers of supporters wherever they marched, the FLN had great difficulties in drumming up public demonstrations of support. An attempt to organise a march in Oran at this time attracted barely 100 participants and in Constantine the party made no public showing at all. Conscious of the threat the FIS posed to their expected domination of the new multi-party system, the FLN took steps to counter it mounting a legal challenge to the FIS's use of mosques for partisan and electoral purposes.

Few concessions, however, were wrung from the government which proceeded with its plans. Chadli and his allies clearly believed that the ideal scenario of a split vote between the FLN and the FIS was likely.

---

34 It was suspected that the FIS march was also part of a deal with the authorities, in which Abassi agreed to not let his followers get out of control.

35 Burgat and Dowell, *The Islamic Movement in North Africa*, pp. 277–8.

On the eve of the local poll the President told one diplomat that he expected the FIS to poll no more than 20–25% of the vote.[36]

The local elections of June 1990

The assumption that independent Algeria's first multi-party local elections were likely to be a two-horse race was confirmed by a number of factors. Two of the most prominent opposition parties announced their boycott of the local elections on the grounds that they had not been given sufficient time to organise themselves before the poll. Both these parties, the FFS (Front des Forces Socialistes) and the MDA (Mouvement pour le Démocratie en Algérie) had been expected to be major forces in the multi-party system since not only had they been active in exile long before the events of 1988-89, but both were headed by one of the "historic chiefs" of the war of liberation. The FFS was headed by the charismatic Hocine Ait Ahmed, whilst the MDA was, of course, led by former President Ahmed Ben Bella. The boycott of these two important parties clearly narrowed the voting options for Algerians. This was further reinforced by the fact that only the FLN and the FIS were able to put up candidates in all the electoral divisions, which implied that there was unlikely to be any breakthrough by any other third force or party.

A third confirmation of the dominance of the two parties came with the release of an opinion poll by the government, following the FIS rally in Algiers in April 1990, which reported that between 40% and 50% of the votes in the local elections were likely to go to the FLN with 20–30% likely to be won by the FIS. The complex links between the government and the FLN must inevitably have cast at least some doubt on the veracity of the poll, but the FLN went into the poll confident of picking up as much as 55–65% of the votes cast. It was consequently a shock both to the FLN and most other observers and participants in the poll when it became clear, as the results of the 12 June voting emerged, that it was the FIS that had achieved the share of the vote anticipated by FLN.

The nature of the poll, which involved combined voting for both commune councils (APCs) and regional wilaya assemblies, made overall

---

36   Author's interview with Hussein Amin, Egyptian Ambassador to Algeria, Cairo, 13.6.94.

voting figures difficult to calculate, but there was no doubting the comprehensive nature of the FIS victory. The party received 54% of the votes cast in the commune elections and over 57% of those in the wilayas. It consequently took control of 853 of the 1539 commune councils and 31 of the 48 wilayas. The victory was further compounded by the disastrous performance of the FLN, which managed to poll barely half of its rival's total, taking just 28% in both sets of results. The remainder of the votes went to the profusion of smaller parties and independent candidates, the largest single party vote being just 2% for the RCD (Rassemblement pour la Culture et la Démocratie).[37]

Once the immediate shock of the results had settled in, there was something of a rush by observers, particularly in the West and the Western media, to try to suggest that the results were in some way inaccurate and misleading. Many pointed to the abstention rate of 35% and suggested that much of this figure and probably a significant slice of the FIS's eventual vote would have probably gone to the FFS and MDA if these parties had participated and given the electorate a wider choice than that between the, for many, equally unappetising FIS and FLN. Other commentators pointed to certain election rules which they argued artificially influenced the results. The existence of a proxy vote, for example, which enabled a man to vote on behalf of his wife, served to effectively double the vote of the FIS, it was suggested. The rule that gave an automatic majority of seats in the APCs to the leading party, irrespective of whether it had achieved a majority of the popular vote in the commune, was also cited as inflating the apparent scale of the FIS's victory. Some simply argued that the strong presence of FIS activists on the streets on the day of the poll influenced or intimidated voters into voting for them.[38]

However, these points were, in reality, of strictly limited significance. The abstention rate on the day of the poll, although significant at 35%, was more or less consistent with non-voting rates in free elections in

---

37 For the full results and analysis of the elections see Jacques Fontaine, 'Les elections locales Algériennes du 12 Juin 1990: approche statistique et géographique', *Maghreb-Machrek*, no. 129 (Juillet–Septembre 1990); see also Keith Sutton, Ahmed Aghrout and Salah Zaimche, 'Political changes in Algeria: an emerging electoral geography', *Maghreb Review*, vol. 17, nos. 1 and 2 (1992), pp. 3–27.

38 Hugh Roberts argues that the absence of Government officials from many voting booths on the day of the poll was a conscious policy to allow the FIS to use such tactics to maximise their vote. Roberts, 'From Radical Mission', p. 462.

most other countries. The participation rate was remarkably high given the negative image voting had inevitably accrued during the years of meaningless elections that occurred before 1988, when voters had had no effective choices put before them but had still been obliged to vote. Even though the FIS did appear to make particular use of the proxy system, the assumption that women were necessarily more inclined to vote against FIS than their husbands was questionable. The FIS had established their own women's section and large numbers of women had often attended FIS rallies and demonstrations in the run-up to the elections. On the issue of the "winner takes all" system operated in the elections, although it resulted in the FIS winning control of a greater percentage of councils than their simple share of the popular vote (they won 65% of the wilaya councils, for example), this did not alter the fact that at both local and regional levels they had achieved a clear majority of the popular vote. Nothing could really dismiss this central reality.

Support for the FIS: social and geographic bases

The election results provided a valuable and unprecedented insight into the nature of support for Islamism in Algeria by providing indications of who exactly had voted for the FIS. More pertinently, it also provided possible evidence as to what had motivated people to cast their votes in such large numbers for a party representing a tendency that had been seen as little more than an extremist fringe movement less than two years previously.

Given the comprehensive dominance of the FIS in comparison to the other parties in the election, it was almost easier (and, arguably, as instructive) to look at who had *not* voted for the FIS in June 1990. The results showed that several areas had clearly not come out strongly for the Islamists. These areas were predominantly the rural south, together with a few pockets in the more urbanised north. The reasons for these areas' resistance to the Islamist tide were relatively easy to identify. In the rural south the majority of the councils were won by the FLN. Here, the dominance of the former single party of state was retained partly because of the continued relative esteem the FLN enjoyed in this traditional area (because of its role in the war of liberation), and because it had escaped many of the social and economic changes and problems that had afflicted the urban north. It was also true that the entrenched FLN control made ballot-rigging more possible. Those pockets of the north which had not voted for FIS were identified as being ones dominated by the country's Berber community: notably the communes of Tizi Ouzou and Bejaia in Kabylia. The established antipathy of much of Kabylia to the Islamist movement and its agenda has already been explored (see Chapter Three) and the election results showed that this sentiment was undimmed. The electoral turnout in the areas of Grand Kabylia and the Soumma Valley (which contained Tizi Ouzou and Bejaia) had been particularly low and reflected a clear response to the boycott call by the FFS which had historically based itself in Kabylia. When people had voted in these areas it had been predominantly for the secularist and Berberist RCD which won clear majorities in both Tizi Ouzou and Bejaia.[39]

On the basis of this evidence it appeared that the FIS vote was concentrated, with the noted exceptions, in the more urbanised north of the country. The election statistics graphically testified to this fact. In Algeria's three biggest cities (all in the north of Algeria), Algiers, Oran and Constantine, the party attracted shares of the popular vote of 64%, 71% and 72% respectively. The particularly urban character of the FIS vote was further emphasised by the fact that the party won control of 90% of the councils and two-thirds of the seats in urban areas with populations of over 20,000. In contrast, its share of seats fell to roughly 40% in areas with fewer than 20,000 inhabitants.

It was clear that the stunning electoral success of the FIS was largely the result of it having attracted the overwhelming support of the people in Algeria's large towns and cities. The reasons why urban Algeria had lent its support so decisively to the FIS were to be found in the declining economic and social conditions in these areas. Urban Algeria had suffered the brunt of the economic crisis that had gripped the country from the mid-1980s – chronic and worsening unemployment, overcrowding and shortages had all become prominent features of everyday life in places like Algiers, Constantine and Oran. It was these areas that had been the focus of the unrest of October 1988. As has been shown, the riots and

---

39   This pattern was also repeated in the Mzab region which voted predominantly for independent candidates. Arun Kapil explains this by stressing the persistence of maraboutist and Sufi tendencies in the more remote areas of Algeria's south and west (which may also help explain the FLN strength in the south) and thus their resistance to more modern and urban Islamism.

demonstrations of that month were at heart an expression of popular rage and disillusionment at the failings of the regime. The continued failure of Algeria's rulers to bring any noticeable improvement in the social and economic conditions after October 1988 meant that this resentment remained. It was thus inevitable that given the opportunity to express their political opinions through the ballot box, this section of the population, together with other large groups in Algerian society who had suffered in the worsening economic and social climate of the late 1980s, would vote heavily to punish the party that represented the existing political establishment: the FLN.[40] The most effective means of humiliating the FLN was thus to vote for that party that was best placed to defeat it. Since late 1989 the only party capable of filling this role was the FIS. As Luis Martinez has observed:

> For the youths who had confronted the forces of law and order at the time of the October 1988 riots, the success of the FIS in the municipal elections of June 1990 in the crowded neighbourhoods and suburbs of Greater Algiers represented an undeniable revenge.[41]

Despite these observations, social and economic deprivation and a consequent desire to reject the FLN were not the only motivating factors for FIS voters on 12 June. A sizeable bloc of people voting for the FIS that day were those who were genuinely attracted to and supportive of the Islamist agenda. To distinguish between these two blocs and thus assess their relative strengths within the FIS vote was clearly unfeasible, and they may have been so closely intertwined as to be indivisible. As one Algerian youth who voted for FIS explained, the FIS's radical and eschatalogical message represented the only perceived alternative in an otherwise bleak future:

---

40   The fact that social and economic hardship were the determining factors in much of the FIS's support was indicated by the fact that the party appeared to perform unusually well in some more rural areas. In the area of Jijel, for example, the FIS took roughly 75% of the seats despite the fact that the area was not particularly urbanised. The probable reason for this was that Jijel was one of the most deprived parts of the country, thus emphasising that deprivation was probably of more importance than urbanisation (even though the two were often synonymous) in understanding the nature of the FIS vote.

41   Luis Martinez: 'L'Environnement de la violence: "Djihad" dans la Banlieue d'Alger' in Remy Leveau, *L'Algérie dans la Guerre* (Brussels, Editions Complexe, 1995), p. 39.

In this country, if you are a young man . . . you have only four choices: you can remain unemployed and celibate because there are no jobs and no apartments to live in; you can work in the black market and risk being arrested; you can try to emigrate to France to sweep the streets of Paris or Marseilles; or you can join the FIS and vote for Islam.[42]

Nevertheless, the massive marches and street demonstrations the FIS had been able to organise in the lead-up to the elections bore witness to the fact that the party had a large, ideologically committed core of supporters. Attendance at the FIS's meetings and mosques was notable for the overwhelming predominance of men between the ages of 20 and 40. This reflected the trend witnessed since the beginning of the decade for younger men in particular to join and support Islamist groups. The continuing decline in the economic means of most young Algerian men meant that the FIS – for the reasons starkly set out by the young FIS voter quoted above – was increasingly able to tap into this numerically huge source of popular support. The huge electoral victories the party had achieved in Algeria's major cities testified to this constituency of support amongst the wider electorate. Core support for the FIS was not, however, limited to unemployed youths. Traders and small businessmen were also found to be, frequently financial, supporters of the party and whilst FIS support electorally had been concentrated in the poorer districts of Algiers, the party also performed well in some of the higher-class areas of the capital. Although having variations in its level of support, the strength of the FIS vote demonstrated once again the breadth of the apparent appeal of Islamism across geographic region and social class as shown by its ability to put up candidates in virtually every division for the elections.

The transformation of the FIS into what was undeniably a mass political party was largely the result of the work of Abassi Madani. As leader, Abassi had quite consciously marketed the party as one of the masses. He regularly referred to the FIS as the "people's party" thus making a deliberate contrast with the FLN which was very much seen as the party of the corrupt elite.

---

42 *New York Times*, 25.6.90.

Ideology and agenda of the FIS

The formation of a political party by Algeria's Islamists and its competition in elections provided the movement – or at least that part of it which had joined the party – with a concrete opportunity to present its agenda to the electorate. Indeed, multi-party democratic politics demanded it.

An analysis of the FIS between its creation in February 1989 through to its victory in June 1990 reveals two main things about its agenda and proposed programme: firstly, the effective absence of any really lengthy or radical political and economic policy programme, and secondly the continued emphasis by the party on a number of specific, largely social, themes. Formal policy statements and documents issued by the party as well as interviews given by senior party figures during this period demonstrate this.

Economic policy

Several documents advancing the FIS's plans for Algeria were issued by the party from its formation and most of these made reference to economic issues. The party's first formal policy document, *Projet de Programme du Front Islamique du Salut*, was unveiled at the meeting officially launching the party on 9 March 1989.[43] Just under a third of its contents were devoted to the FIS's view of and plans for the economy. These statements were largely reiterated in later policy documents.

The plans attracted a significant amount of criticism and scorn from opponents of the FIS and Western commentators alike for their lack of apparent detail.[44] It was more true to say that the plans lacked innovation – balance and moderation characterising their tone and contents with

---

43 For the most detailed analysis of this document see Ahmed Rouadjia, 'Discourses and strategy of the Algerian Islamist Movement (1986–1992)' in Laura Guazzone, *The Islamist Dilemma: The Political Role of Islamist Movements in the Contemporary Arab World* (Reading, Ithaca Press, 1995), pp. 80–6. Rouadjia characterises the forty-nine-page policy statement as "both structurally and thematically disorganised" and observes that it "seems to be much more a justification of Islam combined with a demonstration of national pride than a political and social analysis worthy of a party called to lead a state in solving political, economic and social problems", pp. 80–1.

44 See, for example, *Algérie Actualité*, 4.1.90, and Yahia Zoubir, 'The painful transition from authoritarianism in Algeria', *Arab Studies Quarterly*, vol. 15, no. 3 (Summer 1993) p. 92.

only minor changes and reforms advocated. The unremarkable content of the programme was exemplified by the opening statement of the section dealing with the economy:

> The economic policy of the FIS is founded on the search for an equilibrium between the needs of consumption and the conditions of production, on the complementary relationship between quality and quantity, taking account of demographic growth and of cultural development and the imperative of economic independence.[45]

Such sentiments were likely to be found in the economic programmes of virtually any political party. The one possible exception to this – the stress on economic independence – was in the Algerian context similarly unremarkable because of the nationalism that had traditionally characterised economic relations with the West. Changes and reforms were advocated by the party but these tended to take the form of uncontroversial proposals to better harmonise education with the needs of industry, to introduce more technology and to expand regional trade. More specifically Islamic proposals were contained in the programme but these were largely vague and confined to references that a particular area of the economy or a specific policy should "conform to the spirit of the sharia".[46] A commitment to the establishment of Islamic banks, which banned usury, was expressed but few details of how this was to be achieved were given. Such a nebulous impression of the Islamic content of the party's economic proposals was further added to by Abassi Madani's later assertion that Algeria's economic crisis did not have a material base and would find its solution in the recovery of morality and religious faith.[47]

What was, however, noticeable about the FIS's economic plans was the support they appeared to give to the private sector and the market. Reference was made to the rights and conditions of the worker and an overall need for equity, but the document lambasted the failings of the planned economy which it argued had served "to discourage the spirit of initiative . . . to the profit of mediocrity and incompetence". It

---

45 *Projet de Programme du Front Islamique du Salut*, 9.3.89. Extracts reproduced in Al-Ahnaf, Botiveau and Frégosi, *L'Algérie par ses Islamistes*, pp. 179–87.
46 *Ibid.*
47 *Algérie Actualité*, 19.10.89.

correspondingly spoke of the need "to fix parameters limiting the intervention of the State in industrial ownership and to protect the private sector". More significantly, there was a call for decentralisation of public enterprises and the encouragement of "competition, the agent of plenty".[48] These last two policies were significant in that they represented the main planks of Chadli Benjedid's economic reform programme over the preceding decade. It was their presence within the FIS's programme that helped persuade Chadli Benjedid that the party could be recruited as an ideological ally in his struggle against the anti-reformists within the FLN. This had further been confirmed by Abassi Madani's statement at the beginning of January 1990 that:

> The FIS is more concerned than anyone for these reforms and demands their application.[49]

So whilst the FIS had sacrificed the propaganda tool of the unpopularity of the effects of the reforms, it had not been entirely opportunist in tacitly supporting them. Their inclusion in the programme of March 1989 reflected an established preference for liberal economics in Islamist economic thought across the Muslim world and it was thus simply a case of further emphasising them (as shown in the petition of April 1990) to gain valuable concessions from the regime.[50]

Women, social policy and education

The vast majority of the literature produced by the FIS in the period 1989-90 focused on social, cultural and educational issues and represented a significant departure from current Algerian government policy. The traditional Islamist concerns over the role of women in society and the need to Islamicise and Arabise the education system remained central to the programme of the FIS.

---

48 *Projet de Programme du Front Islamique du Salut*, 9.3.89. Extracts reproduced in Al-Ahnaf, Botiveau and Frégosi, *L'Algérie par ses Islamistes*, pp. 179–87.
49 Interview with Abassi Madani, *Algérie Actualité*, 4.1.90.
50 It has been argued that it was this preference for liberal economics and support for the Government's reform programme that led to the exclusion of Abdallah Djaballah from the FIS at its creation since the Sheikh adopted a far more critical approach (Roberts, 'From Radical Mission', p. 450). However, it is highly unlikely that the leadership of the FIS were aware of any potential deal being struck with Chadli Benjedid as early as the start of 1989.

The party's initial policy document, *Projet de Programme du Front Islamique du Salut*, made clear the new party's view that the Algerian woman's role should primarily be in the home. It indicated that a woman should be given a financial incentive to stay in or return to the home arguing that "her work at home must be legitimately considered as a social and educational function, giving her the right to a pension".[51] The importance of this issue to the party was demonstrated by the FIS's first significant show of force in December 1989 when it participated in the organisation of a counter-demonstration to one held by women demanding the abrogation of the Family Code of 1984 which had reduced the rights and role of women in Algerian society (see Chapter Three). Five months later in April 1990, the role of women was addressed in the fifteen-point petition the party unveiled following their mass rally on the 20th of that month. Point 12 of the list of demands argued for the need to "Assemble the conditions for the protection of the dignity of the Algerian woman" – widely acknowledged shorthand for the return of women to the home and possible curbs on their dress and social relations.[52]

Besides emphasising the importance of women remaining in the home to bring up children and maintain family life, the FIS also argued that this facilitated the creation of more much needed job opportunities for Algeria's young men. Such a policy also supported the party's commitment to sexual segregation in Algerian society, Ali Belhadj arguing that it was actually immoral for men and women to work together in the same office. The ending of co-education was also an expressed priority for the party. Benazouz Zebda, who became recognised as the third most senior figure in the party, claimed that the mixing of the sexes at schools and universities had led to the "proliferation of bastards".[53] At the same time the party also made clear its opposition to birth control.[54]

Overall, social policy together with education, provided the party with most of its favourite themes and it was clear that the FIS aimed to

---

51 *Projet de Programme du Front Islamique du Salut* , 9.3.89, quoted in *Algérie Actualité*, 4.1.90.
52 Text of petition reproduced in Al-Ahnaf, Botiveau and Frégosi, *L'Algérie par ses Islamistes*, pp. 49–51.
53 Interview with Benazouz Zebda, *Algérie Actualité*, 23.2.89.
54 See interview with Abassi Madani, *Jeune Afrique*, 12.2.90.

establish significant control over these areas. As Abassi Madani stated in an interview:

> Our principle concern is with education and the family. It is impossible to achieve an Islamic society without mastering education and this equally demands a healthy and conscientious family.[55]

Apart from the overriding aim of segregation, the other main concern of the party in education was to continue Arabisation and spread it to institutions such as medical schools and schools of technology. It was notable that Abassi Madani rarely used French in public.

Policy on political power and pluralism

The FIS gave very few indications of the sort of political institutions they intended to make use of or indeed create when and if they achieved political power. Abassi Madani referred on several occasions to the party's desire to establish an Islamic state, although precisely what this might entail was never properly elaborated. Until the party began to attract a huge popular following at its demonstrations from the end of 1989, it appears that no serious consideration was given by the party to the prospect of taking power. When asked in October 1989 about the FIS's numerical strength, Abassi Madani gave the surprising reply:

> Our numbers are of little importance, the elections are not our aim. Our aim is the total transformation of the political, economic, social, cultural and civilisational crisis. All of these because we are in clear crisis. Getting out of this crisis is our starting point.[56]

As the elections of June 1990 approached and the party began to realise that the wielding of eventual political power was a significant possibility, specifically political demands became an increasing feature of the FIS's discourse. The petition of April 1990 was dominated by political demands such as the dissolution of the National Assembly with elections to be held within three months, the creation of an independent body to oversee elections, the end of the FLN's monopoly on parts of the media

---

55 *Ibid.*
56 *Algérie Actualité*, 2.5.91.

and the creation of an independent judiciary.[57] However, most of these demands could be seen as merely facilitating, rather than explaining, the party's policy. As one Algerian newspaper suggested at the time, having just attracted such a huge display of popular support, the FIS perhaps decided that it should push to make best use of this support at elections on the grounds that it was "now or never".[58]

The stunning success the FIS had enjoyed in pursuing the electoral path to power and influence also seemed to have silenced that, admittedly fringe, part of the Algerian Islamist movement that had advocated the efficacy of armed Islamist struggle. Some activity was witnessed such as the attack on a court house by a small group of Shi'ite Islamists in January 1990 and the reported involvement of members of Algerian Takfir wa Hijra in the unrest of October 1988, but these incidents were small scale and peripheral to the main movement.[59] Much of this was due to the fact that most members of this tendency were still in prison following their conviction in the wake of Mustapha Bouyali's campaign. Nevertheless, several former associates and sympathisers of Bouyali did assume senior positions within the FIS at its creation, the most high-profile of whom was Ali Belhadj himself, who had been arrested and imprisoned in the 1980s for his involvement with the MAIA.[60] Indeed, despite public disavowals of the use of armed struggle,[61] the party retained considerable sympathy for Bouyali's struggle. Ali Belhadj referred to Bouyali as being part of Algerian Islamism's historic heritage alongside Abdelhamid Ben Badis.[62] Abassi Madani argued that Bouyali had been pushed into the adoption of violence through intransigence and repression on the part of the regime.[63] Collectively, the party called for the release of all Islamist

---

57 Text of petition reproduced in Al-Ahnaf, Botiveau and Frégosi, *L'Algérie par ses Islamistes*, pp. 49–51.

58 *Algérie Actualité*, 26.4.90.

59 The incident at the Palace of Justice in Blida involved six men believed to belong to a Shi'ite organisation called Sunna Wa Sharia.

60 Other founders of the FIS who had also been involved in Bouyali's MAIA included Mohammed Kerrar, Said Guechi, Bachir Fakih and Abdelkader Moghni.

61 Benazouz Zebda, for example, rejected the use of armed struggle, stating that the FIS's fight would be "against delinquency and evil". Interview with Benazouz Zebda, *Algérie Actualité*, 23.2.89.

62 Interview with Ali Belhadj, *Algérie Actualité*, 23.2.89.

63 Abassi claimed: "Bouyali was teaching, was preaching, was thinking that dialogue would succeed . . . He was shocked when the door of dialogue was slammed in his face and he was treated with violence." *Algérie Actualité*, 2.5.91.

prisoners (implying the MAIA) in both the first issue of its paper, *El Mounqid*, and in its petition of April 1990. More tangibly, the FIS organised a show of force of 2,000 of its supporters at a court hearing for some of the Bouyali's followers in October 1989.

One aspect of the FIS's thought and agenda which attracted considerable attention, especially in the aftermath of the June victory, was its attitude towards democratisation and its attendant values of pluralism and respect for the electoral process. Of particular concern to those people who were anxious that the country's democratisation programme be continued were statements made by Ali Belhadj. From the outset the young teacher and preacher made no secret of the fact that he viewed Algeria's new political system strictly as a means to an end rather than as any kind of end in itself.[64] He saw politics as a staging post on the way to Islam and the rule of "divine politics". Whilst this view could be interpreted as expressing, albeit in an unusual way, the legitimate desire of every political party to see introduced its particular agenda and thus one not necessarily inconsistent with the principles of liberal democracy, Belhadj was in fact quite specific in his actual rejection of the idea of democracy:

> Democracy is a stranger in the House of God. Guard yourself against those who say that the notion of democracy exists in Islam. There is no democracy in Islam. There exists only the shura with its rules and constraints . . . We are not a nation that thinks in terms of majority–minority. The majority does not express the truth.[65]

On other occasions Belhadj simply equated democracy with "unbelief".[66] He was similarly forthright and specific in his view on the central concept of multi-partyism and political pluralism, appearing to issue a clear warning to those parties that did not make due reference to Islam:

---

64 See interview with Ali Belhadj, *Al-Bayane*, December 1989 reproduced in Al-Ahnaf, Botiveau and Frégosi, *L'Algérie par ses Islamistes*, p. 71.

65 *Algér Republicain*, December 1989, quoted in Catherine Belvaude, *L'Algérie* (Paris, Karthala, 1991), p. 108.

66 *Le Maghreb*, 20.10.89, quoted in *El Watan*, 15.1.95.

Multi-partyism is not tolerated unless it agrees with the single framework of Islam . . . If people vote against the Law of God . . . this is nothing other than blasphemy. The ulama will order the death of the offenders who have substituted their authority for that of God.[67]

These were not isolated, polemical statements. It became clear that in Belhadj's view, which stemmed from his devout and fundamentalist religious beliefs about the exclusive truth of Islam, there should be no place in Algerian society for anyone who either did not share these convictions or sought to express a dissenting opinion or identity. It was also apparent that these views were shared by a significant section of the party's supporters. Belhadj's hugely popular Friday sermons, which attracted up to 20,000 people each week, were full of denunciations of followers of other religions, liberals, foreign governments and leaders of other parties.

For some of FIS's opponents, the practical implications of these views were felt even before the party was able to wield political power following victory at the ballot box. The PAGS (Parti de l'Avant Garde Socialiste), the successor to the old Algerian Communist Party, clearly occupied a diametrically opposed position in the new party-political spectrum to that of FIS. Indeed, the Islamist party made combating the PAGS, which it saw as a party espousing atheism as part of its communist ideology, a priority. As an almost certain consequence of this, meetings organised by the PAGS in the Spring of 1989, as it waited like the FIS to be officially recognised, became the target of attacks by Islamic militants. Similar attacks occurred against the RCD party, which as the inheritor of the secularist and Berberist traditions and values of the Kabyle Spring of 1980 (see Chapter Three) was likewise viewed as an arch enemy of Islamism. In addition to this new political dimension there was also a rise in this period in attacks on more "traditional" targets of Islamist violence. Unmarried couples, unsuitably dressed women and establishments selling alcohol all appeared to come under renewed threats of violence, particularly once again at the universities, in the period 1989-90. Popular music events in Algiers during this time were cancelled due to

---

67 *Horizons*, 23.2.89, quoted in *Algérie Actualité*, 4.1.90. Belhadj also wanted the Constitution changed to link multi-partyism to Islam.

threats from religious militants and there were cases of vandalism to martyrs' graveyards (tombstones were seen by many Islamists as being "un-Islamic").

The FIS's leadership, however, was quick to deny responsibility for such incidents, blaming "communist infiltrators" as well as the FLN for carrying out the violence to discredit the FIS. Foremost in denying FIS involvement in these incidents was the party leader, Abassi Madani, who actually condemned violence "from wherever it came" and stressed that his party chose "the path of dialogue for the settlement of all questions, whether political, economic, social or cultural".[68] Such language stood in marked contrast to that employed by his deputy, Ali Belhadj, and like Belhadj, Madani appeared to be consistent in his stance. When asked what the discourse of the FIS was, Madani replied simply "Moderation" and added that "Our doctrine is moderate and centrist because Islam is a religion of moderation." In further stark contrast to his deputy, Madani expressed his full commitment to the idea of democracy and when asked about the thorny question of sharia-prescribed punishments, such as stoning for adultery and amputation for theft, he replied that such punishments could only truly be applied in a fully Islamic world where peace, work and security would eliminate the causes of such crime. Again, on the issue of minority rights, there was an unambiguous contradiction of his deputy's views: "We will respect the minority, even if it is composed of one vote."[69]

Such demonstrative differences of opinion and tone within the upper echelons of the party naturally attracted much debate as to the reasons for this. For some, particularly opponents and critics of the FIS, Belhadj's intemperate discourse represented the true face of the party; Madani playing the role of a front man to assuage the fears of would-be voters for FIS, trying to disguise the party's agenda with woolly talk of tolerance and democracy. This strategy was exposed, they argued, when Madani, who was the only senior FIS figure who regularly dealt with the media, was closely questioned and was forced to admit that the party had qualifications to its endorsement of democracy:

---

68 *El Moudjahid*, 26.12.89.
69 Interview with Abassi Madani, *Jeune Afrique*, 12.2.90.

We will consider that those who have been elected by the people reflect the opinion of the people. In contrast, what we will not accept is the elected member who harms the interest of the people. He must not be against Islam, the sharia, its doctrine and its values. He must not be able to make war on Islam. He who is an enemy of Islam is an enemy of the people.[70]

Significantly, in this respect, the leader of the FIS also refused to say what would happen to the PAGS and the staunchly secularist RCD if the FIS came to power. More generally, observers saw the "double talk" by the FIS as a mechanism by which the party could avoid losing its place in the electoral system (still a potential threat if they pushed too far, despite the probable deal with Chadli) through Abassi's emollient public statements whilst Belhadj's hardline rhetoric would retain the party's popularity amongst the militants on the street. As Robert Mortimer observed on Madani and Belhadj: "The contrasting styles of these two leaders combined a soft and hard sell that appealed to a wide range of disaffected Algerians."[71]

A second reason advanced for inconsistencies in the party's line related to a belief that such inconsistencies reflected real divisions that existed right at the heart of the FIS between moderates and hardliners – Abassi and Belhadj being representative of the two tendencies. It was certainly true that the two most senior figures in the party had sharply differing backgrounds and were therefore likely to have divergent views on certain issues. Aged 58 at the time of the FIS's creation, Abassi Madani had had a long history of involvement in nationalist (he had been a member of Messali Hadj's PPA) as well as Islamist organisations. He was also a well educated man and having studied under Malek Bennabi at Algiers University had travelled to Britain in the 1970s to study for a Ph.D. (in Education) at London University. On returning to Algeria, the future leader of the FIS published his thesis (which examined educational problems in Islamic countries) and continued to write and publish on his favourite themes of education, Islam and the deficiencies and problems of Western thought.[72] In contrast to Abassi's varied, cosmopolitan and

---

70 Interview with Abassi Madani, *Algérie Actualité*, 4.1.90.

71 Robert Mortimer, 'Islam and multiparty politics', *Middle East Journal*, vol. 45, no. 4 (Autumn 1991), p. 579.

72 Abassi Madani published three books during the 1980s, all in Arabic: *Al-Mushkilat*

cerebral background, Ali Belhadj was a much more straightforward figure. Twenty-five years Abassi's junior, Belhadj had received a highly religious education (he had been a student of both Abdellatif Soltani and Ahmed Sahnoun) and had gone on to become a schoolteacher of Arabic and religion. His fundamentalist stance and radical pronouncements were perhaps a reflection of his narrow and uncomplicated education and background. It was therefore not surprising that Belhadj's views should appear hardline and uncompromising when compared to the philosophical and temperate statements of Abassi Madani. Nevertheless, despite these differences, both men had developed a close relationship, particularly during October 1988, and it was they who had worked together to form the disciplined and highly successful project of the FIS.

The idea of factions within the FIS was naturally dismissed by the party's leaders when it was put to them. Madani claimed that the idea of factions and tendencies was an essentially Western one and argued that a form of collective responsibility operated in the party with all opinions being subject to the approval of the party's ruling council, the Majlis Shura, meaning that neither he nor Ali Belhadj were able to express their own individual opinions.[73] However, given the divergence of tone it is doubtful that this mechanism of collective responsibility operated as well as Madani seemed to claim. Indeed, despite the apparently well-structured organisation of FIS, there often appeared to exist a gap between the party's grass roots and the leadership: the strategy of the leadership often not being clear to the party members and the latter sometimes acting outside the direction of the leadership (which perhaps supports the claims of the

---

al-Tarbawiyya fi al-Bilad al Islamiyya (Educational Problems in the Islamic World) in 1986; Azmatu al-Fikr al-Hadeeth wa Mubarrirat al-Hal al-Islami (Crisis of Modern Thought and the Islamic Alternative) in 1989; and Al-Naw'iyya al-Tarbawiyya fi al-Marahil al-Ta'limiyya fi al-Bilad al Islamiyya (Educational Quality in the Schooling System of the Muslim World) in 1989. (Transliteration and translation from Cheriet, 'Islamism and Feminism', p. 213). For more details on the thought and ideas of Abassi Madani see Cheriet, and also Ahmed Rouadjia, 'Doctrine et discours du Cheikh Abbassi', Peuples Mediterranéens no. 52–3: Algérie: Vers l'Etat Islamique? (Juillet–Septembre 1990).

73 Interview with Abassi Madani, Jeune Afrique, 12.2.90. When questioned on the subject of his deputy's hostile view of democracy the leader of the FIS resorted to a philosophical answer about the different meanings of democracy since its inception by the Ancient Greeks. Interview with Abassi Madani, Algérie Actualité, 4.1.90.

leaders that the party was not responsible for acts of Islamist violence and intimidation.)

Structures and organisation of the FIS

The precise structure and organisation of the FIS remained largely obscure during the first eighteen months of its political life. When the party filed for official recognition in August 1989 only the names of Abassi, Belhadj and Benazouz Zebda were officially submitted. Unlike most of the other parties, the FIS held no national congress. According to statements made at its founding, the party was officially run by a Majlis Shura consisting of around thirty-five members. However, apart from a few more high-profile figures, the exact composition of the council was unknown. Journalists who tried to discover more about the party received little or no co-operation from the party's leadership. With the exception of the occasional interview by Ali Belhadj and a very few other senior figures, Abassi Madani was the only leader whom the party appeared willing to let speak to the media.

Although Abassi claimed in January 1990 that "the structuring of the FIS is still not achieved", the high degree of organisation and discipline the party appeared to exert at its rallies and demonstrations indicated a significant degree of institutional organisation.[74] More details about the internal workings of the party were to emerge later, but it appears that it was headed by a four-man National Executive consisting of Abassi, Belhadj, Benazouz Zebda and Hachemi Sahnouni. This was drawn from the Majlis Shura which, as indicated earlier by Abassi Madani was the formal decision-making body of the party. Below this the FIS had a highly hierarchical structure of wilaya, commune and even *quartier* branches of the party.[75] This hierarchical structure suggested that authority in the party came from the top down, although the extent to which this occurred with, for example, the selection of local candidates for the June 1990 elections is disputed.[76] Overall though, the mechanisms of the

---

74 Interview with Abassi Madani, *Algérie Actualité*, 4.1.90.

75 For a diagrammatic representation of the structure and organisation of the party see Abderrahim Lamchichi, *L'Islamisme en Algérie* (Paris, L'Harmattan, 1992), p. 102.

76 Hugh Roberts claims that selection of candidates for the elections was by the FIS's Majlis Shura (Roberts, 'From Radical Mission', p. 448), whilst Dévoluy and

party, particularly in terms of decision-making and ideology, remained shrouded in secrecy and thus created the degree of confusion amongst the rank and file referred to earlier.

External influences and support

Examination of and speculation about the FIS's ideology and agenda also prompted questions about the extent to which the party was influenced, and indeed supported, by Islamist movements and governments elsewhere in the Muslim world. Inevitably, significant attention focused, as it had done in the 1980s, on links with Iran. There was, however, little evidence to suggest any real links with the Islamic Republic. Ali Belhadj acknowledged the influence of the Iranian revolution on young Islamists in Algeria, but termed such influence "annoyances" and furthermore expressed his important theological differences with Iranian Shi'ism.[77] Similarly, Abassi Madani, when questioned on the existence of a branch of Hezbollah in Algeria replied:

> Hezbollah? This is nothing but a label. Behind it there is nothing. It is just a minority. Algeria is Sunnite.[78]

Of perhaps more relevance were alleged links with Saudi Arabia. On the ideological level, it was argued that elements of Saudi Wahhabism could be witnessed in both the attacks by militants on tombstones and in supposed plans by FIS to ban women from driving cars. On the practical level there was evidence that the party received significant funds from Saudi sources, both government and individual, including a reported donation of $1 million from a Saudi businessman.[79] Much of this funding was allegedly channelled through an Islamic association called the World

---

Duteil claim that the selection was made by the party's regional offices (Dévoluy and Duteil, *La Poudrière Algérienne*, pp. 126–7).

77 Interview with Ali Belhadj, *Al-Bayane*, December 1989, reproduced in Al-Ahnaf, Botiveau and Frégosi, *L'Algérie par ses Islamistes*, pp. 70–2. Belhadj was also critical of the record of the Islamic Republic claiming that it had "fallen into some traps". Although certain injustices had been eliminated in Iran others, such as the number of executions, had been introduced. Abed Charef, *Algérie: Le Grand Dérapage* (France, Éditions de l'Aube, 1994), p. 35.

78 Interview with Abassi Madani, *Algérie Actualité*, 26.4.90.

79 See *Libération*, 11.8.94.

Daawa League based in Riyadh, which had as one of its senior figures an Algerian – Aboubakr Djabar al-Jazara – and which was reputedly responsible for funding many of the FIS's public events as well as the campaign for the municipal elections.[80] Support also came from the Saudi ulama who sought to promote a form of "moderate" Islamism, capable of participating in power and thus preventing the movement moving towards a more militant Iranian-style Islamism.[81] Rumours that the Saudi King Fahd had attempted to broker a deal between Chadli Benjedid and Abassi Madani in January 1990 spoke of the King being motivated by his fear of the Iranian regime which he perceived to be close to Ali Belhadj.[82]

As evidence of the possible competition for influence between Saudi Arabia and Iran, there were reports of large numbers of cheap books on religious subjects from both Saudi Arabia and Iran appearing in book-shops during this period. Abassi Madani, for his part, denied that the FIS was inspired by any models emerging from Iran, Saudi Arabia or even Sudan. When questioned specifically about Saudi Arabia in early 1990, he stated that there were no official contacts between his party and Riyadh (which, as far as he was aware, still supported the existing regime in Algeria) although he suggested that there might be some now that the FIS had been legalised.[83]

As for links with other countries, the ideological links with Egypt appeared to remain strong. Ali Belhadj cited both Hassan al-Banna and Sayyid Qutb as influences on him. However, that he also cited his former teachers, Soltani and Sahnoun, indicated the importance of domestic Algerian influences.[84] It was suggested that such ideological links with the Arab East were strengthened by the sending abroad, on scholarships

---

80 This was according to a subsequent account given by Bachir Fakih, a member of the FIS's Majlis Shura. Dévoluy and Duteil, *La Poudrière Algérienne*, p. 121.

81 It was suggested that Saudi backing for the FIS was also prompted by a long-standing antipathy to the Algerian regime because of its revolutionary origins, its socialism and its prominent role in Third World politics. There was also a feeling that Algeria was not truly 'Arab' and that this could be rectified by the FIS's programme.

82 It is said that King Fahd actually believed Belhadj to be in the pay of Tehran and thus sought to boost Abassi, whom he portrayed to Chadli as a moderate figure.

83 Interview with Abassi Madani, *Jeune Afrique*, 12.2.90

84 Interview with Ali Belhadj, *Al-Bayane*, December 1989. Belhadj also stated that he liked to read the works of Ibn Taymiyya, the thirteenth- and fourteenth-century

in early 1989, of many of the Islamist students arrested during the unrest of October 1988. Having spent time in countries such as Syria and particularly Egypt, these students returned with new and radical ideas gained from contacts they had established there with local Islamists. This move by the authorities was portrayed as an exercise in removing disruptive elements from the political scene. However, there were suspicions that the idea for the scheme came from Islamist sympathisers within the regime.

Despite the ambiguities of government policy towards the FIS and the probable agreement that Chadli Benjedid had struck with the FIS, the regime appeared sensitive to the potential dangers of allowing the FIS to establish external links and acquire more radical ideas. It was probably for this reason that Abassi Madani was denied access to the International Islamic Conference that the Algerian Government hosted in May 1990 and which was attended by such notable Islamists as Rachid Ghannoushi of Tunisia and Hassan Turabi of Sudan.

The failure of the secular opposition

One of the marked features of the period from October 1988 through to June 1990 was the near total absence of any political grouping that effectively challenged the virtual monopoly exercised over the political scene by the FIS and the FLN. There appeared to be no real third alternative to what many Algerians saw as these two equally unattractive options. This was not due to any shortage of political parties – twenty had formally applied for official recognition in the immediate aftermath of the July 1989 Law on Political Associations. In fact, the sheer number of non-Islamist opposition parties weakened and divided any support such a potentially attractive "third option" might have been able to attract. Most of the secular opposition parties were unable to establish nationwide grass-roots organisations in preparation for the elections. This stood in contrast to their rivals in the FIS, who were able to use the mosque network, and the FLN, which took full advantage of the structures and organisation of the former single party apparatus. The boycott of the June 1990 poll of the two other parties which did appear to have a more

---

Islamic thinker and activist whose ideas had been influential on the Saudi Wahhabist movement, thus potentially supporting the view that Saudi Wahhabism could be identified in some of the FIS's ideas.

established following, the FFS and the MDA, served to accentuate the dominance of the FIS and the FLN which were able to squeeze the potential vote and support of other parties by exploiting the popular fear or dislike of each other.[85]

Tactical support was undoubtedly a prominent feature of both the FIS's and the FLN's vote in the June elections. As already shown, dislike of the FLN made a huge contribution to the FIS's victory in the poll, but it is also true that many of those who cast their vote for the FLN did so not as an endorsement of the record of the party, but out of a desire to block the advance of the Islamists. Although antipathy towards the FLN ran deep in Algerian society, it ran deeper still in some parts against the Islamism of the FIS. The party attracted far stronger reactions, both positive and negative, than the FLN did. A graphic illustration of this was provided by the appearance of Abassi Madani on television during the election campaign, as part of a series of programmes where the main party leaders were questioned by journalists about their aims and policies. The FIS's leader appeared to attract not only a larger audience than that for other leaders but his appearance elicited dramatically varying responses from people watching. In the telephone opinion poll conducted after the appearance of each leader, Madani scored an unremarkable 3.5 out of 10 on a scale of approval. However this figure, an average for all the calls received, hid the fact that out of the 380 calls, 199 gave Madani a score of zero whilst 104 gave him the maximum possible score of 10.[86]

The efforts of both the secular opposition parties and the FLN were also undoubtedly hampered by the high-profile backing the French media gave to them throughout the election campaign and the correspondingly virulent criticism it heaped on the FIS. Such support proved to be entirely counter-productive since it seemed to confirm the FIS's propaganda against the other parties that they were the vehicles of Western and anti-Islamic values. The FLN was particularly damaged in this respect since it had long bolstered itself up on the legitimacy it had gained by winning

---

85 The effect of the absence of Ahmed Ben Bella's MDA with its past emphasis on Islam and the Iranian revolution, on the FIS's electoral performance is uncertain. It was however notable that the FIS's *Projet de Programme du Front Islamique du Salut* was first published in the MDA's newspaper, *Tribune d'Octobre*, on 22 March 1989.

86 *Jeune Afrique*, 19.3.90.

independence from the French. That perceived links with France could be so politically damaging was evidence of the continuing debate and sensitivity to French involvement in and relations with Algeria even after nearly thirty years of independence. Hostility to the former colonial power ran deep in many quarters. Ali Belhadj prompted surprise outside Algeria when he called for English to replace French as Algeria's second official language. However, his preference for the language most widely associated in international Islamist circles with Western cultural imperialism and decadence indicated the important specificity of Algeria's experience and perhaps also an instinct for populism on the part of Belhadj.

Conclusions

There can be little doubting that the events of October 1988 and the changes that occurred in Algeria both subsequently and consequently represented a watershed of opportunity for Algeria's Islamists. It was an opportunity they wasted no time in exploiting to the full. Despite significant bursts of activity at various points during the previous three decades since Algeria had won its independence, the Algerian state had always been able to suppress and control Islamism so that it never really represented any substantial challenge to the political order. That Algeria looked so far away from an Islamist upsurge on the eve of the October unrest suggested that the movement's growth, despite the decline in popular living standards that had occurred in the 1980s, was far from inevitable.

This is not to suggest either, though, that the crisis of October and Chadli's decision to open up Algeria's political system made the Islamist rise unavoidable after 1988. Shrewd decisions and moves on the part of Islamist leaders such as Madani, Belhadj and Sahnouni were clearly important. The movement's swift exploitation of, and high-profile involvement in, the latter stages of the unrest of October, despite having played no part in its instigation, provided a rallying point of dissent to the regime for ordinary Algerians in the absence of any other prominent and coherent grouping. The decision to form a political party solidified this growing support and when the unexpected decision came to allow participation of the FIS in the political system, the new party had the resources and the organisation to ensure that it had no secular competitors in the struggle to provide an alternative in the polls to the unpopular and discredited FLN.

Its exploitation of the offer apparently tendered by President Chadli in early 1990 further boosted itself and its electoral prospects.

The stunning success the FIS experienced in the eighteen months from its creation led many commentators to observe that the Islamist party had assumed the mantle of popular legitimacy that had once been worn by the historic FLN during and immediately after the war of liberation. Lahouari Addi observed that there were remarkable similarities, in terms of their shared emphasis on populism, between the FIS's programme and the FLN's National Charter.[87] However, whilst such comparisons were often overstated, it was certainly true that this was a line that the FIS leadership itself sought to promote. In one of the first interviews he gave following the creation of the FIS in February 1989, Abassi Madani claimed that the new party was simply reclaiming the lost legacy of Algeria's revolutionary struggle against France. "The FIS wants to save the experiences of November (1954) which have been lost," he stated.[88]

It was significant, though that Abassi referred in this context to 1954 rather than 1962. He and the FIS were anxious to emphasise their lineage not so much to the FLN as to the ideological contribution Islam had made to the launching of the national liberation struggle. It was this contribution that had been one of the "lost experiences" of 1954. It was thus unsurprising that the party declared itself to be the inheritors of the tradition of the original Association of Algerian Ulama. The choice of the ageing Sheikh Abdelbaki Sahraoui, one of the members of Ben Badis's original association, to read out the FIS's founding declaration in March 1989 was both deliberate and symbolic.

---

87 See Lahouari Addi, 'De la permanence du populisme Algérien', *Peuples Médi-terranéens*, nos. 52–3 (Juillet–Septembre 1990), pp. 42–3.
88 Interview with Abassi Madani in *Algérie Actualité*, 23.2.89.

5

Islamism and the FIS Centre Stage, 1990–1991

June 1990–March 1991

Reactions to the FIS victory

Despite the shock of the scale of the FIS victory in the local elections, the main political forces in Algeria did not take long to react and prepare themselves for the next stage in the political conflict. For its part, the FIS organised massive enthusiastic demonstrations on the first Friday after the results of the election were announced and Abassi Madani declared himself willing to form a government under Chadli Benjedid. The president of the FIS found himself and his party suddenly the subject of great international as well as domestic attention. As the leader of what was now clearly Algeria's most popular political party, he was besieged by a flow of domestic and foreign journalists and diplomats who came to see him, anxious to hear his plans and thoughts.

The size of the FIS victory had taken all the various factions of the regime by surprise. President Chadli's strategy of encouraging the Islamist party in an effort to prevent a victory by (and thus damage his opponents within) the FLN, had clearly seriously underestimated the popular support for the FIS *vis-à-vis* the former ruling party. Despite this miscalculation, the President appeared to remain robustly confident that having defeated his enemies in the FLN he could also prevent the FIS from potentially threatening his power base. He announced at the end of July 1990 that elections to the National Assembly would take place some time within the first quarter of 1991 and privately reassured foreign diplomats, anxious over the potential consequences of a repeat victory by the FIS in the National Assembly elections, that the party was highly unlikely to do as well in subsequent elections. The local elections were portrayed as being of little consequence, marking the high water mark of Islamist support which would ebb away over the coming months.

One of the reasons Chadli stated for his optimism was his belief that the FIS would struggle to maintain its level of popular support once it took control of the majority of local authorities it had won in the local elections. The party, he argued, would prove incapable of fulfilling the frequently ambitious promises it had made during the election campaign and would consequently suffer increasing popular disillusionment.

The FIS in local government

Considerable international and domestic attention became focused on the activities and performance of the 853 communal (APC) and the 31 regional (APW) councils that the FIS took control of following their June victories. Of greatest concern to most observers was the extent to which the party would seek to impose its vision of an Islamic society on Algeria's daily social fabric and the extent to which this would appear to threaten and impinge individual liberties.

Within weeks of the new local administrations taking over, reports rapidly began to emerge indicating that those councils controlled by the FIS did indeed appear to be set on imposing their strict ideals on local social life and affairs. The Provincial Assembly in Constantine and the City Council in Algiers voted to end co-education. Oran City Council banned a popular "rai" music festival in favour of one committed to "patriotic Islamic music" and suspended subsidies to cultural associations that were not of a religious nature. In Tipasa, the wearing of swimming costumes and shorts on the streets was prohibited. In Jijel the local authority rejected all correspondence not written in Arabic.[1] Across Algeria there were reports of a generalised clampdown on and closing of cinemas, bars and wine-shops in the areas controlled by the FIS. The speed with which such reports appeared in both the national official press and foreign newspapers, however, indicated the readiness of the regime (as well as foreign governments, particularly the French) to try to discredit the FIS. Many of these stories were accurate reflections of what was actually beginning to occur in those areas now controlled by

---

1 See: *The Economist*, 4.8.90; Djillali Liabes, 'La Démocratie en Algérie: Culture et Contre-Culture' in *Peuples Mediterranéens*, no. 52–3: *Algérie vers L'Etat Islamique?* (Juillet–Septembre 1990), p. 47; Dillman, 'Transition to democracy in Algeria', p. 39.

the FIS. However, some were clearly open to question and qualification. It emerged that the bans on swimming costumes and shorts on the streets of Tipasa and the closing elsewhere of alcohol-selling establishments were, in fact, often measures already introduced by the previous FLN-controlled authorities and which had hitherto met with little opposition or comment. Other reports of the so-called "war" FIS councils had declared on rai music François Burgat characterises as being "often distorted by the government, or simply fabricated by the government press".[2]

The reaction of the FIS's leaders when they were questioned about such stories was frequently one of apparent exasperation. The party maintained that contrary to expectations, the FIS was primarily interested in providing effective local services rather than imposing its social values. When Abassi Madani was questioned about what had become known as the "War of the shorts" in Tipasa he responded by arguing that : "The story of the shorts is not the problem. The things that count are the problems of housing, unemployment and money."[3] A similar attitude was adopted by Ali Belhadj on the issue of the supposed clamp down on music: "In Oran there is no drinking water, but we hear talk of rai. Water and housing come before rai."[4]

That the FIS wanted, then, to be judged on their managerial performance and the provision of essential services to the populations in the areas they controlled did not give them any respite from their critics, who were quick to point at the new authorities' failings and inability to deliver the promises of dramatic economic improvement that had been made during the election campaign. Some critics went beyond the standard accusations of incompetence and even alleged nepotism and corruption.[5] These accusations were similarly contested by the FIS and its defenders. On the issue of competence, it was highlighted that within days of the

---

2 Burgat and Dowell, *The Islamic Movement in North Africa*, p. 284.

3 *Le Figaro*, 31.7.90.

4 *Horizons*, 29.9.90. There was evidence, however, that the FIS's concern for ordinary Algerians' living conditions conveniently dovetailed with more ideological concerns. In Bou Ismail in November 1990, for example, the premises of the local Ismaili cultural centre were taken over by the local FIS-controlled authority officially to make way for the construction of houses.

5 See for example Zoubir, 'The painful transition from authoritarianism', pp. 99–100 and *Révolution Africaine*, 20.6.91.

June election FIS workers were on the streets of Algiers clearing rubbish that had accumulated during a long strike in the capital. More importantly, much was made of the fact that the FIS had inherited local administrations which were in a very poor state following years of appalling FLN mismanagement. As Abassi Madani explained: "We have found in the APCs the politics of scorched earth."[6]

The legacy left by previous administrations clearly hampered the ability of the FIS to run effective local administrations. Their efforts were put under further strain by the growing demands of the local populations, increasingly pressurised by failures at the national level to produce economic and social improvements. This made it highly unlikely that even the most competent of local authorities (let alone totally inexperienced ones like those of the FIS) could be expected to make much of an impact in the shorter term, certainly not within the first few months of taking control when accusations of incompetence were at their height.

It was also clear that the government did all it could to frustrate the new authorities and ensure that they made little progress. Only two months before the June elections, the powers of local government had been significantly reduced by the national government and the newly elected authorities were able to enjoy far less financial autonomy than their predecessors, whose accumulated debts were made the responsibility of the new administrations.[7] Speakers from the APCs and APWs at a local government conference organised by the FIS on 28 September 1990, complained bitterly of the lack of co-operation they received from the government and civil servants when they tried to establish agencies and mechanisms to deal with the myriad problems their local areas faced. Six weeks later on 15 November 4,000 FIS councillors presented a petition to the President, formally protesting at the hostile attitude of central government to their administrations.

On the issue of corruption and nepotism, it was argued that the FIS-controlled administrations, far from employing friends or relatives or even party workers frequently appointed people outside of the party in order to make use of the most competent people available.[8] Nevertheless,

---

6 Interview with Abassi Madani, *Algérie Actualité*, 30.8.90.
7 Local councils also complained that public enterprises "threatened" them to get them to pay outstanding debts owed to them.
8 Burgat and Dowell, *The Islamic Movement in North Africa*, p. 285.

there was evidence of FIS councils supplying subsidies to associations closely related to the FIS itself and many critics complained that the local administrations behaved as if they were only accountable to the party and its supporters rather than to the wider electorate. However, it could not be denied that even if there was corruption and nepotism to be found in some authorities, this would not have been on a scale that even approached that witnessed during the previous period of FLN control.

The popularity of these authorities can be seen as one measure of the performance of the local councils. Although any meaningful measure of this could not be achieved until further elections, there did not appear to be any noticeable signs of disenchantment with the local authorities. Most people appeared to continue to blame their worsening economic and social conditions on the central government. Whilst claims by some FIS activists that local people "enthusiastically supported local governments with voluntary assistance and additional taxes"[9] should be treated with scepticism, the inevitable popularity of "Islamic souks" which many authorities, in conjunction with the organs of the party, set up to provide low cost goods to the poor, can not be denied.

Overall, it appeared that the FIS's record in local government in the period following their electoral successes of June 1990 was relatively undistinguished in the wider context. The scale of the tasks its councillors faced and the limited (and reduced) powers that they were able to wield meant that their impact was at best slight. In terms of the changes it tried to make to social behaviour at the local level, whilst many of these were, as demonstrated, subject to exaggeration or fabrication, it seems clear that many local authorities did make identifiable attempts to try and bring social behaviour closer to its own set of norms. In Algiers, FIS-run administrations had collectively demanded not only the banning of the sale and consumption of alcohol in their areas but had also advocated the prosecution of those caught drinking. Numerous attempts had also been made during Ramadan of 1991 to cancel the staging of entertainment events in the capital. Non-Islamists in areas won by the FIS spoke of a tangible "atmosphere of fear" developing in the aftermath of the FIS

---

9   Anwar Haddam, 'The political experiment of the Algerian Islamic Movement and the new world order' in Azzam Tamimi (ed.), *Power-Sharing Islam?* (London, Liberty, 1993), p. 135.

victories of June 1990.[10] However, it seemed that no dramatically draconian social measures were introduced in most FIS-controlled regions and any changes that did occur usually affected only a small minority of the population.

The FIS and the Gulf crisis: the populist option[11]

At the same time as the FIS was dealing in the second half of 1990 with the domestic challenges of local government, events outside of Algeria began to make a rare and important incursion into the national political scene.

The shock of Iraq's invasion of Kuwait on 2 August 1990 and the subsequent dispatch of US troops to Saudi Arabia, was felt – because of the region's Arab and Muslim identity – almost as keenly in the Maghreb as it was in the Mashreq where the crisis itself actually unfolded. In Algeria, the government reacted by calling for Iraq's withdrawal and the removal of foreign troops from Saudi soil. Initially, this position was shared by the FIS which, although particularly sensitive to the presence of non-Muslims so near to Islam's holiest places in Saudi Arabia, wished to offer no support to Saddam Hussein whom they rightly saw as a secular and anti-Islamist Ba'athist. Abassi Madani condemned the "arrogant" and "colonising" behaviour of the United States whilst describing the Iraqi annexation of Kuwait as "unacceptable".[12] Following the Algerian diplomatic tradition of mediation, both Abassi and Ali Belhadj embarked on shuttle diplomacy between Baghdad and Riyadh in an effort to resolve the crisis, hoping particularly to use their links with the Saudis (whose support of the party provided another incentive for not favouring the Iraqis) to good effect.

However, as 1990 drew to a close with no sign of an Iraqi withdrawal and the likelihood of Western military action against Iraq growing, there were increasing signs that the even-handed stance adopted by both the government and by the FIS was out of step with that of the bulk of the

---

10 Author's interviews with eyewitnesses.

11 For a full examination of this subject and the issues involved see Hugh Roberts, 'A trial of strength: Algerian Islamism' in James P. Piscatori (ed.), *Islamic Fundamentalisms and the Gulf Crisis* (Chicago, The American Academy of Arts and Sciences, 1991), p. 143.

12 Interview with Abassi Madani, *Algérie Actualité* 30.8.90

ordinary population. It rapidly became apparent that most Algerians saw Saddam Hussein, despite official discouragement from the FIS as well as the government, as a heroic Arab nationalist standing up to Western threats. This perception was sharpened by the commencement of air strikes against Iraq in mid-January 1991.

The massive popular support which Saddam Hussein enjoyed in Algeria presented the leaders of the FIS with a considerable dilemma. They recognised that they faced the risk of losing the substantial electoral support they had attracted only six months earlier in June 1990, through being seen to be far too balanced in their antipathy towards Iraq and Western military intervention. Furthermore, there were fears of being outflanked by other opposition parties, notably the MDA of Ahmed Ben Bella who had made a high-profile return to the country in September in 1990, and who had been the first to organise public demonstrations and call for the dispatch of volunteers to help defend Iraq. The FIS had clearly underestimated the underlying strength of Arab nationalism in Algeria. Many Algerians saw in Iraq's defiance of the West parallels with their own country's struggle against Western colonialism. Similarly, the string of humiliating reverses that the Arab countries had experienced at the hands of the Israelis over past decades had created an appetite amongst the populations of most Arab states for an Arab leader who sought to turn back this trend. Saddam Hussein's willingness firstly to resist Western pressure to withdraw from Kuwait and, secondly, to launch scud missiles against Israel, therefore ensured his immediate elevation to the status of hero in the eyes of most Arabs and Algerians.

Forced to choose between preserving the loyalty of its popular base and staying true to both its Islamist and anti-nationalist doctrines as well as its Arabian financial supporters, the FIS appeared to make a clear decision to ride the popular impulses of the Algerian people and unambiguously back Saddam. In a multi-party demonstration against the war on 18 January, in which most demonstrators marched under banners calling for peace, the FIS marched under explicitly pro-Iraqi slogans. Furthermore, Ali Belhadj appeared in combat fatigues at the rally and called on the government to open training camps for volunteers to go to Iraq.[13] Whilst such unabashedly populist pitches were primarily aimed at

---

13 The FIS actually organised for several hundred volunteers to be dispatched to the region, but by the time most of them had arrived in training camps set up by

retaining the attention and support of mass opinion, the FIS also made sure that its domestic interests and agenda continued to be advanced. Thus at a FIS-only demonstration on 31 January, calls for a date to be set for the National Assembly elections were mixed in with denunciations of the Western powers and messages of solidarity with Iraq.

The comprehensive defeat of Iraq within a few weeks inevitably brought an effective end to the debate in Algeria and attentions returned more fully to the domestic scene. However, the Gulf crisis as a whole clearly had an impact on the FIS and made revelations about the party's nature and identity. Hugh Roberts argues that the crisis appeared to not only confirm the FIS's "doctrinal shallowness, but also its militancy and political flexibility" as demonstrated by its populist decision to opt for retaining its popular support in preference to staying closer to its Islamist doctrines and Saudi supporters. This choice also marked for Roberts "a major stage in the 'Algerianisation' of the FIS" through its response to domestic rather than foreign (Saudi) and transnational (Islamist) pressures and factors.[14] In making this choice, the FIS was not alone amongst Islamist parties and movements elsewhere in the Muslim world – the majority of Islamist groups taking a far more hostile line towards the Western allies and Saudi Arabia than towards Saddam Hussein and Iraq.[15] However, it was the great scale of the shift in the FIS's line that marked it out from most other Islamist responses to the crisis.

April–July 1991: Crisis and Confrontation

As the war in Iraq and Kuwait drew to a close in the early spring of 1991, the attention of the FIS began to refocus on events inside Algeria

---

the party in Jordan the war was effectively over. For one Algerian journalist, however, Belhadj's call for military volunteers had the second, ulterior motive of creating a well-trained militia for the FIS. *Algérie Actualité*, 24.1.91.

14 Roberts, 'A Trial of Strength', p. 144. Roberts actually argues that because of the relative absence of non-Muslim minorities in Algeria, the FIS were successfully able to blend the idea of pan-Muslim solidarity with the more popular ideas of pan-Arab solidarity, p. 143.

15 For a useful summary of Islamist positions on the Gulf Crisis see Olivier Roy, *The Failure of Political Islam* (London, I. B. Tauris, 1994), pp. 121–2. For a more detailed analysis see James P. Piscatori (ed.), *Islamic Fundamentalisms and the Gulf Crisis* (Chicago, The American Academy of Arts and Sciences, 1991).

and increasingly upon its own internal politics. Very little was publicly known about the internal workings of the FIS during its first two years of life, with even the membership of the party's ruling council, the Majlis Shura, being shrouded in mystery. Throughout 1989-90 Abassi Madani had been the only public voice of the party, with the occasional interview or statement by Ali Belhadj providing an exception to this. However by 1991 this monolithic front that the party had been able to retain began to fissure, not publicly at first, but enough by the middle of the year to be apparent to everyone within the party and beyond.

The emergence of Islamist competition

The first signs of discord within the FIS following its victory in the 1990 local elections emerged over the issue of its relations with and place within the country's wider Islamist movement. As has been shown (see Chapter Four), far from all of Algeria's senior Islamist figures joined the FIS on its creation in February 1989. Although most had involved themselves in the far looser and more apolitical Rabitat Dawa organisation formed the previous November, many had had doubts about the theological and practical need of a specifically political party to further the Islamist movement's aims. However, it was several of these figures who appeared in the wake of June 1990 to rethink their objections and join the field of party-political competition. This did not take the form, though, of responding to an invitation made by Abassi Madani in June 1990 to join the FIS, but rather involved the creation of new and separate Islamist parties.

A number of Islamist-type parties were formed in the latter half of 1990, but only two came to be of any real significance: those formed around respectively Mahfoud Nahnah and Abdallah Djaballah. Both senior and influential figures in the Islamist movement since the 1970s, Nahnah and Djaballah officially transformed their existing apolitical associations into political parties in December 1990. Nahnah's Al-Irchad wal Islah assumed the Arabic acronymed title of HAMAS (Islamic Society Movement) whilst Djaballah's Nahda (Renaissance) association retained its name, although it was frequently referred to by its full French title of Mouvement de la Nahda Islamique (MNI).

The reasons behind the creation of these two new political parties were severalfold. The most obvious, if base, impulse behind the setting up of the parties was the realisation by their founders that the astounding success that the FIS had discovered during the first eighteen months of its existence had pushed all those Islamist figures who had not joined the party to the political and organisational margins. Mahfoud Nahnah and Ahmed Sahnoun's abject failure in trying to prevent the FIS staging its march of April 1990 (see Chapter Four) had been a graphic demonstration of this marginalisation. It was clearly a calculation on the part of Nahnah and Djaballah that the only means of retaining any influence within the broader Islamist movement was to join the party-political fray. For both leaders this meant forming their own parties rather than joining the FIS, since this latter option risked the final abolition and subsummation within the FIS of any remaining independent power bases they possessed.

A second consideration was that the new Islamist parties represented recognisably different strains of Islamism from that embodied by the FIS. Both HAMAS and Nahda were portrayed as essentially more "moderate" expressions of Islamism. A more accurate characterisation was that they operated a far more cerebral and genuinely religious discourse than that held by the FIS – the experience of the Gulf War having further demonstrated the latter party's deepening attachment to political populism. For Mahfoud Nahnah, this more intellectual approach did appear to imply a more moderate and less demotic approach. Although the party's name, HAMAS, was an allusion to the HAMAS of Palestine (the Algerian version was purposely founded on the third anniversary of the Intifada) the choice of name reflected more a desire for popular attention and recognition than an indication of the party's espousal of radical ideas and violent activism.[16] Intellectually, Nahnah proclaimed his belief in an Islam that was "open to the modern world and founded on *ijtihad* . . . " and he made clear his commitment to the establishment of an Islamic state by stages and "based on dialogue, removed from violence (and) from political and religious terrorism".[17] This gradualist approach was also reflected in his far more unambiguous acceptance of the basic tenets of democracy demonstrated by his belief that plurality of thought represented "maturity"

---

16   Nahnah's use of the Arabic acronym HAMAS was in fact slightly different to that employed by the Islamist movement in the occupied territories. In the Algerian context HAMAS stood for Harakat al Mujtama al-Islami (Islamic Society Movement) whereas the Palestinian HAMAS stood for Harakat al Muqawama al-Islamiyya (Islamic *Resistance* Movement).

17   Al-Ahnaf, Botiveau and Frégosi, *L'Algérie par ses Islamistes*, pp. 38 and 42.

and his declared willingness to co-operate with non-Islamist parties at elections.[18] This stood in contrast to the frequently ambiguous signals coming from the FIS. In more specific terms, too, Nahnah and HAMAS appeared distinct from the party of Madani and Belhadj. Al-Irchad wal Islah had had an active women's section and Nahnah was unequivocal in his support of the right of women to work and for an expansion of the Family Code to protect their rights, and he was vociferous in his condemnation of violence against women.

Abdallah Djaballah's Nahda appeared close to Nahnah's HAMAS in terms of this more intellectual discourse, although Djaballah's differences with the FIS amounted arguably to less than those between HAMAS and the FIS. Differences of political strategy towards the institutions of the state and over theological conceptions of ijtihad were cited as demarcating the line between MNI and the FIS, but Arun Kapil, for one, has described them as "purely tactical" and thus a means to preserve Djaballah's independence.[19] In fact, in places, the MNI's discourse appeared as radical as that of the radical wing of FIS, making plain its opposition to the existence of secular parties and its wish to impose the veil on women, stances both Mahfoud Nahnah and (in public at least) Abassi Madani had declared themselves to be against. Like Madani, Djaballah would nonetheless speak more generally of working within the "framework of democracy and pluralism".[20] One way in which the MNI appeared to differ from both the FIS and HAMAS was in its vociferous condemnation of the government's economic reform programme, an issue both other parties had appeared to broadly, if often tacitly, support. Opposing further privatisations of the public sector, Djaballah denounced the liberalising reforms which had been accelerated under the prime ministership of Mouloud Hamrouche since September 1989 as having "opened the national market to domestic wolves and foreigners".[21]

---

18 Interview with Mahfoud Nahnah, *Révolution Africaine*, 10.4.91.
19 Arun Kapil, 'Les partis Islamistes en Algérie: eléments de présentation', *Maghreb-Machrak*, no. 133 (Juillet–Septembre 1991), p. 111. Several years later Djaballah was to state: "Between our brothers in the FIS and ourselves, there have been no fewer than 21 attempts at unification. All have failed because we have not had the same methods and strategies." *Le Matin*, 8.9.94.
20 Lamchichi, *L'Islamisme en Algérie*, p. 107.
21 Al-Ahnaf, Botiveau and Frégosi, *L'Algérie par ses Islamistes*, p. 44.

A third and far more contentious reason advanced for the entry of HAMAS and the MNI into the party political arena was that of encouragement and even orchestration by the regime. It is argued that the formation of both parties was seen by the regime as a means of dividing and splintering the large Islamist constituency that the FIS had been able to monopolise in the June elections. Cited as evidence of official collaboration were meetings both leaders had had with the regime and that both new parties appeared to be well financed following their creation. Whilst such charges ignored the more genuine motivations, detailed above, for forming political parties, there was at least some substance to the claims in the case of Nahnah and HAMAS. In contrast to Djaballah's criticism of official policy in the economic field in particular, Nahnah offered little serious criticism of the regime and even often took its side in subsequent confrontations with the FIS. Nahnah had also enjoyed unusually good relations with the authorities since his release from prison soon after Chadli Benjedid came to power and his absence from the organised agitation of the Islamist movement in the early 1980s (see Chapter Three) was a further indication of his closeness to the regime.

Attempts at unity

That regime manipulation was not the primary motivating force behind the formation of HAMAS (or Nahda) was indicated by Mahfoud Nahnah's expressed belief that the Islamist parties should not compete directly with one another (thus undermining the regime's hope of fracturing the movement). Instead the leader of HAMAS called for a common front between the parties. Soon after the founding of HAMAS, Nahnah organised a conference to this end on 20 September 1990 to which he invited over 300 Islamic associations as well as political parties. However, whilst Djaballah and the MNI were very favourable to some form of "Islamic alliance", the leadership of the FIS made it quite clear that it was not and did not attend the conference.

The FIS officially rejected the idea of an alliance on the grounds of it being essentially divisive. Its leadership maintained that the FIS was the sole legitimate representative of Islamist political activity in Algeria and thus implied that the objective of those Islamists who did not join the party was division. Abassi Madani described Nahnah's initiative as "a call for division under a slogan of unity" and characterised his subsequent decision to create a separate political party as "a stab in the back".[22] Ali Belhadj rejected Nahnah's initiatives on theological grounds referring to a hadith to claim that "there is no alliance in Islam" – Islam having abolished all previous alliances.[23] However, the FIS were far from united on this view. A growing number of the leadership of the party became attracted to the idea of such an alliance. This was often because many of them had belonged to groups established by Nahnah and particularly Djaballah before the creation of the FIS in 1989 and the idea of rivalry and division left them personally and theologically uneasy. Such a view came to be shared by an increasing number of the FIS's rank and file who began to chant slogans and display banners to this end at FIS marches and rallies.

The main opponent of the creation of an alliance was Abassi Madani. The leader of the FIS consistently resisted such a move and this explains the party's failure to respond to Nahnah's overtures. The hostility of Abassi to a common Islamist front was interpreted by some as a result of personal antipathy Abassi felt towards Nahnah as the main proponent of the alliance. The leader of HAMAS's failure to explicitly back the FIS in the 1990 elections, together with his subsequent claim that the FIS victory was one for the wider Islamist movement, clearly irked the president of the FIS.[24] He remained suspicious of the Blida-based leader and his relations with the regime, actually referring to Nahnah in one newspaper interview as "Chadli's man".[25] However, this did not explain why Abassi was opposed to an alliance with Abdallah Djaballah's MNI. Not only did Djaballah enjoy much closer relations with the FIS, but, unlike Nahnah, he had openly called on his supporters to vote for the

---

22 Charef, *Algérie: Le Grand Dérapage*, p. 110.
23 Al-Ahnaf, Botiveau and Frégosi, *L'Algérie par ses Islamistes*, p. 40.
24 At the elections Nahnah had only called on his supporters to vote for 'Islamists' rather than specifically for the FIS, although as Hugh Roberts points out this invariably amounted to the same thing. Roberts, 'A trial of strength', p. 137.
25 Interview with Abassi Madani, *Horizons*, 5.5.91. Abassi's antipathy towards Nahnah was also shared by some of the more radical elements in the FIS. They too suspected his relationship with the regime (particularly with regard to the Bouyali affair – see Chapter Three) and disliked his apparent moderation. Following the party's creation there were incidents of FIS militants tearing down HAMAS posters, interrupting the party's meetings and attempting to prevent Nahnah himself speaking. Violence was also used in attempts by FIS members to wrest control of mosques that were controlled by HAMAS supporters.

FIS in June 1990 and was credited with securing victories for the party in his organisation's heartland in eastern Algeria.

The main reason behind Abassi Madani's opposition to an alliance was that the FIS leader feared it would critically weaken the party's strategic position as well as his own position as leader. At the time of the creation of the FIS, Abassi, Nahnah, Djaballah and, of course, Ahmed Sahnoun, had arguably been the four most senior and influential Islamist figures in Algeria. The fact that Abassi was the only one of the four to become involved in the new party meant that he was able to dominate it. The creation of an "Islamic Alliance" appeared to threaten this dominance and might appear to put both Nahnah and Djaballah on an equal footing once again with Abassi (as indeed was their aim).

There was a strong element of personal ambition on the part of Abassi Madani in this regard, but there was also a concern that any threat to his dominance was a threat to the long-term strategy he had personally forged for the FIS. Abassi's belief and determination that the FIS could win at least a share in political power had been clearly demonstrated by the populist tactics the party had employed during the Gulf War. The involvement of figures such as Nahnah and Djaballah potentially put at risk the "electoralist" strategy Abassi had forged. The more intellectual and religious orientation of both leaders made them more ambivalent towards the aim of full political power as their failure to form political parties before 1990 amply demonstrated. Their involvement might also complicate and weaken Abassi's relations with the reformist elements within the regime, Abdallah Djaballah's hostility to the economic reform programme providing a potentially major impediment to continued co-operation.[26]

As 1991 progressed Abassi Madani came under increasing pressure from both the FIS's Majlis Shura and its ordinary members to respond to the appeals of unity from the other Islamist parties. He became progressively isolated, only able to resist pressure on the issue by relying on the personal loyalty of his deputy Ali Belhadj, whom many claimed was actually personally in favour of an alliance.[27]

---

26 Roberts, 'From radical mission', p. 467.
27 Abdallah Djaballah claimed that Belhadj had supported the idea of a union when it was initially put to him. Pressure for unity also came from Ahmed Sahnoun and the Rabitat Dawaa which continued to meet in this period. From the spring

The internal conflicts within the FIS by the spring of 1991 became entwined and complicated by developments in relations with the regime which had the effect of creating additional fault lines within the party, further weakening the position of Abassi Madani.

The new electoral law of spring 1991

Following the FIS's victory in June 1990 relations between the party and President Chadli and his supporters in the government had clearly cooled, as disputes over local government and the country's stance on the Gulf War had demonstrated. Nevertheless, whilst there appears to have been no renewal of the covert arrangement Chadli had fashioned with Abassi in early 1990 to defeat his enemies in the FLN, the leader of the FIS met discreetly again with the President in the aftermath of the local elections. There the leader of the FIS secured a commitment from Chadli that the regime would proceed to hold elections to the National Assembly in similarly unfettered conditions under which those at the local level had been held. In addition it was alleged that there was an indication from the President that he might even be willing to co-operate and share power with the FIS following the legislative elections.

How genuine this purported commitment from Chadli Benjedid to Abassi Madani was is dubious. Should the FIS repeat its triumph at the local level at national level the President clearly would want to retain good relations with them. However, Chadli did not anticipate this happening and from 1990 worked to ensure that the FIS would not achieve a majority in the elections. By late 1990 his initial hope that FIS difficulties in local government would lead to a decline in the party's popular support showed no clear cut signs of occurring. Similarly, the emergence of HAMAS and the MNI had made no obvious inroads into the FIS's base of popular support. Turnout at HAMAS-organised rallies, for example, was a fraction of that which the FIS could expect to attend its own events.[28] It thus became apparent to the President that he would need to look for other means of reducing the FIS's popular support.

---

of 1991 Sahnoun began to hold weekly meetings to get the parties to present a single list at the forthcoming legislative elections.

28　HAMAS were able to attract 15,000 people to a rally in November 1990 called to commemorate the anniversary of beginning of the liberation struggle in 1954. The FIS were usually able to attract crowds at least ten times that size.

Abassi Madani's personal and political strategy for achieving power had been irreparably damaged. Not only did the FIS look unlikely to gain even a simple majority in elections to the National Assembly, but any presidential ambitions Abassi must inevitably have harboured were similarly threatened by the fear that an FLN victory could pave the way for a fourth presidential term for Chadli Benjedid.[34] Within a few days, the FIS leader appeared to have produced a potential solution to this dilemma. From early April Abassi began to threaten that the FIS might launch a general strike in order to force a change in the new electoral laws.[35] Typical of these, and of the new more radical tone he had adopted was his speech to a party rally in Oran on 1 May:

> We are ready to embark on elections, but with guarantees . . . the first of which is not to act according to these repressive [electoral] laws, as we cannot achieve legitimacy through illegitimacy, unless the President of the Republic complies with the opinion of the Islamic Salvation Front. One of the characteristics of the [FIS] is to demand and to struggle. When making demands does not prove convincing enough, striking to achieve what is right becomes necessary, God willing. It is a general strike, a political strike, not a conventional union one for limited demands.[36]

In issuing such warnings Abassi Madani did not have the official approval of the leadership of the party, having not formally discussed the issue with the Majlis Shura beforehand. His motivations in both making this unilateral move and in not consulting widely were severalfold. First and foremost, Abassi saw a general strike, or the threat of one, as one of the only means of persuading the government to abandon its attempt to electorally hobble the FIS through the election laws. He considered the other two possible options open to the party, that of acceptance of the changes and that of a boycott of the forthcoming elections as being equally damaging. The first of these alternatives would have led to defeat

---

34 Abassi Madani was almost certainly aware that an opinion poll at the beginning of May had shown that nearly 60% of those questioned perceived him to be the most popular party leader, as against 12% for Hocine Ait Ahmed of the FFS and 11% for Abdelhamid Mehri of the FLN. *Algérie Actualité*, 9.5.91.

35 See for example *Summary of World Broadcasts* (*SWB*) ME/1041 A/18, 9.4.91, and ME/1048 A/7, 17.4.91.

36 *SWB* ME/1062 A/14, 3.5.91.

and humiliation for the party, whilst the second risked charges of being unwilling to play the democratic game and may even have led to the sidelining of the party politically. Abassi had witnessed the effectiveness of a general strike that had been called by the main Algerian trade union federation, the UGTA, in the previous March and saw it as a potentially effective political tool. The fact that the idea of a general strike had also been canvassed by a coalition of several of the secular opposition parties also clearly influenced Abassi, not least through the fear of being out-flanked by such a move.

A secondary motivation for Abassi Madani in calling for a general strike was that it could prove to be a useful weapon in his internal battles with the rest of the FIS leadership. Not only would it provide a means of distracting attention from the increasingly pressing issue of alliance with the other Islamist parties, but by leading the strike call Abassi hoped to forge more direct links with the FIS's mass membership and thus strengthen his hand against opponents nearer the top of the party. During the first few days of May, Abassi's opponents had made increasingly public their unhappiness with the independent nature of his leadership. On 1 May, in a move clearly aimed at limiting Abassi, a declaration emerged from the Majlis Shura stating that "Declarations and important political decisions can only be taken by the Majlis Shura."[37] A week later, in an article in *El Mounqid*, the Majlis issued a communiqué restating their desire for a common front with the other Islamist parties:

> The FIS regards, in all sincerity, that the unity of the Islamic ranks is a duty in order to prevent [the emergence of] contradictory political positions capable of thwarting the desired Islamic solution.[38]

Abassi Madani was aware that the party's supporters had repeatedly demonstrated their enthusiasm for mass action through rallies and marches and thus he undoubtedly hoped his general strike call would prove popular and increase his standing with the FIS's rank and file. More generally, such a strategy could also serve to reinvigorate support for the party overall and thus counter any slippage of support that may have occurred since the previous June.

---

37 Charef, *Algérie: Le Grand Dérapage*, p. 112.
38 *Ibid.*

Having more or less unilaterally taken the decision to stage a general strike, Abassi Madani was faced with the difficult task of persuading the Majlis Shura to back him. For many on the FIS's ruling council, the electoral law was not the crucial issue that Abassi perceived it to be. Despite participating in the original party-political project that was the FIS, a significant section of the party's leadership remained more committed to the doctrinal rather than the strategic aspects of the party.[39] Loyal to the original specifically religious objectives of the Association of Algerian Ulama, the achievement of political power was a secondary consideration. As a result, many viewed Abassi's proposal of a general strike with apprehension fearing that such a confrontational policy could threaten the significant gains and influence the party had already achieved. Rachid Ghannoushi, the leader of Tunisia's Islamist party, Nahda, spoke for many in the FIS's Majlis Shura when he tried to dissuade Abassi Madani from pursuing such a course:

> I tried on many occasions to persuade him against such a course of action, telling him, "This path can only lead to prison." I asked him why he wanted to take this risk when the FIS ruled so many councils. "Even if the changes to the electoral districts work against you, the FIS will remain the strongest party" I argued . . . However, he was absolutely convinced.[40]

Abassi Madani worked hard to persuade the Majlis Shura of the wisdom and efficacy of a general strike. Finally, following a stormy meeting of the Majlis Shura on 23 May, (during which Abassi Madani had reportedly threatened to resign if he did not get his way[41]) Abassi was able to declare formally the party's intention to call a general strike to commence two days later on 25 May, having promised members that the strike would only last three days. However, it was reported that as many as seventeen members of the ruling council had opposed the move, leaving Abassi Madani with a bare majority of the thirty-eight-strong membership backing his initiative.

---

39 Roberts, 'From radical mission', p. 468.
40 Author's interview with Rachid Ghannoushi, 18.4.95.
41 This was according to one of his opponents on the issue, Bachir Fakih. See interview with Bachir Fakih, *Horizons* 25.7.91 reproduced in *Maghreb-Machrek*, no. 133 (Juillet–Septembre 1991), pp. 118–9.

The general strike

The strike commenced as threatened on 25 May, the government having remained unmoved by its prospect. It soon became apparent, however, that the strike call had elicited only a very weak response. As one journalist observed, "Shops and cafés stayed open, schools and universities continued giving classes, buses and trains ran on, and the wheels of industry failed to grind to a halt."[42] There were some reports of the petroleum sector being hit by the strike, but the only part of the workforce which appeared to respond to the strike was that working for the FIS-controlled local councils. Officially estimated participation in the strike was just 5%.[43] This figure could not be seen as a reflection of a general reluctance to strike on the part of the Algerian workforce – the general strike called by the UGTA less than three months earlier, in March, had been a recognised success. Moreover, the fact that the FIS's opposition to this earlier strike, expressed through its own trade union organisation, the SIT (Syndicat Islamique du Travail), which called on workers to disregard the UGTA's call, had been comprehensively ignored should perhaps have indicated to the FIS the lack of influence they were able to exercise over Algeria's workforce.

The manifest failure of the tactic of a general strike created another quandary for Abassi Madani. Not only had he tied himself and his leadership of the party closely to the success of the strike,[44] but it also seemed clear that the regime intended to continue with its plans for the legislative elections which were to take place on 27 June – the campaign officially beginning on 1 June. Despite his previous assurances to members of the Majlis Shura, Abassi decided on 28 May, the third and last day of the strike, to extend the strike. Whether this decision was taken following formal reference to the party's Majlis Shura later became the subject of intense debate, with various members of the council claiming that they had not been consulted.[45] Nonetheless, the same day two press agencies received copies of a communiqué apparently signed by the members of

---

42   *The Middle East*, July 1991.

43   This figure was quoted by the Prime Minister but was not seriously disputed despite its origins. *El Moudjahid*, 18.7.91

44   As *Le Monde Diplomatique* observed, "Put purely and simply, an end to the strike would have signified the political end of Abassi Madani." July 1991.

45   See, for example, the conflicting claims by Abdelkader Hachani and Ahmed Merrani in *Algérie Actualité*, 1.8.91.

the FIS ruling council which called for an immediate end to the strike and which attacked the original idea of a strike:

> The call to strike, especially at this time, constitutes a plan which works to the interest of the authorities in undermining the FIS and preventing the achievement of the Islamic way.[46]

Such an allusion to the complicity with the regime of those who called the strike, was made more specific with the allegation of the presence within the FIS of "certain personalities who work for the regime".[47] In response to such a thinly veiled personal attack on himself, Abassi Madani denounced the communiqué as a fake. However, despite the fact that the authenticity of the document was never subsequently proved, there was little doubting that its contents reflected the views of at least some of the members of the Majlis Shura, as was later to become apparent.

Aware that dissent within the party would mount the longer the strike was extended, and that as the strike continued its failure to make any real impact would damage himself and the FIS generally, Abassi Madani decided to change tack. The strike had amply demonstrated that the FIS's main popular support certainly did not lie with Algeria's workers. The leader of the FIS therefore decided that it was time to mobilise what had always been evident was the party's main constituency: Algeria's urban unemployed youth. By bringing this numerous section of the population onto the streets of the capital, Abassi clearly hoped to recreate the same impact its previous marches and demonstrations had had on official opinion. In order to put pressure on the government, Abassi arranged a meeting with the Prime Minister, Mouloud Hamrouche, on May 29 where, as well as restating the FIS's demands, he informed him of the FIS's intention to organise demonstrations in Algiers. Hamrouche refused to make concessions but anxious to avoid trouble and aware of how disciplined earlier FIS marches and rallies had been, he gave verbal agreement to the FIS's peaceful occupation of four sites in the centre of the capital.

---

46 Charef, *Algérie: Le Grand Dérapage*, p. 115.
47 *Ibid.*

Confrontation with the regime

By the fourth and fifth days of the strike, the FIS's supporters had already begun to emerge onto the streets to take part in marches and demonstrations. Despite Abassi's peaceful intent (indicated by the agreement with Hamrouche), tension and friction began to mount in the capital between the demonstrators and the police. The high level of discipline and organisation that the FIS had been able to display for its previous set piece one-day shows of strength proved difficult to maintain over an extended period and clashes became inevitable as May proceeded into June. These clashes became increasingly serious and violent, occasionally involving exchanges of gunfire, and spread across the city as supporters of the FIS began to occupy other districts of Algiers. As the original strike moved towards the conclusion of its second week and injuries and even deaths from the confrontations mounted, riot police moved to dislodge groups of Islamists from the squares in the capital they had occupied as well as from the streets of Islamist strongholds elsewhere in the capital such as Belcourt and Bab el-Oued. These attempts by the state's regular forces of order dramatically gave way on the night of 5 June to the intervention of the Algerian army, which moved armoured cars into the capital to finally end the occupations.

This significant move on the part of the regime, which was accompanied by President Chadli dismissing the Hamrouche government, postponing the elections and declaring a four-month "state of siege", indicated a clear desire to break the impasse. However, despite the use of force against the FIS, the authorities appeared still willing to negotiate with the party's leaders. With battles between Islamists and the army continuing on the streets, Sid Ahmed Ghozali, Hamrouche's replacement as Prime Minister, met with Abassi Madani and Ali Belhadj on 7 June. Later that day the two leaders declared to party supporters gathered at the Al-Sunna mosque in Bab el-Oued that they had won sufficient concessions from the government and thus the FIS would be calling off both the general strike and the protest campaign. As Abassi Madani was to repeat later that day in an interview:

> The talks which have taken place between us and the regime have resulted in the agreement on holding early presidential as well as legislative elections within these (next) six months, God willing. Mr. Ghozali has been appointed Prime Minister of a government which

will supervise free, legitimate elections devoid of any suspicions of rigging. We tell all workers to go back to work tomorrow.[48]

The following day Ghozali appeared on television to confirm this commitment (although he made no specific reference to presidential elections) and indicated that he would be seeking revision of the electoral law: "I promise you that I shall exert my utmost efforts to provide all the necessary guarantees for the organisation of free and clean elections."[49]

Abassi Madani clearly felt that he had won a considerable victory for the FIS. However, this belief came to be short lived as the authorities began to gradually reassert themselves throughout the remainder of June. This reassertion took the initial form of arrests of members of groups on the radical fringes of the FIS widely acknowledged as provoking some of the violence of the first week of June. There was little reaction to this by the FIS, which perhaps felt itself tainted by the activities of these groups, but alarm grew as the arrests and security swoops increasingly targeted members of the mainstream party itself. Tensions mounted as the month progressed and the numbers of FIS members arrested rose. Serious violence, however, did not occur until 25 June when police and army – in what was clearly an attempt to test the strength of the party – moved in to reinstate "symbols of the Republic" (usually the FLN slogan: "By the people for the people") which had been removed from the front of town halls controlled by the FIS and replaced by the words "Islamic Council".

Aware that the authorities and the army seemed to now have the advantage, Abassi Madani, already furious that Chadli and Ghozali appeared to have reneged on their promise to announce a date for presidential elections and reinstate sacked strikers, issued a warning stating that "If the army does not return to its barracks, the FIS will have the right to call for the resumption of jihad like that of November 1954."[50] This combined threat of civil strife and appeal to revolutionary history did not serve to deter the authorities, who finally moved against the leadership of the party itself in the final days of June. Leaders of FIS-controlled councils, and members of the Majlis Shura were detained. Finally, on 30 June, Abassi Madani and Ali Belhadj were themselves arrested.

---

48 *SWB* ME/1094 A/2, 10.6.91.
49 *SWB* ME/1095 A/1, 11.6.91.
50 *Le Quotidien de Paris*, 30.6.91.

The arrest of the party's two most senior figures represented a clear triumph by the authorities who in the space of a month had dramatically reversed their fortunes *vis-à-vis* the FIS. That they were able to move so swiftly and successfully against the party's leadership with such surprisingly little resistance and public reaction (there was some agitation but nothing approaching the near popular insurrection that might have been expected[51]) was largely due to the removal first, by arrest, of the middle tiers of the FIS's organisation. This cut communication links between the top leadership and the mass support and membership of the party on the street. The disruption of the highly structured and hierarchical nature of the FIS had further thwarted attempts to organise mass opposition and reaction to the arrests.

There was a determination on the part of the authorities to portray the crackdown against the FIS as both necessary and within the law. The new Prime Minister, Ghozali, emphasised that "the state of siege did not occur to stifle the Islamic option but to save the country and the citizen".[52] Precisely what the country and the citizen were being saved from was more specifically elaborated at the military tribunal which was convened at Blida at the beginning of July to charge Abassi Madani and Ali Belhadj with specific crimes. The seven charges that were formally levelled at the two leaders included charges alleging organisation of rebellion, the setting up of unauthorised armed forces, the obstruction of the economy and incitement of citizens to take up arms against the state.[53] It was this last charge which, officially at least, was the pretext for the arrest of Madani and Belhadj. Abassi Madani's apparent call for jihad two days before his arrest was offered as explanation for his detention, as was Belhadj's more explicit call at the Al-Sunna mosque a week earlier on 21 June for people to stock up with "arms, explosives and kalashnikovs".[54] In addition to this, more detailed evidence was offered in the case of Belhadj. On the

---

51 There were demonstrations reported in Mostaganem and Constantine but the rest of the country remained quiet.
52 *Horizons*, 21.7.91.
53 It was also widely alleged that the FIS had abandoned its electoral strategy and that the whole pre-planned aim of Abassi Madani's tactics during the crisis was the overthrow of the whole regime. However, the fact (amongst others) that the FIS had nominated candidates for all the electoral districts and had had printed half a million election bills and posters ready for the imminent National Assembly elections indicated that this was not the case.
54 *La Presse*, 21.6.91.

basis of information supposedly obtained by the authorities following the arrest on 9 June of a French convert to Islam, Guyon Didier Roger, it was alleged that the FIS's number two had taken the lead in the setting up of a clandestine armed grouping aimed at destabilising the Algerian state. Belhadj's declaration of 21 June appeared to support such allegations as did his expressed opinion three days earlier that "Islam recommends us to have weapons and to use them against our enemies."[55]

As well as striking at the members and leaders of the FIS, several thousand of whom had been arrested by the end of June, the authorities also moved against the institutional bases of the party. As well as putting pressure on FIS-controlled local councils, the army acted against the mosques. Use of mosques for political purposes had already been prohibited in the previous spring and now many of the preachers of mosques which were known to be collecting centres for financial contributions to FIS were detained. Attendance at mosques, it was officially ruled, was to be restricted to the mosque itself and must not spill into the streets, as had become the norm in many areas. To this end, access to popular and militant FIS-controlled mosques in Kouba and Bab El-Oued was controlled by the army – non-residents of the area being excluded. On 18 August the party's two newspapers, *El Mounqid* and *Al Forkane* were banned for alleged "appeals for civil disobedience and violence".[56]

The regime and the military

The comprehensive nature of the regime's crackdown against the FIS, which went some way beyond measures needed to end Islamist agitation on the streets and the activities of the party's militant fringes, indicated that there had been a shift in official attitudes towards the FIS. The arrest of so many of the party's activists and, most importantly, its two leading figures was evidence of a growing belief within the regime that the FIS needed to be cut back. A significant challenge had been mounted to the regime by the party and the regime needed to respond. For President Chadli this challenge took the form of a threat to his own personal power base, the whole crisis having resulted for the first time

---

55   *SWB* ME/1103 A/15, 20.6.91.
56   Burgat and Dowell, *The Islamic Movement in North Africa*, pp. 297–8.

in the leader of the FIS attacking Chadli personally and moreover, demanding early presidential elections. For other parts of the regime, notably the army, the FIS had made a perceived insurrectionist challenge to the Algerian state itself, something which the army was pledged to defend.

The re-entry of the Algerian army, the ANP (Armée Nationale Populaire) into the political scene was a significant aspect of the crisis. It had formally exited the political stage following its universally condemned role in the bloody repression of the riots of October 1988. It withdrew its representatives from the Central Committee of the FLN in March 1989 and had largely accepted the non-political role it had been accorded in the new Constitution of February 1989. Nevertheless, despite the political changes that swept Algeria after 1988, the ANP remained, not least in its own perception, central to the Algerian regime. A senior general continued to hold the important Defence Ministry portfolio in the government and many senior figures in the regime, not least the President himself, retained close links with the military.

The ANP's view of Chadli's decision to politically liberalise was never unambiguously expressed, but it was certainly extremely wary of the FIS and had voiced its opposition to the party's legal recognition in September 1989.[57] Largely trained abroad in secular states such as the Soviet Union and France, most of Algeria's senior military figures were essentially hostile to the ideas of Islamism, which were seen as a threat to the foundations of the Algerian state as well as to their own positions, should it achieve political power. The chief of the military, General Mustafa Chelloufi, was privately critical of both the FIS and of the government's tolerance of its activities in the run-up to the local elections of 1990. He spoke several times of the army's intention "to defend the Constitution", against elements which "want to exploit democracy", statements which were rightly taken as implicit warnings to the FIS.[58]

---

57   The head of the military, Mustafa Chelloufi, did, however, state the ANP's will-ingness "to protect the enterprise of the installation of political liberalism. . . " Reuters, March 1990, quoted in Abdelkader Yefsah, 'Armée et politique depuis les evénements d'Octobre: L'armée sans hidjab', *Les Temps Modernes: Algérie: La Guerre des Frères*, no. 580 (Janvier–Fevrier 1995), p.161.

58   *Reuters*, and *El Djeich* (a journal of the military), March 1990, quoted in Abdelkader Yefsah, 'Armée et Politique', p. 161.

From the FIS's point of view the antipathy the military felt towards it as both a party and a movement was mutual. Increasingly aware that it was the army rather than the FLN which represented the ultimate potential threat to their political ambitions, the leadership of the FIS were ready to issue counter-threats, when necessary, to those put out by the military. When Chelloufi banned the wearing of the hedjab by women working in military hospitals in April 1990, Ali Belhadj played on the military's fear of infiltration:

> There are in the army, the police, and the gendarmerie, civil servants who adore God and they will be able to remember that.[59]

This mutual hostility persisted even following the replacement of Chelloufi with a figure, Khaled Nezzar, who was generally perceived to be far less fundamentally hostile to Islamism.[60] None the less, Nezzar also proved unreluctant to restate the military's position on any potential threats to the stability of the country. On 13 September 1990 he confirmed the army's willingness to:

> . . . respond to any organised excesses that might jeopardise the national unity of the country . . . [and] would not hesitate to intervene and to re-establish order and unity so that force remains in the hands of the law.[61]

This implicit warning was issued in the growing climate of domestic tension that followed Iraq's invasion of Kuwait at the beginning of August, a period which witnessed a further worsening of relations between the two forces as Ali Belhadj, in particular, raged against the ANP's unwillingness to go to Iraq's defence.[62] With this background of continued

---

59   Burgat and Dowell, *The Islamic Movement in North Africa*, p. 292.
60   Mustafa Chelloufi's dismissal as chief of the military may have been due to what was perceived by the government to his overly hostile attitude towards the FIS. However, it also appears that Chelloufi's claim that the ANP was the 'defender of the constitution' angered Chadli Benjedid who issued a counter-statement claiming that the President and the National Assembly were the proper guardians of the constitution and not the military.
61   *L'Horizon*, 13.9.90 quoted in Zoubir, 'The painful transition from authoritarianism', p.98.
62   Ali Belhadj also made an unambiguous reference to October 1988 (about which the army still felt defensive and vulnerable), speaking of regimes which used their

and rising antipathy, Abassi Madani, whilst formulating his strategy of a general strike in the spring of 1991, felt the need to issue a warning to the military to prevent it intervening if his plans were implemented. Thus, even before the intention to hold a strike was formally announced, Abassi declared that:

> In the event of the military coming onto the streets, we will fight,
> I swear that if a single drop of blood is shed, we will combat the
> military until its complete annihilation.[63]

That this threat was not carried out following the army's eventual deployment on the streets on the night of 5 June was, of course, due to the calling off of both the general strike and the street demonstrations by the FIS following the apparent concessions it had won from the government by 7 June.

How autonomous a role the ANP played in the run-up to the intervention of 5 June was not entirely clear. Although President Chadli clearly welcomed and supported their involvement, how far this involvement was solicited and to what degree it was volunteered is difficult to ascertain. The President had regularly hinted for some time at the possible return of the army if there was a crisis on the streets, but this may have been a simple threat to keep the FIS in line rather than a serious declaration of intent.[64] Nevertheless it was clear that in June 1991 both the presidency and the military were united on the need to restore public order and reduce the power of the FIS. The military backed the striking of a "deal" with the FIS in order primarily to ease the mounting crisis, but whether at this stage the army intended to use the ensuing calm simply to plan its later assault on the party was less apparent. Some Algerian commentators remarked on the fact that the official instructions to remove the slogans from the front of the town halls controlled by the FIS in late June came from the military authorities rather than from the government. This was potentially significant since not only did it indicate the apparent

---

arms against their own people rather than in wars against external aggression. For its part, the ANP through its journal, *El Djeich*, accused the FIS of being the instruments of foreign manipulation.

63   Zoubir, 'The painful transition from authoritarianism', p. 98
64   See John P. Entelis, 'The crisis of authoritarianism in North Africa: the case of Algeria', *Problems of Communism* (May–June 1992), p. 79.

independence of the military, but also it was this incident which was acknowledged as having produced the violent response from the FIS's supporters that led to and was officially quoted as a justification for the subsequent crackdown against the party.[65] Chadli appeared to be in accord with this approach, but vetoed the military's subsequent demand for the FIS to be banned. However, despite Chadli's wishes prevailing on this last issue, the political re-emergence of the military constituted a potentially rival source of authority and power to the President within the regime.

The FIS divided: June–July 1991

The escalating crackdown of June by the authorities and the realisation that Abassi Madani's grand strategy had not, after all, succeeded in its objectives opened up the divisions in the FIS that had been suspended during the height of the crisis. For the first time dissent within the party was aired very publicly. On 23 June, as the arrests of FIS supporters mounted, three founding members of the FIS and members of its Majlis Shura, appeared on Algerian television to call for an opening of dialogue with the authorities. More importantly, they collectively denounced Abassi Madani who in the words of one of them, Bachir Fakih, was "a danger for the FIS and for Muslims". Fakih also stated that he would suspend his membership of the party if Abassi continued as leader of the FIS. The three accused Abassi Madani of being autocratic and of ignoring decisions reached by the Majlis Shura and called on people to heed only the statements of the latter and ignore Madani. Another of the three, Ahmed Merrani, argued that elements within the party were deliberately pushing for violent confrontation with the regime and the third figure, Hachemi Sahnouni, argued that it was imperative that dialogue be opened with the authorities "in order to save the blood of Muslims".[66]

These accusations precipitated a bitter and public war of words between Abassi Madani and his three detractors. The leader of the FIS,

---

65 See *SWB* ME/1109 A/1, 27.6.91. The FIS were subsequently to claim that Abassi had explicitly told the FIS-controlled local councils not to resist the removal of the slogans (he had suggested they film it as evidence) but that the security forces had deliberately provoked confrontations.

66 *La Presse*, 27.6.91.

with the backing of his allies in the Majlis Shura announced the expulsion of both Fakih and Merrani from the party.[67] Hachemi Sahnouni was spared this fate following a public retraction of his criticism and the intervention of his close friend and ally, Ali Belhadj. In response, Fakih denounced Abassi Madani as a "tyrant", accusing him of participating in politics with the sole goal of becoming President. Fakih also alleged that a number of members of the Majlis Shura had formally demanded Abassi's resignation in May.[68] However, despite the seriousness of these allegations and the relative political weight of figures like Fakih (who headed the Oran branch of the FIS) and Merrani (who headed the influential Social Affairs Commission of the party), Abassi was skilfully able to isolate his critics within the party and ensure that their call for the party's membership to ignore his instructions was not heeded. In this he was significantly aided by the public perception that the dissidents were stooges of the regime, an impression that their appearance on state-run television had reinforced.[69]

This did not, however, put an end to dissenting opinion within the upper reaches of the party expressing itself. Three other influential members of the Majlis Shura, Mohammed Kerrar, Said Guechi and Achour Rebhi, who were subsequently joined by Hachemi Sahnouni following his retraction, formed a delegation which opened contacts with the government in an attempt to start dialogue and secure the lifting of the state of siege and the release of the large numbers of FIS members who had been arrested since the beginning of June. Kerrar and Guechi had been part of the faction of the Majlis that had opposed Madani's plans

---

67 Merrani claimed himself that he had suspended his membership of the party and announced his intention to withdraw from politics and concentrate on "study of the Quran" and "adoration of God". *Horizons*, 1.7.91.

68 Charef, *Algérie: Le Grand Dérapage*, p. 116.

69 There were subsequent reports and allegations that the dissenting figures in the Majlis Shura had colluded with the regime. *Le Figaro* (4.7.91) reported rumours that certain members of the Majlis met secretly with government officials with a view to forging a "non-aggression pact" with the FIS. Supporters of Abassi Madani were also to later claim that Mohammed Kerrar, Benazouz Zebda, Merrani, Fakih and Sahnouni had been in contact with General Tewfik, the Head of Military Security, well in advance of the general strike. It was this fact, it was claimed, which explained Abassi Madani's reluctance to refer decisions to the Majlis for fear of telegraphing his strategy to the authorities. See *La Cause*, 5.7.94.

for the general strike and they were also supported in their subsequent search for dialogue with the authorities by Benazouz Zebda, the second vice-president of the FIS and editor of *El Mounquid* who saw it as the only route out of the continuing crisis.

The arrest and imprisonment of Abassi Madani and Ali Belhadj on 30 June, in the midst of these developments clearly exacerbated the growing divisions and factions within the FIS (which some argued encouraged and allowed the authorities to arrest the two leaders[70]) as the struggle appeared to open out from discussion of strategy to that of control of the leadership of the party itself, in the absence of the movement's two most prominent figures.

The question of succession to Abassi's and Belhadj's day-to-day leadership of the party came to be contested by two forces. Within three days of the two leaders' arrest, Mohammed Said proclaimed himself Madani's successor during prayer time at the Oued Koreiche mosque in the casbah of Algiers, claiming that Abassi Madani had nominated him as his successor prior to his imprisonment. This claim was vociferously disputed by members of the Majlis Shura, who although fostering individual leadership ambitions of their own, asserted that Abassi had in fact bequeathed authority to the Majlis itself. Members of the Majlis were particularly incensed at Said's claim to the leadership since he was far from being an established figure within the party. Despite being a noted figure in the Islamist movement, Said had not joined the FIS at its creation (see Chapter Four) and instead had become active in the Rabitat Dawa in which, after Ahmed Sahnoun, he had become the second most influential figure. He had finally joined the FIS in June 1990 at the invitation of Abassi Madani and thereafter rose swiftly within the party.

Antipathy towards Said inside the Majlis Shura was not just limited to his late entry to the FIS (Hachemi Sahnouni even accused him of not possessing a membership card at the time of his leadership proclamation) but was also linked to the fact that he had been the acknowledged leader of the Jazara grouping since the early 1980s. The traditionally secretive and elitist nature of the Jazara (see Chapters Three and Four) made some suspect that Said was attempting to seize the direction of the FIS for the

---

70 The editor of the independent daily, *El Watan*, remarked: "If the FIS had been united, Madani would not be in prison – it simply would not have been allowed to happen." *Trade Finance*, September 1991.

grouping and its shadowy agenda. Such accusations were sharpest from those on the more strictly religious and salafist wing of the FIS who had always been suspicious of the Jazara's pragmatic and nationalistic agenda.

Mohammed Said's "succession" was, however, short lived. Having threatened to launch a jihad unless the party's two leaders were released, he himself was arrested by the authorities on 7 July. Notably, though, the undisputed leadership of the FIS did not then pass to the Majlis Shura but to a young, hitherto low-profile, figure, Abdelkader Hachani, whom Said had nominated as his deputy at the time of his own leadership claim. That Hachani's claim was not disputed, like that of Mohammed Said's, by the other members of the Majlis Shura, was due to several factors. Although not a high-profile figure in the party, Hachani had been a founder member of the FIS and had originally been part of Abdallah Djaballah's organisation, rather than an adherent of the Jazara. This, together with his emphasis on the strictly provisional nature of his leadership whilst Abassi, Belhadj and other leaders were still in prison, helped persuade the Majlis Shura to accept his leadership which it formally confirmed at the end of July.

The nature and orientation of Abdelkader Hachani's leadership of the FIS would later become more apparent (see Chapter Six). However, the struggle over both the direction and latterly the leadership of the party and its outcome had revealed much about the hitherto concealed factions in the party. During the period May–July 1991, the divisions within the party were widely interpreted from the outside as being between moderates and hardliners. The "moderates", represented by figures such as Fakih, Merrani and Sahnouni, were seen fighting to prevent Abassi Madani and his supporters from pushing the FIS into a "hardline" confrontation with the regime. A much more accurate characterisation of the dispute would be, as has been indicated earlier, between those who had more political objectives for the FIS and those who were more content with pursuing specifically religious ends. As Hugh Roberts points out, the struggle could be seen as taking place between religious radicals and pragmatic moderates, with Abassi Madani and his supporters comprising the second grouping.[71] That the chief opponents of Abassi and his tactics were figures who had far from "moderate" backgrounds

---

71   Roberts: 'From radical mission', p. 466.

(compared to the leader of the FIS) undermines the notion of "moderate" opposition to him. Several key adversaries, such as Fakih, Mohammed Kerrar and Said Guechi had been involved in Mustapha Bouyali's insurrectionist MAIA in the 1980s. Hachemi Sahnouni was not only close to Ali Belhadj but had frequently matched the deputy leader of the IS's fiery and intemperate rhetoric and discourse.[72] It was also remarkable that Sahnouni, Fakih and Merrani had, in their famous television appearance, concentrated their attacks on Abassi Madani, the perceived voice of moderation within the leadership, and completely ignored Ali Belhadj whose immoderate pronouncements Madani was forever having to explain and excuse.

The claim of Mohammed Said to the leadership of the party produced another interesting dimension to the internal politics of the FIS. Said's precise ambitions in claiming the helm of the FIS were never fully elucidated during his short (four days) spell as "leader". He himself presented it as a simple and unselfish response to a crisis, stating that: "I am neither an intruder nor a seeker of leadership. [But] Confronted by this vacuum, I have assumed my responsibilities."[73] Nevertheless, the speed with which the move was made and the nature of the Jazara and its agenda must confirm suspicions that Said wanted to steer the FIS in a particular direction. Nine members of the FIS's Majlis Shura had opposed Said's and the Jazara's accession to the party in June 1990 out of hostility towards both the grouping's ideology and possible future intentions. Significantly, this group of nine contained all of the later major critics and opponents of Abassi Madani – Merrani, Kerrar, Fakih, Sahnouni, Zebda and Guechi. Ahmed Merrani, in particular, was unremitting from June 1991 in his accusation that Said, together with Hachani, had perpetrated a "coup" against the leadership of the FIS on the part of the Jazara. However, although Merrani portrayed Abassi Madani as being a fellow victim of such a coup, it was noteworthy that Hachani had been one of Abassi's closest allies in the Majlis Shura and had backed his plans for the general strike.[74] It was thus clear that

---

72   For example, according to one report Sahnouni had declared that if the FIS were to win the planned national elections it would introduce "immediately the Sharia, would ban secular and communist parties and would expel the President", Charef, *Algérie: Le Grand Dérapage*, p. 130.

73   *Ibid.*, p. 117.

74   See interview with Ahmed Merrani, *Algérie Actualité*, 1.8.91.

Hachani's accession to the leadership represented a triumph for Abassi Madani (confirmed by Hachani's stressed reference to the provisional nature of his own leadership, in deference to the imprisoned Abassi) and his allies rather than for some shadowy third faction. If Mohammed Said had planned some "takeover" of the FIS on the part of the Jazara, his nomination of Hachani as his deputy and his loud demands for the release of the FIS's leadership, indicated that his plans were closely allied to and supportive of Abassi Madani.[75] It is clear that Abassi, Said and Hachani all feared the leadership of the party falling into the hands of the more strictly religious radicals of the party who might abandon the whole pragmatic, political and electoral strategy of the FIS. Like Abassi, the Jazara's more intellectual and modernist outlook convinced it of the efficacy and importance of such an "electoralist" strategy.[76]

The FIS as a Party: 1990–1991

The structure of the party

The structure of the FIS changed somewhat following the party's success in the local elections of June 1990 which had seen it enter into institutional frameworks in the public domain. The FIS installed throughout the country a network of its own administrations that largely paralleled the official administrations.[77] Thus executives of the party were established at both wilaya level (Bureaux Executifs Wilaya – BEWs) and at the

---

75 A communiqué signed by Said and Hachani explicitly acknowledged "the authority of Abassi Madani as President of the FIS". FIS Communiqué, 2.7.91.

76 It has been suggested that Mohammed Said and the Jazara backed the general strike as a means of provoking a crisis that would (as indeed it did) split the FIS and allow the Jazara to play a more dominant role. In particular, the forced postponement of the legislative elections would also allow the grouping to nominate more of its own members as FIS candidates when the elections were rescheduled. (See Séverine Labat, *Les Islamistes Algériens: Entre les Urnes et le Maquis* (Paris, Seuil, 1995), p. 115.) However, whilst Said and the Jazara were undoubtedly anxious to exercise more influence within the FIS and were subsequently able to introduce more of their own members as FIS candidates, such a plot credits the Jazara with improbably Machiavellian foresight .

77 In the Chlef region FIS-controlled councils had established "parallel tribunals" to judge private, especially family, law. In Algiers the city hall had been effectively turned into the "national seat" of the movement and was frequently used by Abassi Madani to hold press conferences.

communal level (BECs). These two levels formed the second and third tiers of the party's organisation below that of the supreme BEN (Bureau Executif Nationale) and above those centred around the mosques and the committees of the quarters. The top three levels of the party continued to possess five commissions dealing with the issues of organisation and co-ordination, education, social affairs, planning and programming and information. An "Islamic" trades union body was also established by the FIS, the SIT (Syndicat islamique du travail), which comprised nine different professional sections.[78]

In terms of the decision-making structure of the party, it seemed clear that this was a strictly top-down affair. Both the BECs and the BEWs were answerable to the BEN which dictated policy to the FIS-controlled local councils "of which", Ghania Samai-Ouramdane remarked in 1990, "any freedom of action is not permitted".[79] Officially the BEN was subordinate to the Majlis Shura of the party, which remained the highest decision-making body within the party and which was responsible for all strategic policy. However, as had become apparent, Dévoluy and Duteil characterised the decision-making process of the FIS as oscillating "between a system of hazy consensus and the personal power of its president, Abassi Madani".[80] Such a judgement would seem to have been borne out by the ongoing conflict Abassi had with certain elements of the Majlis Shura during the early part of 1991, as he sought increasingly to make his own policy whilst still formally recognising the Majlis's authority.

Much, however, remained unknown about the precise internal workings of the FIS as a party. As has been indicated, until the crisis of mid-1991, very little was known about the senior figures in the party apart from Abassi Madani and to a lesser extent, Ali Belhadj. The party seemed intent on maintaining this secrecy. When questioned in an interview in August 1990 about the membership of the Majlis Shura, Abassi Madani replied evasively: "You will know them soon."[81] The reasons behind this lack of frankness are unclear, although given the events

78 See Ghania Samai-Ouramdane, 'Le Front Islamique du Salut a travers son organe de presse (El Mounqid)', *Peuples Mediterranéens*, no. 52–3: *Algérie Vers L'Etat Islamique?* (Juillet–Septembre 1990), pp. 158–9.

79 *Ibid.*, p. 158.

80 Dévoluy and Duteil, *La Poudrière Algérienne*, p. 126.

81 Interview with Abassi Madani, *Algérie Actualité*, 30.8.90.

of 1991, it seems likely that it was a policy which aimed at concealing the fractious internal nature of the party from the public gaze.

Support for the FIS

Although there were no elections in this period to back observations up with more empirical data, further information on the composition of support for the FIS did emerge. The opinion polls that were published in May 1991, although not as unambiguous as election results, were able to give added insights into the people who, publicly at least, lent their support to the FIS.

A poll conducted on behalf of *Algérie Actualité* and published on 9 May 1991 recorded not only the levels of support for the various political parties but also revealed the apparent levels of support the parties enjoyed within different sections of the electorate. When broken down into different age groups, the FIS, which had recorded an overall level of support of 38% across all age groups, saw its support vary considerably between the age groups – enjoying the support of 55% of those aged 18 to 19, whilst recording only 28% for those electors between the ages of 50 and 59. The figures revealed a declining level of support for the party across the age bands covering the ages 20 to 59, thus indicating, with the intriguing exception of those aged 60 plus (where the party recorded 36%), that the older a voter was, the less likely he or she was to vote for the FIS. The survey also reported findings about both the educational profile of the FIS's supporters and the relative balance between men and women. On the first category the poll revealed that the party received above average levels of support amongst those voters who had just secondary, primary or no education at all and that it performed particularly badly amongst those with supplementary education. There was also a notable imbalance in the share of men and women expressing support for the party: 44% of men backing it compared to only 32% of women.[82]

---

82 *Algérie Actualité*, 9.5.91. The figures for the support for the FIS amongst the different educational levels were 41% amongst those with no formal education at all; 39% for those with just primary education, 44% for those with secondary and 23% for those possessing supplementary education.

A further poll published by the newspaper three weeks later on 30 May analysed voting intentions, this time by region and occupation. The figures on the regional pattern of the FIS's support did not reveal anything particularly dramatic. The party's declared followers were spread across all of Algeria's four main regions in proportions roughly similar to that of its main rival, the FLN. The party seemed also to enjoy similar levels of support in both urban and rural areas: having recorded an overall level of support of 29%, the figures for the urban and rural zones were 30.5% and 27% respectively. This appeared to demonstrate an evening out of the party's support, since the local elections of June 1990 had shown that the FIS's following was predominantly urban in character. The breakdown of the FIS's supporters by profession revealed the similarly widespread nature of the backing for the party: it being the only party to register responses in all twelve of the categories of occupation in the survey. As with the regional share-out of its potential vote, the FIS's figures roughly shadowed those of the FLN, with the exception of the unemployed, where the Islamist party received a significantly higher proportion of its support than the former single party did.[83]

What explanations could be offered for these findings? The youthful profile of the FIS's voters revealed by the first poll could largely be explained by reference to two factors. Firstly, unemployment was significantly higher amongst the young, producing greater levels of disillusionment with the regime and a corresponding desire to inflict defeat upon the FLN. Secondly, attachment to the memory of the FLN victory in the war against the French was largely absent amongst Algeria's young – those Algerians under the age of thirty having been born after independence and thus having no residual nationalistic respect for the historic achievements of the FLN. The FIS registered its lowest level of support amongst those Algerians who were in their twenties when Algeria gained its independence and were thus those most likely to have been directly involved with the

---

83 *Algérie Actualité*, 30.5.91. The comparison with the profile for the FLN is made not only because it is the only party recording over 10% support but also since the figures regarding the region and occupation in the survey are expressed as percentages of each party's total support rather than as percentages of the region or the occupational group, thus making observations about the relative levels of support between the parties in each category difficult.

revolutionary struggle and the FLN. The poll revealed that the former single party still enjoyed its highest levels of support amongst this latter group, now in their fifties. The apparent anomaly of the recovery in following for the FIS amongst those Algerians over the age of 60 can not easily be explained, but reference to the above-mentioned factors may be useful. Those of retirement age were hit possibly as hard as those without work by the economic crisis that the country continued to experience. This group also remembered a time before independence and before the FLN, thus holding the party in slightly less reverence than the generation below them. The educational profile of FIS supporters, with its relatively low share of those possessing supplementary education (it was the only educational group in which it did not have a lead over the other parties) can probably be linked again to the party's base in the poorer sections of Algerian society, which were likely to be less well educated. The third finding of the first *Algérie Actualité* poll, that a significantly greater percentage of men than women in the Algerian electorate backed the FIS, must be seen as reflecting a belief or fear that women would be worse off under an Islamist-run government. This conclusion is supported by the fact that the party that campaigned on the most aggressively secularist platform, the RCD, received more than twice as much support from women, in the poll, as it did from men (11% compared to 5%).

The findings of the second opinion poll showed, as has been indicated, that the FIS enjoyed an even wider pattern of electoral support across Algeria's regions and in its urban and rural areas than that which it had received in June 1990. There were no notable relative concentrations or absences of support between Algeria's four main regions (although, it should be noted that within these huge regions there were still likely to be variations[84]). The analysis by occupation confirmed this comprehensive spread of support for the FIS, but the party's relatively large proportion of followers from amongst the unemployed (and a corresponding relatively low percentage, compared to the make-up of the other major parties, amongst employees in the state sector) appeared to confirm the link

---

84   The central region of the country contained both areas such as Algiers itself, where the FIS had done particularly well in June 1990, as well as the Tizi Ouzou area, where it had done demonstrably poorly. This appeared to be still the case since the FFS, which was based in Tizi Ouzou, was shown by the poll to find nearly 98% of its support (registered at 10% nationally) in the central region. *Algérie Actualité*, 30.5.91.

suggested above between unemployment, youth and support for the FIS. Overall, the two surveys appeared to construct a picture of the FIS's base of support as continuing to come from the poorer, younger and less well educated layers of Algerian society.

The two opinion polls gave potentially valuable insights into the composition of support for the FIS, but their findings need to be regarded with a certain amount of caution, given the failure of similar polls before the local elections of June 1990 to predict the size of the FIS's victory. However, other more observationally based evidence did seem to back up some of the finding of the polls. The failure of the general strike called by the FIS in May to elicit any significant response amongst Algeria's workforce did, as has already been shown, demonstrate that the party did not enjoy substantial support amongst this part of Algerian society. Conversely, the large numbers of unemployed youths the party was able to mobilise for marches and demonstrations from the beginning of June indicated that this was where the FIS's real strength lay.

Other evidence suggested that the nature of the FIS's following remained consistent with that of previous conclusions about the backing for the party before the June elections. Whilst the bulk of its activist base (as distinct from people who would just vote for the party at an election) was clearly composed of the urban, male unemployed, the FIS continued to have a following in the universities, particularly amongst science and technology students. Similarly, many of the party's leaders were engineers or technicians and it appears that the party enjoyed significant general support from this type of profession. Support for the FIS continued to be found amongst merchants, businessmen and entrepreneurs. It was argued that it was these groups which helped to cushion the financial blow the party received when Saudi funds were withdrawn following the party's decision to back Iraq during the Gulf War. There was also believed to be backing for the party amongst those traders involved in the country's growing black market. One of the reasons advanced for the party's popularity amongst this sector was the perception that the FIS backed free market reforms.

The FIS's attachment to populism ensured that none of these sections of support were taken for granted by the party, particularly the urban unemployed poor, whom the opinion polls had shown formed such an important part of the following of the party. Projects were adopted to aid and thus guarantee the loyalty of the populous bottom rung of the ladder of Algerian society. Ramadan of 1991 saw the establishment of "Islamic" souks where Algeria's poor could buy basic goods at lower than usual prices because the FIS arranged for transportation and retail services to be given free of charge.

Evidence also emerged concerning the size and nature of the support for the other Islamist parties. In the case of Mahfoud Nahnah's HAMAS it appeared that its constituency of support differed from that of the FIS. The opinion polls published in May 1991 indicated that HAMAS attracted a more middle-class, professional following than the FIS, which drew the vast bulk of its popular support from the young unemployed.[85] Whilst HAMAS was able to attract such a constituency, reflecting its more intellectual and less populist discourse, the fact that it made few inroads into this mass popular base of the FIS indicated that the party was likely to stay on the political margins come election time. Despite holding well-attended meetings in the south of Algeria and having notable pockets of support across the country (the party soon had 916 local offices[86]), particularly around Nahnah's hometown of Blida, opinion polls indicated that FIS support was roughly ten times that of HAMAS.[87] In the case of Abdallah Djaballah and Nahda, although initially observers believed that the party had significant support in the east of Algeria around Djaballah's traditional base in Constantine, opinion polls in the spring of 1991 showed the party as failing to register even 1% of voting intentions.[88]

Programme and agenda

Despite the inevitable surge of interest in the nature and content of the FIS's political programme following the party's victory in June 1990, precise details remained difficult to identify and many of the old contradictions and ambiguities remained.

---

85 *Algérie Actualité*, 30.5.91.
86 Of these local offices, 133 were women's sections.
87 HAMAS recorded levels of support of 2% and 3% respectively in the two polls. *Algérie Actualité*, 9.5.91 and 30.5.91.
88 *Algérie Actualité*, 30.5.91 and 9.5.91.

Pluralism and democracy

Chief amongst these issues was the party's stance on pluralism and democracy. Besieged by the national and foreign press in the wake of the local elections, Abassi Madani, as the chief spokesman for the party, continued to reiterate his line of liberal toleration of diversity. Questioned on other parties' stated fears about their possible fate under a (now more likely) FIS-led national government, he claimed that "The other parties are not our enemies, but our brothers", arguing that they would, in fact, have a vital role to play under a future FIS government:

> Islamic rule is not against opposition. There was opposition in the time of the Caliphs and the companions of the Prophet. How would we be able to discover our errors if there was not an opposition to point them out to us? Must we relive a scenario like October 1988 to correct our mistakes?[89]

That the FIS had accepted co-existence with other parties in local government, he argued, was evidence of the genuineness of this stance. Fears about a return to the one-party state he therefore maintained were groundless and he pointed, in this context, to the participation of the communist PAGS in the electoral process and asked, with reference to Stalin, Mao and Ceausescu: "Who has mocked liberties as much as the communists?"[90]

On the issue of the imposition of the sharia and specifically its implication for women, Madani claimed that it would only be introduced gradually. He stated emphatically that he would "never, never" impose the wearing of the veil on women, arguing that whilst the party strongly believed that this was the correct form of dress for women:

> The problem is one of education. It is not one able to be resolved with penal sanctions . . . We struggle against the illness not against the person who is ill.[91]

Such apparently unambiguous statements continued to contrast sharply with those emanating from other parts of the party's leadership.

---

89 Interview with Abassi Madani, *Jeune Afrique*, 25.7.90.
90 *Ibid.*
91 *Ibid.*

Hachemi Sahnouni, the party's second vice-president, stated on 8 May 1991:

> In the case of [the FIS achieving] a majority at the next legislative elections, we suspend the constitution, we ban secular and socialist parties, we immediately apply the sharia [and] we immediately get rid of the President of the Republic.[92]

Such sentiments closely echoed statements made by Ali Belhadj at this time and the deputy leader of the FIS continued to attack the notion of liberal democracy. Writing in *El Mounquid* the FIS's deputy leader declared:

> In Islam sovereignty belongs to the divine Law; in democracy, sovereignty belongs to the people, to the mob and to charlatans.[93]

Once again these were not isolated utterances confined to a few radical individuals. As one observer commented on Sahnouni's statement, "Declarations of this sort had been the common currency of FIS preachers these last two years."[94] Nor did it appear that these views were restricted to figures within the party's leadership. Banners declaring "Death to Democracy" appeared at FIS demonstrations during June 1991.[95]

Abassi Madani continued to be pressed by the media on the continuation of such divergent views on these critical issues within the leadership of the party. One interviewer put to him the reported view of Ali Belhadj that democracy was a vehicle for communism and Berberism. The FIS president replied that he had not heard his deputy express such a view but if he had then he believed that it was a "theoretical point of view", there being "several conceptions of democracy".[96] On another occasion Madani defended Belhadj by claiming that the young imam's aggressive rhetoric when preaching (when most of his more extreme statements were made) was not a true reflection of his overall character, maintaining that in reality "Belhadj is very gentle. The problem is that

---

92 *El Watan*, 4.8.91, quoted in Kapil, 'Les Partis Islamistes en Algérie', p. 104.
93 *El Mounquid*, no. 23, reproduced in Al-Ahnaf, Botiveau and Frégosi, *L'Algérie par ses Islamistes*, p. 93.
94 Kapil, 'Les Partis Islamistes en Algérie', p. 104.
95 *The Tablet*, 20.7.91.
96 Interview with Abassi Madani, *Jeune Afrique*, 25.7.90.

he doesn't show it."[97] It was clear that despite the tactical need to retain the support of the party's radical militants, the president of the FIS was discomforted by his deputy's rhetoric. One broadly sympathetic political figure privately challenged Abassi on Belhadj's belligerent proclamations:

> I told Abassi to tell Belhadj not to say such radical things. Abassi reddened with embarrassment and replied that he had told him many times to do so, but he could not control him.[98]

Economic policy

On the subject of the economy and economic policy the FIS's stance appeared to shift during this period. Its initial policy programmes, though lacking in detail, had favoured, in accordance with much established Islamic economic thought, more liberal economic practices (see Chapter Four). As previously explained, it was this stance which allowed the party to strike a deal with President Chadli to help support him and his allies against those elements in the FLN and the regime who were opposed to his liberalising economic reforms.

Although this economic doctrine attracted the electoral and financial support of merchants and entrepreneurs, Abassi Madani appeared to repudiate this existing position in an interview at the beginning of May 1991 when he launched a blistering attack on the government's reform programme:

> . . . there will never be reforms. These things called reforms are in fact nothing other than an operation to enable the regime to steal from the pockets of citizens, make the poor still poorer and trying today to exhaust the money of the wealthy.[99]

He criticised the government for failing to help traders and businesses with exports whilst "opening all the doors and according all the facilities" to foreign competition, a policy he termed "a dangerous deviation from Algerian history". He directed his fire also at the International Monetary Fund which he blamed for much of the escalating problems and poverty

---

97 *Le Figaro*, 31.7.90.
98 Author's interview with senior Algerian political figure.
99 Interview with Abassi Madani, *Horizons*, 5.5.91.

in Algeria saying that it had blocked national solutions to the crisis and having "dictated its conditions and orders" had left the Algerian people to "pay the bill".[100]

The reason behind this startling *volte face* by the leader of the FIS could be discerned by the date that these remarks were made: early May 1991. April 1991 had seen the unveiling of the regime's new electoral code. It was this event which, as has been shown, provoked the breach between Abassi Madani and the President whom he believed had deceived him. Not only, therefore, did Abassi's fury lead him to attack Chadli himself and call for early presidential elections, but also clearly led him to dramatically terminate his tacit support for the President's economic reform programme.

As for the FIS's own economic policy, little of any real substance was added to its original proposals (see Chapter Four) and the party proceeded to be increasingly vague about its own position. Earlier in 1991, before Abassi's outburst in May, the party held a symposium on the government's reform programme but as one Algerian journalist attending remarked: "one tried in vain to identify the content (of the FIS's economic view and programme)."[101] This ambiguity and lack of definition on policy was a clear reflection of the increasingly populist direction in which the FIS moved following June 1990 and which had been exemplified by its behaviour in the Gulf War. Because of its desire to maintain its breadth of popular support, the party was forced into making often inconsistent statements. Thus in the same interview Abassi Madani would promise new housing and an expansion of social security as well as committing the party to "seriously reducing taxation".[102]

Foreign links and influences

The question of foreign links and influences on the FIS continued to be an issue in this period as its domestic enemies and many foreign commentators sought to uncover a "foreign hand" behind the activities of the party.

---

100 *Ibid.*
101 *Algérie Actualité*, 14.3.91.
102 Interview with Abassi Madani, *Jeune Afrique*, 25.7.90.

Saudi Arabia

The issue of links with Saudi Arabia came to the fore during the Gulf crisis with the party appearing to turn its back on its alleged Saudi sponsors and FIS militants swapping the Saudi flags that had often been seen at rallies for banners supporting Saddam Hussein and Iraq. Whilst such a development could be interpreted as demonstrating the absence or weakness of the FIS's Saudi links, the announcement by the Saudi Prince Sultan Ibn Abdelaziz on 26 March 1991 that his country had been funding the party was judged by one observer as revealing a fact that was "a secret to nobody".[103] The timing of the declaration, following the end of the Gulf War, was undoubtedly chosen by the Saudis, angered by the FIS's backing of their enemy in the war, as being that which would cause maximum damage to the FIS, showing it to have not only backed the losing side in the conflict but having also been supported by foreign money. The accusation of foreign sponsorship was clearly damaging in a country where national independence was so highly regarded and, in the face of appeals in the press for stricter prohibitions for foreign funding of political parties, Abassi Madani strenuously denied the accusation stating that it was "a lie without foundation" and if Prince Sultan did in fact say this "he did not mean it".[104] The president of the FIS claimed that the party had not received a penny from any known state and alleged that such accusations were part "of a vast plan to destabilise the FIS".[105] All the available evidence, however, suggested that the FIS had been backed by Saudi funds. Ali Belhadj, less politically cautious than Abassi, hinted through references to money and treachery at the truth of the allegations in a bitter attack he had launched against the Kingdom shortly before (and in possible anticipation) of the Saudi revelations of March 1991: "Saudi Arabia and Kuwait are more dangerous than the Jews, for they use money and Islam to achieve their own ends. They are traitors."[106]

Iran

There continued to be little effective evidence of any real links between the FIS and Iran, despite the latter's declared interest in seeing an Islamic

---

103   Al-Ahnaf, Botiveau and Frégosi, *L'Algérie par ses Islamistes*, pp. 35–6.
104   *Ibid.* p. 36.
105   *El Moudjahid*, 3.4.91.
106   *El Watan*, 19.3.91.

regime established in Algeria.[107] During the crisis of June 1991, the Iranian Ambassador in Algiers had been summoned to the Algerian Foreign Ministry to explain his country's ties with the FIS. However, Ali Belhadj's already explained theological differences with the Islamic Republic (see Chapter Four) clearly served to limit any such potential links. Abassi Madani, who was more willing to praise aspects of the Iranian regime, when asked about links with Ali Akbar Mohtachemi, a leading Iranian radical and key figure in the pan-national Hezbollah, asked in return who Mohtachemi was. When told ("the spiritual guide of the Iranian revolution"), he replied that he was still unaware of him.[108] This denial appeared to be more genuine than that issued over links with Saudi Arabia. In fact, Iran and Hezbollah seemed to exercise their greatest influence with small specifically Shi'ite groups such as Sunna wa-Sharia. One foreign diplomat noted the emergence of at least five mosques in late 1990 which were financed and encouraged by the Iranians.

Egypt

A third country which had alleged links with Algeria's Islamists, although not at state level, was Egypt. Around the time of the June 1990 elections Egypt's Ambassador to Algeria, Hussein Amin, was informed by the Egyptian intelligence services of links being established between Egypt's radical Islamist groups such as the Gamaat Islamia and Al-Jihad and members of the FIS. In a move to halt such contacts, Hussein Amin reintroduced visa requirements for Algerians wishing to visit Egypt, in June 1990, so that FIS members could be vetted. This was swiftly reversed, however, on the orders of Egyptian President Hosni Mubarak who Amin believed had been put under pressure by complaints from Chadli Benjedid.[109]

Contact between the FIS and the more constitutionalist and less radical sections of the Islamist movement in Egypt, such as the Muslim Brotherhood, were minimal. Adel Hussein, the Secretary-General of the

---

107 See Mohammed Mohaddessin, *Islamic Fundamentalism: The New Global Threat* (Washington, Seven Locks Press, 1993), p. 87.

108 Interview with Abassi Madani, *Algérie Actualité*, 4.7.91.

109 Author's interview with Hussein Amin, Cairo, 13.6.94. Amin believed that Mubarak was heavily influenced by Chadli, who he believed wished to aid a FIS victory in the electoral process. However, it seems likely that the Algerian President took the imposition of visa requirements as a slur on Algeria generally.

Egyptian Labour Party, under whose banner the Muslim Brotherhood competed in elections, stated that despite both groups' participation in elections, links between his party and the FIS were "very limited".[110] For the FIS's part, Abassi Madani expressly stated that "the FIS is not a movement of the Muslim Brothers, its position is different."[111] This lack of contact and co-operation could be explained by the close relations Mahfoud Nahnah continued to enjoy with the Egyptian Muslim Brotherhood, the leader of HAMAS having originally established links with the organisation in the 1960s.

On a more theological level, the replacement of Sheikh Muhammed Ghazali (see Chapter Three) with Sheikh Yussef Al-Karadawy, a fellow Egyptian, as rector of the Abdul Qadir mosque, in early 1989, was seen by some observers as having a significant influence on the development of the Algerian Islamist movement. More of an intellectual than his predecessor, Al-Karadawy deepened the roots of Islamic ideas in Algeria although his more moderate approach made only limited headway against the more hardline and fixed views of Abassi Madani and Ali Belhadj.

General

In general, although the FIS enjoyed good relations with foreign Islamists – prominent Islamists from Egypt, Kuwait and Jordan being invited to a conference the party organised on the Intifada in December 1990 – it was anxious to play down and deny foreign links and influences. This extended even to relations with Islamists in other parts of the Maghreb. Despite the presence of Rachid Ghannoushi, the influential leader of the Tunisian Nahda party, in Algeria during 1990 and 1991, links with the Tunisian and Moroccan movements were similarly denied.[112] The use of any "models" for a future FIS-run Islamic government was also rejected. When questioned in an interview about the possible use of the examples of Iran and Saudi Arabia in this context, Abassi Madani replied:

> Neither one nor the other. Our only model is the Prophet. We are equally guided by the rightly-guided Caliphs. The systems of which

---

110 Author's interview with Adel Hussein, secretary-general of the Egyptian Labour Party, Cairo, 19.6.94.

111 Interview with Abassi Madani, *Algérie Actualité*, 30.8.90.

112 See *Le Figaro*, 31.7.90.

you speak are not able to be of any use to us. We respect them, certainly, but we have our own model.[113]

The determination to be seen to be pursuing a rigidly independent line free from any foreign influence and support can be seen as evidence of the nationalistic influence of the Jazara on the thinking and stance of the FIS, or more likely a simpler populist desire to appear as a party beholden to its grass-roots supporters. Nevertheless, the FIS was notable for being virtually the only significant Islamist grouping in Algeria which did not assume a name already used for or by another Islamist group outside of Algeria. HAMAS (the occupied territories), Takfir wa Hijra (Egypt), Nahda (the more usual name for the MNI – Tunisia) as well as many smaller groups, chose names that reflected the importance of outside images and symbols.

Beyond the FIS: the Secular and Militant Challenges

The militant fringe

The political reforms of 1989 had resulted in Algerian Islamism largely shedding the covert forms it had assumed during the preceding two decades and manifesting itself in more overt structures such as religious associations and political parties. However, there remained elements of the movement that preferred a more clandestine existence, particularly those groups that espoused achievement of Islamist aims through force.

Initially it appeared that the opening of the electoral option to Islamism had totally eclipsed the idea of a need for armed insurrection – such as that attempted by Mustapha Bouyali – particularly following the FIS's comprehensive election victories of June 1990. Nonetheless, the period 1990-91 produced evidence to suggest that such groups, although numerically small, were still present and occasionally active. Beginning in 1990 a number of violent acts occurred including several armed robberies, attacks on drinkers in a bar in Baraki, an assault on a military barracks in Blida and an exchange of fire with police in December 1990. These incidents were often attributed, particularly by the media, to supporters

---

113   Interview with Abassi Madani, *Jeune Afrique*, 25.7.90.

and members of the FIS, but it subsequently became clear that responsibility predominantly lay with Islamists associated with the various radical groups, particularly Takfir wa Hijra, which had been in existence since the 1970s (see Chapters Two and Three). Augmented and now dominated by the returned volunteers from the war in Afghanistan, groups such as Takfir became gradually more active, particularly in the Belcourt district of Algiers.[114]

The militants of Takfir and other similar groups had explicitly rejected, on ideological grounds, the constitutional and peaceful path to the achievement of an Islamic state that the Islamists in the FIS had apparently embraced. However, despite this divide, it became clear during 1991 that Takfir was associating itself increasingly closely with the FIS. A violent battle which took place for control of the Abi Obeida mosque in Bachdjarah in May 1991 was fought between HAMAS militants and members of Takfir who had allied themselves with the FIS in the struggle against Mahfoud Nahnah's party. Takfir also participated in the FIS's protests against the electoral law the following month, their presence at demonstrations being apparent, according to one observer, by the way its supporters marched in tight squares with clenched fists wearing combat fatigues under their traditional Islamic dress. The transformation of the largely peaceful demonstrations into bloody confrontations with the security forces has been blamed on the actions of Takfir militants who were also reported as being responsible for the shooting of five members of the police and army on the first night of the curfew.[115]

It was thus unsurprising that it was members of Takfir and other Afghan veterans who were the initial targets of the arrests and security sweeps carried out by the government from the beginning of June which reportedly uncovered arms caches belonging to the group (who themselves claimed to possess in excess of four thousand guns). The army moved decisively to try and crush the organisation, in what became known as the "Battle of Belcourt", on the night of 30 June–1 July, seeking to flush

---

114 The organisation was also reported to be present in a belt to the south of Algiers comprising areas such as Baraki, Eucalyptus and El Harrach, although the leader of the group, reported to be El-Wahrani, lived in Belmourdes to the east of the capital.

115 *The Middle East*, July 1991.

its supporters out of their stronghold in the Khaled Ibn Walid mosque (known locally as "Kabul") in what proved a largely successful operation.

That the FIS was not altogether happy with Takfir's association with its activities was revealed by the lack of protest coming from the party's leadership when the latter's members became the first to be arrested by the authorities at the beginning of June. This was in spite of the alleged links between the group and Hachemi Sahnouni, the FIS's second vice-president. There was clearly a feeling that the provocative role of the group did not generally serve the ends of the party. Nevertheless, despite their defeat in Belcourt and the arrest of a large part of its membership (claimed to number 16,000),[116] Takfir had reportedly regrouped itself in another stronghold in Béni Mered to the east of the capital.

The continued failure of the non-Islamist opposition

Part of the reason for the scale of the FIS victory in the local elections of June 1990 was seen to be the lack of an effective secular alternative for Algerians to vote for – those secular opposition parties that did exist having either boycotted the poll or proved too small, fractious and narrowly based to mount a real challenge to the FIS and the FLN. It was hoped by many outside observers that the entry of the two large opposition parties that had boycotted the 1990 poll, the MDA and the FFS, together with a greater unity of purpose on the part of all the opposition parties, galvanised by the results of June 1990, would break the monopoly the FIS and the FLN had so far established over the electoral process.

The return of Ahmed Ben Bella, the MDA leader, to Algeria from exile in September 1990 attracted considerable domestic and foreign media and popular interest and speculation. It was thought that the first President of independent Algeria and one of the original "historic chiefs" of the liberation struggle might be able to provide a charismatic alternative to the FIS – his revolutionary nationalistic credentials together with his endorsement of Islamism (see Chapter Three) offering the necessary political ingredients for a winning political platform. The MDA had been the first political party to back Iraq and call for volunteers to be

---

116 Takfir's own claim in a communiqué sent to newspaper editors in February 1991.

sent there during the Gulf crisis and this had led to worries amongst the FIS's leaders that their party might be being outflanked.

Ben Bella's populist instincts, however, were increasingly equated in the eyes of most Algerians with simple opportunism. Chief amongst such opportunism was his stance towards the FIS itself which saw wild fluctuations over a short space of time as he appeared to be deciding whether he stood to gain most by rallying to the FIS or against it. When he returned to Algeria in September 1990 he strongly criticised the intolerance and excesses of the Islamist movement, stating that he differed "absolutely" from the FIS on their position towards women and found the party's apparent belief that they were the sole representatives of Islam "intolerable".[117] Just over six months later on 8 May 1991, the leader of the MDA called on people to vote for the FIS in order to defeat the FLN and the regime in the forthcoming legislative elections and subsequently even proposed an alliance with the party.[118] This change of tack might conceivably have been taken as a genuine change of conviction and strategy on behalf of Ben Bella were it not for the fact that in the wake of the May–June crisis, just a few weeks later, he was declaring the government "credible" and the recourse to the military "necessary".[119] The lack of credibility Ben Bella and the MDA consequently appeared to have with the electorate was indicated by the opinion polls carried out in May 1991 – the party failing to register 2% support in either survey.[120]

More genuinely popular was the FFS led by another of the original "historic chiefs" of the war of independence, Hocine Ait Ahmed. A demonstration organised by the party in Algiers in December 1990 was able to attract the support of an estimated 500,000 people. However, whilst this was an impressive show of strength by the party, it appeared unlikely that the FFS would be likely to build on this support since its power base, despite its fervour, was largely restricted to Kabylia and Algeria's Berber population. This was illustrated by the fact that the

---

117 Interview with Ahmed Ben Bella, *Jeune Afrique*, 26.9.90.

118 See *Le Monde*, 11.5.91; Anne Dissez: 'Les partis "democrates": l'impossible coalition', *Les Cahiers de L'Orient*, no. 23 (1991), p. 100. Ben Bella was later to deny he issued such a call claiming that his relationship with the FIS was "not good". *SWB* ME/1072 A/12, 15.5.91.

119 Dissez, 'Les partis "democrates" ', p. 100.

120 The actual figures for MDA support in the two polls were 0.7% and 1.98% respectively. *Algérie Actualité*, 9.5.91 and 30.5.91.

focus of the rally in December 1990 had been to protest against the government's plans to expand its Arabisation programme. Thus whilst galvanising significant support within Berber areas, particularly Kabylia, it looked unlikely that the FFS could attract enough support on its own to challenge the two major parties.[121]

Given the shortcomings of the FFS and the MDA, the most viable alternative for those Algerians who were not Islamist and were opposed to the government was the construction of some form of united front for the secular opposition parties. Such an attempt was made in 1990-91 by some of the largest opposition parties and various smaller parties that had fought separately against each other in the June 1990 elections, to form an alliance for the upcoming legislative elections.

Seven parties participated in this initiative with the hope that an eighth, the FFS, would also join them. However, this "Group of Eight", as it became known, gradually broke up as differences of policy, strategy and personality emerged to frustrate efforts to create a coalition of the parties. The inclusion of the well-supported FFS as part of the group was clearly crucial to its success but despite an extended courtship this was never achieved. One of the main reasons for this was undoubtedly the presence of the RCD within the coalition which drew its main base of support from the same source as the FFS – the Kabyle Berbers. The RCD had attracted the bulk of the Kabyle vote that had not responded to Hocine Ait Ahmed's boycott call in June 1990. Despite drawing on the same base of support there was considerable rivalry and even hostility between the two parties. Many of the supporters of the RCD, including its leader Said Saadi, had originally been members of the much older FFS which had been established by the charismatic Hocine Ait Ahmed in his native Kabylia in 1963 when the wartime FLN had broken into warring factions in the aftermath of independence. The RCD was essentially a product of the events in Kabylia in the spring of 1980 (see Chapter Three). Ait Ahmed's failure to return to Algeria from exile at this important juncture had been heavily criticised by Saadi and his allies who went on to launch the RCD in the wake of October 1988. For his part, the

---

121 The concentration of the FFS's support was confirmed by the opinion poll published on 30 May 1991 which showed that 98% of the party's support came from just one of Algeria's four regions (the centre, which contained Kabylia). *Algérie Actualité*, 30.5.91.

leader of the FFS was extremely wary of the new party and suspected and accused it of collusion with the authorities as part of an official attempt to damage and split the popular FFS. It was this rivalry that prevented the FFS from committing itself to the "Democratic Alliance" and Said Saadi suspected that withdrawal of his party would be a condition for FFS participation in the alliance.

The inclusion of the MDA, which had an Islamist fringe, also created problems. Four MDA members started a hunger strike to protest at (amongst other things) the party's alliance with militantly secularist parties, such as the RCD, which, in their view, did not recognise Islam. A final stumbling block was the government's plans for the new electoral law revealed in the spring of 1991. This forced the parties to contemplate what stance they should adopt in the event of a second ballot producing a run-off between FIS and FLN candidates. For at least two of the parties, the PRA and the MAJD, the defeat of the corrupt governing party, the FLN, was imperative and thus, in such a situation, the opposition candidate, even if belonging to the FIS, must always be backed to remove the government.[122] The militant secularism of the RCD compelled it, in contrast, to back any candidate capable of defeating the Islamists of the FIS which it saw as a far greater threat to Algeria than the FLN. Such a fundamental division on strategy and who the main enemy of the proposed alliance should be, therefore seemed to ensure that a common front between the parties could not be achieved.

The continued failure of the secular opposition parties to attract significant amounts of support away from the FLN and particularly the FIS (opinion polls revealed that even combined support for these parties was still well below that for either of the two major parties) was due to their own failure to attract the core of the Algerian electorate: the poor and unemployed. For Ahmed Rouadjia, their essential constituency was rather different and largely " . . . confined to the narrow universe of the cultured 'petite bourgeoisie' of the big cities".[123] Thus the FIS was free to

---

122   PRA – Parti du Renouveau Algérien; MAJD – Mouvement Algérien pour la Justice et le Dévelopment. Ironically, the MAJD was lead by the former FLN Prime Minister (1988–89), Kasdi Merbah, who had primarily formed the MAJD to combat his former party whose failings he now bitterly denounced.

123   Ahmed Rouadjia, 'Le FIS: à l'épreuve des élections legislatives', Les Cahiers de l'Orient, no. 23 (1991), p. 76.

gather up the support of the populous bottom ends of Algerian society whose opposition to the regime was clear. The FLN continued to exploit the extensive networks of patronage within the state enterprises and institutions. The opposition parties were also unable or unwilling to use their more educated constituency to construct viable alternative programmes for the governing of Algeria, a fact that was often ignored by those commentators who accused the FIS of lacking a political and economic programme of any real substance.

Conclusions

The year that stretched from the party's victories in the local elections in June 1990 through to the crackdown on its activities the following June witnessed the FIS taking centre stage in the unfolding drama of Algeria's ambitious programme of political reform. Whilst a strong showing had been expected from the party in the local elections, the scale of their triumph had not, which had meant that attention had been more widely focused on other parties and actors. The achievement of 55% of the vote signified to everyone that the FIS was the clearest beneficiary of the political reform programme and thus stood the greatest chance of wielding most political power following future national and presidential elections.

It was this prospect of real political power that animated both the internal and external dynamics of the FIS in the period 1990-91. Abassi Madani became convinced, in the wake of June 1990, that the party's primary objective must be the achievement of maximum political power through the ballot box with all other considerations making way for this greater goal. This explains both the FIS's populist swing towards backing Saddam Hussein during the Gulf War and its precipitation of the crisis of May–June 1991. The first was necessary to ensure that the party retained its mass electoral following and the second was viewed as essential to prevent the regime effectively blocking the party's path to political power through changes to the electoral law. In pursuing such a strategy, Abassi Madani exposed rifts between himself and those in the FIS who did not see the achievement of political power through elections as the primary objective of the FIS. Several senior Islamist figures had argued at the time of the FIS's creation that the party should primarily concern itself with the traditional Islamist goals of religious preaching and teaching rather than with politics. One of these figures, Mohammed Kerrar, subsequently explained that this proposal had been defeated by younger, more radical figures who favoured the idea that the party should aim to exercise political power.[124] These dissenting figures nevertheless joined the party, clearly hoping to influence its direction. The crisis of mid-1991 brought these differences to the surface once again, with another of Abassi's sternest critics during the crisis, Ahmed Merrani, arguing that the FIS had still been originally created to participate in party-political competition as a vehicle for propagating the Islamist movement's ideas rather than with the objective of actually taking political power.[125] The expulsion of both Kerrar and Merrani from the FIS in July 1991 was final testimony to the victory of Abassi's belief in the primacy of the political over the purely religious in the strategy of the party.

For Abassi, victory rather than mere influence was the essential aim and ultimate prize for the party. Whilst he may well have been motivated in part by personal ambition, it was notable that firstly, his policy was the one carried through and, more importantly, enthusiastically backed by the party's rank and file on the streets. Secondly, it was his allies that were victorious in the struggle for the party's leadership against those who sought to return the party to a more narrow and religiously hardline agenda.

The spring of 1991 also witnessed the severing of the links and co-operation between the FIS and the presidency that had operated since January 1990. The precise effect that the crisis of May–June had had on the nature, structure and stance of the regime and its composite factions was not fully apparent in the immediate aftermath of the crisis. The use of force, however, in early June and more portentiously the re-entry of the ANP into the political scene, indicated that a new configuration was emerging (see Chapter Six). In the wake of the local elections, President Chadli Benjedid had correctly perceived the FIS to be the main threat to him, as was shown by the increasing pressure he put on the party in local government and ultimately in the amended electoral law of April 1991. It remained to be seen whether he would continue to perceive the FIS in this way following the comprehensive repression the party had suffered during June and July 1991.

---

124 Dévoluy and Duteil, *La Poudrière Algérienne*, p. 115.
125 Interview with Ahmed Merrani, *Le Figaro*, 12.1.92.

6

The Brink of Power: The FIS and the Legislative Elections, 1991–1992

The Political Scene, July–December 1991

The crisis of June 1991 created the greatest disturbance to the Algerian political landscape since October 1988, surpassing the fall-out emanating from the FIS's surprise victory in the local elections of June 1990. The crisis had a significant impact on both the Islamist movement and the regime and both sought to reorder and regroup themselves in the wake of the dramatic events of the summer.

The regime and the government: July–December 1991

The regime was generally acknowledged to have emerged from the crisis in a superior position to the FIS – given the repression the Islamist party had been subjected to – but events had also forced it to change and reconstitute itself. The fall of Mouloud Hamrouche's government at the height of the crisis in early June and the appointment of Sid Ahmed Ghozali in his place brought to an end Hamrouche's twenty-month-old reformist administration. More fundamentally, it signified a further breach in the separation of the state from the FLN as a political party. Ghozali's new administration contained a large number of new and independent technocrats in preference to members of the FLN who were largely excluded from the new government. The breach with the former ruling party was finally and fully confirmed on 28 June when Chadli Benjedid resigned from the post of president of the FLN. These developments represented an attempt by Ghozali and Chadli to distance and disassociate themselves and the new government from the previous regime. The new Prime Minister, in particular, reinforced this impression by proceeding to verbally attack the FLN on every possible occasion.[1] It appeared that

---

1 See Charef, *Algérie: Le Grand Dérapage*, pp. 204–5.

the President had abandoned his attempts to transform the FLN into his own vehicle or "presidential party", believing that by appearing more consensual and independent he would possibly attract broader popular support.[2]

The image of independence that the regime wished to display, however, was belied by clear indications that Chadli had allied himself with other forces within the Algerian state. The exit of the overtly reformist Hamrouche and his replacement by Ghozali, who had played a significant role in the economic strategy of the Boumedienne era, indicated that more conservative forces had returned to the fore. Such forces were not, however, primarily constituted by the old enemies of Chadli's economic reforms in the FLN. The Algerian army's re-entry on to the political scene in early June 1991 to quell the street protests of the FIS had signalled its intent to at least have more of a say in political developments. It was the military that had primarily demanded the departure of Hamrouche as Prime Minister – for reasons of his perceived failure to manage the escalating crisis rather than through any antipathy to his programme of political and economic reforms[3] – and it was the military which began from the summer of 1991 to exercise more influence with the regime.

The ANP's primary concern with public order was reflected in the appointment of two senior generals to the two positions most closely associated with security. Khaled Nezzar became Defence Minister in July and Larbi Belkheir was appointed Interior Minister in October. However, despite this involvement in the government no attempt was made by the military to frustrate the political policy of the Ghozali administration. Having failed to persuade President Chadli to ban the FIS the military did not interfere with initiatives to restart the electoral programme that had been suspended following the disturbances of the summer. Despite his "Boumediennist" past, Sid Ahmed Ghozali and his government did

---

2   Roberts: 'From radical mission', pp. 469–70.
3   Yefsah, 'Armée et politique', p. 163n. Yefsah rightly dismisses suggestions that the army had primarily demanded Hamrouche's resignation because his anti-corruption initiatives had threatened some of its senior figures. Whilst this may have been a consideration, the desire to restore order on the streets and political stability was more important. (*Ibid.*, pp. 163–4) As Hamrouche was later to reveal (at the trial of the Abassi Madani and Ali Belhadj in July 1992) his dismissal as Prime Minister had immediately followed his expressed opposition to the decision to send the security forces into the areas occupied by the FIS's supporters.

much to display liberal and reformist credentials over the following months, casting some doubt on suggestions that the changes to the regime heralded a return to old-style Algerian politics. Two inter-party conferences were organised on 30 July and 24 August, supposedly to provide a forum for dialogue between the regime and the various political parties, in an effort to try to establish some consensus on the future course of Algeria's political development and reform. Although there was widespread scepticism about the aims and sincerity of these moves (the FFS boycotted the first conference and the FIS both – although dissident figures such as Mohammed Kerrar, Bachir Fakih and Ahmed Merrani attended) and the conferences achieved little consensus on the electoral law, they did result in an eventual declaration that the aborted legislative elections should take place before the end of the year.

It soon became apparent that both Ghozali and the presidency were intent on proceeding with the electoral programme. On 29 September the regime lifted the state of siege which had been declared in June – several days earlier than planned. This was seen as an indication on the part of the regime that it wished to return as swiftly as possible to the electoral process. Ghozali also embarked on a concerted attempt to reform the most controversial aspects of the electoral law of the previous April. September and October witnessed a fierce battle between the Prime Minister and the National Assembly, as the exclusively FLN-composed legislature sought to resist efforts to reduce the number of electoral constituencies, to remove the right of husbands to vote on behalf of their wives, and to make it easier for independent candidates to stand for election – all measures perceived by the APN to be hostile to FLN interests. Despite threats of resignation from Ghozali if the reforms were not endorsed, the new electoral law emerged from the Assembly on 13 October with few of the changes for which he had hoped. Constituency numbers were reduced from 542 to 430 (rather than to the preferred original number of 295) and there was no concession on the issue of proxy voting. In response to this relative failure, the Prime Minister attempted to get the presidency either to have the electoral bill put to a second reading or to organise a referendum on the subject. Chadli refused both requests and announced on 15 October that the first round of the legislative elections would take place on 26 December.[4] However,

---

4   The APN was so opposed to Ghozali's proposed reforms to the electoral law

Ghozali was subsequently comforted by the fact that the Constitutional Court, to whom Chadli had referred the proxy vote rule, ruled on 29 October that the rule was "null and void" on the grounds that it conflicted with other legal articles.

The intended place of the FIS in the regime's renewed commitment to the electoral process appeared initially uncertain. The government had made no indication of wishing to ban the FIS despite the comprehensive repression of the party in June and July. It gradually became apparent that having failed in its attempts to help the dissident members of the Majlis Shura win control of the party, the regime's new approach was to try and "build bridges" with the new leadership of the party whilst keeping the old leadership firmly under lock and key. This new policy was exemplified by Ghozali himself in an interview in which he sought to draw a distinction between the old and new leaderships of the FIS when questioned on the possible banning of the party:

> It is not a question of banning any party. We made clear the distinction between the party and certain of its leaders who have chosen a dead end.[5]

More tangible evidence of the policy was seen in August when Ghozali authorised the freeing of several hundred lower-ranking FIS militants arrested in June and made efforts to persuade employers to take back some of the 12,000 workers who had been sacked for responding to the FIS's strike call in May. No move, however, was made to release any of the of the party's more senior members and heavy publicity was

---

because many deputies felt that they would damage the electoral prospects of the FLN of which they were all still technically members. They were in favour of retaining the proxy vote because it was believed to work to the FLN's advantage in the deeply traditional south of Algeria where the party had performed strongly in 1990. Its support for a larger number of constituencies reflected its desire to retain the gerrymander of the original electoral law of April 1991 which created proportionately more electoral districts in the FLN-supporting areas. Despite the reduction in seat numbers eventually achieved by Ghozali, large disparities between electorates in various districts persisted. For example, the average electorate size in the southern Saharan wilayate of Illizi was 3,633 compared to that for Algiers which was 49,777 (there were similarly large figures for Oran and Constantine).

5   *El Moudjahid,* 18.7.91.

given to the discovery of 20,000 documents of an allegedly "subversive nature" found at a printing works at Blida and signed by Ali Belhadj.[6]

The government kept up attempts at dialogue with the FIS despite the refusal of new leadership of the party to take part in the two inter-party conferences in July and August. The minister responsible for the electoral law asserted in an interview in September that he had retained links with the party throughout the crisis and had contacts with both the old Majlis Shura and the new Provisional Executive Bureau (BEP).[7] It appeared that the regime was anxious that the FIS participate in the forthcoming elections to the National Assembly. In a clear concession to the party the authorities released Mohammed Said from prison on 7 December. A week earlier it had also released Abdelkader Hachani, the provisional leader of the FIS, who had been taken into custody by the authorities on 28 September. Hachani's release was viewed by one Algerian newspaper "as an appeal to the FIS to participate in the elections".[8]

These moves did not mean, however, that the new government was any better disposed towards the FIS than its predecessor. Ghozali had included in his new cabinet of technocrats and independents two women renown for their anti-Islamist views which, in Robert Mortimer's view, "served notice that he intended to preserve a liberal secular regime".[9] Nor was it implied that the regime would henceforth be more tolerant of Islamist violence and street activism. Periodic warnings were issued by the regime throughout the autumn of 1991 about the consequences of an attempted return by the FIS to the tactics of confrontation of the previous May and June. When President Chadli announced the date of the elections on 15 October, he stated that despite the continuation of the electoral process "neither the citizen nor the state will accept behaviour outside the constitution and the law."[10] Similarly, when the FIS announced its intention to hold a series of marches across Algeria on 6 December, Abdelkader Hachani was summoned to the Interior Ministry and warned of a possible bloodbath if the party went ahead with its plans.[11] This robust stance reflected the influence of the army on the government.

---

6 Ibid.
7 *Horizons*, 5.9.91.
8 *Algérie Actualité*, 13.2.92.
9 Mortimer, 'Islam and multiparty politics', p. 590.
10 *Financial Times*, 16.10.91.
11 All marches by political parties were in fact banned in the run-up to the election.

Having failed to persuade Chadli to ban the FIS in June–July 1991 and having gone along with his plans to proceed with the elections, Algeria's military chiefs were intent on seeing that the FIS could not repeat its challenge of the previous May and June. The appointment of General Larbi Belkheir as new Interior and Local Authorities Minister in October 1991, with responsibility for overseeing the elections, indicated this resolve on the part of the ANP, as did a law passed on 5 December which allowed the regional *wali* administrations to call upon the military in the event of a crisis.

None of these developments appeared to aim at explicitly discriminating against the FIS, merely to restrain its excesses, and the regime's commitment to continuing with the electoral process seemed uncompromised. Why the regime had retained this commitment and in particular why it was so anxious to secure the FIS's participation in the process, given the crisis of mid-1991, was a matter of some debate. Chadli and Ghozali continued to publicly express their belief in the virtue of persisting with democratisation. Ghozali's battles with the National Assembly over the electoral law and his stated view that "You either have 100 per cent democracy or zero per cent . . . You can't have exceptions to democracy", when questioned on FIS participation, appeared to bear witness to this conviction.[12]

The reality was that both men still adhered to the strategy of going ahead with the elections in the hope and expectation of an inconclusive result, with no single party achieving a majority. Such a result would allow the President (and possibly the Prime Minister[13]) to play the influential role of adjudicator and kingmaker. This divide and rule strategy was bolstered by the heightened prospect of a failure on the part of the FIS to secure a majority in the legislative elections. The disappointing opinion poll ratings for the FIS of earlier in the year (see Chapter Five) were confirmed by Chadli's own polls in the autumn of 1991, which continued to suggest that the FIS would not secure more than 30% of the vote. This, aided by the absence through imprisonment, of a large part of the party's leadership, encouraged the regime to believe that the FIS could be safely allowed to compete in the elections. As François Burgat comments:

---

12 *Financial Times*, 28.6.91.
13 There were suggestions that Ghozali harboured such ambitions for himself. See *Jeune Afrique*, 4.9.91.

The general staff and the chancelleries in Algiers seemed convinced that the elections were pushing towards that equilibrium that was the dream of all the leaders in the region: an Islamist party that was domesticated and whose integration in the institutional system would not call the political survival of the regime into question.[14]

Ghozali and Chadli were also convinced that the exclusion of the FIS, which was still clearly the most popular opposition party, from the electoral process would greatly undercut the perceived legitimacy of the elections and would provide the FIS with an excuse to adopt a more violent path of opposition to the regime.

It was therefore concluded by the regime that continuation with the elections on the broadest possible basis represented its best course of action. Such an approach was perceived as preferable to either the exclusion of the FIS or the abandonment or suspension of the process altogether in the wake of the June crisis, both of which would have led to violent confrontations with the Islamist movement.

The FIS July–December 1991

Recovery

The crisis of June 1991 affected the FIS far more than it had the regime. Despite the initial apparent victory of securing in the first week of June both the fall of the Hamrouche government and promised concessions on the electoral law and presidential elections, the subsequent crackdown by the army, culminating in the arrest and detention of Abassi Madani, Ali Belhadj and many of the party's senior figures, swept away any perceived earlier gains. The attendant splits in the party and the battle for its control during and immediately after the crisis had, in the eyes of both the regime and the other opposition parties, ended "the myth of the invulnerability of the FIS".[15]

Despite these significant reverses, the FIS was able to regroup itself effectively over the late summer. A conference was held at Batna at the end of July which gathered together the remaining members of the party's

---

14 Burgat and Dowell, *The Islamic Movement in North Africa*, p. 299.
15 *Jeune Afrique*, 11.9.91.

Majlis Shura with representatives from nearly all the regional BEWs. The meeting produced a decisive victory for the supporters of Abassi Madani over the dissenting voices in the party. Not only did the conference reaffirm the leadership of Abassi and Ali Belhadj and formally recognise Abdelkader Hachani as provisional leader, but it also succeeded in suspending and marginalising most of the leading dissidents. Having already formally expelled Ahmed Merrani and Bachir Fakih from the Majlis on 25 June following their appearance on national television, the Majlis confirmed at Batna the suspension of Benazouz Zebda, Hachemi Sahnouni and Mohammed Kerrar from the Majlis. The one remaining notable dissident, Said Guechi, escaped this fate but realising the direction that events were moving in, left the conference before its conclusion. This, together with the complete absence from the conference of Zebda and Sahnouni, gave Abdelkader Hachani and his allies the narrow majority they needed to achieve their aims.

In place of the excluded figures the party co-opted twelve new members onto the Majlis Shura as representatives from the regions.[16] These new members included, significantly, Mohammed Said (still at that time in official custody). Hachani characterised these changes as "strictly functional" but it was clearly an attempt to bolster his and his allies' majority on the party's ruling body.[17] Two close allies, Rabah Kebir and Othman Aissani, were appointed to senior positions within the party – Kebir becoming responsible for political affairs whilst Aissani became a new vice-president. The new additions to the leadership of the FIS represented a shift from the profile of the original leadership which had been characterised by predominantly older and essentially religious figures. The new leadership was notable for its relative youth (Hachani and Kebir were both under 40 years of age) and its high levels of education. In place of the pious outlook and priorities of many of the original founders of the party, figures such as Hachani and Rabah Kebir were to take a more pragmatic and political approach to the objectives

---

16 Part of the reason for the victory of Hachani and his allies during the conference had been the support given lent them by the regional representatives of the FIS. Their support had been deliberately courted by Hachani prior to the conference in order to outvote hostile elements in the Majlis Shura. Their support was further guaranteed by the fact that arrests of many FIS members had allowed Hachani to nominate new representatives.

17 Interview with Abdelkader Hachani, *Algérie Actualité*, 1.8.91.

of the FIS. Such an outlook placed them close to the line that had been adopted by Abassi Madani and indeed it was clear that the now imprisoned leader of the FIS had previously nurtured many of them as potential future leaders and allies. Contrary to the accusations of hostile critics none of these new figures belonged to the Jazara (most in fact being former members of Abdallah Djaballah's organisations) and Mohammed Said remained the only figure from the grouping to join the reconstituted Majlis Shura. Nevertheless, the post-Batna leadership of the FIS represented a consolidation of the alliance between the supporters of Abassi Madani and the Jazara – both supporters of a more pragmatic, political line.[18] Members of the Jazara came increasingly to the fore in the regional branches of the FIS, in particular, in the wake of the Batna conference, but their younger and better-educated orientation frequently made them indistinguishable from figures such as Hachani, Kebir and Aissani.

The new provisional leader of the party (who carried the official title of president of the BEP) worked hard over the weeks following the conclusion of the Batna conference to convince the party's grass roots that he and the new Majlis Shura remained loyal to the line of Abassi Madani and Ali Belhadj. This together with the recuperation that the party as a whole was undergoing in the aftermath of the events of June, meant that nationally the FIS kept a very low profile throughout the summer of 1991.

By the beginning of the autumn, the FIS had sufficiently recovered itself to begin to look outwards again and it rapidly became apparent that although the leadership of the party may have received a severe blow during the crisis of the previous spring, the base of the party's activist support remained intact. Over the following months the FIS was able to demonstrate its continued ability to mobilise large numbers of its supporters. Within a week of the lifting of the state of siege on 29 September, the FIS staged a rally at the 20th August Stadium in Algiers which was attended by "scores of thousands" of people. Four weeks later on 1 November an estimated 300,000 participated in a march held by the party through the capital.[19]

---

18 In supporting a more political line the Jazarists seemed to be deviating from the apoliticism of their intellectual mentor, Malek Bennabi. However, this shift could be explained by either the group's pragmatism or its antipathy to salafyism.

19 *Jeune Afrique* 20.11.91

The debate over participation

The impressive displays of strength by the FIS in the autumn of 1991, however, concealed an intense debate and uncertainty within the new leadership of the party over future strategy. Central to this debate was the response the party should adopt to the government's apparent determination to continue with the electoral process. Initially, in the immediate wake of the June crisis, the FIS's rejection of the regime's invitation to the government–party conferences of 30 July and 24 August seemed inevitable and understandable given the recent crackdown on the party and the imprisonment of its leaders. It branded the conferences as disingenuous attempts on the part of the regime "to retrieve its lost credibility".[20] However, as time progressed and as the FIS was not officially banned, the state of siege was lifted and Ghozali made plain his desire for the FIS to participate in the elections, the party faced more of a dilemma over whether it should respond to the Prime Minister's overtures and announce its participation in the elections.

Abdelkader Hachani had publicly reaffirmed the FIS's commitment to the electoral route to power by stating in August: "We can not arrive in power other than through free and proper elections."[21] However, he and the new leadership of the party made clear their conditions for rejoining the electoral process. Whilst initial demands included the lifting of the state of siege and the reappointment of workers sacked for their participation in the FIS-organised general strike of the previous May, the central demand was and remained the release of Madani, Belhadj and the other senior leaders of the movement. This primary precondition for participation was continually restated whenever the question of FIS involvement in the elections was raised. Moreover, Hachani stated that the party would not only boycott the elections but would also "exert every available means, within the framework of the law, so that there will be no elections".[22]

The determination to prevent the holding of the elections if pre-conditions were not met revealed the nature of the dilemma the FIS

---

20 FIS communiqué quoted in Lavenue, *Algérie: La Democratie Interdite*, p. 163. The FIS also suspected that Ghozali had organised the conferences with the intention of opening up the divisions within the party.

21 Interview with Abdelkader Hachani, *Algérie Actualité*, 1.8.91.

22 John P. Entelis and Lisa J. Arone, 'Algeria in turmoil: democracy and the state', *Middle East Policy*, vol. 1 (1992), p. 33n.

faced – in view of the government's determination to proceed with the elections even in the event of a FIS boycott. Neither boycott nor participation represented satisfactory stances for the party. Participation without securing concessions from the regime would appear like compromised capitulation and weakness, whilst a boycott risked marginalisation for the party and possibly invited repression from the regime which could portray the party as being in reality anti-democratic. Amongst the leaders, Rabah Kebir believed that Ghozali's overtures towards the FIS were not genuine and that in reality the Prime Minister hoped for a boycott by the FIS:

> The government pretended that it wanted everyone to join the elections and it did not want it to seem that the FIS was excluded. If the FIS did not participate in the elections it wanted it to appear that it was the FIS's fault.[23]

The debate over participation was played out within the leadership of the party with more detailed strategic and tactical considerations being raised on both sides. Those who favoured participation argued that it offered the ultimate prize of political power. Since it appeared that the FIS's essentially urban support had remained solid, they argued, this would be able to provide the party with, at the very least, a significant voice in the new National Assembly and might even be sufficient to secure an absolute majority. Furthermore, it was argued that failure to participate would result in the FIS's support shifting, perhaps irretrievably, to the other smaller Islamist parties such as HAMAS and the MNI who intended to run candidates in the election.[24]

Such a view was disputed by those within the leadership who feared that support had already begun to slip towards the other Islamist parties and that this, together with the adverse impact of the June crisis, would mean that the achievement of a majority by the FIS was an unrealistic scenario. Being simply the largest party was not to be seen as an advance for the Islamist cause, as Hamza Kaida observed of the opponents of participation:

---

23 Author's interview with Rabah Kebir, 27.9.95.
24 See interview with Rabah Kebir, *Algérie Actualité*, 31.10.91, quoted in Lavenue, *Algérie: La Democratie Interdite*, p. 126.

For them, an electoral failure is not to be dismissed. It would be fatal, for it would strike the FIS at its base, constituted by activists mobilised by their rejection of the system, and would make the movement an ordinary opposition party. In abstaining to participate in the elections, the FIS would continue, instead, to channel discontent and would nullify the results because of the poor turnout . . . [25]

Whilst this debate continued, attempts were made to win concessions from the regime. Concessions were of particular importance to those within FIS who backed participation and who saw them as a means of strengthening their case in the internal debate within the party. On 7 September Abassi Madani, Ali Belhadj and the six other senior imprisoned FIS leaders embarked on a short hunger strike in an ultimately unrewarded effort to pressurise the authorities, through the fear of creating martyrs, to release them or at least have themselves accorded the status of political prisoners.[26] A second attempt to win concessions took the form of trying to persuade the government to let the imprisoned leaders appear before a civilian rather than a military court. President Chadli appeared at one time to hint that this might be possible and that the leaders might even be released following a deliberately public and humiliating admonishment in front of the court, but no concessions were eventually achieved on the issue.

The FIS leadership proved anxious to portray itself as operating within the law during this time. This was demonstrated by Hachani's statement quoted earlier about preventing the holding of the elections by using "every available means, *within the framework of the law*". Such an approach was designed not only to persuade the regime to make some form of goodwill gesture, but also to avoid giving the regime and the army any excuse to crack down on the party. On 20 September, Hachani stated that FIS activists would not respond to provocation, having disavowed violence and actions that might undermine security.[27] A week later when Hachani himself was arrested by the authorities following Friday prayers at the Bab El-Oued mosque, the loudspeakers

---

25 *Jeune Afrique*, 20.11.91.
26 The hunger strike was eventually called off following the visit of a religious delegation who advised the prisoners to abandon the strike.
27 See *SWB* ME/1184 A/16, 23.9.91.

at the mosque appealed to worshippers not to respond to provocation from the heavy police and army presence around the area.

In spite of the attempts at and displays of restraint on the part of the FIS, Madani and Belhadj remained in custody. With no public concessions to justify their participation, the FIS continued to decline to join in the electoral process even after the campaign for the first ballot for the National Assembly formally commenced on 5 December. Then, on 14 December, just twelve days before voting was due to take place the party issued a statement declaring:

> To take a step towards the establishment of an Islamic state . . . the FIS will take part in the forthcoming legislative elections.[28]

The decision demonstrated that the ongoing debate within the FIS had been resolved, but it was uncertain what, at this late stage, had decisively shifted the debate within the party. It was clear that the arrangement of forces on either side of the debate over participation was not a random affair and continued to reflect the divisions in the FIS that had first come to light in the aftermath of the June crisis.

Ironically – given the closeness with which the debate over participation echoed that which had occurred in the party over the general strike in May – it was Abdelkader Hachani and his allies who pushed for participation. The explanation for this paradox lay in the fact that whilst Hachani and new senior figures in the leadership such as Rabah Kebir and Othman Aissani had supported Abassi Madani's overall political and electoral strategy, they were even more pragmatically inclined than the official leader of the FIS and recognised that the tactic of confrontation had clearly failed in May and June.[29] Against Hachani and his allies was ranged a considerable rump within the party's Majlis Shura which remained supportive of many of the more traditional and religiously

---

28 *Guardian*, 16.12.91.

29 The provisional leadership of the party was in contact with the original imprisoned leadership, through lawyers and family visitors. However, whilst it is known that the imprisoned leadership was divided on the issue of participation in the elections, the exact opinions of Abassi and Belhadj are unknown. Once the party had announced it was joining the elections senior figures such as Abdelkader Moghni claimed that both men backed the decision. See *Jeune Afrique* 9.1.92; Charef, *Algérie: Le Grand Dérapage*, p. 234.

radical views which had suffered a substantial defeat at Batna. Despite the expulsion of some of the leading figures in this tendency, this grouping was still influential, particularly with elements of the party's rank and file. Their opposition to participation in the elections was due as much to their hostility to the new leadership of the FIS and the increased influence of the Jazara as to any of the more tactical arguments they advanced.

The final decisive shift in the debate over participation came with the release by the authorities of both Hachani and Mohammed Said within a week of each other in October–November. This development (as the Ghozali government clearly intended) not only reintroduced two powerful voices for participation back into the internal debate within the party, but also gave Hachani, in particular, much greater weight and credibility within the FIS as someone who had suffered for the party. Throughout November and early December, as well as embarking on a campaign to persuade the party, Hachani remained in contact with the regime as he made public and private hints that the FIS would compete in the elections in an effort to induce further concessions from the authorities. It was also notable that, following his release, Hachani refrained from repeating the FIS's call for early presidential elections. In response to these overtures, the FIS's two main newspapers, *El Mounqid* and *Al Forkane*, banned since August, were allowed by the authorities to publish again on 18 November.

It was evident, even before the official announcement on 14 December, that Hachani had already decided that, even without the achievement of the central concession of the release of Abassi, Belhadj and the other imprisoned leaders, the FIS should participate in the elections. The party had selected candidates for all 430 constituencies to be contested in the election in advance of any other party and at a rally on 6 December Hachani had spoken of the achievement of an Islamic state through the ballot box.[30] The holding of the December rally itself represented evidence of the defeat of the faction within the FIS which was deeply opposed to participation. Hachani's decision to hold a rally in preference to the planned march, following the warning by the Interior Ministry

---

30 The FIS had actually submitted Abassi Madani, Ali Belhadj and its other imprisoned leaders as candidates for the election and as possible means of putting pressure on the government. However, their candidatures were officially rejected on the grounds that candidates had to register in person.

of bloody consequences if a march took place, marked a rejection of the hardline alternative to participation which favoured confrontation with the regime on the streets.

The militant fringe

There was evidence during late 1991 which suggested that parts of the Islamist movement, including FIS members, had already begun to turn to more violent alternatives to participation. The weeks preceding the declaration by the FIS that it would enter the elections witnessed a number of violent incidents involving Islamists. Political opponents of the FIS suffered attacks from Islamists. Ahmed Ben Bella had his meetings disrupted by stone-throwing Islamists and on 1 November Islamist militants attacked a residence of the FLN where the ex-Prime Minister Mouloud Hamrouche was holding a meeting.[31]

Far more serious was a spate of related incidents that occurred on Algeria's eastern borders at the end of November. Beginning with exchanges of gunfire with militants in the El Oued region following discoveries by the police of significant caches of arms, these incidents culminated in an attack by an estimated sixty armed Islamists on a border post at Guemmar on 29 November, resulting in the deaths of three policemen. These events, which the government claimed were indications of a planned and widespread Islamist terror campaign against the state, were acknowledged to have been instigated by Aissa Messaoudi, also known as Tayeb al Afghani, whom the police had been seeking to hunt down. Although, as his *nomme de guerre* suggested, Messaoudi was connected with the extremist wing of the Islamist movement involving Afghan veterans in groups such as Takfir wa Hijra (see previous chapters) which were not controlled by the FIS, there were indications that Messaoudi did, in fact, have connections with the FIS. Several captured members of Messaoudi's group made dubious televised "confessions" in which they claimed to belong to the FIS, but it was separately established that Messaoudi himself was an active member of the FIS trade union – the SIT.[32]

---

31 Hugh Roberts suggests, perhaps improbably, that these attacks were orchestrated by Ghozali and Chadli to sabotage the electoral chances of both the MDA and the FIS. Roberts, 'From Radical Mission', p. 473.

32 The authorities claimed to have finally wiped out the group following an attack by the security forces on 9 December.

Despite the regime's ongoing efforts at this time to persuade the FIS to participate in the elections, much was made by the authorities of this link to the party. The Defence Minister, Khaled Nezzar, appeared on television to accuse the FIS publicly of being directly or indirectly involved – a charge both the FIS and the SIT were quick to rebut, claiming that it would not serve the party's interests to be involved in attempts at violent insurrection.[33] Abdelkader Hachani reasserted the legalist line of the FIS stating: "Violence is not part of our methods. The FIS operates inside the law."[34] Nevertheless, the provisional leader of the FIS was clearly unsettled by the incident and was concerned at the possibility that the regime might use it as an excuse to act against the party. In an effort to head off any such moves, Hachani argued that "You don't punish the whole family for the misdemeanours of some members" – a statement that appeared to implicitly acknowledge FIS involvement in the incidents.[35]

The incidents in the El Oued region were not the only testimony to the existence of a section of the FIS that dissented from the FIS's official overall strategy of participating in elections. The Batna conference of July witnessed the exclusion not only of those individuals who had attempted rapprochement with the regime, but also of two members, Said Mekhloufi and Kameredine Kherbane, who had in contrast advocated a more confrontational approach to the authorities. At the beginning of 1991, Mekhloufi had published and distributed a pamphlet entitled "Principles and Objectives of Civil Disobedience". As well as promoting civil disobedience, Mekhloufi and his pamphlet implicitly criticised the whole "democratic" electoralist strategy of the FIS by asserting amongst other things that "The point of view of the majority has not any value" and "It is not the opinion of the majority which represents truth and justice, but God." He indicated that more direct methods should be employed by Islamists to force the regime to relinquish power.[36] He was publicly criticised by Abassi Madani at the time, but it was not until the opportunity of the Batna conference six months later that supporters of

---

33   See BBC African World Service News, 9.12.91; *Jeune Afrique*, 11.12.91.
34   Charef, *Algérie: Le Grand Dérapage*, p. 221.
35   BBC African World Service News, 10.12.91. Hachani had initially tried to suggest that the incidents may have been the result of an intra-army feud.
36   Charef, *Algérie: Le Grand Dérapage*, p. 190. For a fuller treatment of Mekhloufi and the contents of his pamphlet see *ibid.*, pp. 189–95.

the electoral strategy were able to oust Mekhloufi and his close ally Kherbane from the Majlis Shura. It was notable that although neither Mekhloufi nor Kherbane were directly linked to the incidents that were to occur later in the year, both, like Aissa Messaoudi, had served as volunteers in the war in Afghanistan.

The First Ballot: 26 December 1991

The FIS campaign
Despite its late entry into the electoral contest, the FIS worked in the twelve remaining days before the first ballot to ensure that the party would attract a maximum level of support. The party fielded candidates of an unusually high level of education (a quarter of them had postgraduate qualifications[37]) and fought a highly professional campaign, opting for lower-profile activities such as door-to-door canvassing and continuing its social action programmes in the poor areas to attract support. Sermons in mosques were used to get across the party message rather than the more usual medium of mass rallies. Particular attention was focused on the multitudinous young urban unemployed, who frequently made up 60% of their age group and whose desperation at the still declining socio-economic conditions in Algeria and disillusion with the regime could be turned, as it had in June 1990, into votes for the FIS. The FIS also continued to make much of the revealed corruption of the ruling FLN.[38]

---

37 The FIS fielded more postgraduate educated than any of the other parties contesting the election. This was a result of the accession of Abdelkader Hachani and his allies to the leadership who favoured younger, well-educated candidates like themselves. There were said to be a large number of members of the Jazara amongst the candidates. For details on the education levels of the parties' candidates see Fawzi Rouziek, 'Algérie 1990–1993: La démocratie confisquée?' in Pierre Robert Baduel (ed.), L'Algérie Incertaine (Paris, Edisud, 1994), p. 43. For details on the backgrounds of FIS candidates fielded in Algiers see Séverine Labat, Les Islamistes Algériens, p. 123.

38 The FLN, in response, portrayed itself throughout the campaign as a "hostage" of the political system and claimed that itself, as a party, had been the true initiator of political reforms after 1988.

The results

When the results of the 26 December poll began to appear it once more became apparent that the hopes and expectations of the regime and the other parties, that the FIS would struggle to get more than 35% of the vote, were woefully misplaced. For the second time in eighteen months the FIS triumphed massively. The party took over 47% of the total votes cast, even further ahead of its nearest rival – once again the FLN, which secured less than 24% of the vote – than it had been in 1990. No other single party succeeded in winning more than 10% of the votes cast. Indeed, it appeared that the voting patterns of the local elections had persisted at the national level: the FIS totally dominating the urban north (taking over 50% of the vote in Algiers, Constantine and Oran and most other large towns[39]); the FLN performing best in the large southern Saharan wilayate; and the wilayate of the Kabyle rejecting both the FIS and the FLN and voting for a third party – this time Ait Ahmed's FFS.[40]

What made this victory even more comprehensive than these voting percentages suggested, was the number of seats in the new National Assembly the FIS had been able to secure. It rapidly became clear, as the results were announced, that the electoral system, despite the efforts of the outgoing FLN-dominated Assembly, had dramatically favoured the main Islamist party. Of the 430 seats contested 231 were won outright in this first ballot by candidates who had been able to win 50% or more of the vote in their individual constituencies. The remaining 199, where no single candidate had achieved a majority, were to proceed to a decisive second ballot to be contested by the leading two candidates from the first ballot. It was a shock to everyone in Algeria, perhaps even to the FIS itself, when it was revealed that the FIS had won no fewer than 188 of the 231 seats decided at the first ballot. For the FLN, which the system had supposedly favoured, the outcome of the election in terms of seats was a disaster: the party secured just 16 seats outright. This was less than

---

39 The FIS received shares of the vote of 58%, 62% and 65% in Algiers, Oran and Constantine respectively.

40 For voting statistics see Keith Sutton and Ahmed Aghrout, 'Multiparty elections in Algeria: problems and prospects', *Bulletin of Francophone Africa*, no. 2 (Autumn 1992), pp. 76–7. Full and comprehensive voting statistics of the results were, however, never fully published. Only those relating to successful or near-successful (that is, proceeding to the second ballot) were fully released. Sutton and Aghrout, p. 65.

the FFS, which had managed to scoop 25 and which had the second highest tally behind the massive gains of the FIS. No other party managed to win a seat outright – the only other seats decided by the first ballot were three gained by independent candidates.

The results also made it clear that all the factors suggested in the period since the 1990 elections to indicate that the FIS would fail to hold onto the support it had garnered in those elections, had proved to be of little significance. The return of the parties who had boycotted the 1990 polls had little effective impact. Hocine Ait Ahmed's FFS had managed to attract over 500,000 votes and had even beaten the FLN into third place in Algiers, buts its votes were still heavily concentrated in the Kabyle and came overwhelmingly from those who had either abstained or voted for the RCD in 1990.[41] Ahmed Ben Bella's MDA won a derisory 2% of the popular vote. Similarly, the much vaunted incursion of the smaller Islamist parties into the FIS's vote was in the event marginal: Mahfoud Nahnah's HAMAS took 5.4% to the MNI's 2.2%.[42] The supposed mobilisation of women – freed by the abandonment of the procuration vote rule against the "threat" the FIS posed to women's rights similarly never materialised. Despite the FIS's strong backing for the retention of the procuration rule (Hachani having described its abandonment as "in reality a development for the worse"[43]) it actually appeared not to hinder and possibly aided the party. In traditional areas where, regardless of political or religious views, women voting was frowned upon, one Algerian journalist noted that the only women voting in any numbers on polling day were those from FIS-supporting households.[44] It appeared that the FIS instructed its supporters to ensure that all their female relatives went to the polling booths.[45] The much highlighted failings of the FIS-run local councils also seemed to have made no effective difference as voters clearly continued to blame their

---

41 Over half of the FFS's vote came from the Kabyle wilaya of Tizi Ouzou and Bejaia alone. The party performed relatively well in Algiers mainly because of the significant Kabyle Berber population in the capital.

42 The FIS even managed to secure five times the vote of HAMAS in Blida, the hometown and stronghold of HAMAS's leader, Mahfoud Nahnah.

43 *El Moudjahid*, 9.9.91.

44 *Algérie Actualité*, 2.1.92.

45 The abandonment of the procuration rule undoubtedly contributed to the overall fall in turnout. Many women were not permitted, or more likely not able, to take time to vote.

declining social and economic well-being on the central government. Once again the FIS had done particularly well in those areas of Algeria that were most disadvantaged.[46]

The implications

The results of the 26 December ballot clearly had profound implications for the political future. Having won 188 (nearly 44%) of the seats in the first round of voting, the FIS needed to win just 28 out of the remaining 199 seats to be contested in the second round of voting to achieve an absolute majority in the new National Assembly. Given that it was the leading party in 144 (and was the challenging party in another 43) of these remaining seats, it also seemed entirely feasible that the FIS eventually could win the 99 seats required to give it a two-thirds majority in the Assembly which it could use to press for changes to the Constitution. Furthermore, in the likely event that supporters of HAMAS and the MNI in the first round would cast their votes for FIS candidates in the second round, Keith Sutton and Ahmed Aghrout have estimated that the main Islamist party would sweep two-thirds of the remaining seats.[47] Had supporters of the two smaller Islamist parties voted for their larger cousin in the first round the FIS would have achieved 55% (a majority) of all the votes cast – a percentage that almost exactly equalled that gained by the party in June 1990.[48] Overall, as Sutton and Aghrout conclude:

---

46 For a detailed analysis of the relationship between social and economic disadvantage and support for the FIS see Jacques Fontaine, 'Quartiers défavorisés et vote Islamiste à Alger' in Pierre Robert Baduel (ed.), *L'Algérie Incertaine* (Paris, Edisud, 1994).

47 Sutton and Aghrout, 'Multiparty elections in Algeria', p. 66. On the issue of whether the other Islamist parties' leaderships would have encouraged their supporters to vote for the FIS in the second round, Abdallah Djaballah, leader of the MNI, claimed that no such decision was taken because he believed that the electoral process would be aborted before a second round could be held. Author's interview with Abdallah Djaballah, London, 7.10.94. Nevertheless, Djaballah, despite failing to win a seat in the first ballot, was prominent in calling for the results of the election to be respected – forming a committee and even writing to the President to achieve this end.

48 Exact parallels with 1990 are, however, misleading. Due to a lower turnout in 1991, the combined vote for the three Islamist parties was still nearly half-a-million votes lower than that achieved by the FIS eighteen months earlier. Nevertheless, it was interesting to note that on both occasions Islamists appeared to attract a near identical share of the vote.

As the FIS were within 5% of an overall majority in many of the undecided seats, any result other than a FIS government after January 16th (the date fixed for the second ballot) seemed very unlikely.[49]

Reactions to the Ballot:
December 1991–January 1992

The secular opposition

For the secular opposition the elections had once again demonstrated their failure to break the dominance of the FIS and the FLN at the ballot box. Between them they had taken only just over 20% of the vote (if the figures for HAMAS and the MNI are excluded) and won just 28 seats. Once again it appeared that these parties' discourses had had little influence on the mass of illiterate young who constituted so much of the electorate. The reactions to their relative failure and the massive gains of the FIS varied considerably between the parties.

For several of the secular opposition parties it appeared imperative that the electoral process must now be suspended and the second round of voting cancelled to prevent the FIS achieving a majority in the new National Assembly. Foremost among parties taking this line was the RCD which had won less than 3% of the vote in the elections (and thus could be seen as having nothing to lose) and the communist PAGS. Both parties, which had applauded the June crackdown by the authorities against the FIS, clearly saw the threat a FIS majority posed to their own militantly secularist vision of Algeria as a far greater evil than the suspension of the electoral process.[50] Working with other similar-minded groups and parties such as Kasdi Merbah's MAJD, the UGTA, various women's associations and elements of the League of Human Rights (LADH), "Committees for the Support of Republican Algeria" were created to call for the abandonment of the second ballot.[51] The first communiqué of the national Conseil National de Sauvegarde de l'Algérie (CNSA) declared, "It is improbable that democracy will be saved by those who denounce

---

49 Sutton and Aghrout, 'Multiparty elections in Algeria', p. 66.
50 The PAGS had always opposed the legalisation of parties based on religion.
51 These committees almost certainly had the backing of senior figures in the establishment.

it [the FIS]."[52] Said Saadi, the leader of the RCD, called for strikes, demonstrations and the use of "any means, including violence" to prevent the holding of the second round of voting which he claimed would "bury Algeria . . . It would condemn us to chaos."[53] A similar line was adopted by Abdelhak Benhamouda, leader of the UGTA, who declared:

> We are legalists, but if the institutions do not fulfil their functions, it is our duty to resist and to participate in all initiatives aimed at countering the advance of the Islamists.[54]

A different line, however, was taken by the largest and most successful secular opposition party in the elections, the FFS. Its leader, Hocine Ait Ahmed, called on the day after the first ballot for the continuation of the electoral process. Despite being as politically opposed to the agenda of the FIS as most of the other parties, he argued against annulment of the elections stating that: "A crisis of democracy cannot be solved other than through more democracy."[55] Accordingly, his strategy to block the likely FIS victory in the second round was to mobilise the "democratic camp" and ensure that it turned out in maximum numbers to vote in the deciding 199 second ballots. An impressive rally and "March for the Defence of Democracy" was organised by the FFS together with the LADH and women's associations, and was attended by an estimated 300,000 people on 2 January. At the rally Ait Ahmed called for the mobilisation of the 6.3 million Algerians who had abstained or spoilt their papers in the first ballot. Together with the fact that the FIS's total vote had fallen by 1.2 million since 1990 it was highlighted that over three-quarters of the electorate had *not* voted for the FIS on December 26 and thus could potentially be mobilised.[56]

---

52   *Algérie Actualité*, 30.12.92.
53   *Daily Telegraph*, 2.1.92; *Financial Times*, 2.1.92.
54   *Jeune Afrique.* 24.1.92.
55   Lamchichi, *L'Islamisme en Algérie*, p. 84. Ait Ahmed also argued that it was essential to proceed with the elections in order "to avoid civil war". Charef, *Algérie: Le Grand Dérapage*, p. 247.
56   There was an unusually high number of spoilt ballot papers from the first poll, 924,906, which was almost certainly due to the complicated nature of the ballot paper itself. Hugh Roberts argues that this complexity was deliberately contrived by Larbi Belkheir to sabotage the FIS's vote. Roberts, 'From radical mission', p. 475.

The leader of the FFS also alleged that over 900,000 polling cards had not been distributed before the election, thus disenfranchising a significant 10% of the electorate. For some this and other irregularities on polling day held out hope that a legal block to the FIS's advance could be found. In all, 341 complaints about irregularities in individual constituencies had been lodged with the Constitutional Council which had the power to annul and rerun elections in individual constituencies if the complaints were upheld. The majority of such complaints (174) came from the FLN which made a variety of allegations of malpractice against the FIS. It was alleged that the FIS had used intimidation and impersonation as well as arbitrary disqualifications of voters by its local council officials, who were responsible for the running of the ballots, in attempts to maximise their vote and minimise that of their opponents. Although some of the FLN's complaints (against, for example the FIS's provision of transport to the polling booths) were rather spurious, the fact that the local councils, most of which were controlled by the FIS, were in charge of the electoral process inevitably gave potential substance to the allegations.[57] It was also alleged, with undoubted justification in certain areas, that FIS-controlled councils struck off election lists the names of voters who had abstained in 1990 and that the failure to distribute the 900,000 polling cards, the supposed duty of local authorities, was also a deliberate tactic by the FIS.[58] Other parties including the MAJD and the FFS complained that the FIS had made use of fraudulent ballot papers and deliberately misrecorded votes to aid their victory.[59] Nevertheless, despite the large number of complaints lodged with the Constitutional Council, it was unlikely that a sufficient number would have been upheld to make an effective difference to the FIS's tally of seats.[60] As Jean-Jacques Lavenue observes, the legal paths to blocking the FIS were largely wishful thinking on the part of their advocates:

---

57   See *El Moudjahid*, 22.1.92.

58   See *Financial Times*, 2.1.92; Charef, *Algérie: Le Grand Dérapage*, p. 239.

59   It was alleged that the FIS were able to overcome the obstacle of having significant numbers of illiterate supporters by using an initial false ballot paper. This would be filled in by the party beforehand, then given to the supporter who would use it to vote with and who would then bring back the legitimate paper he had been given, so that the party could fill it out for the next illiterate supporter who would repeat the process. See Charef, *Algérie: Le Grand Dérapage*, p. 237.

60   In refusing to overturn the results of the first ballot, the Constitutional Court

... it rapidly became apparent that neither the annulment of the disputed results, nor the mobilisation of the first-round abstainers ... would probably be sufficient to prevent the FIS from obtaining a majority in the second round.[61]

The FIS between the ballots

The comprehensive nature of the FIS's victory in the first ballot and the virtual certainty of the party achieving a majority at the second ballot (and, through that, its first taste of national political power) excited the party and clearly vindicated all those who had argued for participation in the elections. Whilst delight and exuberant expectation at the prospect of power were evident amongst the FIS's rank and file in the wake of the results of the 26 December vote, the party's leadership was more restrained in its response to the startling victory they looked set to achieve.

Tactics and strategy

The reason for the FIS leadership's measured response to the party's victory was due to a realisation on the part of the senior figures in the leadership that the prospect of assuming power risked the intervention of the military. The FIS had enjoyed a delicate and tacit truce with the ANP since the events of the previous June when the army had made amply clear its continuing antipathy towards the FIS and the implications of its programme. It had subsequently appeared that the military would probably have been willing to tolerate a FIS presence in the new National Assembly. However, it was far from certain that it would adopt a similar attitude towards a FIS majority in the Assembly and particularly not one of a size significant enough to be able to change a constitution that the army had pledged itself to defend and uphold. It was in reference to this consideration that Abdelkader Hachani warned crowds of party supporters that "victory is more dangerous than defeat" and thus urged them to show once again moderation and restraint and so avoid giving the army an excuse to move against them and curtail the electoral process.[62] Similarly another senior figure, Othman Aissani, argued that the period

---

ruled that challenges to the results were justified in as few as a dozen individual constituencies.

61 Lavenue, *Algérie: La Democratie Interdite*, p. 174.
62 *Algérie Actualité*, 9.1.92. This response by Hachani revealed that he had probably

between the two ballots was the most vulnerable time for the FIS. Once the party had secured a majority in the second ballot, the unambiguous legitimacy this would bestow on the FIS would prevent both the army intervening and the President siding with it if it did. He also reminded the party that it had been when Abassi Madani and Ali Belhadj had warned the military against intervention that the ANP had moved to arrest both leaders.[63] Hachani made it quite clear in a press conference following the 26 December poll that he did not anticipate confrontations with the military:

> There is no conflict between us and the armed forces. It is a supposition which has no foundation. We say to the army, it is God who has led us to power through the people, and it is time for the army to protect the people's choice and we believe the army will not hold back in doing this.[64]

The leadership sought to eschew partisan and triumphalist predictions of how they would operate once in the National Assembly. Hachani spoke openly of the party's readiness to co-operate with both the presidency and other parties in the APN, calling at one point for the formation of a coalition government.[65] Despite the struggle between the two parties that had been the central feature of the election, it appeared there was considerable evidence, both before and after the first ballot, that the FIS and at least elements of the FLN would be willing to co-operate in government. The FLN's leader, Abdelhamid Mehri, had admitted in November that the FIS "were a fact of Algerian political life" with which he hoped he could form a government of national unity to guarantee for the country "a period of stability of 2 or 3 years".[66] For the FIS, Abdelkader Hachani declared his willingness to work with the FLN, claiming that the FIS was willing to make use of all the available expertise in Algeria.[67]

---

neither expected nor unambiguously welcomed the massive scale of the FIS's victory.

63 Dévoluy and Duteil, *La Poudrière Algérienne*, pp. 53–4.
64 *Independent*, 30.12.91.
65 *Jeune Afrique*, 9.1.92.
66 *Le Monde Diplomatique*, 12.91.
67 *El Moudjahid*, 30.12.91. Hachani also mentioned the FFS in this context.

Particular attention had focused, in this context, on the linking role certain senior figures on the "Islamic" wing of the FLN might play in any future such arrangement. Most prominent of these were the former Prime Minister, Abdelhamid Brahimi, and the former Foreign Minister, Ahmed Taleb Ibrahimi, who had actually helped found a "Committee of Support for Political Prisoners" in October 1991 which called for the release of Abassi Madani and the other imprisoned FIS leaders. This development signified not only the movement of the Islamic wing of the FLN towards the FIS, but, more importantly, clearly reflected the more nationalist orientation of the FIS itself. The accession of Mohammed Said, the leader of the Jazara, to the Majlis Shura in July 1991 had had an impact on the party's new, younger and more pragmatic leadership. The Jazara's more nationalist ideas had become increasingly evident in the FIS in the autumn of 1991. Abdelkader Hachani had officially marked the nationalist anniversary of the beginning of the liberation struggle on 1 November whilst Abassi Madani had previously explicitly boycotted the celebrations. The new leadership of the FIS also abandoned traditional Islamist distrust of Berber culture – embracing the Jazara's belief in the importance of the Berber heritage in the Algerian national identity as well as reflecting the Kabyle origins of many Jazara members (most notably Mohammed Said himself). The FIS even began to use the Berber language, tamazigh, in its own literature and propaganda. Abdelkader Moghni of the FIS underlined this new link with the FLN, in particular, and nationalism generally, when he criticised those whom he claimed "want to sow discord between the FIS and the *patriots* of the FLN [Italics added]".[68]

A consensual approach was also adopted towards the presidency. The FIS realised that Chadli's behaviour and role was not only vital in the inter-election period, but that he would still wield considerable constitutional and political powers *vis-à-vis* the National Assembly even if the FIS achieved an absolute majority in the chamber. Hachani affirmed that although his party would call for presidential elections following the conclusion of the legislative ones, it would not seek to impose or force this objective, saying that the party could "leave this for later".[69] This implied, as Hachani also stated explicitly, that the FIS were prepared to

---

68   *Algérie Actualité*, 9.1.92.
69   *Independent*, 30.12.91; Dévoluy and Duteil, *La Poudrière Algérienne*, pp. 52–3.

co-habit with Chadli following the legislative elections. Hachani declared that "there would not have to be a problem with the President of the Republic".[70]

The fact that many of these statements declaring the party's willingness to co-operate with other political forces were often carefully qualified, indicated that the party still intended to push through its own political programme. Hachani's willingness not to press for early presidential elections was thus conditional on the FIS having "all the real guarantees to apply our programme, so as not to betray people who voted for us and our aims."[71] Similarly, whilst the FIS's leadership affirmed that it would respect the Constitution, Hachani stated that he would be "obliged to modify it" if the people demanded it.[72] Despite similar promises to accept the National Assembly's rules once there, Abdelkader Moghni indicated the party's desire to reduce the President's powers by loosening his control of the Defence and Foreign Ministries.[73] This was all quite within the FIS's constitutional rights, but it demonstrated the party's determination to make full use of the political power it looked set to seize at the second ballot.

There were, however, indications that the party was also intent on introducing changes that went beyond and outside the Constitution. The prospect of the world's first democratically elected Islamist government had attracted considerable foreign media attention to Algeria. Anxious to pick up on any immoderate statements made by members or leaders of the FIS, these journalists reported much that appeared to cast doubt on the liberal and pluralistic credentials of the party. Plans and desires, once in power, to establish popular tribunals to try the party's enemies; to ban the secular parties and secular press and to allow only divorced, widowed and orphaned women to work, emerged.[74] Hachani moved to explicitly deny many such stories stating, on the first issue, that there would be "no popular tribunals, nor settling of scores, nor a bloodbath".[75] However, his statements on the FIS's supposedly moderate and tolerant

---

70 *El Moudjahid*, 30.12.91.
71 *Independent*, 30.12.91.
72 Dévoluy and Duteil, *La Poudrière Algérienne*, p. 55.
73 *The Times*, 31.12.91.
74 See *Financial Times*, 30.12.91.
75 *Jeune Afrique*, 9.1.92.

plans for Algerian society were, like his statements on co-operation with other political forces, carefully qualified:

> The FIS will guarantee individual and collective liberties *in the framework of Islamic law* and will tolerate the existence of parties other than Islamic ones[76] [Italics added].

Similarly, he spoke of upholding "the freedom of the press *in keeping with our Arabo-Islamic principles*".[77]

The reasons for these qualifications and indications of a much more hardline FIS agenda, which may have seemed dangerously provocative to the army, were connected with the fact that the party still had to keep its own radical constituency in check by assuring this constituency that the FIS still planned to radically transform Algerian society. This was a balancing act the party had kept up throughout the autumn of 1991. During Abdelkader Hachani's imprisonment in October, Rabah Kebir and Abdelkader Moghni (who, following Ali Belhadj's arrest, had assumed the influential position of main preacher at the Al-Sunna mosque in Bab El-Oued) had (possibly consciously) recreated the roles played by Abassi Madani and Ali Belhadj in 1989–91 with Kebir's public moderation being combined with Moghni's radical denunciation in the mosques of democracy as "blasphemy".[78] Similarly, after the first ballot, it was at the Friday sermons in the mosques that the most uncompromising speeches and declarations by the senior figures in FIS were made to the party's militant faithful. The day after the first ballot, a Friday, Mohammed Said warned that Algerians "must change their customs regarding clothing and food" and another senior figure declared that the other parties and those who voted for them "must announce (their) repentance publicly".[79] On the following Friday, 3 January, at Bab El-Oued, Abdelkader Hachani himself was heard to pronounce that: "these elections have demonstrated that there are only two parties – the Party of God and the Party of the Devil" and similarly also affirmed: "Our fight is between Islamic purity and democratic impurity."[80] Most alarming of all, perhaps, was the

---

76 *Ibid.*
77 *El Moudjahid*, 30.12.91.
78 *Jeune Afrique*, 20.11.91
79 *Independent*, 2.1.92; *Guardian*, 28.12.91.
80 *Algérie Actualité*, 9.1.92; *Financial Times*, 11.1.92.

statement by one of the FIS's election candidates that once the party had achieved an Islamic state the place for the supporters of democracy would be (in the words of one Algerian newspaper) "at the end of a rope".[81] Such statements appeared to contradict the president of the BEP's other pronouncements on the importance and intrinsic value of democracy.

Where the real convictions of the leadership lay was uncertain. Ibrahim El-Bayoumi Ghanem believes the conflicting messages reflected the difficulties the new more moderate post-June 1991 leadership faced in retaining its radical rank and file support whilst remaining committed to a more thoughtful and genuinely pluralistic agenda. Bayoumi quotes Hachani, in particular, as stating on the vital issue of the FIS's willingness to cede power in a future election that:

> If the majority of the people voted against the sharia and Islamic Government, it would be through a failure of the FIS not because of the apostasy of the people. Therefore we must cede power to someone else.[82]

However, there were many who doubted that this was in fact the case and that the immoderate statements, as in the case of Abassi Madani and Ali Belhadj, were the true face of the FIS which would be fully revealed once they had fully secured their victory at the second ballot. Even if the party's leadership may have had more liberal and democratic convictions, it was questionable whether they would have been capable of restraining the radical and populist impulses of the party's militants both in parliament and on the streets once the second round of voting had occurred.[83]

The agenda of the FIS

The now very real prospect of the FIS achieving political power increased popular and media attention on the party's plans once in government. Besides the collection of often contradictory statements made by individual

---

81 *El Watan*, 3.8.94.
82 Author's interview with Ibrahim El-Bayoumi Ghanem, National Centre for Social and Criminological Research and observer at 1991 legislative elections in Algeria. Cairo, 26.6.94.
83 It appeared that this was already occurring. Several hundred Islamists, some armed with knives, tried to disrupt the opposition march and rally of 2 January.

FIS leaders, there were more tangible indications of the FIS's programme in the wake of their victories in the first ballot for the National Assembly. The party issued a sixteen-page manifesto following the first round of voting, which purported to give a more detailed and defined account of the FIS's agenda. The document declared the party's intention to extend Islamic sharia law to a highly comprehensive number of aspects of Algerian public and private life: family law, schools, associations between men and women, the police force, the army and factories and firms. More specifically, the document indicated the party's desire to regulate women's dress and work (expressed as an intent to "reinforce the faith in women's morality") and "combat" sexual promiscuity. On the institutional level the document called for reform of government at all levels.[84]

The period following the first ballot also saw the FIS indicating, usually under questioning from foreign journalists, its priorities, once in government, on less emotive and more technical issues such as the economy and foreign policy. Overall, the party appeared to stick to its general commitment to a mixed economy, Rabah Kebir condemning equally the "impious capitalism of the last few years and the state socialism that had preceded it".[85] Correspondingly, Hachani argued that he had no objections on "religious grounds" to privatisation of Algeria's state-owned industries and enterprises but was opposed to the selling-off of "publicly-owned strategic industries". He was, however, much more critical of foreign involvement in Algeria's ongoing programme of economic liberalisation, terming the new hydrocarbons law in Algeria, which permitted foreign companies to exploit the country's oil and gas resources, a "transaction of shame". He was equally hostile to the ECU 400 million loan made by the European Community the previous autumn to aid Algeria's economic recovery, which he denounced as being "made by countries who are enemies of Islam".[86] Nevertheless, this antipathy to foreign involvement in Algeria which reflected the new influence of more nationalistic Jazarist views within the leadership, were tempered by commitments to maintain

---

84 *Financial Times*, 8.1.92.
85 *Independent*, 28.12.91. Kebir subsequently stated, "We didn't fully support Chadli Benjedid's economic reforms. . . . His programme for reform was unclear. In terms of decisions, sometimes it was socialist, sometimes capitalist. We rejected this because we were seeking a rational solution to solve Algeria's economic problems." Author's interview with Rabah Kebir, 27.9.95.
86 *Financial Times*, 8.1.92.

relations with the IMF and other foreign creditors as well to standing by Algeria's existing international treaties and agreements. Hachani assured journalists at a press conference that "Algeria is not going to be isolated from the world."[87] The FIS's leaders were clearly acknowledging that if they did achieve power they could not afford to alienate the outside world if they wanted to attempt to solve Algeria's grave economic problems. It subsequently became known that discreet contacts had been established by officials of the FIS with Western governments and multinationals to assure them that their investments in Algeria would be respected by any future FIS government.[88]

The regime and the prospect of a FIS victory

The most important of all the reactions to the results of the voting on December 26 was that of the regime itself.

President Chadli Benjedid

From the outset it appeared that the FIS's triumph in the first ballot and almost certain achievement of a majority in the second, whilst not being his preferred or expected result, did not unduly alarm and perturb President Chadli Benjedid. There was no indication that he wished to either interrupt or delay the second round of voting. Two days before the election, he had declared himself prepared to cohabit with an opposition government and he did not seem to demur on this statement once it became apparent that such a government would almost certainly be one exclusively dominated by the FIS.[89] There were also persistent reports that either personally or through an intermediary Chadli had secretly begun negotiations with the FIS on the framework of a cohabitation agreement with a FIS-dominated National Assembly and government. The FIS's announcement that it would not seek an immediate presidential election

---

87 *Financial Times*, 8.1.92; *Independent*, 30.12.91. Hachani also criticised foreign media reports forecasting the "Iranisation" of Algeria. *El Moudjahid*, 30.12.91.

88 *Financial Times*, 30.12.91.

89 In response to a question put to him before the election about the possible implications of a FIS victory, the President had replied: "We will respect the will of the people. There will not be any competition between the president and the government . . . I do not believe there will be any problem if the Constitution is respected." Charef, *Algérie: Le Grand Dérapage*, p. 236.

was cited as evidence of such a deal having being struck between the party and the President.[90]

The explanation for Chadli's adoption of this response to the FIS's electoral advance, which appeared to go against the advice of his closest advisors, was to be found in Chadli's awareness that as President he was far from being in a politically weak position *vis-à-vis* the FIS. Even if the Islamists were able to secure a majority in the National Assembly, the presidency still, constitutionally, wielded considerable political powers. These included the ability to appoint and dismiss governments and ministers as well as the ultimate authority to dissolve the Assembly itself. Institutionally, both the army and the bureaucracy were subject to his control and both clearly were far more likely to back him rather than the FIS in the event of clashes and confrontations with a FIS-controlled Assembly and government. Moreover, despite agitation by the FIS for presidential elections to be held as soon as possible after the conclusion of the legislative ones, Chadli still had two years of his presidency to run until his current mandate ran out in December 1993. It was thus perhaps hoped by him that he would be able to control and even use and weaken the FIS and therefore neutralise the threat of an Islamist agenda being applied in Algeria.

It was possible that a further explanation for Chadli's espousal of the idea of cohabitation was that the President viewed it as the legal and proper response to the latest development in the programme of political liberalisation and democratisation that he himself had instigated in 1988-89. Thus a personal commitment to seeing the process through perhaps played a role, with Chadli's own honour, which he had vested in the programme originally, being at stake. This interpretation of the President's stance was not necessarily incompatible with the more probable explanation that Chadli wanted to continue with the electoral timetable in order to retain his position. It is certainly possible that Chadli believed that he could best ensure the survival of his "democratic project" by

---

90 The reports and rumours circulating about such a deal varied from stories of Abdelaziz Khelloufi, the secretary-general of the presidency, or more neutral figures acting as intermediaries for Chadli in negotiations with senior figures in the FIS; through to a story about Chadli himself supposedly meeting FIS leaders at a ski resort near Blida at the end of November. See Lamchichi, *L'Islamisme en Algérie*, pp. 174–5; Dévoluy and Duteil, *La Poudrière Algérienne*, pp. 43–4.

pressing ahead with the second ballot and then using his powers to curb the potentially anti-democratic excesses of the FIS.

The Algerian military

Chadli's sanguine response to the results of the first ballot was not reflected in the Algerian military's assessment of the implications of the election. Whether or not the scale of the FIS's victory had been anticipated by the senior figures in the army, it was clearly not welcomed by them.[91] The historic antipathy between the Algerian military and the country's Islamist movement has already been explored (see Chapter Five), but the now very real prospect of FIS dominance of the government and the National Assembly sharpened both the nature and intensity of the army's hostility to the FIS and its agenda.

For many senior figures in the military, a FIS government would spell disaster, politically and economically, for the Algeria they had pledged themselves to defend. There were considerable fears for the already highly fragile condition of the country's economy. Fear of the FIS coming to power threatened to further deepen the nation's colossal debt (estimated at $25 billion in December 1991[92]) through capital flight and the cancelling by foreign petrol companies, of agreements aimed at increasing exploitation of Algeria's oil and gas resources.

Politically, the Algerian military felt certain that the FIS would bring instability and conflict to large areas of Algerian life – developments that the ANP had historically pledged itself to prevent. The FIS's victory in the first ballot had, as has been shown, produced great alarm amongst significant sections of Algeria's population and there were indications that many opponents of the FIS were already preparing for armed conflict with a future Islamist government. Of particular concern were the ethnically distinct areas of Mzab and Kabylia which had decisively rejected FIS candidates at the elections of 1990 and 1991.[93] The threat of civil

---

91 Abed Charef argues that the noticeable change in the demeanour of Larbi Belkheir between the closing of the polls, at which point he had declared himself to be "very satisfied" with the voting, and the official announcement of the results, when he had seemed tired and worried, indicated that the Belkheir, at least, did not anticipate the scale of the FIS's victory. Charef, *Algérie: Le Grand Dérapage*, pp. 238–9.

92 *MEED*, 27.12.91.

93 The Mzabite areas had predominantly voted for independent candidates in both

war could not be ruled out. An external conflict was also seen as possible if a new and radical Islamist regime chose to provoke one of Algeria's neighbours. It was also probable that, despite the ANP's past, at least some of the senior figures in the military had become committed to the goal of democratisation as the best avenue for Algeria to achieve the traditional goals of development and modernisation to which the ANP had always been publicly attached.

More crucially and more importantly for the military were fears it held for its own integrity and survival if the FIS were able to achieve a majority in the National Assembly. There was considerable concern amongst the senior figures in the army that once in power the Islamists would waste no time in seeking to use their new political powers to attempt to neutralise their traditional foes, and only truly powerful enemies, in the general staff of the military. Such fears were also shared by more junior officers who also saw themselves as the potential targets of the rumoured "popular tribunals" and who, having often had a secular and frequently foreign military training were similarly anxious for the survival of a modern and secular state.

The military were not reassured by Chadli's confidence that he could keep the Islamists in check with the use of his constitutional and institutional powers. They doubted his strength of will and ability to constrain the Assembly and feared he might "defect" to the Islamist camp to preserve his own position. Despite both Chadli's and Abdelkader Hachani's vehement denials,[94] the ANP were already highly suspicious of the rumours and reports circulating about the President conducting secret discussions with the FIS. One such report alleged that the dismissal of the senior personnel in the army had been conceded by Chadli in return for a cohabitation agreement with the party. The leaders of the military were not persuaded by arguments that Abdelkader Hachani's post-Batna conference leadership of the FIS was significantly more moderate than the leadership the military had helped imprison the previous June. They were aware that the FIS continued to be influenced by directives coming (via relatives and lawyers) from Abassi Madani and Ali Belhadj in prison in Blida and also believed that whatever the intentions of the leadership

---

elections, whilst the Kabyle, as has been shown, supported the RCD in 1990 and the FFS in 1991.

94　See *Algérie Actualité*, 30.12.92.

of the party, the FIS's rank and file would force the party to implement a radical agenda once in power.

The leaders of the military were conscious that their own position and room for manoeuvre could be sharply reduced once the second ballot had taken place. Any move the military might make against the FIS after the conclusive second ballot could put severe strains on the integrity of the army – the loyalty of the troops being confused and possibly divided by the election of an apparently legitimate new Assembly. The declared intention of the FIS to secure the release of all its members and supporters, arrested in June 1991 and prosecuted by military courts under the state of siege, represented a clear challenge to the all-important authority of the military. Given these factors, then, it was clear that if the military were to move against the FIS and somehow block their achievement of a legislative majority, it would have to do so before the holding of the second round of voting scheduled for 16 January.

The *Coup d'État*: January 1992

The military plot
A covert meeting was held at the end of December to discuss the options available to the military. It was attended by all the senior military figures in the country including Khaled Nezzar, the Defence Minister; Abdelmalek Guenaizia, Chief of the General Staff; leaders of the navy, the Gendarmerie and the security services; and the commanding colonels of the military regions. Little time was lost in agreeing that the FIS's path to electoral victory should be blocked and discussion then focused on how this was to be best achieved. Whether through a genuine attachment to constitutional legality or, more likely, for tactical reasons, it was decided that the FIS's progress to victory should, as far as possible, be blocked by using constitutional mechanisms rather than by physical force.[95]

Chadli Benjedid, as President, held the key to such moves. It was his determination to press ahead with the second ballot and then cohabit with the FIS that so alarmed the military and he was clearly the main obstacle to any plan aimed at averting a FIS government. For Nezzar,

---

95 For a full account of the army's plots and plans see Dévoluy and Duteil, *La Poudrière Algérienne*, pp. 41–52.

Guenaizia and the other figures at the secret meeting, it was therefore evident that Chadli had to go. His resignation would not only remove the personal obstacle he represented but would also help force the suspension of the second round of the election. In order to persuade the President of the necessity of his resignation a comprehensive petition of military officers began to be compiled to demonstrate to Chadli the strength and solidarity of feeling within the armed forces.

The second question to which the military leaders gave attention was who should then replace Chadli as President. According to the Constitution, in the event of the death or resignation of the President, the presidency should provisionally pass, until proper elections could be held, to the president of the National Assembly. This, however, constituted a problem to Nezzar and his colleagues. The outgoing president of the Assembly, Abdelaziz Belkhadem, despite being a member of the FLN, was perceived as being far too sympathetic to the FIS. Not only was he a recognised member of the FLN's Islamic wing but his efforts to act as peace broker during the crisis of June 1991, which had involved him in several meetings with the leaders of the FIS, had earned him the sobriquet of the "valet of the FIS". Such a figure, with an established reputation for seeking compromise with the Islamists, was clearly even more unacceptable to the military than Chadli and therefore a way (preferably constitutional) had to be found around this obstacle. It was decided that Chadli, in addition to tendering his own resignation, must also be persuaded to dissolve the existing National Assembly before resigning, and thus prevent the triggering of the constitutional mechanism which would lead to Belkhadem succeeding him as President. Succession to the presidency would then pass, by the military's calculations, to Abdelmalek Benhabyles, the head of the Constitutional Council and a far more acceptable figure to the military than either Chadli or Belkhadem.

The decision to pursue this strategy was concluded at another meeting of the senior figures in the military on 4 January. According to a source close to the presidency, Khaled Nezzar went from this meeting to the offices of the President where he then spent the night persuading Chadli of the unavoidable necessity of his resignation. Having listened to Nezzar (significantly a figure, like the other leading plotters, whom Chadli had appointed and seen as an ally) and having seen the list of 181 military officers who signed the petition requesting his resignation,

Chadli, having first secured assurance that he would be replaced by a strong regime, then agreed to step down.[96]

However, the military plotters' plans for a "constitutional coup" suffered something of a setback after they had successfully persuaded Chadli of their designs. By 5 January it had become clear that the president of the Constitutional Council, Abdelmalek Benhabyles, had refused to co-operate with the military's plans to let him become interim President. According to Benhabyles he could not assume the presidency since the Constitution only provided for the president of the Constitutional Council becoming President in the event of the death, not the resignation, of an incumbent President.

This development finally forced the military leaders to abandon their plans to utilise the proper provisions of the Constitution to achieve their aims. They remained, however, anxious to maintain, what François Burgat terms, "a legalistic facade".[97] Thus it was planned that following the official announcement of his resignation, Chadli would cede power to the High Council for Security (HCS) which would appoint his successor. Attachment to the appearances of constitutionality was supposedly maintained since the HCS was an existing body and was provided for in the Constitution. However, its defined role in the Constitution was simply to act as a consultative body to the Head of State on issues of state security and was clearly not intended to act, even in a provisional capacity, as an executive or legislative body. The planned defence for this constitutional deviation, though, was to be that the Constitution itself did not provide for the simultaneous absence of both the National Assembly (having been dissolved by Chadli – supposedly five days before his resignation[98]) and the President. Therefore extraordinary powers needed to be granted to other constitutional bodies such as the HCS which itself would specifically

---

96 Dévoluy and Duteil, *La Poudrière Algérienne*, pp. 68 and 70. There are differing accounts of the chronology of these developments. Paul-Marie de la Gorce claimed that the military finalised their plans on 7 or 8 January and did not manage to persuade Chadli to step down until a few days later – the President still convinced of the wisdom of carrying on up until 10 January (see *Jeune Afrique*, 16.1.92). The chronology offered by Dévoluy and Duteil has been used in the main text since it is the most detailed, it appeared later (and is therefore more likely to be more considered and accurate) and quotes a source close to the presidency for its details.

97 Burgat and Dowell, *The Islamic Movement in North Africa*, p. 302.

98 This was not made public, however, until after Chadli's resignation itself.

assume the powers of the National Assembly. The real explanation for the emergence of the HCS into the political foreground was that it was dominated by senior military officers including Nezzar, Guenaizia and Larbi Belkheir, the Minister of the Interior.

The "coup", 11–16 January 1992

Finally, on 11 January, just five days before the second ballot was due to be held, the military's rapidly constructed plan to thwart the FIS was launched with the appearance of President Chadli Benjedid on national television. In a quiet voice and what one observer described as "sober informality",[99] Chadli announced his resignation to the nation, declaring that:

> Given the difficulty and gravity of the current situation, I consider my resignation necessary to protect the unity of the people and the security of the country.[100]

The following day the HCS stepped to the fore, as planned, and issued a statement announcing "the impossibility of continuing the electoral process until necessary conditions were achieved for the normal functioning of institutions".[101] Tanks and troops moved onto the streets to guard important points and buildings in Algiers. On the same day the HCS announced the appointment of a Haut Comité d'Etat (HCE) which would function as a collective successor to President Chadli. Despite the constitutional provisions that presidential elections must follow within forty-five days of the death or resignation of a President, the HCE assumed, on the claimed advice of the Constitutional Court, the presidential mandate Chadli had "won" in 1988 and which was due to formally expire in December 1993.

The HCE was revealed as comprising five figures: Khaled Nezzar; Ali Kafi, the leader of the Veterans Association; Tijani Haddam, the rector of the Paris mosque; and Ali Haroun, the Human Rights Minister in Ghozali's government. The fifth figure, and the one who was to assume

---

99   *Guardian*, 13.1.92.
100 *Middle East International*, 24.1.92.
101 *Guardian*, 13.1.92.

the leadership of this new collective presidency, was Mohammed Boudiaf, a veteran leader of Algeria's war of liberation, who had been forced into exile in Morocco by Ben Bella in 1964. Boudiaf duly returned to the country, after an official absence of twenty-eight years, on 16 January to assume the daunting task that Algeria's military leaders had bestowed on him.

The composition of the HCE indicated what impression the military planners of the "coup" wished to give. One observer noted that each member represented "a symbolic piece of the collective field" of Algeria.[102] Ali Kafi, as secretary-general of the veterans association, the ONM (Organisation Nationale des Mujahidin) was chosen to provide the historic link with the experience of Algeria's birth through the war of liberation. Ali Haroun, a doctor in law and Human Rights Minister, clearly represented the new regime's desire to portray itself as concerned about legality and human rights, despite the nature of its accession to power. The choice of Tijani Haddam was an evident attempt to give the regime a degree of religious legitimacy and thus perhaps limit the inevitable backlash and condemnation from the Islamists. This last choice of the rector of the Paris Mosque also reflected a desire to emphasise the modern and liberal tendency that Haddam supposedly exemplified. Significantly, Ahmed Sahnoun, the leader of the Rabitat Dawa and senior figure in the Islamist movement, had also been approached to take this "religious" seat on the HCE, but had refused. The presence of General Khaled Nezzar on the HCE, as Defence Minister and the figure widely perceived as the "brains" behind the "coup", needed little explanation.

The choice of Mohammed Boudiaf, as the head of the new collective presidency, was perhaps the most significant of all. It appears that Nezzar and his fellow conspirators were aware of the need to give the regime a fresh image and an enhanced sense of legitimacy, to counteract the negative impression of the coup and perhaps even to reconstruct some kind of popular support for the regime (which had all but vanished over the preceding years). A number of different names were discussed but the choice of Mohammed Boudiaf, with his high-profile historic revolutionary record, was felt to give the new regime the image of legitimacy it required. More importantly, though, it was realised that Boudiaf's long absence from Algeria cleared him of any suspicion of the corruption that was

---

102 *Jeune Afrique*, 24.1.92.

popularly perceived to be endemic within the Algerian establishment and regime, and which had so aided the FIS's electoral triumph.[103]

Reactions

News of the effective *coup d'état* by the military against Chadli, the electoral process and ultimately the FIS, came as no surprise to many inside and outside Algeria. As François Burgat observed: "The uncertainty concerned only the time when they would make their move – before or after the first round of voting."[104] Indications of the plans of the military were evident in advance of the formal announcement of Chadli's resignation on 11 January. Abdelkader Hachani voiced his concern on 8 January over troop movements across Algeria and the parallel lack of apparent preparation by the authorities for the holding of the second ballot scheduled for 16 January:

> We want to know what justification there is for this deployment. If it is because of the second round, why have they deployed in regions where seats were decided at the first poll?[105]

For the FIS these fears were confirmed by the train of events that began with Chadli's resignation. A journalist accompanying Hachani on an internal flight he was making at the time, noted the FIS leader's tense if unsurprised reaction to the news of the President's resignation, when informed of it mid-flight.[106] Rabah Kebir later stated: "We expected that the army may cancel the elections, but our expectation was not 100%."[107] The party's leadership was clearly aware of the importance of formulating

---

103   There is some uncertainty as to when the decision to appoint Boudiaf was actually taken – his choice as the new figurehead for the regime appearing to come only after Abdelmalek Benhabyles' refusal to assume the presidency. However there were claims that Boudiaf had already met with senior military figures, during a secret visit to Algiers beforehand, and had discussed a plan to install him as President. See Charef, *Algérie: Le Grand Dérapage*, p. 260. According to Dévoluy and Duteil, the decision finally to contact Boudiaf was taken on 8 January. Dévoluy & Duteil, *La Poudrière Algérienne*, p.83

104   Burgat and Dowell, *The Islamic Movement in North Africa*, p. 298–9.

105   *Financial Times*, 9.1.92.

106   *Nouvel Observateur*, 16.1.92.

107   Author's interview with Rabah Kebir, 27.9.95.

a careful response to these developments and the need to prevent the initiative they had won slipping, or being seized, away from them. Thus whilst initially dismissing Chadli's resignation as "a piece of theatre"[108] (which it nonetheless took the credit for[109]) it was not until 13 January, following a secret meeting in the suburbs, that the FIS formally responded to the developments of the previous three days. The statement issued by the party declared Chadli's resignation to be unconstitutional and the new "regime" illegitimate and the result of a comprehensive conspiracy. Attention was drawn to the purely consultative function the Constitution accorded to the HCS which consequently had no legal right to take over the reins of power. This treasonable act by a small clique, the statement declared, was a betrayal of both God and the Algerian people and one against which all Algerians should stand together.[110]

The relatively restrained tone of the statement, especially with regard to action to be taken against the new regime, was remarked on by many observers who expected a far more robust response, perhaps even a call to arms, from the Islamists who were witnessing a transparent attempt to rob them of their electoral victory. However, the FIS felt that their strength and therefore their legitimacy had been proven during the first round of voting and there was no need for a confrontation yet. In addition there was the ever-present concern that the military were simply waiting for another excuse to crack down upon and this time possibly ban the FIS altogether. Accordingly, the FIS continued to restrain itself and avoid confrontation with the regime in the same fashion as it had since June 1991. A rally to be held by the party on hills outside Algiers was cancelled in the wake of Chadli's resignation, and Abdelkader Hachani, whilst calling on the party's supporters to oppose the coup, promised that the FIS "would pursue the application of its programme in a peaceful manner and rejects the use of violence."[111] An official communiqué from the party on 17 January called on the population not to respond to provocations from the security services, a message that was backed by more hardline senior figures in the party such as Abdelkader Moghni, who implored

---

108 *Independent*, 13.1.92.
109 See *SWB* ME/1280 A/5, 17.1.92.
110 *MEED*, 24.1.92.
111 Lamchichi, *L'Islamisme en Algérie*, p. 238.

crowds at the Al-Sunna Mosque not to "furnish them with the opportunity they are waiting for".[112]

Besides these initial reactions, the FIS was aware of the need to develop a clear strategic response to the coup. Correspondingly, the party announced at a press conference at Algiers Town Hall on 15 January three proposals which it was putting to the regime. Firstly, that the electoral process be allowed to continue. Secondly, that the presidency should be assumed by Abdelmalek Benhabyles until the National Assembly elections were concluded, at which point the new president of the Assembly would take over as head of state. Presidential elections should then be held as soon as possible. Thirdly, that all political prisoners, including the FIS leaders at Blida, should be released.[113]

The FIS also entered into discussions with other political parties which rejected the coup. This perhaps surprising move may have reflected the sincerity of Hachani's earlier calls for inter-party co-operation and even a coalition government in the National Assembly, but more likely it demonstrated the FIS's realisation that it must construct as broad a front as possible against the regime so as to undermine its legitimacy. Whilst some parties, such as the RCD and the PAGS openly and unambiguously applauded the termination of the electoral process, other parties, notably those which had won seats in the first round, shared the FIS's opposition to the coup. Hocine Ait Ahmed of the FFS refused to deviate from his unwavering commitment to democracy and the elections, despite having been approached to co-operate with the plotters before the coup. He was now willing to co-operate with the FIS in order to attempt to have the cancellation of the elections reversed. More interestingly, the FLN joined the FIS and the FFS in opposition to the HCE which the party's leader, Abdelhamid Mehri, branded as "anti-constitutional", thus emphasising the separation of the party from the core of the regime.[114] Meetings between the leaders of the three parties took place through the 15th and 16th of January, the FIS announcing on the first day its intention to form a parallel parliament consisting of the 231 deputies elected in the first round of voting.

---

112   Lamchichi, *L'Islamisme en Algérie*, p. 238; *Guardian*, 18.1.92.
113   *SWB* ME/1280 A/5, 17.1.92.
114   *Middle East International*, 24.1.92.

Repression and dissolution of the FIS, January–March 1992[15]

It soon became clear "that the initiative was fast slipping away from the FIS", as one Western journalist noted during Abdelkader Hachani's speech to the party's faithful after prayers on Friday 17 January.[116] Indeed, in what increasingly appeared to be a replay of the events of the previous June, growing numbers of FIS militants began to be arrested by the authorities. This accelerated following the first reported attack on the regime by Islamists, which occurred on the night of 18 January when an army barracks was attacked at Sidi Moussa to the south of Algiers, resulting in the death of a soldier. On 22 January Hachani himself was arrested after calling on soldiers to "give up their allegiances to despots" – á statement interpreted by the authorities as an illegal incitement for the army to mutiny.[117] The editor and various staff on the newspaper which printed Hachani's call to the soldiers, El-Khaber, were also arrested. Hachani's successors to president of the Executive Bureau of the FIS, Othman Aissani and Rabah Kebir were also detained as soon as each attempted to assume the position following the arrest of the previous holder. Several FIS deputies elected to the National Assembly in the first round of voting in December also began to be arrested.

The regime also struck, as it had done in June 1991, against the institutional and organisational bases of the party. On 22 January Sid Ahmed Ghozali, who had remained Prime Minister (having fully supported the coup) announced measures that banned all political activity, including all speeches "of a political nature", at mosques.[118] Decrees were passed prohibiting worshippers spilling onto streets outside mosques, and the army began to turn away people trying to attend the most popular mosques. It was as the army moved to replace the imams of the estimated

---

115   For a detailed chronology of the official moves against the FIS see Lamchichi, *L'Islamisme en Algérie*, pp. 238–45.
116   *Daily Telegraph*, 18.1.92.
117   Lamchichi, *L'Islamisme en Algérie*, p. 239.
118   *Independent*, 24.1.92. Ghozali had established close links with the military and attempted to portray himself as the civilian spokesman of the new regime. He publicly made much of the "irregularities" of the first ballot and bolstered the appearance of the legitimacy of the regime when he appeared on television to claim that he, as Prime Minister, had ordered the tanks and troops onto the streets in the wake of the coup. *Jeune Afrique*, 16.1.92; *Middle East International*, 24.1.92.

8,000 mosques controlled by the FIS that the first violent conflicts with the Islamist movement began. In Batna on 5 February clashes erupted following the sentencing of an imam for breaking the government's ruling on politics in mosques (this was the pretext for most of the arrests and replacements of imams) which heralded similar incidents across the country, particularly in the capital, as supporters of the FIS – with few senior figures left at liberty to urge restraint – came onto the streets to challenge the authorities' ruling.[119] Clashes over the weekend of 7 to 9 February left, according to medical services, 40 dead and at least 300 injured as firearms began to be used by both sides.

Finally, on 9 February in the face of a mounting tide of violence against them, the authorities announced a state of emergency. Furthermore, the Minister of the Interior, Larbi Belkheir, announced the beginning of legal procedures to officially dissolve the FIS on the grounds that it had attempted insurrection against the state. Whilst dissolution of the FIS had clearly been the ultimate objective of the military from the start, it appeared that the new president of the HCE was less committed to this end. Up until 3 February, Mohammed Boudiaf denied that he wanted to ban the party but insisted that the FIS must operate within the framework of the law. Six days later he declared that although he did not wish to dissolve any party which respected democracy, dissolution was inevitable since "the FIS wanted to use democracy to destroy it".[120] It was clear that Boudiaf had been swayed by both the mounting violence and pressure from the military. Having been dissuaded once – by President Chadli in June 1991 – from breaking up the FIS, the ANP was determined that this time their will should prevail.

Ignoring appeals from the remaining leadership of the FIS to halt the arrests and the repression of the party, the regime moved swiftly to defeat and dismember the FIS in the wake of the 9 February announcements. Making full use of the extensive extra-ordinary powers the state of emergency granted the security forces, which included wide-ranging powers of arrest and curtailment of rights of association, the military began large-scale arrests of FIS militants. Five new "detention centres"

---

119 It was suggested that the military leadership looked for deliberate excuses to arrest Hachani, Kebir and the other leaders because they wished to remove their restraining influences in the hope that more radical elements could come to the fore thus provoking a confrontation and justifying a full repression of the party.

120 *MEED*, 14.2.92; *Middle East International*, 21.2.92.

were set-up on 17 February in the Sahara to house the between 5,000 (the official figure) and 30,000 (the FIS's estimate) Islamists arrested in the security swoops as clashes continued to occur across the country. In response, the remains of the FIS leadership attempted to regroup support for the party by organising a rally for 14 February but evidence of the intent of the military to prevent this occurring forced the plan to be abandoned to avert a bloodbath.[121] It proved to be the last major act of the party. The FIS was formally dissolved, following the completion of the procedures instituted by the Interior Ministry, by an Algiers court on 4 March 1992. It was found guilty of multiple violations of the law. However, as Abderrahim Lamchichi remarked, by this stage there was not much left of the FIS to dissolve:

> . . . its seat in Algiers had been shut, its newspapers banned, its 250 town halls confiscated, its principal leaders imprisoned, its militants interned in security camps . . . [122]

Conclusions

The events of January to March 1992 finally brought to a close Algerian Islamism's brief three-year foray into the arena of party political competition for political power. The cancellation and annulment of the elections by the "new" regime formally signalled an end to Algeria's wider and similarly short-lived experiment with democratisation and political pluralism.

The period since the events of the summer of 1991 had seen the FIS regroup itself under a younger, more pragmatic and nationalistically oriented leadership that ensured that the party continued with the electoralist strategy pursued by Abassi Madani. It was, ironically, the remarkable success that this strategy once again enjoyed at the ballot box

---

121 The fact that this decision by the FIS leadership to call off the rally was largely followed indicated the strength and endurance of the communication lines in the party – the order being mainly disseminated through the mosques following prayers on the previous Friday.

122 Lamchichi, *L'Islamisme en Algérie*, p. 86. The military had closed down the Algiers headquarters of the party shortly before the announcement of the state of emergency on 9 February.

on 26 December, that proved to be the undoing of both the strategy and the FIS. As Hugh Roberts observed, the FIS were confronted in the wake of the ballot with "not an electoral triumph but a strategic disaster".[123]

This disaster took the form of provoking the one force that could bring a lasting halt to the whole electoral process and the FIS's chance of some national political power into doing precisely that. Having re-entered the political arena in June 1991, the Algerian military leadership had allowed themselves to be persuaded by President Chadli that permitting the FIS to continue to function represented the most sensible option for the retention of civil peace and stability in the country. The results of the first ballot demonstrated that the President's calculations and reassurances about the reduced strength of the FIS had been wildly inaccurate. Chadli's willingness to countenance a FIS-dominated National Assembly which could plunge Algeria into chaos and facilitate a concerted assault on the army's privileges and senior personnel pushed the leaders of Algeria's military to act.

The resolution of the army and their apparent effectiveness in carrying out the curtailment of the electoral process and the subsequent dismemberment of the FIS did, however, obscure one important fact. The results of December 1991 had demonstrated the remarkable resilience of the FIS. Despite suffering serious internal splits, the banning of its newspapers and the removal of many of its leaders, including its two most senior figures, the party had still nearly gathered as many votes as all the other political parties combined. It had lost some 1.2 million votes since June 1990 but had still managed to retain the support of more than three and a quarter million Algerians – nearly a quarter of the total electorate. By simply discarding the electoral process and sweeping away the institutional manifestations of the FIS, the leaders of the Algerian military risked provoking a substantial section of the Algerian population by ignoring the demands and concerns they expressed in voting so massively for the FIS.

---

123   Roberts, 'From radical mission', p. 474.

7

The Descent into Conflict, 1992–1993

The new regime

Boudiaf's initiative, January–June 1992

The formal dissolution of the FIS at the beginning of March 1992 signalled the effective closure of the period 1989–92 in which Algeria had sought to open up its political system and in which the Islamist movement had come to play such a central role. The indefinite abandonment of the electoral process by those in power in Algeria, closely followed by the official exclusion of what had clearly been the most popular political force, indicated a clear breach with the main features of the preceding three-year period. The ending of this period also implied a need, on the part of the regime which had established itself in January, to provide a workable alternative path for Algeria in place of the turbulent one that had been taken by Chadli Benjedid.

The "new" regime that replaced Chadli at the apex of the Algerian state was (as has been shown) formally represented by a collective five-man "presidency" – the HCE. The creation of the cabal of senior military officers that had executed the effective *coup d'état* of January 1992, the HCE was generally expected to function as a predominantly civilian front for the leaders of the ANP. It therefore surprised many when the new head of the HCE, Mohammed Boudiaf, began to play a prominent and clearly leading role in the reconstruction of Algerian political life in the aftermath of the dramatic events of the opening months of 1992.

Boudiaf was aware of the colossal task that confronted the Algerian authorities and was conscious of the need to act in three particular areas to set Algeria back on a stable path. Civil order, the economy, and political legitimacy were all issues that presented the regime with significant challenges and which the new president sought to address. Clear initial priority was given to the re-establishment of public order on Algeria's streets following the abrupt prorogation of the legislative elections. As has been shown (see Chapter Six) the new regime appeared to deal swiftly and effectively with the protests and violence that did occur as a result of its actions through mass arrests of both the leadership and much of the militant support of the FIS.

The parlous state of the Algerian economy represented a far greater, but in Mohammed Boudiaf's view no less urgent, challenge to the government. For the new President improvement in the economic situation was a priority. It was Boudiaf's conviction that the strength of the Islamist tide which the FIS had ridden so successfully over the previous three years was a clear product of the economic crisis that had continued to grip Algeria through that same period. Rapid economic improvement, he reasoned, would therefore would serve to cut back Islamism as swiftly as it had risen.[1] In order to achieve this goal, however, huge obstacles needed to be overcome. There had been no tangible or lasting improvement in the Algerian economy over the three-year period since popular anger at its spiralling decline had first erupted in October 1988. The emphatic success of the FIS at the ballot box in both 1990 and 1991 – and the corresponding failure of the FLN – was clear testimony to the fact that the vast majority of ordinary Algerians had witnessed no improvement in their quality of life. The Algerian economy continued to struggle under a colossal external debt of $25 billion which by 1992 entailed a debt service ratio of over 70%, which in turn massively hampered official efforts to ameliorate the social and economic lot of the population. Negative economic growth and high unemployment (particularly among the young) continued to be major features of the economy.[2] A crisis meeting of the cabinet had been convened on 21 January which sought, in the words of Sid Ahmed Ghozali (who continued as Prime Minister) to draw up "concrete steps to relaunch the economy".[3] There was, however, no break with existing economic policy as the government appeared to continue the drive to liberalise Algeria's economy in pursuit of a market economy – objectives that the new President was to explicitly endorse.[4] The official recovery plan launched at the end of March heralded the removal of subsidies on all but a few staple foods resulting in massive price rises and clearly, for the foreseeable future, ongoing public hardship.

---

1   Interview with Mohammed Boudiaf, *El Moudjahid*, 17.5.92.
2   *MEED*, 27.12.91.
3   *Ibid.*, 31.1.92.
4   Charef, *Algérie: Le Grand Dérapage*, p. 338.

Boudiaf's third and most complex objective was to remake Algeria's political field. The new President made it clear that there would be no early return to the programme of elections started under his predecessor. He stated that new elections to the National Assembly would be held within two years but only if "the circumstances are right for true democracy".[5]

The President made it similarly plain that there would be no place for the FIS in any future elections. Boudiaf had appeared initially reluctant to ban the party in March, but once the decision was taken and enacted he was steadfast in his defence of the move. He argued that the FIS had put itself outside both the law and society by its actions, stating that it had shown itself willing to "stop at nothing to monopolise power" and had made murder "part of their philosophy of taking power". Boudiaf also made clear his determination that the party should not be allowed to return to the political field, ruling out any future possible re-legalisation by asserting that: "It has not left any chance of reconciliation. Absolutely none."[6] The President argued that the provisions of the 1989 Constitution, which banned the establishment of political parties based solely on religion, justified this stance and promised that future revisions to the Constitution would reinforce this prohibition, thus excluding the possibility of a return of any political grouping substantially similar to the FIS.

At the same time as attempting the exclusion of Islamism from the political field, Boudiaf was aware of the importance of winning over and avoiding the alienation of those three and a quarter million Algerians who had voted for the FIS on 26 December. The regime had made plain its tough response to unrest and violent opposition. This had been demonstrated by the handing out of thirteen death sentences to Islamists involved in the attack on the border post at Guemmar in November 1991 and the President's threat to send another 10,000 people to the detention camps in the Sahara if deemed necessary for the salvation of Algeria.[7] However, these hardline responses were also mixed with clemency. Charges brought against Abdelkader Hachani and Rabah Kebir were publicly rejected by the courts when they came to trial (although

---

5   *MEI*, 21.2.92. Boudiaf also indicated that presidential elections would be held before those for the APN.
6   Interview with Mohammed Boudiaf, *El Moudjahid*, 17.5.92.
7   *Guardian*, 18.4.92.

both were still detained) and the regime progressively released many of the estimated 9,000 people detained in the security clamp down of February–March, whom Boudiaf described as "simple stone-throwers".[8]

Attempts were also made by Boudiaf and the HCE to widen the political base of the regime to boost perceptions of their own legitimacy. They were aware that both the *coup d'état* of January and the HCE were widely seen as illegitimate, having been explicitly condemned by the three parties which had attracted the most votes in the first ballot (the FIS, the FLN and the FFS). The regime consequently attempted to draw in former members of other political parties and tendencies. In a clear appeal to the constituency of the FIS two moderate Islamists, Sassi Lamouri (ex-HAMAS) and Said Guechi (co-founder and former member of the FIS) were appointed to ministries in the new government. In addition, Hashem Nait Djoudi, former general secretary of the FFS, was appointed as Transport and Telecommunications Minister. In an attempt to fill the void left by the dissolution of the National Assembly, a National Consultative Council (CCN) was created. Launched on 22 April 1992, the CCN aimed to include a range of prominent personalities who would advise the government despite not enjoying any formal powers. However, attempts to tempt figures from other parties to join this body proved less than successful. Hocine Ait Ahmed, the leader of the FFS, turned down the government's offer of the chairmanship of the Council.

Boudiaf believed that still more active steps needed to be taken to win the confidence and support of the Algerian population. He perceived a need to construct some form of popular alternative political framework that was capable of gathering the sort of support and legitimacy that the FIS had so clearly succeeded in attracting. To this end he attempted to create a mass popular organisation in the country at large aimed at mobilising support for the regime. Launched at the end of May 1992 the Rassemblement Patriotique National (RPN) was heralded by the President as "the framework to discuss difficulties at all levels of national life with the authorities".[9] It encapsulated Boudiaf's overall strategy for regaining political consensus and legitimacy. The RPN represented a clear attempt on the part of the President to revive the concept of the mass political organisation that had been at the heart of the historic FLN (of which

---

8   *Jeune Afrique*, 2.4.92.
9   *MEI*, 10.7.92.

Boudiaf had been one of the founders) and which had been subsequently utilised by Houari Boumedienne in the 1970s. Incorporating twelve other – albeit insignificant – political parties the RPN began to set up branches across the country as Boudiaf made a concerted pitch for the sort of personal and direct legitimacy that had been able to achieve during his presidency.[10] Boudiaf mounted extended tours across Algeria to popularise and explain both the RPN and his ideas generally. It was during one of these tours at Annaba that he was assassinated on 29 June 1992.

The death of Boudiaf

The death of independent Algeria's fourth President, gunned down by one of his own bodyguards whilst making a speech, came as a profound blow to a country which was still in a state of shock following the turbulent events of early 1992. In the initial aftermath of the killing it was widely assumed, particularly abroad, that the assassination must have been the work of Islamists. However, despite the alleged Islamist sympathies of the bodyguard responsible for the killing and the obvious interest many Islamists would have in murdering such a resolute opponent, most Algerians did not believe that this was the case. Instead, the widespread conviction was that the assassination had actually been planned and facilitated by senior figures *within* the Algerian regime itself – the result of an irreconcilable clash of interests inside the ruling elite.

The original choice of Mohammed Boudiaf to head the HCE had been one that the leaders of the *coup d'état* of January had hoped would obscure the constitutional manipulations of their ouster of Chadli Benjedid and effective cancellation of the electoral process. Several other candidates had been considered for the post but it was felt that Boudiaf's unique combination of historical standing and legitimacy (as one of the original founders of the FLN) together with a past unsullied by the failings of Algeria's independent history (having been in exile since 1963) made him the best available figurehead for the new regime. Most of the senior figures in the military were of the view that Boudiaf would act as a pliant spokesman for their own (often individual and conflicting)

---

10 The largest party to join the RPN was the Parti National pour la Solidarité et le Développement (PNSD) which had attracted just 0.7% of the vote in the December elections.

interests. None of them appeared to consider that the new President, who had been a member of the PPA, a central figure in many of the FLN's internal bodies during the liberation struggle (such as the GPRA) and had even formed his own opposition party in exile, might want or try to implement his own agenda for Algeria's future. It was Boudiaf's efforts to strike an independent role for himself and his ideas that brought him into fatal conflict with others in the regime.

Boudiaf's initial period in office had raised few problems within the regime as he backed the army's crackdown on and eventual dissolution of the FIS. However, unease grew as the new President's ambitions to forge an independent course which sought to provide a more radical break with the past and present political order became more apparent. Boudiaf expressed his disappointment with a cabinet reshuffle in February indicating that he felt it was not sufficiently radical and he attempted to introduce his own staff to the presidency as an intended *cordon sanitaire* against the influence of other figures within the regime. The creation of the RPN was perceived as an attempt by the President to create a personal political vehicle for himself separate from the rest of the regime.[11]

Of more direct concern to many figures within the regime were the specific initiatives Boudiaf appeared to be using his position to launch. The leadership of the ANP, in particular, was concerned that the President was seeking to undermine their position both literally and in terms of policy. Boudiaf's long exile in Morocco, together with a visit he paid to King Hassan II in May 1992, prompted fears in the military that he was preparing to settle, in Morocco's favour the long-running dispute that had existed between Algeria and Morocco over the Western Sahara issue in which the ANP had invested much personal prestige.[12] More worrying still were rumours that Boudiaf would seek to replace the powerful figures at the head of the military with individuals who were more favourable to his leadership.

---

11 See Charef, *Algérie: Le Grand Dérapage*, pp. 336–9; Hamid Barrada: 'Le système a assassiné Mohammed Boudiaf' in *Reporters sans Frontières: Le Drame Algérien* (Paris, La Découverte, 1994).

12 Algeria had experienced difficult relations with her western neighbour Morocco over most of the period since independence. Border disputes between the two states in the 1960s developed by the 1970s into conflict over Algeria's support for the independence movement within the former Spanish territory of Western Sahara which Morocco wished to annex.

The most consistently cited reason for why Mohammed Boudiaf had managed to attract such extreme animosity within the regime, however, was his crusade against corruption. The embezzlement of vast sums of money from Algeria's national coffers had become a potent popular symbol of official venality and failure and had played a major role in both the defeat of the FLN and the victory of the FIS in the elections of 1990 and 1991. Numerous initiatives had been launched under Chadli Benjedid to deal with this seemingly endemic practice, but they had enjoyed little confidence amongst a public who believed that everyone in the senior echelons of the regime was involved in lining their own pockets. The opening of a fresh drive against institutional graft by Mohammed Boudiaf in 1992 was, however, greeted with more optimism. Boudiaf's long absence from Algeria cleared him of any suspicion of involvement in corruption and it appeared that the new President was intent on making progress on the issue which he saw as vital to the revival of public confidence in the regime. Heightened confidence in the sincerity of Boudiaf's anti-corruption drive was accompanied by growing unease within the Algerian regime that the President would not hesitate in exposing senior figures suspected of corruption. This unease grew to alarm in April 1992 when Mustapha Belloucif, a former senior general, was arrested and charged with embezzlement. Although Belloucif was regarded by many as being a symbolic scapegoat, there was significant concern within the upper echelons of the military and the administration that other senior figures would be exposed and indicted. It was this fear that most Algerians came to believe prompted unnamed influential figures to plan and facilitate the assassination of Mohammed Boudiaf on 29 June 1992.[13]

Overall, it appeared that it was Boudiaf's unwillingness to play the role of spokesman and front man for the perpetrators of the January *coup d'état* that led to his death. The leadership of the ANP had not calculated on their chosen candidate for the head of the HCE making a concerted bid to implement his own vision for Algeria, independent of the wishes of other forces and individuals within the regime. It was

---

13   For a fuller account of the reasons behind and suspicions surrounding Mohammed Boudiaf's assassination see Dévoluy and Duteil, *La Poudrière Algérienne*, pp. 190–215.

this desire for independence that cut short both Boudiaf's life and his ambitious plans for a route out of the crisis of January 1992.

The death of Mohammed Boudiaf and the suspicions surrounding it threatened to push Algeria even deeper into political crisis and malaise. Popular disillusionment and cynicism towards the country's rulers climbed following the violent removal of a figure many Algerians felt had had the necessary charisma and credibility to renew Algeria's fractured political life. This in turn foreboded a revival in the deep-rooted anti-regime sentiment that had underlain the rise and popularity of the FIS. Figures from the now dissolved FIS had been swift to deny responsibility for Boudiaf's assassination, but this did not prevent other elements in the party recognising that it was a development that might work to their advantage. As one communiqué purporting to come from the party declared in the wake of the assassination:

> The FIS announces the good news to the Algerian people and the inevitability of the materialisation of their hopes of the installation of an Islamic state.[14]

The Islamist movement and the FIS: the aftermath of dissolution

Initial reactions

The announcement by Larbi Belkheir on 9 February of the initiation of legal proceedings to officially dissolve the FIS had led to a desperate rearguard action by what remained of the party's leadership to dissuade the authorities and prevent this happening. Following the failure of these efforts with official confirmation of the dissolution order by the Court of Algiers a month later, a number of the few remaining unimprisoned FIS leaders (including four members of the party's Majlis Shura) appeared at the Arqam mosque in the southern Algiers suburb of Chateau Neuf on 4 March. In front of an estimated gathering of 5,000 and in contravention of the authorities' ban on political messages at mosques, an official communiqué declaring the FIS's official reaction to the dissolution order was read out. The communiqué stated that the party had not been surprised by the move and robustly asserted that:

---

14   *Le Monde*, 2.7.92.

The FIS represents a case, a nation, a religion and a history which will not die away due to a mere dissolution decision.[15]

More ominously the statement went on to declare that:

The dissolution of the FIS is a return to rule by the sword and domination by a self-interested elite which opens up the state to unpredictable consequences and dangerous developments, as long as the country remains in the control of a gang who has no respect for the sharia or the constitution.[16]

The exact implication of "unpredictable consequences and dangerous developments" was uncertain at this time. The communiqué remained consistent with established FIS practice of avoiding making any appeal for public unrest beyond calls for people to remain "steadfast". Leaders of the FIS had, however, continually warned the authorities for some time about the possibility of unrest. Abdelkader Hachani spoke of the dangers of the radical base of the FIS escaping the moderating influence of the leadership of the party and Mohammed Said spoke dramatically of the leadership having "an unpinned grenade in its hands".[17]

Popular reaction to the FIS's dissolution appeared remarkably muted. Small groups of Islamists tried to protest in Constantine and the outskirts of Algiers but were swiftly dispersed by tear gas and gunfire from the security forces. More structured forms of protest against the decision, such as the formation by Islamist students of the Mouvement Universitaire pour la Defense du Choix du Peuple (MUDCP) were similarly clamped down on.[18] This lack of apparent public reaction to events was the result of the efficiency of the security operation by the regime against the FIS and the Islamist movement. As had been the case in June–July 1991, the large scale arrests of both senior and intermediate leaders of the party had deprived the FIS of its usually impressive powers of mobilisation.[19] A call for a mass demonstration on 5 May, issued by Rabah Kebir from

---

15   FIS Communiqué, no. 21, 5.3.92.
16   *Ibid.*
17   Charef, *Algérie: Le Grand Dérapage*, p. 384.
18   Following the clampdown on its campaign of passive resistance the leadership of the MUDCP was reported to have told its members to "pursue the struggle by other means". Charef, *Algérie: Le Grand Dérapage*, p. 384.
19   By April 1992, 109 of the FIS's victorious candidates in the December 1991 ballot (including those proceeding to the second round) were held in detention along

house arrest, was an acknowledged failure as the authorities ruthlessly broke up the few attempts made to respond to the call.

Clandestinely issued calls for armed resistance purporting to come from the FIS appeared over the following few months.[20] Whilst these elicited no direct and immediate popular response, there was a clear and progressive increase in violence generally during this period. Increasing clashes between the police and armed militants occurred in Algiers and bombs exploded outside newspaper offices and at Constantine University in early May. There were also a growing number of assassinations of members of both the security forces and the judiciary. By the beginning of August seventy police officers had been killed through attacks on individual officers and small stations.

These attacks appeared to indicate that resistance to the regime, albeit on a relatively small scale, was becoming increasingly organised, despite the disarray of the FIS and the absence of an unambiguous endorsement of a strategy of armed resistance by any of its senior figures. The reason for this apparent paradox was that it was groups outside the formal frame-work of the FIS that had initiated organised armed resistance to the regime.

The formation of the armed groups

The manifest failure of the FIS's "legalist" strategy, following the January coup, strengthened the conviction of those radical Islamist elements that had remained outside the party, that only force of arms could achieve an Islamic state. These elements became the immediate spearheads of attempts by the wider Islamist movement to attack and bring down the new regime by force.

Elements of the shadowy Takfir wa Hijra and the various veterans of the Afghan war that belonged to the organisation or operated close to it were at the forefront of the initial attacks on the security forces in early 1992. These elements had already demonstrated their eagerness to confront the regime through attacks on the security forces during the

---

with 28 presidents of APWs, 200 presidents of APCs and 528 members of APWs who had assumed office following the FIS's victories in the elections of June 1990. *Jeune Afrique*, 2.4.92.

20 An example of such calls appeared in a clandestine newspaper of the FIS on 20 April 1992 which issued an appeal "to pass on word of arms". The veracity of this message was, however, questioned by some members of the FIS who pointed to the fact that it was unsigned. *Jeune Afrique*, 13.8.92.

disturbances of June 1991 and the subsequent assault on the border post at Guemmar in November 1991 (see Chapter Six). However, the vigour with which the security forces responded to the activities of these groups in the opening months of 1992 struck them hard and following the deaths and arrests of several prominent figures, including Aissa Messaoudi (leader of the Guemmar attack) who was arrested in February, the various groups associated with Takfir had been forced by the summer to retreat from their urban bases around Algiers to the rural maquis.

Despite their established tradition and experience of armed resistance Takfir wa Hijra and the Afghans soon came to be overshadowed in the maquis by the materialisation of a far more important grouping. The year 1992 marked the reappearance of several of Mustapha Bouyali's key lieutenants in the maquis under the banner of the MAIA, or just MIA (Mouvement Islamique Armé) as it was increasingly known. This re-emergence indicated an intention to relaunch the guerrilla war the grouping had waged against the Algerian government between 1982 and March 1987 when Bouyali had finally been killed by the security services and most of his small, but dedicated, band of followers imprisoned. The release of the last of those convicted of being involved with Bouyali and the MIA on 29 July 1990 following an amnesty led to the gradual and clandestine re-formation of various cells of the organisation. This culminated in a reconstitution of the MIA itself in January 1991. Despite the flight of some figures abroad and the adhesion of some others to the FIS, senior figures in the old MIA such as Abdelkader Chebouti, Mansour Meliani, Azzedine Baa and Mouloud Hattab remained in Algeria and had kept their distance from the FIS. At odds with the constitutionalist strategy of the FIS, they continued to hold to the martyred Bouyali's belief in the efficacy and importance of armed struggle. The crackdown of mid-1991 by the Algerian authorities on the FIS strengthened the case and even support of these figures who began to form small groups in preparation for armed resistance. They preferred not to attack the regime openly, as elements of Takfir wa Hijra and the Afghans did, in 1991, but began following the January *coup d'état* to launch individual operations against the security forces and by the summer of 1992 the veterans of the MIA had moved to become the main source of organised armed resistance to the regime.[21]

---

21 It is possible that elements associated with the MIA were involved in the clashes

A third, and vital, strand to the organised armed Islamist opposition to the regime was that associated with the two dissident members of FIS, Said Mekhloufi and Kameredine Kherbane. Formally ejected from the party's Majlis Shura at the Batna conference in July 1991 following their advocacy of a return to armed struggle, Mekhloufi and Kherbane continued to enjoy an important array of contacts with a wide variety of Islamist elements, both inside and outside Algeria. Kherbane had been a former head of the Arab Mujahidin in Peshawar in Pakistan during the war in Afghanistan and through this had numerous connections and friends throughout both the Muslim and Western worlds. For his part, Mekhloufi, also an Afghan veteran, had close and cordial relations with Kamel Assamer, leader of Takfir wa Hijra, and had spent time in Jordan in 1990-91 as the chief co-ordinator of the Islamist effort to send volunteers to fight for Iraq during the Gulf crisis of that period. These connections together with the important positions the two had held within the FIS as members of the Majlis Shura (Mekhloufi had also been head of security for the party) meant that both had the potential to play crucial co-ordinational roles: between the various and disparate components of the Islamist movement, the various emerging elements of the armed resistance and ultimately between the armed groups and the FIS itself.

Attempts at co-ordination

Attempts at co-ordination between the various factions began as early as mid-January 1992 when Said Mekhloufi and several radical figures close to him met with the Bouyalistes Abdelkader Chebouti and Mansour Meliani in Zbarbar in the mountains. Despite the atmosphere of suspicion that prevailed at the meeting, it succeeded in establishing an important precedent and the group met again two weeks later at the beginning of February, when they were joined in their discussions by a prominent "Afghan". The beginning of the first violent clashes with the security forces at the start of February 1992 (not unconnected with the February meeting) and the subsequent clampdown by the regime sharpened the debate in later meetings. The various representatives felt

---

that occurred near the Tunisian border in late 1991. Several armed Islamists captured by the authorities 'confessed' to being involved in an organisation called the Armed Islamic Movement. It was also likely that there was significant overlap between groups associated with the MIA and Takfir wa Hijra.

impelled to move on from emphasising their own strength and importance *vis-à-vis* the others to more serious discussions of how the armed factions could arm themselves and how they could form some form of unified national structure. A meeting held during Ramadan, again in Zbarbar, attracted a still-widening range of radical figures representing the increasing number of independent armed groups. Despite the strong belief of some figures that priority should be given simply to out and out armed struggle, rather than co-ordination, a concerted attempt was made at this meeting to give the burgeoning guerrilla resistance to the regime some unity of organisation. Operational sectors comprised of armed cells were consequently designated and at the national level it was agreed that the leadership of a new unified organisation would include a variety of posts which would be shared out between the various groups. In recognition of the central role being played by the MIA in the maquis – due to their organisation, experience and use of hideouts and arms caches surviving from the 1980s – the post of "national emir" was offered to the most prominent and powerful figure in the MIA: Abdelkader Chebouti.[22]

The decisions taken at the Zbarbar meeting and the posts allocated did not, however, represent the conclusion of an organised and fully co-ordinated common front amongst all the armed groups against the regime. Several factors worked to ensure that despite the growing overall level of violence against the regime there remained only minimal operational co-operation and co-ordination between the various groups. The increasing effectiveness of security force operations against the guerrilla groups in the rural maquis during the spring and summer of 1992 hampered attempts at communication between the different, often geographically isolated groups. In addition these operations succeeded in damaging and splintering many of the organised groups, creating new groups and cells and thus further complicating the process of co-ordination. A second and ultimately more important factor inhibiting unity was the reluctance of many of the groups to submit themselves to central authority. This did not just apply to the growing number of small isolated bands which had emerged and which did not align themselves to the major groupings represented at the meetings, but equally to several individuals, even within the MIA, who attended the meetings but still wished to retain the independence of their own groups.

---

22 Dévoluy and Duteil, *La Poudrière Algérienne*, pp. 147–9 and pp. 172–3.

Another meeting of the major groups was convened on 1 September at Tamesguida in a final endeavour to unite their efforts. Abdelkader Chebouti, in particular, was concerned that attacks, notably a bloody bomb attack on Algiers airport on 26 August, had been carried out without his agreement. He argued that this could alienate ordinary Algerians and create schisms between the groups. In response to these fears, Nourredine Seddiki, the representative of the Afghans and Takfir wa Hijra formally agreed to unite under the banner of the MIA. The groups Seddiki represented had been decimated by the security forces during the summer offensive and he thus saw little practical point in remaining technically independent. One influential independent group leader, Allal Mohammed (also known as Moh Leveilley), having rejected an offer of a post in the organisational structure drawn up at the Ramadan meeting (because of suspected ambitions to lead the entire organisation) proposed the creation of a Majlis Shura. However, these promising indications of greater unity were almost immediately cut short and shattered. The security forces, having learned of the location of the meeting from a prominent activist captured just a few days earlier, launched a surprise assault against Tamesguida whilst the meeting was still in session. Although both Chebouti and Seddiki were able to escape the attack, Allal Mohammed and his senior lieutenant were killed. More importantly, the confusion and suspicion which the attack provoked amongst all the armed groups ensured that the Tamesguida meeting would be the last of its type for the foreseeable future and from the autumn of 1992 the various armed factions continued to operate largely independently of each other.

The role of the FIS

The precise role and attitude of the FIS itself towards the armed struggle conducted by other elements within the wider Islamist movement was initially unclear and was result of the confusion and disruption that had been inflicted on the party in the opening months of 1992. The arrest of so many of its senior figures, and the forcing of the remainder of its leadership and membership underground following the formal official dissolution of the party at the beginning of March, meant that authoritative statements from the FIS became more difficult to identify. Of the group that had formed the provisional leadership of the party following Abassi Madani and Ali Belhadj's imprisonment in June 1991,

Abdelkader Hachani, Rabah Kebir and Othman Aissani were all arrested by the authorities, whilst Mohammed Said went into hiding.[23]

Mohammed Said continued to be active in clandestinity, working closely with Abderrazak Redjam, another member of the FIS's BEP (as head of the Information Bureau). In concert with Ikhlef Cherrati, a former assistant to Othman Aissani and an expert in propaganda techniques, both became involved in the work of various clandestine media which sought to put the Islamist message across and to condemn the regime. Newspapers such as *Minbar El-Djoumma* and *Ennafir* were established and a radio station, Idaat El-Wafa, began transmitting at the beginning of August 1992. It soon became apparent, not least from the detailed information that they supplied, that these media had established close links with elements of the armed resistance. "Radio Wafa", as it became known, transmitted, in addition to sermons and communiqués, reports on the "activities of the MIA", and at times it appeared to be actually transmitting in the name of the MIA itself.[24] However, whilst both the newspapers and the radio listed and justified the killings of members of the security forces, neither Said, Redjam (who continued to sign both *El-Minbar* and official FIS communiqués) nor Cherrati explicitly called for further attacks on the regime either through these media or personally.[25] Despite allegations that all three had joined the MIA, there seemed to be a marked reluctance on the part of all of them to depart from the established FIS line that the party was neither perpetrating nor demanding violence against the state.

Other figures outside the central core of the leadership of the party, however, departed from this plank of FIS policy with far greater ease and several became quickly involved in the armed groups. Benazouz Zebda and Hachemi Sahnouni, both of whom had been ejected from the party's Majlis Shura in July 1991, accompanied Said Mekhloufi in his initial meetings with members of the MIA and Takfir wa Hijra in January and

---

23 Mohammed Said was subsequently convicted *in absentia* to ten years in prison for distributing subversive tracts.
24 *Algérie Actualité*, 16.2.92 and 2.3.93.
25 An example of this stance of justifying but not actually calling for attacks on the security services was provided in a statement by Redjam on 13 March 1992: "The FIS held out the hand of dialogue, but the authorities responded with state violence. It was this which drove the children of the people to resort to means other than that of dialogue." *Jeune Afrique*, 23.12.93.

February 1992. Various other FIS figures including former APC presidents and National Assembly candidates elected in December 1991 became directly involved with the armed groups. Amar Lazaar, the FIS mayor of Guemmar, became co-leader of the armed group led by Chebouti around Lakhadaria. Two other members of the FIS, Soussene Said and Hocine Abderrahim, became important linking figures between elements of the FIS and the armed groups. Both former companions of Bouyali, they had joined the FIS and had been elected under its banner – Said as president of the Bouzaréah APC and Abderrahim as a deputy in the December 1991 elections. The extent of Soussene Said's knowledge of and links with the various groupings was revealed when he was captured and interrogated by the security forces in August 1992. Information he revealed led to the spectacular attack on the summit held between the armed groups at Tamesguida on 1 September. Abderrahim, a former aid to the FIS leadership, had, according to information supplied by Soussene, been appointed as head of the Algiers cell of the MIA by Chebouti. He was later convicted and executed for his alleged role in the bombing of Algiers airport on 26 August.

The unclear and ambiguous position and message of the FIS, resulting from its official dissolution, was both eased and complicated by the emergence of a number of FIS exiles abroad who began to be active and to speak on behalf of the party in the later part of 1992. Two figures rapidly came to prominence: Anwar Haddam, who had been elected as a deputy for the FIS in the December elections, and more importantly Rabah Kebir, who had miraculously escaped house arrest and fled the country in September 1992. Establishing themselves in the USA and Germany respectively, Haddam and Kebir both set about the task of lobbying popular and official opinion in the West for the FIS's cause. They sought to draw particular attention to the iniquities of the Algerian regime: primarily its cancelling of the elections and, as its campaign against the armed groups intensified, its increasingly dubious human rights record. Both figures assumed "official" titles. Kebir referred to himself as the official representative of the FIS abroad, whilst Haddam described himself as head of the "FIS Parliamentary Delegation to the USA and Europe" which purported to represent the FIS "parliamentarians" elected in December 1991. These titles led many to conclude that far from being in confusion and disarray, the FIS was rapidly reconstructing itself. As one observer saw it, Mohammed Said had moved to become the recognised leader of the FIS in the wake of the events of early 1992, Abderrazak Redjam had become his deputy and Kebir and Haddam had assumed important positions abroad.[26] That all four of these figures came from the young, technocratic group, often associated with the Jazara, that had assumed leadership of the party at the Batna conference of July 1991 further reinforced this impression. However, it was unlikely that such close co-operation existed between the various elements, given both the clandestinity Said and Redjam worked under and the remoteness of the representatives abroad. This was demonstrated by statements issued by Anwar Haddam and Rabah Kebir, both of whom called into question the role played by the media established by Said and Redjam. Haddam described as being "linked to us . . . but it does not represent our policy".[27] Kebir went further and explicitly denied the right of the newspaper to speak on behalf of the FIS.[28]

Haddam and Kebir's qualification and even denial of links with organs such as *Minbar El-Djoumma was* primarily the result of a desire on the part of both of them to distance themselves from the rather equivocal stance taken by the various media connected to Said and Redjam on the issue of violence against the regime. Both were anxious to promote as attractive and innocent an image of the FIS abroad as possible – an image that stood to be damaged through being perceived to be endorsing bombings and assassinations. In addition, Kebir in particular still held out hope that the regime could still be persuaded to negotiate with and rehabilitate the FIS – a hope that risked being similarly negated by violence from Islamists. He continued to reiterate the line that had been established by the FIS at the time of the December elections and which he had held to even after his arrest and the dissolution of the party. In April 1992 he affirmed that the FIS remained "attached to legality and public political action" and stated that "the methods of the FIS remain political unlike those of the regime . . ."[29]

The divergence of views on the endorsement of violence revealed not only the differences that existed between the various senior figures in the FIS but more importantly raised the issue of who should be seen as

---

26 See *Libération*, 14.3.94.
27 *Independent*, 13.5.92.
28 Charef, *Algérie: Le Grand Dérapage*, p. 385.
29 *Ibid.*, p. 310.

the official voice of the FIS. Both Kebir and Said clearly felt that they had legitimate claims in this regard. This apparent crisis of legitimacy appeared to be resolved by the intervention of the figure who was formally recognised by both factions, inside and outside Algeria, as the legitimate leader of the party: Abassi Madani. In a statement smuggled out of the prison at Blida, Madani declared that henceforth Rabah Kebir should be "the sole authorised spokesman of the FIS abroad". Moreover, he ordered that the issuing and signing of official FIS communiqués and statements should be the exclusive right of Kebir, and specifically instructed that Abderrazak Redjam, who had continued to sign such communiqués, should no longer do so.[30] Abassi's decision to endorse Kebir in this way was largely due to the senior position Kebir had held in the party over the period of the legislative elections but was probably influenced by the fact that Madani's two sons were close allies of Kebir as fellow exiles in Germany. The official endorsement of Kebir did not, though, ease the divisions and rivalries within the segmented Islamist movement. Despite having come from the same group that took on the leadership of the FIS in the summer of 1991, Said and Redjam clearly balked at the new exclusive authority vested in Kebir and continued to use the clandestine newspapers and radio within Algeria to assert their authority. Anwar Haddam was also unhappy with Kebir's new status. Statements issued from his base in Chicago, where he worked with an estimated forty exiled Algerian Islamists, became increasingly critical of Kebir and his allies in Germany. He accused Abassi Madani's sons of trying to establish a family hegemony over the FIS and Kebir himself of being sympathetic towards some form of compromise with the regime.[31] Like Said, Redjam and Cherrati, Haddam adopted an increasingly ambiguous and equivocal line on the issue of violence in a departure from his previous statements which whilst expressing understanding of the violence had argued that this was not a path endorsed by the FIS.[32] In

---

30 *Algérie Actualité*, 23.3.93.
31 *Ibid.*, 16.11.93.
32 In May 1992 Haddam had declared: "The armed groups support the free choice of the people. They have chosen a certain way. We in the FIS don't want that. We don't want violence. But more and more people are calling for that. They (the armed groups) are our brothers in Islam. We understand their feelings." (*Independent*, 13.5.92). A few months later he remarked: "We have no interest in inheriting a country torn apart by civil war." *Jeune Afrique*, 13.8.92.

making this shift Haddam was clearly seeking to bolster his own popular legitimacy with the armed groups inside Algeria whilst simultaneously undermining the legitimacy bestowed on Rabah Kebir who stuck to the line originally held by Haddam.

In spite of the endorsement of Abassi Madani, Kebir gradually found himself politically isolated both inside the FIS and within the wider Islamist movement. His differences with Mohammed Said, Redjam and Haddam represented ruptures with close political associates, and it was clear that he was unlikely to find fresh allies outside this grouping. Kebir's new authority was explicitly rejected by more traditionalist figures in the FIS such as the 83-year-old sheikh Abdelbaki Sahraoui (one of the founders of the FIS) who declared from France that "Kebir is illegitimate . . . He is not mandated to speak in the name of our organisation."[33] This lack of recognition by members of the FIS for the official endorsement of the party's leader, Abassi Madani, indicated that Kebir stood little chance of gaining the support of those Islamists who had never been a part of the FIS and thus felt no need to recognise Madani's authority. This was particularly true of many of the armed groups. Ikhlef Cherrati frequently came into conflict with his allies in the MIA over the issue of legitimacy. Cherrati explicitly drew his authority from Abassi and the original leadership of the FIS whilst Chebouti, Azzedine Baa and other senior figures who had never joined the FIS looked further back to their association with Mustapha Bouyali for their legitimacy.

The issue of legitimacy came to the fore again in January 1993 when a statement emerged from the prison at Blida, this time from Ali Belhadj, who declared:

> If I was outside the walls of this prison. I would be a fighter in the ranks of army of brother Abdelkader Chebouti.[34]

---

33 *Jeune Afrique*, 30.9.93. Sahraoui also appeared equally hostile towards Redjam and Said, possibly also because of their Jazarist connections, condemning the French version of *El Minbar*, *La Critère* as "a rag" (*Le Monde*, 18.11.92). There were even some suggestions that Sahraoui and Kamreddine Kherbane (who enjoyed close relations as fellow exiles in France) had 're-grouped' the salafi tendency of the FIS, sidelined since 1991, in France and had even supplanted allies of the Jazarist there. Dévoluy and Duteil, *La Poudrière Algérienne*, p. 287; *Jeune Afrique*, 11.11.93.

34 *Jeune Afrique*, 21.1.93.

The statement had a dual significance. Firstly, it represented a clear endorsement of the armed struggle by the FIS's original deputy leader. Secondly, it appeared to indicate the FIS's recognition of and unity of purpose with Chebouti's MIA. It was not made clear whether Abassi Madani fully subscribed to his deputy's position, but it appeared to contrast with Abassi's recent endorsement of Rabah Kebir – a figure reluctant to applaud the armed struggle. It was possible that once again Abassi was acting to ensure that the FIS displayed a moderate, pragmatic face to the outside world in particular (Kebir being charged with winning support for the party's cause in the West) whilst Belhadj busied himself with securing robust rank and file support for the party with his more hardline and uncompromising rhetoric. However, whilst in 1989–91 uncertainty had persisted over which line represented the real nature of the FIS, Rabah Kebir, bereft of allies was steadily pulled towards adopting a less moderate stance. Initially attempting to suppress Ali Belhadj's expression of solidarity with Chebouti and the MIA by failing to make Belhadj's letter public (copies of it were, nevertheless, distributed in Paris by Kameredine Kherbane), Kebir relented by the time a second similar letter reached him and fully publicised it.[35] A further step was taken in February 1993 following an assassination attempt against Defence Minister Khaled Nezzar when Kebir, whilst not claiming FIS responsibility for the attack, remarked that:

> This can be considered a clear warning from the mujahidin to the tyrants who openly fight God and his Prophet.[36]

The strengthening of links between the FIS and elements of the armed resistance heralded further attempts to unite the entire Islamist movement, politically and militarily, in the struggle against the regime. In March 1993 the establishment of a unified military command for a number of the armed groups was announced. It was to be headed by a troika of Chebouti, who became the supreme commander; Said Mekhloufi, who had been operating his own independent group and became head of operations; and Azzedine Baa of the MIA, who became the command's deputy leader. For the first time a political representative was also

---

35 *Ibid.*
36 *The Economist*, 20.2.93.

nominated – Mohammed Said being named as head of the interior political leadership.

The efforts at unification came to full fruition six months later with the announcement of the formation of an "Executive Authority of the FIS Abroad", which appeared to establish a unified political structure for the hitherto fractious individuals active abroad. A four-man leadership was unveiled headed, significantly, by Rabah Kebir as president, with Kameredine Kherbane as vice-president. Abdallah Anas (a prominent Afghan) and Anwar Haddam assumed unspecified responsibilities. The creation of these bodies appeared to represent the final unification of the three important strands of the Islamist movement that had emerged in the wake of the January coup and now shared the senior posts in the new bodies: the MIA, the Afghans and the FIS itself.

The emergence of the GIA

The creation of bodies such as the Executive Authority of the FIS and the unified military command of the MIA did not, however, fully represent the unification of all of the major elements of the Islamist movement. They incorporated most of the major ones that had been in existence in the early months of 1992, but by 1993 there had emerged a powerful and influential tendency that remained firmly outside of these new bodies. The Jammat Islamiyya Mousalaha, the Armed Islamic Groups (usually referred to by the French acronym – GIA), which became the main embodiment of this tendency, represented a faction of opinion that espoused a far more radical response to the crisis that beset the Islamist movement in the wake of the January coup and accordingly gathered to it those Islamists who shared such radical convictions.

Origins
In essence the GIA drew its inspiration, as well as its members, from that part of the Islamist movement that rejected the idea that an Islamic state could be installed by constitutional and legal means, believing instead that force of arms was both morally and practically the right way to achieve this aim. As has been shown, many elements that held this conviction joined the FIS in 1989 despite its explicitly constitutionalist and electoral strategy. The blocking of the constitutionalist path by the regime in January 1992 caused most of these elements to break their

tactical alliance with the party and join those seeking armed confrontation with the government. Despite the effective renewal of this alliance in 1993, with advocates of armed resistance such as Chebouti and Mekhloufi willing to come together with "political" figures such as Kebir and Redjam on a new agenda of political unity and limited armed struggle, there remained those for whom armed struggle of an increasingly unlimited nature had become a political and ideological imperative which prevented them from joining the new structures.

This radicalism and commitment to armed struggle inevitably led to suggestions that groups such as Takfir wa Hijra and Bouyali's original MIA were the forerunners of the GIA. However, although there were links of ideology and personnel the more concrete origins of the organisation did not emerge until after the coup of January 1992.[37] The fragmented nature of early armed resistance to the regime inevitably led to the formation of groups espousing varying ideologies and headed by individual figures eager to establish their own leadership and ideology over the other groups. Personal ambition and ideological differences played a significant part in the formation of the dissident grouping that first set itself up as a radical alternative and which was the first to formally employ the term GIA. This initial GIA was formed by Mansour Meliani, the former Bouyalist, who used the name for the three small groups he had gradually drawn together under his leadership by July 1992. Meliani had been a close associate of Abdelkader Chebouti, the two having fought alongside Bouyali in the 1980s and been imprisoned together. However, following bitter rivalry between the two for leadership of the reformed MIA, Meliani broke with Chebouti in January 1992, and withdrew his cells from the overall leadership that Chebouti was establishing over the armed movement. Meliani's GIA, however, lasted barely a few weeks before Meliani himself was arrested by the security forces on 28 July 1992 and his groups dispersed.

The idea of the GIA did not die with the arrest of Meliani. The name continued to appear in small clandestine newspapers and was formally revived in January 1993 by another radical and independent figure:

---

37 One Algerian journalist dates the origins of the GIA back to the formation in June 1990 of an organisation entitled Youm El-Hissab (Redemption Day) by individuals from Takfir wa Hijra, including Nourredine Seddiki, and former MIA figures such as Azzedine Baa. *El Watan*, 28.2.94.

Abdelhak Layada.[38] A lieutenant of Allal Mohammed, Layada had assumed control of the group they led following the death of Allal Mohammed in the security force ambush of the armed groups' summit at Tamesguida in September 1992. Like Allal Mohammed, Layada sought to become the supreme commander of all the armed groups, and kept his distance from attempts to draw him and his supporters into a Chebouti-headed unified command. Layada brought in two further groups and having been encouraged by military setbacks Chebouti's MIA had suffered in the autumn of 1992, officially declared his independence from Chebouti and announced that his new GIA would no longer obey orders issued by him.[39]

Ideology

The secession of Layada, although provoked by personal rivalries and ambitions, swiftly developed into something of far greater substance in terms of both ideology and strategy. Encouraged by the prominent role enjoyed by Omar El-Eulmi, a radical ideologue who became the GIA's "spiritual guide" on its creation, the new GIA exhibited an extremely radical ideology from the outset. Central to its ideology was a fundamental and unequivocal rejection not only of constitutional Islamism but of the whole idea of democracy itself. El-Eulmi had joined the FIS and had at one stage been a member of the party's Majlis Shura and a senior figure in the Islamist trade union, the SIT. He had disappeared from the ranks of the FIS in mid-1991, marginalised and alienated by the rise in influence of the Jazarists. He appeared briefly again before the legislative elections of December 1991 to declare publicly that an Islamic state could not be achieved other than through force of arms.[40] Such sentiments

---

38 Layada, however, denied authorship of several tracts that appeared in the name of the GIA during this time. *Algérie Actualité*, 2.11.93.

39 Antipathy to Abdelkader Chebouti's overall leadership of the armed struggle, which had also been evident at earlier meetings of the armed groups and in Mansour Meliani's break with Chebouti, was not simply a result of personal ambition and ideological differences on the part of the dissident voices. Many of the senior figures in the armed groups felt that, despite his experience, Chebouti was too cautious and uncharismatic a figure to effectively lead a unified command. This was particularly true of figures such as Allal Mohammed and Abdelhak Layada who were younger and whose groups were more active and who were therefore less willing to show deference towards Chebouti's background and experience.

40 *El Watan*, 28.2.94. El-Eulmi had also been the main spokesman for the FIS/SIT during the general strike of May–June 1991.

were reiterated a year later in December 1992, shortly before the formal recreation of the GIA, by Layada who asserted that:

> We reject the religion of democracy. We affirm that political pluralism is equal to sedition. It has never been our intention to participate in elections or enter parliament. Besides, the right to legislate belongs solely to God.[41]

Methods and campaigns: the use of terror and assassination

What increasingly began to mark the GIA out from the other armed groups, as 1993 progressed, was a willingness to translate this extremist rhetoric into actual policy. The struggle against the regime by the various armed groups during the first year following the imposition of the HCE was characterised predominantly by guerrilla warfare against the security services and by sabotage and bomb attacks against state-run and related institutions.[42] The GIA demonstrated that it was willing to expand the armed struggle in much more extreme and sinister directions.

March 1993 witnessed a series of assassinations of junior government ministers and members of the National Consultative Council (CCN) which had originally been established by Mohammed Boudiaf. Assassination had become an established instrument of the armed groups by 1993, but it had been used almost exclusively against members of the security services and those government members directly involved in the anti-terrorist struggle. The assassinations of March 1993 marked an effective expansion in the definition of those apparently seen as "legitimate" targets to include anybody more generally a part of, or representing, the regime. Writers, journalists and those involved in the media became increasingly the targets of assassination attempts. Increasingly, figures who were neither involved with nor supportive of the regime but who were seen as opposed to Islamism, particularly the secularist press, also became subject to attack.

---

41 *Jeune Afrique,* 27.1.94.
42 Such attacks against post offices, financial institutions, telephone exchanges (with the notable exception of the airport bombing of 26 August 1992 where it was argued that their warning had not been acted upon quickly enough by the authorities) usually took place outside working hours to avoid casualties.

That it was the GIA which was primarily responsible for these attacks and the escalation and expansion of the armed struggle was fairly clear. The early months of 1993 had seen the circulation of cassettes in various mosques, containing calls for no mercy to be shown to anyone collaborating with the regime and the authorities, it being necessary "to kill all the agents of the regime".[43] The suspected author of these calls was Omar El-Eulmi, who also issued more explicit fatwas authorising the killing of not only members of the security services and the government in the name of the GIA but also of individual intellectuals and journalists. Most notable of these named individuals was Taher Djaout, a poet and journalist who had been a strong critic of the Islamists and who was shot dead by gunmen in May.

The reasons for these attacks were mixed. Whilst the killing of all of those perceived to be opposed to the idea of an Islamic state had obvious roots in the GIA's radical ideology and was reminiscent of the stance taken by several extremist Islamist groups elsewhere in the Muslim world, notably in Egypt, there were other tactical and strategic reasons for these campaigns. For some observers the shift away from attacks on the security services represented an attempt to enforce public support for the armed groups (and undercut support for the regime) through the simple use of terror. However, it seems more likely that the campaign of assassinations was part of an endeavour on the part of the GIA to accrue notoriety and support through the killing of high-profile individuals who clearly represented "softer" and more accessible targets than members of the security forces. Through this the GIA appeared to be making an attempt to seize both the political and operational initiative from the other armed groups.

A further expansion of the conflict came with the targeting by the GIA of foreign nationals living in Algeria. Hitherto physically untouched by the escalating conflict in the country, Algeria's estimated 70,000 foreign residents first became involved in the struggle when two French surveyors were kidnapped and killed on 20–21 September 1993 near Sidi Bel Abbès. These deaths were followed in October by the deaths of two Russian military advisers and three foreign contract workers employed by the state oil company SONATRACH. The responsibility

---

43ʳ Charef, *Algérie: Le Grand Dérapage*, p. 387. The cassettes also called for no clemency to be shown to "the fathers of families, women and the elderly".

for these killings became known at the end of October when three kidnapped French nationals were released by the Algerian security forces following the storming of a prayer hall on 30 October. A note given by the kidnappers to one of the freed captives (whom the kidnappers had apparently planned to release with the note) signed by the GIA and addressed to the country's foreigners, explained the new strategy of targeting foreigners:

> Leave the country. We are giving you one month. Anyone who exceeds that period will be responsible for his own sudden death. There will be no kidnappings and it will be more violent than in Egypt.[44]

This assault on the expatriate community living in Algeria, as with that against prominent Algerians, had both ideological and strategic motivations. Like their radical counterparts in Egypt, the GIA aimed to rid Algeria of "corrupting" non-Islamic influences. More importantly, they also sought to weaken the regime by frightening off the foreign companies and foreign investment that the government was relying on so heavily to improve economic and social conditions and so undercut support for the armed groups. The fact that an estimated 3,000 foreign nationals left the country within days of the release of the note warning them to quit Algeria by the end of November, and continued to leave as killings of foreigners began and continued following the expiry of the deadline, indicated that the strategy's initial intention was succeeding.[45]

Structure

In June 1993 *Echahada*, a clandestine newspaper which first appeared in January 1993 and which was clearly controlled by the GIA, set out the structure of the organisation. Abdelhak Layada was listed as the party's leader and co-ordinator as well as a member of the groups' four-strong Majlis Shura. Other issues of *Echahada* claimed that the GIA contained an "Islamic Legislative Committee" led by an Islamic scholar, which was

---

44   *The Times*, 20.11.93. Foreigners, particularly tourists, had been targeted by Egypt's radical Islamist groups since the summer of 1992.

45   The GIA explicitly claimed responsibility for these attacks, vowing that it would continue to pursue the "enemies of Allah" – thus emphasising the religious dimension of the campaign.

charged with pronouncing fatwas in conjunction with the actions of the armed cells of the organisation.[46]

It was doubtful, however, that the GIA was in fact structured and ordered to such a high degree. One observer concluded that the GIA was in reality a flexible federation of at least four ideologically similar but distinct groups operating in different regions.[47] Nevertheless, the organisation, such as it was, did appear to display a significant degree of cohesion and resilience surviving both the death of El-Eulmi at the hands of the security forces in April 1993 and the arrest of Layada by the authorities in Morocco the following July. Despite the removal of the group's two most important and charismatic figures, the GIA was still able to continue its campaign of assassinations and, moreover, to launch its offensive against Algeria's foreign community. The absence of both Layada and El-Eulmi did not lead to the GIA reducing the radical tone of its pronouncements or activities. Sid Ahmed Mourad (also known as Djaffar Afghani and a former lieutenant of Meliani[48]), who assumed the acknowledged leadership of the GIA following Layada's arrest, made plain his commitment to the extremist line established by Layada and El-Eulmi. He declared in an underground newspaper in November 1993:

> Our jihad consists of killing and dispersing all those who fight against God and his Prophet.[49]

More specifically he added:

> The journalists who fight against Islamism through the pen will perish by the sword.[50]

Abdelkader Hattab, who became the effective number two in the GIA under Mourad, expressed similar sentiments in a leaflet gruesomely entitled "Throat-slitting and murder until the power is God's."[51]

---

46 *Algérie Actualité*, 7.12.93.
47 *Jeune Afrique*, 27.1.94.
48 This emphasises the continuity of personnel between Meliani's initial GIA and Layada's later organisation.
49 *Jeune Afrique*, 27.1.94.
50 *Ibid.*
51 *Jeune Afrique*, 11.11.93.

As the GIA rose to increasing prominence there were accusations from a variety of quarters that the group was simply a front and a puppet for other interests and groups. A persistent charge, particularly from Islamists, was that the GIA had become a cover for units of the security forces to perform two tasks. Firstly, that of discrediting the Islamist movement in general and the FIS in particular through the brutality of their attacks on usually unarmed individuals. Secondly, and more ominously, it allowed the security forces to eradicate prominent critics of the regime, particularly journalists and intellectuals, whilst blaming it on the Islamist opposition. However, although it was increasingly apparent that the security forces were involved with the GIA, this involvement overwhelmingly took the form of infiltration by the security forces. Such infiltration was facilitated by the recruitment strategy of the GIA which drew its members predominantly from the young unemployed. This made it relatively easy to introduce informers into the groups and explains the repeated successes the authorities had in eliminating the senior figures of the group.[52]

The almost inevitable counter-charge by the Algerian regime was that the GIA was simply a convenient cover for the worst excesses of the FIS itself and its allies and was in reality an integral part of the FIS.[53] However, this accusation too had only a passing element of truth to it. Whilst there was some evidence of links between the two factions, mainly abroad, the central reality within Algeria was that the GIA had become by late 1993 a substantial threat and rival to the FIS.

Relations with the FIS

The original leadership of the GIA aimed through its activities to seize both the political and operational initiative of the armed struggle from the FIS and its allies in the armed groups. Motivated by both rivalry and extremist ideological purity the GIA pushed itself increasingly into conflict with the more mainstream elements of the Islamist movement.

Politically, the GIA, from its revival in January 1993, sought to distinguish itself from the FIS. Unlike all the other armed groups which either explicitly or implicitly drew their legitimacy from or deferred

---

52 Layada had been particularly keen to recruit young members as they were less likely to contest his authority.
53 The regime naturally accused the FIS of being behind each attack and assassination.

politically to the FIS, the leadership of the GIA made clear its rejection of the party. It is possible that this had been encouraged by Ali Belhadj's endorsement of Chebouti, Layada's rival, in December 1992, but statements issued by Omar El-Eulmi attacking former members of the FIS's BEP such as Redjam, Said, Kebir and Cherrati contained clear elements of hostility towards the pragmatic tendencies of the Jazara to which all of these figures were linked. In addition to accusations of un-Islamic compromise and moderation, El-Eulmi also charged these figures with having joined the FIS "for love of power" and accused Rabah Kebir and other leaders of the FIS abroad of being responsible for the alleged disappearance of funds gathered abroad to support the armed struggle.[54]

In common with the terror campaigns, the stance of the GIA towards the FIS did not essentially change with the removal of Layada and El-Eulmi from its head in 1993. Sid Ahmed Mourad continued to denounce senior figures in the party and furthermore began to heap scorn on both Abassi Madani and Ali Belhadj.[55] The formation of unified military and political structures by the FIS, the MIA and various individual Afghans in 1993 increased the political stakes for the GIA which saw the initiative slipping away from itself. This possibly explained the timing of its decision to launch the campaign against foreigners, begun just a week after the announcement of the formation of the Executive Authority of the FIS Abroad on 14 September.

Up until the formation of the Executive Authority it had been the FIS that felt it was losing the initiative to the GIA. The leadership of the party, already riven by its own splits between moderates and hardliners, even endorsed many of the GIA's assassinations out of fear of being sidelined in the struggle against the regime.[56] Anwar Haddam commented on the killing in June 1993 of Mohammed Boukhobza, an academic and a member of the CCN, that: "It is not a question of it being a crime, but a sentence of death carried out by the mujahidin."[57] Similarly,

---

54 *Algérie Actualité*, 27.4.93. El-Eulmi also stated that those FIS figures living abroad should return to Algeria and participate in the jihad. Charef, *Algérie: Le Grand Dérapage*, p. 387.

55 See *Jeune Afrique*, 23.12.93.

56 Omar El-Eulmi had explicitly referred to these fears by claiming that the leaders of the FIS had been "eclipsed" by the calls for jihad he had issued through recordings on cassettes distributed in Algiers. *Algérie Actualité*, 27.4.93.

57 *Jeune Afrique*, 1.7.93.

Abderrazak Redjam remarked on the first wave of assassinations of junior ministers and members of the CCN that occurred in March 1993 that:

> What is unfolding is not terrorism but a blessed jihad that's legitimacy is founded on the duty to establish an Islamic state and also on the *coup d'état* perpetrated against the choice of the people.[58]

The opening of the campaign against foreigners living in Algeria was, by contrast, met with condemnation by several FIS figures. Influenced by the disastrous impact this development had on the Islamist case they were pleading in the West (and also by the effect this might have on their own status and welcome in the West) senior figures abroad, such as Haddam and Abdelbaki Sahraoui, demanded the immediate and unconditional release of the three French hostages kidnapped in October.[59] Nevertheless, and despite the formation of a common political front in September, members of the new Executive Authority of the FIS Abroad and the leadership of the party inside Algeria itself continued to justify the killings of minor officials, journalists and intellectuals. Both Haddam and even Rabah Kebir began to argue that these categories of people had become "combatants" and thus legitimate targets by supposedly siding with the regime. Members of the CCN and local administrators appointed in the place of sacked and imprisoned elected FIS officials had similarly become liable to assassination because they had "usurped" the rightful and elected authority of the FIS.[60]

Endorsement of the killings by FIS leaders represented not only a desire to avoid being outflanked by the GIA but also a need to justify the operations of the FIS's own armed groups which had also begun to target individuals not directly involved in the anti-terrorist campaign.[61]

---

58 Charef, *Algérie: Le Grand Dérapage*, p. 386.
59 *Algérie Actualité*, 2.11.93.
60 'Human rights abuses in Algeria: no one is spared', Middle East Watch (January 1994), pp. 56–9.
61 Rabah Kebir, for example, had detailed procedures that were operated before assassinations of individuals were carried out, including the convening of committees of Islamic scholars to decide guilt, the ascertaining of facts about the case and the issuing of warnings. "We can say that these [procedures] are really akin to courts" he asserted. (Middle East Watch, p. 54n, p. 55 and p. 59). However, whilst such knowledge of these procedures suggested complicity of the FIS, it

Figures such as Haddam and Kebir were anxious to show they were not out of touch with the armed groups, but they were more concerned to show that the FIS itself was not responsible for much of the violence. In condemning the attacks against foreigners, Kebir stated that: "The popular movement is very difficult to control."[62] And in an implicit reference to the GIA, he indicated that the FIS did not control all the armed groups:

> Among those who responded to state violence there were undoubtedly members of the FIS . . . [But] the organisations and groups [that] came into being to defend the will of the people and resist the violence of the state . . . cannot be said to be the FIS.[63]

For its part the GIA was considerably more forthright in its disavowal of links with the FIS. A communiqué issued in its name on 20 November 1993 declared that it "did not represent the armed wing of the FIS" and affirmed that it was an "independent group".[64]

Conflict between the GIA and those close to or part of the FIS also took more direct forms than simple political and strategic manoeuvrings. In addition to denouncing individuals such as Redjam, Kebir, Chebouti and Cherrati, Layada and El-Eulmi had also issued death threats against these and other figures on the grounds of treason.[65] These menaces were never actually carried out, but the first indications that the leaders of the GIA were serious in their antipathy and rivalry towards the leaders of the FIS came with the arrest by the authorities of Ikhlef Cherrati on 26 February 1993. It was widely believed that Cherrati had been betrayed to the security forces by either Layada himself or one of his lieutenants. The death of Sid Ahmed Lahrani, a leader of one of the GIA groups, in a prepared police ambush just a week later, sparked a series of betrayals

---

seems probable that Kebir was attempting to give a legalistic facade to what were almost certainly fairly arbitrary killings, whilst at the same time attempting to claim that they were under the direction of the FIS, a claim that was at best dubious.

62 *Financial Times*, 25.10.93.
63 Middle East Watch, p. 54n.
64 Agence France Presse, 20.11.93, quoted in Middle East Watch, p. 54.
65 *Algérie Actualité*, 23.3.93. In his communiqué, no. 5, Layada also specifically included figures not associated with Jazarist ideas such as Mekhloufi, Azzedine Baa, Benazouz Zebda and Hachemi Sahnouni in his death threats.

to the authorities between the two sides. As the tension increased, Radio Wafa stopped transmitting, following death threats from Sid Ahmed Mourad and his deputy Abdelkader Hattab, and by the end of the year it had begun to appear that the dispute between the two sides had spilled over into direct conflict. Armed clashes occurred between units of the GIA and the MIA in an area to the south-east of Algiers in late November which resulted in the deaths of nearly thirty Islamists.

The regime and the anti-terrorist struggle, 1992–1993

The death of Mohammed Boudiaf at the end of June 1992, albeit welcomed in various shadowy parts of Algeria's ruling elite, deprived the regime installed in January of the vision the assassinated President had had for extricating Algeria from the crisis that had enveloped it. No attempt was made to continue the dead President's political strategy that had been embodied in his launching of the RPN and no comparable strategy was drawn up in the wake of his death to deal with the problems of political legitimacy and support that Boudiaf had identified and sought to rectify. Some attempt was made to find another charismatic outsider to front the regime, but the choice of Belaid Abdessalem as a new Prime Minister with enhanced powers in place of Sid Ahmed Ghozali was not comparable to the original appointment of Boudiaf as President.[66] Although a respected figure who had been progressively marginalised during Chadli Benjedid's presidency, Abdessalem had played a key role in Houari Boumedienne's governments (as one of the central architects of the programme of heavy industrialisation) and had remained an important figure in the FLN, facts that deprived him of the sort of uncompromised image enjoyed by Mohammed Boudiaf.[67] Abdessalem shared Boudiaf's conviction that economic deprivation underlay popular support for Islam, but in contrast to the former President he did not

---

66 Following the death of Boudiaf, many of the powers of the presidency were shifted to the post of Prime Minister. The now more symbolic role of President passed to another member of the HCE, Ali Kafi.

67 Before deciding to recall Mohammed Boudiaf as President the leaders of the January coup had considered Belaid Abdessalem as a possible candidate for the post. His name had been suggested by Sid Ahmed Ghozali who had served under him in the 1970s.

appear to believe that substantial political initiatives needed to accompany initiatives in the economic field. Moreover, he differed sharply with Boudiaf's belief in further liberalisation of Algeria's economy. A long-standing critic of Chadli Benjedid's economic reform programme, the new Prime Minister sought a return to the *dirigiste* economics of the Boumedienne era, reimposing state controls on foreign trade and injecting large sums of money into Algeria's unreformed state companies.[68]

The one part of Boudiaf's programme that was continued in the aftermath of his death was his commitment to eliminating violent resistance to the regime and this became the central plank of the government's policy. In military terms the "anti-terrorist struggle" by the regime met with considerable initial success. The repression of the FIS and the mass arrests of the first half of 1992 had proved very effective. Most of the senior figures in the Islamist movement were rounded up and there was no orchestrated mass resistance to the new regime and its crushing of the FIS. The success of the authorities in retaining control of the streets in urban Algeria resulted in the flight to the rural maquis of those Islamists intent on armed resistance.[69] Although this retreat gave the armed groups access to the more defensible heartland of the old maquis of the war of liberation, as well as to the arms caches and bases of the more recent maquis of Mustapha Bouyali, these factors did not provide them with any real advantage. The retreat to the rural areas cut off the armed groups from each other and, more importantly, isolated them from the essentially urban base of support that the FIS and Islamism drew on. It also allowed the security forces the opportunity to isolate and track down the groups in an environment unhindered by the restrictions of an urban setting. Army units equipped with helicopters, rocket propelled grenades and even tanks pursued the Islamist groups with significant effectiveness during the summer months of 1992. Good intelligence about the bases the fighters were likely to use, as well as about individual Islamists and their contacts, meant that numerous armed groups were

---

68 Michael Willis, 'Algeria's troubled road to political and economic liberalization' in Gerd Nonneman, *Political and Economic Liberalization: Dynamics and Linkages in Comparative Perspective* (London, Lynne Rienner, 1996), p. 211.

69 As Larbi Belkheir, the Interior Minister, claimed in mid-June, "the security forces have succeeded in dislodging from Algiers and the big cities the Islamist outlaws, this explains their retreat to the mountainous regions." *Algérie Actualité*, 18.6.92.

broken up and destroyed across the country.[70] Important figures such as Mansour Meliani and Soussene Said were captured and the surprise attack against the meeting at Tamesguida in September narrowly missed netting most of the heads of the armed groups but still secured the elimination of the powerful Allal Mohammed and several of his key lieutenants.

The significant victories by the security services proved unable, however, to stem the activities of the armed groups which continued to grow and spread despite the setbacks of the summer. The break-up of larger groups led to the formation of smaller, more numerous and more secretive independent groups on whom it proved far more difficult to gather intelligence. The reverses the armed resistance had suffered during the summer of 1992 had led to a gradual flow of guerrillas back to the urban areas of Algeria where recruitment, support and anonymity were far easier to achieve. The passage of time since the dramatic events of the opening months of the year had allowed Islamist and more general opposition to the regime to coalesce and organise itself. Antipathy to the regime continued to be fuelled by growing popular disgust at both the failure of the new regime to deliver any significant improvement in social or economic conditions and the perceived complicity of the regime in the assassination of the charismatic Boudiaf.

The persistence of Islamist violence, which the Algerian military had originally thought would end following the containment of street protests and the elimination of the inevitable but small number of armed activists, prompted the regime to enhance its security policy.[71] The final months of 1992 saw the regime introduce a number of further measures aimed at eliminating the armed opposition.[72] On 2 October a raft of new security measures were announced aimed at strengthening the arsenal of legal measures which the government could use against the terrorists. Panel courts of anonymous judges were introduced, periods of detention without trial were increased and the minimum permissible age

---

70 The good intelligence was the reputed result of the patient accumulation of information on Islamists and their organisations over several years by General Mohammed Médiènne, the director of military security.

71 Larbi Belkheir, as Interior Minister, had predicted in April that the liquidation of the armed groups would be achieved in "a matter of weeks or, in the worst case, a matter of months". Charef, *Algérie: Le Grand Dérapage*, p. 298.

72 The strengthening of security policy in the autumn of 1992 was in large part a reaction to the bombing of Algiers airport at the end of August.

for prosecution was lowered.[73] Mid-February 1993 saw the first sitting of special anti-terrorist courts which enjoyed wide-ranging sentencing powers, including the death penalty. The first executions, out of nearly fifty pending (and the first for nearly four years in Algeria) were carried out on two Islamists involved in an attack on a naval base in the previous February.[74] Large-scale security sweeps began again in urban areas. Nearly 1,200 Islamist activists were arrested during October and November 1992 and on 6 December a curfew was imposed on Algiers. This last measure was accompanied by operations by special police and army units in an attempt to clamp down on increasing Islamist activity in the city at night. On 9 February 1993 the state of emergency that had been declared a year earlier was formally extended for another twelve months, and four months later in June the curfew was extended to three more regions – Cheliff, M'Sila and Djelfa – in addition to Algiers.

There were also efforts on the part of the regime to finally shut down the remaining institutional bases of Islamism and the FIS. On 29 November 1992 new measures were announced which gave the authorities the power to close down the various private companies, labour organisations (notably the SIT), and cultural and charitable organisations which the government saw as providing a network of support for the FIS. Belaid Abdessalem accused the SIT, in particular, of "being the true nucleus of the armed organisation of the dissolved party" and of operating "an explicit strategy of penetration" towards other labour organisations.[75] In addition the last remaining locals councils controlled by people elected under the FIS's banner in June 1990 were dissolved by the government on the grounds cited by the Interior Minister, Mohammed Hardi that "these assemblies had been transformed into logistical bases for subversion."[76] Within two weeks of the 29 November decree nearly 300 APWs and APCs had had their powers transferred to executive delegation committees

---

73 This last measure was aimed at combating the increasingly young age of Islamist activists.

74 A total of 26 death sentences had been passed on Islamist militants (mainly belonging to the MIA) in the three-month period between 3 March and 3 June 1992.

75 *Alger Républicain*, 29.11.92.

76 *El Moudjahid*, 16.3.93. There were accusations, for example, that the president of the FIS-controlled APC in Jijel had used the mayoral budget to buy arms. See *Algérie Actualité*, 2.12.92.

appointed by the government.[77] In late December the government also moved to demolish a number of prayer rooms that had been established by the FIS and which in the view of the Religious Affairs Minister Sassi Lamouri were "used by murderers who do not hesitate to kill in order to gain power".[78]

The regime's determination to defeat the Islamist groups militarily, was reflected in both its increasingly robust statements to this effect and by the promotion of figures who were resolutely committed to the anti-terrorist struggle. General Mohammed Lamari, a figure well known for his hardline anti-Islamist views, was appointed to head the special anti-terrorist unit at the Defence Ministry in September 1992. Ten months later in July 1993 Lamari was promoted again, this time to the head of the armed forces as a whole, replacing General Mohammed Guezmaizia who was rumoured to harbour doubts about the campaign of continued repression.[79]

The robustness with which the ANP and the security forces dealt with the armed resistance, however, obscured certain anxieties that existed within the regime about the conflict. One of the main doubts and concerns held by senior figures in the Algerian regime concerned the continued cohesion and integrity of the military in the face of what was clearly becoming a long-running struggle. The loyalty and stability of the army was inevitably seen as vital to the regime's survival in the face of the Islamist assault.

Initially, there appeared to be very limited grounds for concern. The army, which had stayed loyal throughout the period of the January coup and its aftermath, witnessed few or no desertions or defections to the armed groups. General Nezzar's assertion at the end of June that "the deserters can be counted on the fingers of one hand"[80] was something of an underestimate but there was no significant flight to the maquis.[81] A

---

77 It was members of these committees who became particular targets for Islamist assassinations, many being sent miniature coffins or pieces of shrouds with Quranic funeral rites written on them as a warning.

78 *Daily Awaz*, 24.12.92.

79 Lamari had been dismissed in mid-1992 from his post as Land Army commander for advocating too hard a line against opposition, when the government was still intent on winning over the support of moderate Islamists.

80 *El Moudjahid*, 28.6.92. At the same time, however, Nezzar affirmed that only 17 members of the armed forces had defected!

81 The only noteworthy defections were a small group of paratroopers who joined

more potent potential hazard to the army was of rebels remaining within the ranks of the military and providing both intelligence and a destabilising influence for the Islamist resistance. Several high-profile terrorist operations such as the airport bombing in August 1992 and notably the assassination attempt against Khaled Nezzar in February 1993 were of sufficient complexity and planning as to indicate the use of specialised information from within the military itself.

Evidence of the fear of internal complicity with the Islamists came with the prosecution of seventy members of the armed forces (who included two officers) at the end of 1992 on charges of having plotted against the state. At the same time reports emerged indicating that as many as 200 lower-ranking officers had been dismissed from the military on suspicion of having Islamist leanings.[82] This preventative action on the part of the regime reflected a growing concern that a split could develop within the military itself, occurring between the senior and junior officer corps. Such fears were based on observations about the backgrounds of the two corps. A large proportion of Algeria's senior officers had experienced the nationalism of the liberation struggle and its aftermath and been imbued with its ideals of modernisation, which were reinforced by having spent time training abroad in the Soviet Union and the West. In contrast, most junior officers had been educated under Algeria's Arabisation programme of the 1960s and 1970s and thus often emerged with a more Islamic and traditional outlook. There were also fears that many junior officers with little political or financial stake in the regime (unlike the senior officers) might feel that they had little to lose by siding with the Islamist opposition. It was these Arabised officers that undoubtedly made up the bulk of an estimated total of 500–800 officers, subalterns and junior officers that reports suggested deserted to the maquis during the course of 1993. No reliable estimates existed for the number of "other ranks" that similarly defected in this period but given the numbers of officers thought to have joined the maquis desertions from these sections of the army seemed likely to have run into four figures.[83]

---

the maquis with their weapons in late March 1992.

82 Details of prosecutions and dismissals were never officially acknowledged because of the ANP's natural desire to down play the issue.

83 One journal issued by FIS activists in exile claimed that by 1994 as many as 20-42,000 members of the armed forces had defected to the maquis. See *Echoes of*

Support for Islamism, 1992–1993

Counting Islamists: the initial base

The official dissolution of the FIS in March 1992 and the subsequent suppression of Islamism made it difficult to assess the strength of support for the party and the Islamist movement generally from 1992. The three and a quarter million votes the FIS had attracted in the first ballot of the legislative elections in December 1991 had given a very tangible indication of the level of support the Islamists enjoyed. However, a survey carried out by the Algerian national research centre argued that only half of those who had voted for the FIS in 1991 actually espoused its central objective: the achievement of an Islamic state. The rest had voted for the party as the best means of punishing and jettisoning the ruling order.[84] Although such findings were inevitably open to scepticism, it could not be denied that the depth of unpopularity of the regime and the FLN had contributed massively to the success of the FIS. Therefore, if it were to be assumed that this assessment was broadly correct (it may in fact have been over generous to the FIS), it appeared that the Islamist goals of the FIS enjoyed the electoral support of just over one and a half million Algerians – about 12% of the adult population.

The armed groups

Expressing support for the FIS at the ballot box or sharing the party's aim of the establishment of an Islamic state, did not, of course, indicate a belief in the efficacy of taking up arms to achieve this, much less a willingness to participate in such an action. Therefore at the outset of their campaign the armed groups' were only likely to have the active support of a section of the aforementioned and notional 12% of the population which had backed the FIS's agenda in December 1991.

Given the fragmented and clandestine nature of the armed groups, any assessment of the numerical membership of these groups, let alone the popular support they enjoyed, was difficult to gauge. In the early period of the spring and summer of 1992, the membership of the groups

---

the Truth, May 1994. This claim was, however, inevitably improbable since defections on this scale would have resulted in an escalation of the conflict to the level of a full-blown war – something that did not subsequently occur.

84 *Financial Times*, 30.1.92.

appeared relatively small scale. One Algerian newspaper estimated in the summer of 1992 that roughly twelve groups had emerged over the preceding few months, each consisting of up to a few dozen members, indicating an overall strength of a few hundred for the armed groups.[85] However, foreign intelligence sources judged there to be at this time around 800–1,000 "hard-core terror fighters" in just the Algiers area.[86] The well-executed campaigns by the security forces during 1992 appeared to have only a limited impact on the armed groups which, despite frequent decimation, demonstrated remarkable resilience and even began to increase in number from 1993. This proved them clearly capable of continually attracting and involving new members in the war against the regime.

The attraction of youth: the urban male

The overwhelming majority of new recruits to the armed groups were young men. This was not simply a function of the military and operational needs of the armed groups, but also reflected the relative popular support Islamism enjoyed amongst this section of the Algerian population. The lack of education and prospects enjoyed by the country's youth, who found themselves to be amongst the main victims of Algeria's continuing economic and social decline, meant that they had been easy recruits for the FIS's populist message. Economic and social conditions in Algeria singularly failed to improve and demonstrably worsened after 1992 with Algerians under the age of 30 making up 84% of the country's unemployed (estimated at around 30% of the working population) by the end of 1993.[87] Consequently, whether through boredom, frustration or anger, young Algerians remained more susceptible than most to the propaganda and recruitment initiatives of the armed groups. The youthful profile of those captured or killed by the security forces in clashes with the Islamist groups bore testimony to the support of the young for the armed struggle. In March 1993, for example, the majority of those killed by security forces in an attack by armed Islamists on a barracks at Boughezoul were aged between 18 and 20 years old. The average age of most of the members of the armed groups appeared to be no higher than 25.

---

85 *Algérie Actualité,* 13.8.92.
86 *Independent,* 30.6.92.
87 *MEI,* 17.12.93.

The expansion in the activities of the armed groups from the latter part of 1992 was a result of the groups reconnecting themselves with the main reservoirs of discontented youth that existed in the urban centres. It had been the poor suburbs of Algiers which had provided the main initial bases for attacks against the regime in the opening months of 1992 and following the failure of the decampment by the armed groups to the rural maquis, these areas became the focus of insurgent Islamist activism once again. The GIA, in particular, concentrated its activities in Algeria's central urban areas. This not only allowed it to carry out the type of operations it desired (mainly assassinations) but also kept in touch with the fertile base of support amongst the young urban unemployed from which it drew the vast majority of its recruits. The sheer number of jobless males (*hittistes*[88]) on the streets of the urban centres meant that, besides formal recruitment, their numbers would allow a high degree of cover and anonymity for GIA operations. Perpetrators of attacks were able to "melt" into similarly aged and dressed crowds. Many of these *hittistes* served "apprenticeships" with the armed groups: watching, driving and storing for them before formally being admitted to a cell or a unit. An added advantage for the urban groups was that unlike their counterparts in the rural maquis, logistical problems were few – young members simply returning to their families for food and shelter.

Other social bases

Support for the armed struggle was not confined to young jobless men in the cities. Whilst they clearly made up the greater part of it, other sections of the population also lent their support. There was evidence of a more middle-class element to the Islamist campaign. Large numbers of civil servants and teachers were to be found amongst the several thousand Islamists still detained in the Saharan prison camps at the end of 1992 and according to the Algerian security services in mid-1993 close to 300 teachers could be found in the ranks of the armed groups.[89] In April 1993 professionals such as doctors and teachers dominated a group of

---

88 The term *hittistes* derives from the Arabic word for wall, *hit*, and refers to the habit of young unemployed men of spending the majority of their time leaning against walls.

89 The exact figures quoted for those detained in the camps were 1,186 civil servants and 1,219 teachers. *Algérie Actualité*, 2.12.92.

nearly fifty Islamists which was arrested by the authorities during an apparent attempt organised by the MIA to sabotage a gas pipeline near the southern town of Laghouat. Intrusions into the telecommunications network (including one which penetrated the Interior Ministry network) and the extensive use of fax machines to transmit messages and communiqués also appeared to indicate that the armed groups enjoyed the expertise and advice of educated Algerians.

Another area of society identified by the security services as being a hotbed of Islamist activism was the black market. This clandestine section of the economy continued to be substantially controlled by the Islamists who frequently relied on it as a source of funds. Many of the armed groups turned to more violent means of securing funds for their campaigns such as protection rackets, bank raids and general theft. However the massive increase seen in these crimes across Algeria from 1992 was also largely the result of the more general breakdown of law and order and government control that had been precipitated by the conflict between the armed groups and the government. Collapsing living standards had also provided a further impetus for crime in this period.

Geographic bases

Geographically, the armed groups initially operated predominantly in the east and centre of the country, but gradually spread into the west as well. The strength and presence of the armed groups in individual areas was frequently determined by the activities of the security forces. The various shifts between the urban areas and the rural maquis, detailed earlier, were largely the result of the intensity of operations by the regime in each theatre.

Armed Islamist activism was notably strong in two particular areas of the country. The poor, south-eastern suburbs of Algiers such as El-Harrach, Bachdjarah and Eucalyptus provided the initial bases for operations by armed militants and by 1993 these densely populated areas became the focus of much of the GIA's recruitment and activity. The small towns of the Mitidja plain to the south of Algiers, such as Sidi Moussa, Meftah and Larbaa, also came to be closely associated with the armed groups. Abdelkader Chebouti was himself from Larbaa and much of the MIA's campaign during 1992-93 was centred on this region. The influence the armed groups were able to exercise in these areas was often considerable and testified to their strength and support. In many of these areas no attempt was made by the authorities to revoke many of the measures that had been introduced by the FIS councils after 1990.[90]

The General Population

The importance of winning the backing of the mass of the ordinary population to their side in order to defeat the regime clearly figured in the calculations of the armed groups. The example of the revolution in Iran in 1978-79, where Islamists came to power on the back of a genuinely popular revolution, provided an unignorable precedent for them. However, despite the steady flow of recruits to the Islamic militias, there was little evidence of the Islamists being able to mobilise large numbers of people in street demonstrations in the way that had contributed so decisively to the fall of the Shah in Iran.[91]

The apparent reluctance or indeed unwillingness, of significant numbers of the Algerian populace – even those who must have voted for the FIS – to demonstrate their support for the Islamist opposition was a notable feature of the growing conflict. Despite the worsening economic and social conditions for most Algerians during this time, the attitude of ordinary people to the regime was accurately described by one observer as one of "passive hostility rather than active support for the fundamentalists".[92] The majority of Algerians seemed to avoid involvement or association with either side in the conflict, realising that in the increasingly violent and bloody battle any expressed sympathies were liable to invite retribution from the other side. As one Algerian journalist remarked one year into the conflict: "The street remains strangely impassive, as if this does not concern it."[93]

The neutrality of the great majority of ordinary Algerians in the struggle between the Algerian regime and the armed groups failed, however, to prevent the conflict growing significantly during the two years following the HCE's accession to power. The numbers of those directly

---

90 In the Mitidja town of Médéa, for example, a ban on alcohol introduced by the local FIS-controlled council remained.

91 Mohammed Said, in particular, was said to have originally placed his hopes in the mass mobilisation of the FIS's supporters in the wake of the coup. However, the success of the government in stifling popular dissent forced him to reconsider future strategy.

92 *The Middle East*, July 1993.

93 *Algérie Actualité*, 23.2.93.

involved with the armed groups grew from an estimated few hundred in early 1992 to possibly as many as 20,000 by the end of 1993.[94] A more tangible and depressing indication of the expansion of the conflict could be seen in the numbers of people dying as a result of the struggle. A total of approximately 600 people were killed by either the armed groups or the security forces during the course of 1992. By the close of 1993 this grim total had risen to roughly 3,000.[95]

Foreign support for the Islamist cause

The barring of the FIS's path to victory through the cancellation of the electoral process in January 1992 provided Islamist movements and governments everywhere with a powerful and symbolic cause. The FIS's domination of the first ballot of the National Assembly elections had furnished both Algeria's Islamists and Islamism generally with an unprecedented sense of popular and legal legitimacy. The effective confiscation of the FIS's certain victory had been met with dismay and outrage by Islamists across the world. In the eyes of many the January coup was confirmation of the iniquity of Algeria's secular ruling elite, which, like similar elites across the Muslim world, was intent on blocking both Islamism and the popular will. Support for Algeria's betrayed and cheated Islamists thus became a priority for Islamists worldwide.

Iran

Iran continued to be the target of most official Algerian suspicions and accusations over aid and support to the country's Islamists. The new HCE had recalled its Ambassador to Tehran in the immediate aftermath of the coup of January 1992 amid complaints that a "virulent press campaign" had been mounted by Iran against Algeria, together with allegations that Tehran had contributed $3 million to the FIS's recent election campaign.[96] Although these charges were denied and dismissed by the Iranians, relations between the two countries declined throughout 1992

---

94 In late 1993 *Algérie Actualité* reported that the security forces were looking for approximately 22,000 activists. This total was in addition to the numbers of Islamists already killed or imprisoned by the regime.

95 'Political killings in a human rights crisis', Amnesty International (AI MDE), 28.1.94.

96 *Independent*, 24.1.92.

resulting in a complete severing of diplomatic ties with Iran by Algeria in March 1993.

The Algerian authorities alleged that Iran had had a direct hand in training, funding and supplying the armed Islamist groups in their struggle against the regime. In November 1992 Qasim Naamani, an attaché at the Iranian Embassy in Algiers, was expelled along with nine others for allegedly co-ordinating efforts to send Algerian Islamists to Hezbollah training camps in Lebanon. One Algerian newspaper claimed that Naamani had been the official liaison between the Majlis Shura of the FIS and Mohammed Kasem Khansari, the mullah with responsibility for the Maghreb states at the Iranian Foreign Ministry.[97] There were also accusations that the Iranian Embassy had let Islamists use their facilities to print their clandestine newspapers and communiqués.

The truth of these claims was difficult to judge, although it was clearly in the interests of the Algerian government to emphasise the foreign links of the Islamists in order to discredit them in the eyes of nationalistically minded Algerians and to reassure people that the Islamist struggle had only limited domestic support. Iran continued to enjoy strong links with the very small radical Shi'ite groups (see earlier chapters) but these groups remained marginal in influence because of their size. There were, however, links with more prominent Islamist groups. Takfir wa Hijra had had links with the Islamic Republic since the 1980s and several of its senior figures had visited Tehran and Kameredine Kherbane travelled there on several occasions from 1992. Iran undoubtedly did help supply at least some weapons and material to the armed groups in Algeria after 1992, but the ideological influence and leadership it hoped to exert was restricted, as before, by its Shi'ite theology. This was often frequently acknowledged by the armed groups. In a statement issued by the GIA in late 1993 Sid Ahmed Mourad commented on links with Iran by simply stating simply that "Iran is Shi'ite".[98]

Egypt

The issue of links between Algeria and the influential Islamist movement in Egypt, revolved mainly from 1992 around attempts by the two governments to co-ordinate efforts to prevent links being established between

---

97   *Algérie Actualité*, 30.3.93.
98   *Jeune Afrique*, 27.1.94.

the two movements. Egypt had itself witnessed a resurgence of Islamist violence from the Summer of 1992. In November 1992, Sassi Lamouri, the Algerian Minister for Religious Affairs, led a delegation to Cairo where he met with his Egyptian counterpart, Mohammed Ali Maghoub, to discuss ways of combating the Islamist threat. For Algeria, Lamouri secured an agreement from Egypt to reopen a mission bureau of Al-Ahzar University (the esteemed Islamic university) in Algeria and to send around fifty professors and imam instructors to work, under the guidance of the Ministry of Religious Affairs, against "Shi'ism and fundamentalism".[99] It was no coincidence that it was shortly after this meeting Algeria that announced its expulsions from the Iranian Embassy and Egypt launched verbal attacks on alleged Iranian interference in its domestic politics. The Egyptians were also willing to lend, on a limited scale, more tangible support to Algeria's anti-terrorist struggle, supplying from 1993 much needed spares for Algerian army equipment. Co-operation between the two countries' security services remained close and in March 1994, citing security reasons, Egypt announced that the number of Algerian pilgrims allowed to travel across Egypt to attend the Hajj in Mecca would be reduced by more than 90%.

Tunisia and Morocco

Algeria's two Maghrebi neighbours, Morocco and Tunisia, were clearly likely to be affected by the growing crisis across their borders. Algeria had traditionally been the dominant state, politically and geographically, in the region. For Tunisia's President Abidine Ben Ali, developments had vindicated his unease over Chadli Benjedid's programme of political liberalisation. He robustly supported the Algerian regime's suppression of the Islamists which he had foreshadowed with his clamp down on Tunisia's own Nahda party. A more ambiguous stand was taken by the Moroccan government. Several Algerian newspapers claimed that Algeria's western neighbour provided the main route for Islamist funds, materiel and personnel into Algeria. Although bribery of border officials was seen as the primary means of operating this route, El Watan argued that the Moroccan authorities themselves had "closed an eye" to the networks of supply on their territory.[100] Nevertheless, the Moroccan government

---

99   Ahmed Rouadjia, 'Le FIS: est-il enterré?' in *Espirit*, no. 6 (1993), p. 100.
100   *El Watan*, 15.2.94.

arrested the GIA's Abdelhak Layada in July 1993 and allowed the Algerian authorities to extradite him back to Algeria.

Other Arab states

Other states that appeared to have links with the conflict in Algeria were Jordan, Saudi Arabia and Sudan. In Jordan these links took the form of contacts with the country's Muslim Brotherhood. Said Mekhloufi spent time there in the summer of 1992 cementing links with the Jordanian Brotherhood which offered to send a team of lawyers to Algeria to defend Abassi, Belhadj and the other FIS leaders during their trial in July 1992. Saudi Arabia become once again, following the hiatus of the Gulf War and its aftermath (see Chapter Five), a source of funds for the Islamists. Individual Saudis were approached by Algerian Islamists for support. This support was frequently provided despite official assurances to the contrary that were given to the Algerian Defence Minister, Khaled Nezzar, when he visited Riyadh. For its part, Sudan was regularly accused by the Algerian regime of supplying the armed groups inside Algeria, and although there was no real concrete evidence for this, Algeria recalled its Ambassador to Khartoum in March 1993.

Overall, it appeared that there was a concerted effort on the part of certain Islamists to set up international sources of support for the armed struggle. Figures such as Kameredine Kherbane accompanied by Abdallah Anas travelled from country to country seeking funds and training for the struggle. In contrast to these efforts and the approaches made to individual Saudis – which came predominantly from those on the salafi wing of the Algerian Islamist movement – it was argued that Djazairist-aligned figures such as Rabah Kebir preferred to accept funds only from other Algerians, therefore enabling them to retain their nationalist credentials. Indeed, it was argued that through domestic "donations" and crime the FIS and its allies were more or less financially self-sufficient. For his part, Kebir stated on relations with other foreign Islamist movements that:

> There are some contacts, but only discussions, not close relations. Sometimes we meet some of them in Europe, by chance. Our members are under siege abroad, so we cannot move freely and contact other Islamic organisations.[101]

---

101   Author's interview with Rabah Kebir, 27.9.95.

Conclusions

The *coup d'état* of January 1992 marked the effective failure of the attempt by Algeria's Islamists to exercise political power and influence through the ballot box. The dissolution of the FIS in March 1992 and explicit assurances from the regime that neither it nor any similar successor party would not be permitted to rejoin any future electoral process, appeared to confirm Islamism's exclusion from the constitutional political arena.

The failure of the constitutionalist option constructed and pursued by Abassi Madani and others from 1989, whilst mourned by some Islamists, vindicated those elements in the Islamist movement who had either explicitly rejected or otherwise tactically gone along with the electoralist strategy of the FIS. The cancellation of the elections and the dissolution of the FIS were signals to these elements that the movement should resort to the more fitting means of acquiring power through armed struggle. These elements had long been present within the broader framework of the Algerian Islamist movement. Many drew their ideological inspiration from ideas and experiences established abroad, particularly through those who had served as volunteers in the Arab Mujahidin in Afghanistan. The ideas and methods of radical Islamist thinkers and activists elsewhere in the Muslim world (especially in Egypt) also had an impact.

Algeria's Islamists did not have to exclusively turn abroad, though, in search of a tradition that espoused violence against the state in order to achieve religious ends. Mustapha Bouyali's five-year campaign against the Algerian authorities in the 1980s not only provided other Islamists with a precedent and example, but also supplied the armed groups of the 1990s with figures who had actually fought alongside Bouyali and who shared his aims and ideas. Mustapha Bouyali himself drew much of his inspiration from that most important of all Algerian experiences of which he himself had been a part – the war of liberation against the French. For many in the armed groups, 1992 represented the resumption of the struggle of 1954–1962. Like the mujahidin of thirty years earlier they were waging a jihad against unjust and unIslamic rule which they similarly hoped to overthrow through force of arms.

Parallels with the original independence struggle were indeed strong. The shifting of the armed campaign between the rural maquis and the urban areas in response to pressure from the security forces echoed the various operational shifts that had occurred in the 1950s. The competition over who should officially speak for the FIS and who should control the armed groups, had much in common with the power struggles within the FLN during the war of liberation. In both cases individuals and faction based variously abroad, in prison and in the maquis fought with each other for influence and control. Similarly the desire to establish organisational hegemony over the struggle could be seen in both the FLN's ruthless war against Messali Hadj's PPA in the 1950s and in the clashes that escalated between the armed allies of the FIS and the GIA during 1993.

By the close of 1993 it remained to be seen whether the campaign by Algeria's armed Islamists would result in the final capitulation of the existing regime and whether this struggle, like that thirty years earlier, would take a further six years to achieve its final victory and conclusion.

8

The Search for a Solution, 1993–1996

The upsurge in violence that accompanied the passing of the first anniversary of the *coup d'état* of January 1992 and the official dissolution of the FIS two months later, testified dramatically to Algeria's failure to solve the crisis that had been engendered by these two events. The hopes of both the HCE and the FIS in early 1992 that each would swiftly capitulate to the other's pressure and wishes had proved unfounded. The opening and escalation of an armed struggle between the regime and elements of the wider Islamist movement indicated that no recognisable victory for either the Islamists or the regime would be likely in the medium term.

Regime initiatives
The failure of the Algerian government to control the security situation and defeat the threat posed by the armed Islamist groups during 1992 and 1993 forced the regime to contemplate the adoption of a more political strategy towards the crisis in addition to the simple military/security one that had formed the core of its response to events since the death of Mohammed Boudiaf.

Boudiaf's assassination at the end of June 1992 had resulted in the abandonment of the dead President's plans to marshal support behind the HCE through mass popular participation in the planned Rassemblement Patriotique National (RPN). However, whilst military defeat of the armed groups became the explicit priority of the regime from mid-1992, there were indications that Algeria's rulers remained conscious of the need to secure political support for their rule. In the immediate aftermath of Boudiaf's death, Boudiaf's successor as head of the HCE, Ali Kafi, had declared that he would "not spare any effort in involving all the existing forces of the nation in the search for a way out of this crisis".[1] It soon

---

1   Le Matin, 15.9.94.

became clear that Kafi, in speaking of the involvement of "all the existing forces" was not referring to the creation of the sort of mass political party envisaged by his predecessor, but rather was suggesting that the regime establish contacts with Algeria's existing political parties.

From the Autumn of 1992 the Algerian government tried to enter into discussions with the major opposition parties but their efforts met with little success over the following months. Virtually without exception, the political parties remained highly sceptical about both the motivations and the prospects of official overtures towards them. Most of the leaders of the parties were aware that neither Ali Kafi nor the new Prime Minister, Belaid Abdessalem, had ever been enthusiastic supporters of Chadli Benjedid's original project of political liberalisation through multi-partyism. They were consequently suspicious of official attempts to involve them in discussions and dialogue, fearing that the regime sought only to use them as a political shield to boost its own negligible legitimacy. A further disincentive to involvement came from the increasing pressures the authorities put on many of the opposition parties through restrictions placed on their newspapers, premises and activities.

A second more fundamental obstacle to comprehensive talks between the government and the opposition parties materialised in the shape of the opposition parties' demand that there should be a swift return to the electoral process precipitously abandoned in January 1992. Moreover, nearly all of them stated their preference for the honouring of the results of the first ballot of 26 December 1991. Of the seven parties which had received more than 100,000 votes in the first ballot only one (the RCD[2]) had not condemned the subsequent annulment of the voting. The leaderships of the FLN, the FFS, HAMAS, the MNI and the MDA had joined with the FIS in early 1992 in demanding that the results of the election be respected. They remained committed to this stance even after the formal dissolution of the FIS in March. Despite their many differences with the FIS all of these parties made clear to the government their view that any realistic solution to the ongoing crisis had to involve at least representatives of the FIS. Abdelhamid Mehri of the FLN argued

---

2   In contrast to the other major parties, the RCD remained implacably opposed to the participation of the FIS in any dialogue. Although this stance was supportive of the regime's line, the RCD's antipathy to *any* dialogue with Islamist parties created further problems for the regime's attempts to arrange multi-party discussions because of its unwillingness to have contact with the MNI and HAMAS.

in May 1993 that "certain parts of the Islamic movement are ready for dialogue and they should not be ignored. The greater the delay, the more opportunities are given to extremists."[3] By mid-June 1993 all five parties had separately called for the participation of the FIS in the formal multi-party talks that the regime had continued to seek to organise.

The demand that the FIS be included in the dialogue process created considerable difficulties for the regime. The exclusion of the FIS from the legal political field had clearly been the main aim of those who had carried out the *coup d'état* of January 1992. Many of Algeria's senior military officers had regretted their decision not to have forced Chadli Benjedid to ban and dissolve the party during the crisis of June 1991 and thus had no intention of giving any political space to the FIS. Following the party's official dissolution, President Boudiaf had explicitly ruled out the possibility of the FIS ever being allowed to re-enter the legal political field and the regime continued to hold to this stance.

In excluding the FIS from the political stage Algeria's rulers were aware of the need to appease the party's bereft following. Efforts were made throughout 1992 to appeal to Islamist opinion by showing relative leniency to many of those held in detention by the authorities. Eight thousand of the estimated nine thousand activists detained by the authorities in the camps in the Sahara were released by the beginning of 1993. Many were released under new security laws introduced in October 1992 which granted amnesties to those prisoners convicted of non-violent offences or those deemed to have quit "terrorist" groups. More importantly, the trial of Abassi Madani, Ali Belhadj and the other leaders of the FIS arrested in 1991, which finally took place in July 1992 resulted in much lighter sentences than might have been expected. Abassi and Belhadj were sentenced to twelve years each in prison, with the other defendants receiving sentences ranging from between four and six years each. The FIS leaders were convicted of conspiring against the state but significantly were cleared of the more serious charge of plotting an armed insurrection. The sentences were interpreted as a gesture to the Islamists as were other sentences handed out by the courts. Benazouz Zebda, the former vice-president of the FIS, was notably acquitted of charges filed against him and the special anti-terrorist courts introduced by the government passed a range of sentences ranging from death sentences

---

3   Charef, *Algérie: Le Grand Dérapage*, p. 494.

through to light sentences and occasional acquittals in an effort to achieve an impression of fairness.

The regime also tried to appeal to Islamist sentiment by reverting to the established practice of attempting to portray itself in a more Islamic light. The most dramatic example of this came in a speech made by Belaid Abdessalem on 11 February 1993 when the Prime Minister made a critical reference to "secular-assimilationists".[4] The use of a term long used by Algeria's Islamists to identify their secular enemies, indicated that Abdessalem appeared to want to distance himself from the support of parties such as the RCD, the PAGS and elements of the Francophone elite, which the Islamists accused of being the mainstay of the regime.[5] More direct appeals to Islamists were made as well. In September 1992, Mohammed Hardi, the Interior Minister, called on "Islamist brothers who are of good faith and who back the project of an Islamic State" to "distance themselves totally from terrorism".[6] In what was a clear bid to separate Islamism and Islamist sentiment from the campaigns of the armed groups, Hardi also indicated that such a separation could accelerate the revival of the electoral process. Despite this, though, the regime reaffirmed its determination that the FIS could play no part in political processes. In March 1993 Ali Kafi let it be known that the HCE had considered entering into dialogue with the FIS at the beginning of 1992, but had decisively rejected the idea.[7] The regime justified this exclusion by publicly associating the party with the growing campaign of violence. In a speech formally marking the first anniversary of the HCE's assumption of power on 14 January, Ali Kafi restated the regime's intention to "continue the debate with political parties" but stressed that "We shall exclude from such an endeavour all those who perpetrate or adopt violence to attain power."[8]

The regime persisted throughout 1993 in its efforts to achieve multi-party dialogue in spite of the reluctance of most of the legal opposition

---

4   *Jeune Afrique*, 25.3.93.
5   The Prime Minister's use of the term "secular-assimilationist" greatly angered and alarmed many secular Algerians, some of whom suggested it had encouraged the unleashing of the wave of assassinations of Algerian intellectuals that occurred the following month in March 1993.
6   Interview with Mohammed Hardi, *El Watan*, 3.9.92.
7   Charef, *Algérie: Le Grand Dérapage*, p. 425.
8   *SWB* ME/1588 a/18-20, 16.1.93.

parties. Attempts at the beginning of the year collapsed following the withdrawal of nearly all of the major parties, most of whom were frustrated at the regime's insistence on concentrating on the construction of interim political structures rather than on the preferred agenda of the establishment of a timetable for the return to elections. A new initiative was announced in September 1993 with the creation of a National Dialogue Commission. This Commission set itself the specific task of achieving a consensus with the opposition parties on the nature of the new governing body that the HCE had pledged itself to cede power to when its own two year "mandate" (inherited from Chadli Benjedid) expired at the end of the year. It was publicly hoped that the work of the Commission would culminate in the holding of a "National Recon-ciliation Conference" attended by all the political parties and other national organisations which would then choose a successor to the HCE. However, efforts to produce a consensus with the parties continued to founder over demands for an election timetable to be set and on the issue of the participation of representatives of the FIS in the dialogue.

The impasse in the dialogue process appeared to be partially broken at the end of November, when a statement from the presidency declared that the regime would be willing to talk to movements hitherto excluded from the multi-party talks. Clearly referring to the FIS, the statement made the single qualification that only individuals who had not broken the law could be invited to participate in the dialogue.[9] One of the generals who sat on the Commission went further and declared:

> . . . there are leading figures of the dissolved FIS, who respect the law, and who would like to express themselves on behalf of this tendency, the way will be open for them to take part in the dialogue.[10]

This concession, accompanied by hints that curfews and house arrests might be reduced, appeared to have born few fruit, however, by the time of the convening of the National Reconciliation Conference in January 1994. No representative of the FIS was invited to attend and the Conference failed to attract any of the major parties which had boycotted the event chiefly on the grounds that it was a disingenuous and pointless function without the participation of the FIS. In the face of these absences

---

9 *MEI*, 3.12.93.
10 *SWB* ME/1869 MED/12, 11.12.93.

the regime appeared to abandon any pretence that the Conference would somehow play a role in producing a new political consensus. Instead the regime used the Conference as a platform to announce the formation of a new three-year transitionary regime. It was revealed that this new regime would be overseen by a new state presidency until elections could be held at the end of the three-year period. The announcement that the new incumbent of this new state presidency would be the existing Defence Minister, General Liamine Zeroual, seemed to confirm the popular belief that the HCE and its military backers had merely reinvented themselves under a new guise.

It was therefore of some surprise to many observers when the new President appeared to reiterate the offer made by the National Dialogue Committee at the end of 1993 to widen the dialogue to include figures from the FIS. Within a week of being formally sworn in, Liamine Zeroual declared on 7 February that he was committed to "reverting to the path of democratic elections" and moreover stated that:

> We realise that the political crisis cannot be solved except through dialogue and the participation of the national political and social forces *without exception*.[11] (Italics added)

The response of the FIS

The position of the FIS
The FIS's response to the public overtures that emerged from the regime over the period of the National Dialogue Commission was neither immediate nor clear. The period in the immediate wake of the cancellation of the elections in 1992 had seen the party joining with most other parties in denouncing the move and demanding the reinstatement and honouring of the results. It had also made numerous appeals for dialogue with the HCE in order to resolve the crisis. The dissolution of the party by the regime at the beginning of March meant inevitably that the FIS's official policy became less clear and more ambiguous as the party had difficulty speaking with one voice, its leaders divided between foreign countries, Algeria's prisons and the various internal underground networks. The

---

11   *SWB* ME/1917 MED, 9.2.94.

rise in importance of the armed struggle and of actors such as Chebouti, the MIA and the GIA further complicated matters and reduced the significance of the strictly political aspect of the FIS.

Senior figures in the FIS continued to refer to the possibility of dialogue even from clandestinity and exile even after the formal dissolution of the party. At the beginning of July 1992 *Minbar El-Djoumma* stated that the FIS was willing to respond to "a serious and responsible dialogue" but added that it the party did not "beg for dialogue in order to gain some small concession from the regime".[12] For his part, Rabah Kebir set out the party's conditions for dialogue with the regime in an interview with a French newspaper in September of 1992. The four conditions stated were: the liberation of all detainees; an end to all arbitrary arrests; reparation for all injustices committed (with all FIS members who had been elected to official posts to be reinstalled); and the organisation of the second round of the elections to the National Assembly.[13] This statement represented a formal response on the part of Kebir to the various statements issued by the regime concerning multi-party dialogue, particularly that issued earlier that month by Mohammed Hardi, promising "Islamist brothers of good faith" that the electoral process might be revived. Kebir additionally affirmed that he had a mandate from the party to participate in "sincere dialogue".[14]

The emergence of dissent

The openly expressed hostility on the part of the regime to any discussions with the FIS meant that the issue of participation in dialogue with the regime never came to the fore. However, the shift in the HCE's position on this in the autumn of 1993 threw down a serious challenge to the FIS and its newly confirmed allies amongst the armed groups. The overtures from the National Dialogue Commission rapidly exposed the central fault line that existed between those who saw the armed struggle as a means of putting pressure on the regime to permit the FIS's re-entry into the political system and those who saw it as the sole and proper means of establishing an Islamic state by militarily overthrowing the illegitimate authority of the HCE.

---

12   Charef, *Algérie: Le Grand Dérapage*, p. 425.
13   *Le Monde*, 18.9.92.
14   *MEED*, 16.10.92.

Foremost amongst this latter group was Said Mekhloufi, who had been ejected from the FIS in July 1991 over this very issue. Despite having supported the familiar conditions that Mohammed Said and others voiced, through Radio Wafa and other media, for dialogue with the authorities, the actual possibility of such a dialogue drew a strong reaction from Mekhloufi. He issued a communiqué on 4 October which denounced certain "Jazarists" for having approached him to establish contacts with the emerging National Dialogue Commission.[15] In this and subsequent communiqués, he reprimanded figures such as Kebir and Benazouz Zebda for having supposedly responded to overtures from the regime and reaffirmed his belief in the "armed struggle" until the achievement of an "Islamic Republic". He also claimed that the Jazarists, at the initiative of Abderrazak Redjam, were planning a new conference at Batna to unite the movement and formulate a response to the regime.[16]

It rapidly appeared that the so-called "Jazarists" were far from united on how to react to the National Dialogue Commission's initiative. In public, at least, a common front was initially maintained. Rabah Kebir declared on 1 November that:

> The leaders of [the FIS] do not ask for a ceasefire . . . Neither slogans about dialogue nor repression are able to disunite us or discourage us.[17]

A similar response came from Abderrazak Redjam who issued a statement which declared that the FIS "rejects all dialogue and reconciliation" with the "putchist junta".[18] However, the tone of Redjam's assertion, in its rejection of reconciliation (he also stated that there could "not be dialogue with the junta until victory (and) the establishment of an Islamic State"[19]), was far harsher than that of Kebir and soon this difference in tone developed into differences of substance. These differences threatened a resurrection of the old rivalries that had arisen between Kebir on the one hand and Redjam and Mohammed Said on the other. More specifically they represented Said and Redjam's closer involvement with the armed

---

15 *Algérie Actualité*, 30.11.93.
16 *Ibid.*, 7.12.93.
17 *Le Monde*, 21.9.94.
18 *Ibid.*
19 Charef, *Algérie: Le Grand Dérapage*, p. 498.

struggle inside Algeria which had perhaps influenced them to adopt a more uncompromising line towards the regime.

These differences became acute and undisguised by December when Kebir responded publicly to the National Dialogue Commission offering a negotiated end to the conflict and setting out the conditions for the attendance of representatives of the FIS at the National Reconciliation Conference. Whilst restating earlier demands that the leaders of the party be released, security measures be relaxed and reparation for abuses perpetrated against the party be made, the head of the Executive Body of the FIS Abroad significantly made no mention of the need to respect the election results of December 1991. This had hitherto been a primary demand and was intended to be seen as a concession to the regime.[20]

Rabah Kebir was not the only senior FIS figure who responded publicly and potentially positively to the approaches of the National Dialogue Commission. In early December six founding members of the FIS, including most notably Hachemi Sahnouni, published a communiqué stating that FIS participation in the forthcoming National Conference was conditional on the approval of the party's Majlis Shura which should be reconvened for that purpose. One of this group of six subsequently went further claiming that one of them had actually already met with Ali Belhadj and secured the deputy leader of the FIS's approval to enter into dialogue with the authorities. However, whilst Sahnouni subsequently confirmed that he had been the member of the group which had met with Ali Belhadj on 17 October, he stated that Belhadj had not yet made clear his position on dialogue since the Commission had at that point only just started its deliberations.[21]

These receptive responses to the idea of dialogue were not shared by other elements within the FIS and its allies. Ali Belhadj appeared to slightly clarify his position towards dialogue in an open letter to the National Dialogue Commission in which he rejected the legitimacy of the Commission and railed against the iniquities of the regime.[22] For his

---

20 *Daily Telegraph*, 18.12.93; *MEI*, 7.1.94; Kebir stated that the dropping of the demand for the 1991 results to be respected was to overcome the regime's public stance that the election had been rigged by the FIS and to show that the FIS was not afraid to submit itself to fresh elections. Author's interview with Rabah Kebir, 27.9.95.
21 *Algérie Actualité*, 14.12.93.
22 Labat, *Les Islamistes Algériens* pp. 245–6.

part, Redjam, having already repudiated Kebir in November for calling for what he termed a modern set of "Evian Accords" to end the conflict, issued a further statement in December calling for a continuation of the armed struggle and dismissing the National Dialogue Commission as a government manoeuvre to gain cross-party backing for its repression of the FIS.[23] Radio Wafa, (controlled by Redjam and Mohammed Said) rejected in its broadcasts all dialogue and any truce with the regime unless the FIS was totally rehabilitated. This reference to an (albeit unrealistic) condition suggested some movement towards the position of Kebir and Sahnouni, but the fact that calls for "jihad" against "interlopers" who called for an end to the violence, were also broadcast, suggested otherwise.[24] Redjam warned those other parties already participating in the dialogue that they too could be open to attack by militants.[25] Said Mekhloufi made his threats more plain, and stated openly that he would not hesitate to kill both Abdallah Djaballah and Mahfoud Nahnah for the participation of the MNI and HAMAS in these and earlier talks.[26]

The Zeroual initiative: December 1993–March 1994

The declaration by Algeria's new President, Liamine Zeroual, at the beginning of February 1994 that dialogue should seek the involvement of all political forces "without exception" did not signify the launching of a specifically new initiative on the part of the government. It formed part of a wider attempt by the Algerian regime to find a political solution to the country's deepening malaise that focused on the new President.

General Liamine Zeroual had entered the government in July 1993 as Defence Minister. He replaced Khaled Nezzar, the central figure in the *coup d'état* of January 1992, whose deteriorating health had forced him to bow out of the government and seek a successor for his role. Nezzar's choice of Zeroual as the holder of the key Defence Ministry portfolio was somewhat unexpected. Zeroual had not been drawn from

---

23 *El Watan*, 22.11.93; *MEI*, 7.1.94. The Evian Accords were the set of agreements signed by the FLN and France in 1962 which formally drew the War of Independence to a close. They were subsequently depicted by some Algerians as having contained too many concessions to the French.
24 *Algérie Actualité*, 28.12.93.
25 *MEI*, 7.1.94.
26 *El Watan*, 22.11.93.

the clique of senior military officers who had designed the ouster of Chadli Benjedid and the cancellation of the electoral programme. Instead he had come out of retirement to assume the post. Still only in his early fifties, Zeroual had been appointed deputy Chief of Staff in the 1980s but had been dismissed by President Chadli in 1989 following a dispute between the two men over plans to reorganise the armed forces. Following a brief period as Ambassador to Romania, Zeroual returned to Algeria and officially retired in 1990. His recall by Nezzar, under whom he had served when deputy Chief of Staff, signified another attempt by the regime to present a new face to the population. Zeroual's absence from the political scene since his dismissal in 1989 was seen (as Boudiaf's since 1963 had been) as a potential advantage. Zeroual's "outsider" status also allowed Nezzar to present him as a compromise candidate in preference to other senior military figures whose candidatures were mutually unacceptable.

Liamine Zeroual's elevation to the new presidency six months after his appointment as Defence Minister gave a clear indication that his path to office had been planned in advance. The architect of Zeroual's accession was clearly Khaled Nezzar. Although enjoying the reputation of being the strong man of the HCE, Nezzar was in fact the first amongst the senior figures in the regime to conclude that wide-ranging dialogue, even involving representatives of the banned FIS, represented the best course forward for Algeria. Too unwell and compromised to perform the role himself, Nezzar selected his former deputy for the task of finding some form of political solution to the crisis.

Zeroual and the FIS

Official reactions from senior figures in the FIS to the National Reconciliation Conference of January 1994 which formally appointed Liamine Zeroual as President were initially predictably dismissive. Rabah Kebir ridiculed the Conference as the product of "theatrics to seek legitimacy".[27] However, in contrast, the appointment of Liamine Zeroual received a cautious welcome. The FIS's representative in Sweden stated that Zeroual was a potential De Gaulle with the ability to push the army "out of the era of Chadli".[28] This response was echoed by other FIS figures, including those around Rabah Kebir who himself later stated: "I did not know

27 *Guardian*, 31.1.94.
28 *El Watan*, 3.2.94.

Zeroual personally, but those people who did know him spoke well of him and expected him to do some good."[29]

The relative warmth of the reception that Zeroual's appointment received in Islamist circles was the result of hope there that it provided much more of a break with Algeria's existing rulers than had been the case with either Mohammed Boudiaf or Belaid Abdessalem. This optimism was encouraged not so much by the new President's four-year absence from the ruling councils of Algeria's regime between 1989 and 1993, but by his background and career up until his dismissal in 1989. Zeroual's military career had had two notable features that marked him out from the vast majority of other figures who came to occupy senior positions in the Algerian military from the 1980s. Firstly, Zeroual had entered the military through having joined the ALN (Armé de Libération Nationale) – the armed wing of the FLN – at the age of 16 during the liberation struggle in the 1950s. By contrast, many of the other senior officers in the post-war ANP had originally become involved in the War of Independence through being part of the *French* military, only joining the ALN through (largely late) defections to the nationalist cause. The second factor that distinguished Zeroual from his military peers was his educational background, both before and after the liberation struggle. Unlike most of his Francophone colleagues Liamine Zeroual's preferred language was Arabic. This preference was reflected in his military training after 1962. While most other senior military figures spent significant periods in the 1970s in military academies in France, Zeroual spent just six months in France, passing more time in military institutions in the Soviet Union and Jordan.

The importance of these two distinctions was not just that they conferred on Zeroual the image of an uncompromised patriot. Much more importantly, they gave him immunity against the charge made by many of the regime's opponents that those ruling Algeria after 1992 were simply a Francophone elite. Islamists, in particular, had alleged that the fact that so many of the senior military figures in the regime (notably Generals Nezzar and Guenaizia) had originally been members of the French army during the war of liberation indicated that Algeria was now been run by the lackeys of France. Thus the *coup d'état* of January

---

29   Author's interview with Rabah Kebir, 27.9.95.

1992 had effectively re-established French colonial rule over Algeria. This belief in the domination of the Hizb-Fransa (Party of France), whatever its truth, became an immensely powerful concept after 1992 and became a central part of opposition and Islamist propaganda against the regime – the role of France in Algerian politics still proving capable of provoking widespread nationalistic feeling. Liamine Zeroual's exemption from the charge of being part of the Hizb-Fransa conspiracy was not only a passive function of his background. There was evidence that he had actively resisted pro-French influences in the Algerian military. The dispute he had with Chadli Benjedid in 1989, which had led to his dismissal, was said to have concerned Zeroual's resistance to plans to reorganise the Algerian military along French lines.

Overtures and releases

The more flexible approach the Algerian regime had begun to adopt towards dialogue with the FIS from the autumn of 1993 appeared to indicate that Liamine Zeroual's influence was already making itself felt. In addition to the positive statements made by members of the National Dialogue Commission, more tangible demonstrations of goodwill were shown by the Algerian authorities. Several hundred Islamists detained without trial were released in January. These releases were welcomed by Rabah Kebir, but the representative of the FIS abroad felt compelled to add that on their own they were not sufficient to get the FIS to join either the dialogue or the forthcoming National Reconciliation Conference. "We must have the release of all political prisoners, first and foremost our leaders", he demanded.[30]

Optimism following the official appointment of Liamine Zeroual as President at the end of January seemed to be fully vindicated when within a month the reconstituted regime appeared to respond to Kebir's primary demand. On 22 February two of the seven leaders of the FIS held in prison since the summer of 1991, Ali Djeddi and Abdelkader Boukhamkham, were quietly released from Blida jail. The releases confirmed that the authorities had entered into discussions with the imprisoned leadership of the FIS in Blida. It was not until some weeks later that it was revealed that Liamine Zeroual himself had played a central

---

30   *Financial Times*, 21.1.94.

role in establishing these contacts and had even visited the prison in December, in his then capacity as Defence Minister.[31]

The failure of the initiative

The releases appeared to be a clear indication that dialogue and possibly even some form of truce might be in prospect. In the wake of Djeddi's and Boukhamkham's release, there was widespread speculation that Abassi Madani and Ali Belhadj might also be set free. The government made no attempt to deny this possibility. General Tayeb Deradji, widely believed to be in charge of discreet contacts with the two premier leaders of the FIS, remarked on suggestions that they might be released: "If it puts an end to the violence, then why not?"[32] However, optimism that an agreement could be struck faded with a presidential statement on 30 March which announced that the dialogue had failed and that the struggle against terrorism would now continue "without a break".[33]

In the aftermath of the collapse of this initiative both the FIS and the regime alleged that each other had reneged on commitments made when Zeroual had met with the FIS leaders at Blida. According to the government, Djeddi and Boukhamkham had failed on their release to call publicly for an end to the campaign of violence by the armed groups, having previously agreed to this as a condition for their release. For its part, the FIS claimed that Zeroual had gone back on commitments to free most of the party's leaders, to release Madani and Belhadj to house arrest, to close down the detention camps in the Sahara by mid-March and to lift the ban on the FIS.[34]

Reactions to failure: the regime

The failure of the first attempt at dialogue with the FIS since the party's dissolution was a setback for Liamine Zeroual, who had made this

---

31 It was also revealed that in addition to establishing contacts with the seven FIS leaders held in Blida jail, the authorities had also approached Abdelkader Hachani in the hope that he might provide an alternative source of authority.

32 *Jeune Afrique*, 31.3.94.

33 *Ibid.*, 21.4.94.

34 It emerged that the government had actually planned to release four of the seven imprisoned leaders but two, Nourredine Chigera and Abdelkader Omar, had declined to be freed because of restrictions set by the authorities on their movements within Algeria once released.

initiative the centrepiece of his political strategy. The attempt at dealing with the FIS had inflicted damage not just on his plans for breaking the impasse and halting the escalating conflict, but had also exposed serious rifts inside the regime and amongst its supporters. The break that had been made with the policy of not admitting the FIS back into the political arena, which had been adhered to since the party had been dissolved by Mohammed Boudiaf, provoked serious opposition amongst those opposed to Islamism and who saw Zeroual's initiative as a betrayal of those who had struggled against the terrorism of the armed groups. *El Watan*, a daily newspaper highly critical of Islamism and firmly opposed to dialogue with the FIS, argued on 1 March that the release of Ali Djeddi and Abdelkader Boukhamkham had struck a hard blow at the morale of "troops and other Algerians who believe in democracy in this country".[35]

Opposition to Zeroual's initiative also came from more weighty sources within the regime itself. One of the obstacles that the attempts at holding talks with the main legal opposition parties in 1993 had encountered was the issue of the participation of HAMAS and the MNI. Although the most vocal opposition to the two parties' involvement had come from the RCD, it was strongly suspected that important elements within the military were similarly hostile to discussions with *any* Islamists. It was the opposition of this latter element that was believed to be behind a suspension of official dialogue with HAMAS and the MNI in early 1993. Secret meetings of army chiefs held in mid-March 1994 saw the growing strength of a dissident pole within the military, led by Mohammed Lamari, the Chief of Staff, which believed that the only solution to the Islamist threat to the regime was eradication, as opposed to the conciliation proposed by Zeroual and his supporters. Lamari's stance also had powerful allies within the civilian administration including Redha Malek, the Prime Minister (who had replaced Belaid Abdessalem in August 1993) and Selim Saadi, the Interior Minister, both known for their hardline anti-Islamist views.

As Zeroual's initiative gathered pace in early 1994, these dissident elements within the regime, although unable to openly express dissent, worked to mobilise opposition against Zeroual's dealings with the FIS. As Prime Minister, Redha Malek permitted a number of marches and demonstrations to take place on 22 March, which although ostensibly protesting

---

35   *El Watan*, 1.3.94.

at the escalating level of violence sweeping the country, invariably became platforms for elements (such as the RCD) calling for a halt to the regime's contacts with the FIS. Dissent within the army at Zeroual's policy was demonstrated through a series of shifts in the prosecution of the campaign against the armed groups. The month of Ramadan (February–March) 1994 witnessed a significant retreat on the part of the security forces from areas of Islamist strength allowing in some areas the armed groups to effectively take control. The end of the Muslim holy month, however, saw a substantial "counter-offensive" launched by the security services in both urban areas and the rural maquis. An estimated 350 suspected militants were killed in three weeks of operations. It was argued that the initial abandonment of areas to the armed groups was part of a "strike" tactic by the "eradicator" faction in the military in protest at the softening line being taken by Zeroual. It also undoubtedly represented a faltering in the purpose and morale of the military whilst discussions with the FIS continued and the "eradicator" and "conciliator" factions within the military leadership argued their respective cases. The subsequent counter-offensive by the security forces reflected either a clarifying of purpose with the failure of the dialogue or a triumph, within the military, by General Lamari and his supporters who favoured an iron-fist policy against the groups.

When the President's initiative finally collapsed at the end of March, much of the credit for its failure went to the pressure exerted by figures such as Mohammed Lamari and Redha Malek on Zeroual, who appeared not to have expected such fierce opposition to his plans. The failure of the initiative of early 1994 did not, however, signify a full defeat for Zeroual and his policy of conciliation towards the FIS, nor a victory for Lamari, Malek and the "eradicators". The President reordered personnel in both the government and the military in April and May 1994 to replace many of the senior opponents of dialogue with figures more supportive of his policy of dialogue. Redha Malek's government resigned on 11 April and Zeroual appointed Mokdad Sifi, widely viewed as a malleable technocrat, in Malek's place. Salem Saadi, who had been appointed at the same time as Malek in August 1993 as part of a generally more hardline administration, was similarly replaced as Interior Minister by a more pragmatic figure. In his reshuffle of the security forces and the military Zeroual replaced officers commanding the police and the Constantine military region and ensured that men loyal to him took over the Oran and Blida regions and the command of the army and the airforce.[36] Mohammed Lamari, however, retained his position and actually had his powers enhanced with Zeroual ceding several of his own powers as Minister of Defence to the Chief of Staff. This failure to move against his most powerful opponent was interpreted in some quarters as an indication that the President did not feel sufficiently strong to take on Lamari and felt the need to placate him with new powers. However, it was also likely that Zeroual was anxious not to disrupt the prosecution of Lamari's robust anti-terrorist campaign, seeing it as a means of putting pressure on Islamists to negotiate.

Reaction to failure: the Islamist camp

The GIA and dialogue: violence and hostility

The most vehement Islamist opposition to the idea of dialogue with the government came from the GIA. From its creation the GIA had never hidden its total hostility to any means other than armed jihad to achieve the goal of an Islamic state. The opening of its campaign of assassinations against intellectuals and members of the CCN in the spring of 1993 coincided with the beginning of the HCE's first real attempts at multi-party dialogue and was clearly designed to halt this process. The assassination of the former Prime Minister Kasdi Merbah in August 1993 was thought by many to be the work of the GIA because of covert attempts Merbah had been making to bring both the government and the FIS to the negotiating table.[37] The GIA were particularly hostile to any group or individual who tried to speak on behalf of the Islamist movement. Mohammed Bousilimani, a founding and senior member of HAMAS was kidnapped, tortured and killed by the GIA in December

---

36 These changes were perceived by some as Zeroual seeking to promote and strengthen the role of Arabophone officers within the military *vis-à-vis* Francophone officers and thus further counter the real or perceived dominance of Hizb-Fransa.

37 Other theories behind the assassination suggested that Merbah had been murdered by elements within the regime which, like the GIA, were totally opposed to the idea of dialogue with the FIS. Another prevalent theory suggested that the former Prime Minister had been killed, again by elements from within the regime, to prevent him revealing damaging information on individuals he had compiled and retained during his time as Chief of Military Security between 1979 and 1988.

1993 largely because of the central part his party had been playing in the ongoing dialogue with the regime and in attempts to involve the FIS.[38]

The first indications that some figures from within the FIS might be willing to talk to the regime were met with dark warnings and threats of violence from the GIA. A communiqué issued by the grouping on 21 November 1993 threatened to kill senior figures in the FIS over a supposed "manoeuvre destined to establish contacts with the authorities" naming Redjam, Mohammed Said and Said Mekhloufi in particular. For the two senior figures of the party abroad, Anwar Haddam and Rabah Kebir, the communiqué grimly prophesied that: "Even if they cling onto the walls of the Kaaba, they will suffer the worst of deaths."[39] The advent of the National Reconciliation Conference saw an upsurge in violence from the GIA which was directed against the FIS as well as the regime. This campaign continued into the new year as speculation grew over whether the FIS would deal with the authorities and death threats were issued against Ali Djeddi and Abdelkader Boukhamkham following their release at the end of February (which undoubtedly contributed to their subsequent reluctance to participate in dialogue with the authorities).

The prospect of a deal between the regime and the FIS also heightened the rivalry between the FIS's allies in the armed groups and the GIA. The leader of the GIA, Mourad Sid Ahmed issued a communiqué on 6 February claiming that 70 members of the MIA had been "executed" by the GIA.[40] Three weeks later, on 27 February, Sid Ahmed was himself killed when security forces stormed a house in the Bouzaréah district of Algiers where senior GIA figures had been meeting. That the security forces were clearly well informed about the location of the meeting and that the house belonged to a former member of the executive bureau of

---

38   It was suggested that Bousilimani had been kidnapped in an attempt by the GIA to get a fatwa from an authoritative religious figure, such as Bousilimani, to support the groupings' argument for jihad and thus maintain unity within its ranks. Bousilimani's refusal to agree to this, even under torture, led to his eventual murder. (*El Watan*, 2.2.94.) HAMAS and its leader, Mahfoud Nahnah, in fact appeared to enjoy the closest links of all the major political parties with the regime, particularly in attempts to create a forum for national dialogue which would involve elements from the FIS. Indeed, they appeared to know about the negotiations that had taken place with the FIS before the other parties.

39   *El Watan*, 22.11.93 and 28.2.94.

40   *SWB* ME/1917 MED, 9.2.94.

the FIS suggested that it was sources close to or within the FIS which had provided the security forces with their intelligence.

Defections to the GIA

The collapse of the attempt at dialogue between the authorities and the FIS and President Zeroual's intention to resume the anti-terrorist struggle "without a break" forced the FIS to reappraise its political strategy. The failure of the initiative confirmed the fears of many in the FIS who doubted that the regime would ever be prepared to make real concessions in negotiations. There was thus an increase in the number of defections to the GIA as members of the FIS became convinced that the GIA's strategy of militarily defeating the regime was the only way forward.

Defections to the GIA achieved greatest significance at the beginning of May, when Abderrazak Redjam and Mohammed Said announced that they were joining the grouping. They were soon joined by Said Mekhloufi. The scale and importance of the defections was further emphasised by a statement issued a few days later by Rabah Kebir and the leadership of the party abroad. It declared that Anwar Haddam was no longer able to speak on behalf of the FIS because he had joined the GIA.[41] The defection of the maverick Mekhloufi, who had made known his opposition to the policy of dialogue, was of no great surprise. The adherence of Redjam, Said and Haddam was more unexpected, not least because of the steady flow of death threats that had been issued by the GIA against these three figures over the preceding months.[42]

No precise reasons for the defections of Haddam, Redjam, and Mohammed Said were stated. There were, however, two likely explanations. It is probable that the trio perceived the base of popular support for Islamism to be shifting decisively away from the FIS and towards the GIA and thus feared being sidelined. The release of Ali Djeddi and Abdelkader Boukhamkham from prison in February had also posed a potential threat to the primacy of Said and Redjam's leadership of the FIS inside Algeria as Djeddi and Boukhamkham became the clear focus of

---

41 *Nouvel Observateur*, 11.8.94; *El Watan*, 3.8.94.

42 As recently as April, Cherif Gousmi had signed a communiqué accusing Mekhloufi of being a member of the security services, Redjam of being guilty of "treason" and Mohammed Said of being the son of a *harki* who had opposed the original creation of the FIS in 1989. (Gousmi had himself originally been a member of the FIS.) *Algérie Actualité*, 12.7.94.

government attempts at achieving a political settlement. Defection to the GIA therefore appeared to be a means of preserving their position and authority within the wider Islamist movement. The second, more sophisticated, reason advanced for Said, Redjam and Haddam joining the GIA was that it was part of some form of strategy aimed at politicising and moderating the GIA with the possible eventual aim of drawing it into negotiations. It was notable that Mohammed Said, in particular, had an established reputation for joining and then becoming a leading figure in Islamist groupings having already achieved this in both the Rabitat Dawa and, more significantly, in the FIS itself.

The FIS counter-offensive: the formation of the AIS

The defection of so many senior figures put the remainder of the FIS's leadership under pressure to respond. Rabah Kebir publicly responded with a degree of equanimity, stating that Said and Redjam were free as individuals to join the GIA if they wished but that this did not commit the FIS as a whole.[43] However, there was considerable anger at the nature of the defection. Of particular concern to Kebir and the rest of the FIS's leadership (notably those in the prison in Blida) was that the defections had been portrayed by those defecting as a unification of the FIS and other elements under the banner of the GIA. The GIA had even indicated that Abassi Madani and Ali Belhadj would become members of its Majlis Shura.[44] This was seen as a presumptuous and unacceptable subsummation of the politically far more substantial FIS into what had been, until comparatively recently, a small extremist grouping. The proclaimed unification also threatened to dispense with the name of the FIS, thus losing the important symbolic associations and degree of popular legitimacy that the party had accrued since 1989.[45] The unification was thus denounced and rejected by both senior FIS politicians as well as the leaders of its allies in the armed groups.[46]

---

43   *Echoes of Truth*, August 1994.
44   *Algérie Actualité*, 12.7.94. A statement issued by the FIS's allies in the armed groups argued that neither Abassi nor Belhadj had been consulted on this. (*Ibid.*) Ali Belhadj was later reported by one Algerian newspaper to have explicitly condemned the unification. *El Watan*, 3.8.94.
45   See *Echoes of Truth*, August 1994.
46   A statement by the soon-to-be reconstituted AIS stated that the GIA unification ignored the fact that the FIS already had its own armed wing (the AIS). *Algérie Actualité*, 12.7.94.

The FIS leadership was aware that condemnation of the GIA and disassociation from it were insufficient responses to the challenge the GIA presented. Those in the FIS who continued to hope for a deal with the regime knew that the increasing strength of the GIA reduced the chances of such a deal being struck. Firstly, there was the fear that by negotiating the FIS could lose more popular support to the GIA. Secondly, there was the concern that the hardliners within the regime could point to the increasingly bloody and indiscriminate campaign being waged by the GIA as reason why no compromise with any Islamist group should be contemplated.

The leadership of the FIS therefore perceived there to be a need to create an armed wing for itself to prevent the GIA dominating the armed struggle and thus threaten the credibility of any commitments the party might make in negotiations with the regime. The structures that had been set up by the FIS and the MIA in 1993 to control the armed struggle had operated only very loosely and had suffered with the growing defections to the GIA, particularly that of Said Mekhloufi, who had been head of operations under these arrangements. There was consequently a more concerted attempt by the FIS in 1994 to draw together various armed groups and unite them under the explicit banner of the FIS. The FIS was aided in this task by the liberation of significant numbers of Islamist activists who had been imprisoned by the authorities. These releases came not only from the gradual release of detainees from the camps in the Sahara, but more importantly from a mass prison breakout from Tazoult prison in March 1994 which freed nearly a thousand Islamist activists, including several senior figures. The time spent in both the camps and prisons strengthened not only the Islamist convictions of those imprisoned but established links between groups and individuals which were retained after release when many joined or returned to the armed groups allowing greater communication and co-ordination between the various groups.

The result of the efforts at unifying the armed groups was revealed in July when the creation of an Armé Islamiques du Salut was announced. Increasingly known by its initials, AIS, this new grouping was made up of elements of the old MIA together with a number of other hitherto independent groups and groupings.[47] Foremost of these was the

---

47   The title "Armé Islamiques du Salut" (AIS) had been used for the armed groups

Mouvement pour l'État Islamique which joined the AIS after protracted negotiations and brought in the two regional "Emirs" of the movement from the east (Madani Merzak) and the west (Ahmed Ben Aicha) of the country. Together with other smaller groups from the still very fragmented armed resistance the forces of the AIS were formally united under the leadership, once again, of Abdelkader Chebouti.[48]

The creation of the AIS differed from past attempts at uniting and unifying the Islamist struggle in that, for the first time, the armed struggle within Algeria was explicitly subordinated to the political leadership of the FIS. Although anxious to retain a degree of autonomy, both Madani Merzak and Ahmed Ben Aicha (who had actually been elected as a deputy for the FIS in the December 1991 elections) affirmed that supreme authority belonged to Abassi Madani and Ali Belhadj. The choice of name for the AIS (which had already been occasionally employed since 1993 by the groups allied to the FIS) with its inclusion of the word *Salut*, was intended to underscore the affinity and loyalty of the new grouping to the FIS.

The GIA response: the formation of the "Caliphate"

Sensing that the political and military initiatives were beginning to shift back in the direction of the FIS with the creation of the AIS and the affirmation of the primacy of the two historic leaders of the party, the GIA looked for ways to raise its own profile. Militarily, this was done by stepping up their campaign against foreigners in Algeria. The most notable result of this was an assault on 3 August on a residential block in the Algiers suburbs housing French Embassy staff, which resulted in the deaths

---

loyal to the FIS since 1993. The whole process of unifying the armed groups had been made easier since the summer of 1993 by the authorities' gradual release of detainees from the prison camps in the Sahara. This was so because while in detention, the groups and individuals had an opportunity not only to form links with one another, but also to strengthen their Islamist conviction by symbiosis.

48 Chebouti's title as "general" and commander of the AIS was, however, largely symbolic due to his increasing ill-health and the desire for the two regional emirs of the old MEA to retain a significant degree of autonomy. Chebouti's declining influence aided the process of subordinating the armed struggle to the political authority of the FIS since despite enjoying close relations with many of the party's senior figures, he had never been a member of the FIS and had always been opposed to its constitutionalist strategy.

of five Frenchmen. In the political field, the GIA tried to consolidate the political capital it had gained through the defections of senior FIS figures in May.

At the beginning of August, Anwar Haddam appeared to formally announce his adherence to the GIA, having hitherto only been accused by the leadership of the FIS of having joined the grouping. He declared that FIS party militants were joining forces with the GIA as a result of a decision taken by Islamist field commanders at a meeting held in April (thus probably explaining the timing of the other defections at the beginning of May). In response, Rabah Kebir publicly reiterated that the FIS would continue to exist as the FIS.[49] The political initiative of the GIA went one step further at the end of August when it announced, in a communiqué released on 26 August, the formation of an Islamic government or "Caliphate". Asserting that this Caliphate "will manage the affairs of the *umma* in the framework of a state governed by the law of the Almighty", the communiqué went on to list the personnel in this supposed "Islamic government-in-waiting". In addition to the post of "Commander of the Faithful", which went to the leader of the GIA, Cherif Gousmi (who had assumed the leadership following the death of Mourad Sid Ahmed in February), eleven ministries and their heads were detailed. Mohammed Said was named as head of government, Anwar Haddam was made responsible for foreign affairs and Said Mekhloufi became the provisional Interior Minister.[50]

The creation of a credible political leadership to rival that of the FIS threatened to greatly bolster the GIA in its struggle with the FIS–AIS. However, the potential impact of the announcement was sharply reduced by the haste with which many of the named ministers sought to disassociate themselves from the declaration. In a communiqué sent to a national newspaper on 27 August, Said Mekhloufi and a close ally announced their withdrawal from the GIA's Majlis Shura claiming that the grouping deviated from Islamic precepts and legitimised reprehensible acts.[51] Other figures disputed their involvement with the GIA and even attempted to rejoin the FIS. Anwar Haddam denied all knowledge of the GIA's "Caliphate" and his inclusion in it, claiming it was a deliberate

---

49 *MEI*, 5.8.94; *El Watan*, 3.8.94.
50 *Le Monde*, 28/29.8.94.
51 *El Watan*, 28.8.94.

invention of the Algerian and French security services.[52] He refuted the claim that he was or ever had been a member of the GIA and asserted that he had only ever spoken in the name of the FIS.[53] There was also evidence of considerable dissent between the various named members of the GIA's Caliphate. At the same time as announcing his secession from the GIA, Said Mekhloufi claimed that the formation of the Caliphate had in fact been part of an attempt by Mohammed Said to take over the GIA for the Jazara and stated that he had in his possession an audio tape which proved this.[54]

Continued competition

The collapse of its attempt to mount a more political initiative pushed the GIA into looking for other means of advancing their struggle both against the regime and the FIS–AIS. More importantly, it sought to prevent these two adversaries talking to each other. Operationally, the GIA continued to be both robust and resilient, despite the regular loss of successive leaders (the grouping had survived the disastrous blow of the security forces raid on its February meeting in which it lost nine senior personnel in addition to Mourad Sid Ahmed). It had established itself as the dominant armed group within Algiers and the surrounding region. The adherence of the MIA, in particular, to the AIS had given the FIS's armed wing primacy in the eastern and western regions of the country, but the GIA still maintained a presence in these regions too.[55] The regime's post-Ramadan counter-offensive had pushed some of its units out of the capital and into the rural maquis which was largely controlled by the AIS. This inevitably led to clashes between the two groups and although these led to important casualties on the GIA's side (notably Abdelkader Hattab and nine of his lieutenants in July[56]), the GIA remained able to

---

52   *Le Monde*, 28/29.8.94.
53   Paul Schemm, 'Hope for Algeria?', *Middle East Insight* (September-October 1994).
54   *El Watan*, 28.8.94; *Le Matin*, 27.9.94.
55   According to FIS sources, at the end of 1994 the AIS controlled the majority of the armed groups in both the east (55%) and the west (65%) of the country, but only 20% in the centre due to the predominance of the GIA. Labat, *Les Islamistes Algériens*, p. 259n.
56   It was alleged that Said Mekhloufi had actually been responsible for the deaths of Hattab and his men. If this was the case, it was indicative of violent dissensions between the more established elements of the GIA and new adherents such as Mekhloufi. It would also explain Mekhloufi's announced exit from the GIA at

prosecute well-planned attacks in the capital, such as that against the French Embassy staff residence.[57]

The GIA's need to maintain a high profile and, more importantly, receive more substantial leadership was demonstrated in its kidnapping of two Arab diplomats, the Omani and Yemeni Ambassadors, in July. Released unharmed a few days after their capture, the diplomats carried a message to the authorities. It offered an end to the assassination campaign against foreigners in return for the release of the seminal leader of the GIA, Abdelhak Layada, who had been imprisoned since his successful extradition from Morocco the previous autumn. The demand for Layada's release was a recognition by the GIA of its need for leadership. Layada's charismatic influence had been instrumental in uniting the GIA's constituent groups originally and could possibly galvanise once more the GIA's still fairly loose structures. The authorities' failure to respond to this offer led to the killing of sixteen foreigners over the following two weeks. This demonstrated that even if it lacked leadership and unity, the GIA was still able to carry out its threats.[58]

The increasingly extreme nature of the GIA's campaign appeared to serve the interests of the newly unified FIS–AIS. It made the latter seem a more moderate and pragmatic alternative to the GIA, both for ordinary people and the regime. The FIS and the AIS condemned the GIA's increasing use of violence against the ordinary population (which it used as a means of control) and in a communiqué released on 31 August the AIS explicitly distanced itself from a campaign recently launched by the GIA which threatened schools with arson unless they changed their curricula, organisation and pupil dress codes to comply with "Islamic" requirements.[59] Rabah Kebir, in an interview with a Western newspaper,

---

the end of August. *El Watan* suggested that disputes over territory and arms lay behind the killing of Hattab. The newspaper (which benefited from well-informed sources in the security services) also voiced the suspicion that Mekhloufi had in reality never joined the GIA and it was his anger at the claim had led to the confrontation. *El Watan*, 1.8.94.

57   There even appeared to be competition between the GIA and AIS in certain areas over the control of protection rackets and businesses.

58   *MEI*, 5.8.94; *Jeune Afrique*, 4.8.94; *Nouvel Observateur*, 11.8.94.

59   *Libération*, 7.9.94. These threats, which were carried through against some 500 schools between June and September alone, resulted from a failed attempt by the GIA to initiate a school strike in imitation of similar tactics used during the liberation struggle. The precise demands of the GIA on schools were that they

made clear that the FIS differed from the GIA on the important issues of the killing of foreigners, which it opposed, and participation in elections, which it remained in favour of.[60]

The second attempt at dialogue, 1994

The competitive manoeuvring that occurred between the various parts of the Islamist movement during mid-1994 coincided with renewed attempts to find a solution to the wider crisis.

Political initiatives: May–August 1994

Despite the collapse of the first attempt at dialogue with members of the FIS and the consequent stepping up of the anti-terrorist campaign, President Zeroual remained intent on not excluding the possibility of further dialogue with the party. His replacement in April and May of hardline figures opposed to dialogue with the FIS with pragmatic personnel who were personally loyal to him, was an indication of this intent. For the FIS, Rabah Kebir remained uncertain as to how genuine Zeroual's commitment to finding a solution was. He was unsure whether the President's policy of "talking peace, whilst waging war" was due to Zeroual being constrained by other forces within the regime or whether it was the result of a deliberate policy of deceit.[61] Nevertheless, Kebir cautiously welcomed Zeroual's dismissal of the anti-Islamist Prime Minister, Redha Malek, and described it as "a positive act in the context of the search for a negotiated settlement" and emphasised that the FIS was ready for such negotiations.[62]

President Zeroual still faced considerable potential opposition to his plans for political development from figures in the military, particularly those officers close to Mohammed Lamari who were supportive of his

---

should end mixed classes and the teaching of music, and that girls should no longer participate in gym classes and should wear hedjab.

60 *Le Monde*, 6.8.94. The leadership of the FIS abroad were particularly concerned by the effect the GIA's campaign against foreigners would have on international opinion. They feared that it would not only destroy foreign sympathy for the struggle against the regime, but would also damage important overseas relations for any future Islamist government.

61 Author's interview with Rabah Kebir, 27.9.95.

62 *MEI*, 29.4.94.

policy of eradication. At a stormy meeting in July with the chiefs of staff, the President announced new plans to relaunch attempts at national dialogue which would once again aim to include Islamists. In support of his proposals he pointed to the evident failure of the "total security" policy launched at the end of Ramadan which had been the favoured approach of the "eradicators". This had failed to noticeably curtail the activities of the armed groups and had simply added to the violence and bloodshed which had increased dramatically since the beginning of the year.[63] On August 8 Mokdad Sifi, the new Prime Minister, announced that the government would, once again, be taking up dialogue with the political parties, although no mention was made, at this stage, of participation by the FIS.

Overtures from the FIS

Attempts to include the FIS in the dialogue had in fact begun in April, within weeks of President Zeroual's formal acknowledgement of the failure of the new year initiative. The instigator of contacts this time, however, was the FIS. Persuaded perhaps by the initial effectiveness of the security forces' post-Ramadan offensive that military victory for the AIS was simply not possible, the leadership in Blida prison started to send letters to the presidency indicating terms on which dialogue and an agreement could be reached.

The first letters came from Ali Belhadj, on 7 April and 22 July. They stressed primarily the importance of freeing the remaining leaders of the FIS before any progress could be made or meaningful dialogue take place.[64] Zeroual and the authorities did not respond directly to these letters, but made it plain that the primary condition they attached to engaging in dialogue with members of the FIS was the latter's renunciation of violence. Movement on the issue came with the sending of two further letters from Blida prison, this time from Abassi Madani. FIS figures abroad stressed the importance of these letters being signed by the leader of the FIS himself (rather than just his deputy) and they

---

63 *Le Point*, 10.9.94.
64 *Libération*, 15.6.94; *Le Monde*, 23.8.94. Apart from the central demand of his and the other leaders' release, Ali Belhadj called for a "return to legitimate laws" (the sharia?) and greater public information. He even challenged the President to a televised debate.

provoked far greater attention from the authorities than either of those sent by Belhadj.[65]

Both sent in the last week of August, the two letters resulted in government representatives being dispatched to Blida to attain clarification of various points following the receipt of each letter. Whilst awaiting this clarification the authorities made known the contents of the letters which listed general principles, proposals for a political solution and practical measures to be taken to achieve this solution. That the letters contained moderate and clearly serious proposals that did not fundamentally conflict with conditions set out by Zeroual for parties wishing to participate in elections encouraged the President and the conciliators in the regime. The President had made it plain that together with an ending of violence respect for the Constitution and acknowledgement of the irreversibility of democracy were conditions for a return to dialogue. In his letters Abassi Madani had appeared to specifically address these last two issues expressing his commitment:

> To abide by: party pluralism and to allow free opinion and to encourage diversity of programmes and forms of interpretation; the freedom of initiative and the acceptance of the changes of government through elections . . . [66]

Also to support the constitution which is "applicable in the way provided for in the constitution itself . . ."[67]

Stressing that the letters had been unsolicited by the authorities, Zeroual made known the contents of the letters and publicly described several elements contained within them as "positive" and said that they represented a significant "first step" by the FIS.[68] However, Abassi and Belhadj, together with the three remaining leaders in prison, made it clear to the presidency's emissaries that no political initiative could be contemplated whilst they remained in prison. On the evening of 13 September Abassi Madani and Ali Belhadj were released to house arrest whilst the other three detained leaders were simply allowed to go free.

---

65 *Le Monde*, 6.9.94.
66 *SWB* ME/2095 MED/2, 8.9.94.
67 *Ibid.*
68 *SWB* ME/2096 MED/12–13, 9.9.94.

Opposition from both sides: the "eradicators" and the GIA

The releases of the FIS leaders were heralded as marking a possible beginning of an end to Algeria's bloody conflict, but they were far from welcomed by those on both sides who were resolutely opposed to the idea of dialogue. Leila Aslaoui, a minister in the government renowned for her anti-Islamist views, resigned on 19 September in protest at the releases. Opposition to the developments from within the regime also made use of figures outside the government to voice their own grave reservations. In collusion with Mohammed Lamari, Redha Malek, the former Prime Minister, spoke out publicly about what he regarded as a "unilateral concession" on the part of the regime which "put in deadly danger the Republic". He criticised Zeroual for appearing to suspend his condition that Abassi Madani unambiguously condemn terrorism before being released.[69] The anti-Islamist press, notably *Le Matin*, highlighted the fact that the releases had not reduced the violence and argued that Abassi and Belhadj "no longer controlled the armed groups".[70] Criticism was also voiced from those political parties who were similarly hostile to any compromise with the Islamists of the FIS. Said Saadi, the leader of the RCD, reacted to the releases of the FIS leaders by observing that: "A part of the army is ready to go for a walk on the backs of the democrats."[71] Even the FFS, which had long stipulated inclusion of the FIS in dialogue as a condition for its own participation, maintained its distance from discussions because of stated fears that a "secret pact" had been concluded between the FIS and the government.[72]

The reaction of the GIA to the release of the FIS leaders was judged as being crucial. Efforts had been made in the official media over the preceding months to distinguish between extremists and pragmatic moderates in the Islamist movement in an effort to increase popular acceptance of dialogue with the FIS as representatives of the latter tendency. However, the authorities still clearly hoped that the GIA could be persuaded by the FIS to halt their campaign. Rabah Kebir maintained that 80% of Islamist violence could be stopped by the FIS's leadership

---

69 *Jeune Afrique*, 22.9.94.
70 *Le Matin*, 15.9.94.
71 *Jeune Afrique*, 6.10.94.
72 *Le Monde*, 16.9.94. The FFS's reluctance to become involved in dialogue also had much to do with the increasingly fierce challenge to its base of support that the RCD had been mounting in Kabylia.

since current or former cadres of the FIS could be found at the heart of virtually every armed group (including, presumably, elements of the GIA).[73] In a communiqué following the releases the AIS formally reaffirmed their allegiance to the leadership of the FIS, stating that "The Chiefs of the FIS are the Chiefs of Jihad in Algeria" – a clear gesture of support for the leadership's negotiating position. However, the communiqué also called on the "brothers in the centre" to organise themselves "in order to design a national command and bar the way to manipulations by the junta and its services". This clear appeal to the GIA (who dominated the "centre", the Algiers region, of Algeria) was, however, vigorously rebuffed by the GIA. On 14 September, the day after the releases, the GIA condemned all compromise with the "apostate regime" and restated their established credo of "Neither reconciliation, nor truce, nor dialogue."[74] As a more tangible indication of the GIA's attitude towards events, Islamist violence demonstrably increased in the aftermath of the releases, culminating in the detonation of a car bomb in Algiers on 12 October as dialogue began.

The demands of the FIS

The FIS did not join the next round of multi-party talks scheduled for 20 September, despite hopes of early participation in formal dialogue. The party remained concerned about the lifting of both the ban on the FIS and the state of emergency, and an amnesty for the substantial numbers of Islamists still in prison. However, the main blockage to further participation by the freed leaders in talks to break the impasse and end the conflict was the demand that they be allowed to freely consult with the wider leadership of the party. It became evident that this implied direct consultations not only with the leadership of the party abroad and other individuals still imprisoned, but also with the leaders of the armed groups. As the freed leaders had declared in a final joint letter before their release:

> Since we are asked the opinion of the leadership it is right that we reunite the leadership to give it . . . All the leadership: the military leadership imprisoned or at liberty, inside the country or outside.[75]

---

73 Le Monde, 21.9.94.
74 Jeune Afrique, 22.9.94.
75 Jeune Afrique, 2.9.94.

This demand, which had been present in virtually all the FIS's previous conditions for dialogue, did not just represent a tactic on behalf of the party to wring more concessions from the government. It also reflected a genuine need on the part of the party to unite its ranks behind it before beginning negotiations thus preventing the development of possible splits and schisms. As Rabah Kebir explained:

> A simple appeal for a truce, even if it comes from Abassi, will not stop the bloodshed. We must gather together all our cadres in both political positions and in the armed groups.[76]

The collapse of the initiative

The demand that the FIS be permitted to reunite its leadership proved unacceptable to a regime which was already under pressure from its hardliners over excessive concessions to the FIS.[77] Three sets of meetings between the released leaders and government representatives on 15 and 29 September and 23 October failed to resolve the issue and at the end of October the regime formally announced the failure of the initiative. As with the collapse of the first attempt in the previous March, the government's statements were full of recriminations and accusations of bad faith on the part of the FIS. In sharply worded statements President Zeroual alleged that Abassi Madani and Ali Belhadj had "gone back on their undertakings" which had formed the basis for their release. They had also refused to issue a call to end the violence until they were released from house arrest.[78]

More seriously, the regime released the texts of two letters allegedly found on the body of the commander of the GIA, Cherif Gousmi, killed on 26 September by the security forces. Purportedly signed by Ali Belhadj, the letters seemed to reveal the close nature of links between the GIA and the FIS's number two. They thanked Gousmi and the GIA for contributing to pressures on the regime which led to his and the other FIS leaders' release. They also urged Gousmi to "reach an agreement" with the AIS and proposed that: "Pressures must be brought to bear

---

76 *Le Matin*, 25.9.94.
77 This was despite rumours that the regime itself had been in contact with FIS leaders living abroad. See *Financial Times*, 5.9.94 and *Guardian*, 6.9.94.
78 SWB ME/2140 MED/11–15, 30.11.94, and ME/2142 ME/17–20, 2.11.94.

from outside by you through military operations and statements and by us . . . through information and guidance." Zeroual presented these letters as clear evidence that the FIS leadership was "trying to bolster extremism and encourage crime". Furthermore: "With such behaviour those concerned have demonstrated that they only have a dictatorial view of democracy" and therefore they should no longer be allowed to participate in dialogue with the regime and the other law-abiding forces.[79]

Whether both sets of allegations had any substance or were simply covers for the regime to justify their abandonment of the dialogue over the real issue of allowing the FIS to consult its wider leadership, was uncertain. Kamel Guemazi, one of the three FIS leaders completely freed on 13 September, had asserted on 20 September, well in advance of the collapse of the initiative, that the authorities had in fact set no preconditions for their release.[80] This was undoubtedly the case given Zeroual's avoidance of the issue of explicit renunciation of violence in the probable hope that the releases would prompt subsequent concessions on the part of the FIS. The veracity of the letters found on Cherif Gousmi's body was difficult to judge, but the texts of the letters revealed by the authorities (if accurate) did appear to indicate that these were not the first that had been sent from the deputy leader of the FIS to Gousmi.[81] The explanation for such contacts clearly lay in attempts by the FIS to establish links with the GIA in order to harness them to the FIS's negotiating position. Both Abassi Madani and Ali Belhadj had appealed to the AIS during 1994 to avoid confrontations with the GIA[82] and as one senior FIS figure remarked to a Western academic while discussions between the FIS and the government were still in progress during October:

> The reality is that the GIA are present on the ground and that they are representative. To not take this into consideration would be like failing to take into account the army . . . Our concern is not so much the winning back of the GIA cadres, but to arrive at a consensus

79 *Ibid.*
80 *Independent*, 20.9.94.
81 In one of the letters Belhadj stated: "This is my first contact with you from the prison of house arrest." *SWB* ME/2140 MED/12–13, 31.10.94.
82 *Nouvel Observateur*, 11.8.94.

with them concerning the religious basis for a strategy to resolve the crisis.[83]

The leadership of the FIS were clearly aware of the GIA's hostility to the idea of dialogue. The fact that the letters found on Cherif Gousmi's body were from Ali Belhadj may have been an indication that these contacts were an individual initiative on the part of Belhadj (as opposed to one endorsed by the other leaders). However, it was more likely that the FIS leadership were conscious that Belhadj enjoyed a substantial amount of respect from elements within the GIA. The FIS number two had been nominated for a portfolio in the grouping's Caliphate in August whilst Abassi Madani had been notably ignored. However, despite a brief indication in the group's newspaper *Al Ansar* that the GIA "partially" accepted the terms set out for dialogue by Ali Belhadj, the increasing level of violence that accompanied the discussions indicated that the GIA held to its established position of rejecting categorically any negotiation with the regime.[84]

Zeroual's response: presidential elections

The collapse of Liamine Zeroual's second attempt to bring a negotiated end to the conflict came as a blow to the President and his allies. The President's credibility had been heavily invested in achieving such a settlement and the formal termination of negotiations with the FIS leadership at the end of October threatened to plunge Algeria back into deep and bloody stalemate. Zeroual therefore used the occasion of the fortieth anniversary of the start of the liberation struggle on 1 November to launch a new political initiative aimed at shoring up his damaged authority. To the surprise of many Zeroual in his presidential speech to the nation on 31 October 1994 announced not only the inevitable redoubling of efforts against "terrorism" but also the regime's intention "to organise presidential elections before the end of 1995".[85]

Reaction to the announcement was nearly universally sceptical. For most Algerians, the continuing level of violence ruled out the prospect

---

83 Labat, *Les Islamistes Algériens*, pp. 284–5.
84 *Libération*, 20.9.94. It was also suggested that the upsurge in violence during October 1994 may also have been attributable to rejectionist elements within the regime itself.

of any proper or fair election being able to be held and the proposal was widely treated as an empty gimmick designed to obscure the collapse of the attempt at dialogue. Representatives of the FIS shared this analysis, Anwar Haddam describing it as an act of desperation on the part of Zeroual.[86] More ominously, the Chicago-based spokesman indicated that the party would actively seek to prevent such elections taking place:

> There cannot be elections and there will not be any elections. That is a promise. There will quite simply not be any elections under such circumstances. The armed struggle will be certainly stepped-up. Algeria is in a state of war.[87]

Haddam's grim forecast appeared to be fully borne out in the closing weeks of 1994 as Algeria witnessed a further upsurge in violence as nearly a thousand deaths in the opening week of November made it the bloodiest single period in Algeria since the beginning of the conflict three years earlier.

The Rome Accord

The growing fear that, with the failure of a second attempt to find a negotiated solution, Algeria was on the verge of a full civil war prompted efforts from all sides to find a way out of the impasse. For the first time since the beginning of the crisis, the political parties took the lead. Having failed in their attempts to influence the government in officially sponsored talks over the preceding two years, the principal legal opposition parties launched their own initiative. The move was spearheaded by the FLN and FFS. The abrogation of the electoral process in January 1992 had led the two parties to overcome their historic differences and to co-operate increasingly closely to demand the reinstatement of elections. The FLN's final breach with the regime had come in January 1992 with Abdelhamid Mehri's decision to join with the FFS and the FIS (as the three parties which had won seats in the first ballot of December 1991) in denouncing the abandonment of the electoral process. The leader of the FLN's continued criticism of the regime's security policy and insistence that any

---

85 *SWB* ME/2142 MED, 2.11.94.
86 *The Times,* 2.11.94.
87 *SWB* ME/2142 MED, 2.11.94.

political solution must involve the FIS further removed the party from the regime and aligned it with the position of the FFS.

In the autumn of 1994 both the FLN and the FFS had agreed on a project to organise a genuinely national dialogue which would involve all the political forces and which would result in the drawing up of some form of national "contract" to chart a course out of the crisis. Aware that the regime would not permit any such independent gathering within Algeria, a conference was rapidly convened under the auspices of the St Egidio Community at Rome, which had hosted conferences to resolve crises in other countries (such as Mozambique) and which offered to provide a similar service for Algeria. Invitations were issued to all the major political parties and to the government itself. Predictably the regime declined to attend but representatives from HAMAS, the MDA, Nahda, and several smaller parties as well as the FLN and the FFS travelled from Algeria to attend.

Clearly crucial to the endeavour was the issue of FIS representation at the conference which had been the obstacle to any domestically organised meeting. No FIS figure within Algeria was permitted by the regime to leave the country, which meant that the representatives of the party abroad would need to attend. Invitations were issued to Rabah Kebir and Anwar Haddam. The attendance of both of these figures threatened to be problematical. Haddam's presence was controversial because of his equivocation on violence and the operations of the GIA, but it was hoped that his radical connections might aid acceptance by the armed groups of any eventual agreement.[88] It was also hoped that the presence of the more moderate and technically more senior Kebir would curb Haddam's radicalism. This last hope though was stymied by fears from Rabah Kebir that whilst he was able to travel to Rome from his base in Germany, he might not be allowed back into Germany.[89] At the last minute it was agreed that Abdelkrim Ould Adda, a member of the

---

88 Haddam's stance on violence had forced the abandonment of original plans to hold a conference in London – the British government having made it clear that they would not issue him with an entry visa.

89 The German government had come under increasing pressure from Algiers over the status and activities of Rabah Kebir. Although an attempt to extradite him had failed in 1993, the German authorities continued to try and restrict his activities and were clearly uncomfortable with his presence.

FIS's Executive Bureau Abroad and a close ally of Kebir would represent Kebir at the conference.

The conference was convened on 21 November and lasted two days. No formal contract resulted from the gathering but the majority of the participating parties signed a joint communiqué and stated their intention to meet again within a few months to draw up a formal document. Of the major parties only HAMAS and the PRA declined to sign the final communiqué with the FLN, the FFS, the MDA, Nahda and most importantly, the FIS endorsing the preliminary conclusions of the meeting.[90] No official comment on the meeting was passed by Algiers but the Algerian Ambassador to Rome condemned the gathering as "interference in internal Algerian affairs".[91] For its part the FIS was clearly pleased at the apparent alliance that was being forged with the other opposition parties. It allowed Anwar Haddam to declare at the close of the conference:

> The crisis is not due to divergences between the FIS and the Government. It is clear today that it is the whole political class, the civil society, that demands a return to the political process.[92]

A second meeting in Rome was duly organised for January 1995. Having successfully achieved FIS participation in the first meeting, particular efforts were made in the run-up to the second gathering to secure support from the party for the planned national contract. Aware that only support from the original leadership of the FIS would appear credible to the regime and moreover, seem legitimate to many in the armed groups, Abdelhamid Mehri visited Abassi Madani and Ali Belhadj in prison before travelling to Rome. Presenting to them a list of proposals that were to be put to the conference, the leader of the FLN received in response a letter from the two leaders which detailed their demands and concessions.

---

90 HAMAS and the PRA were believed to be unhappy about the role of the armed groups in a planned future settlement (the full nature of which was to be revealed in January). Nourredine Boukrouh, the leader of the PRA, subsequently complained that "there was no debate" at the November meeting. *Le Soir d'Algérie*, 9.5.95.
91 *Le Monde*, 23.11.94.
92 *Ibid.*

No indication of the contents of the letter from Abassi and Belhadj was given before the second Rome conference convened on 8 January, but following five days of discussions, the participants were able to present on 13 January a jointly signed document.[93] The "Platform for a political and peaceful solution to the Algerian Crisis" constituted a proposed programme aimed at resolving the impasse in Algeria. The six-page document outlined the disastrous nature of the crisis, declared a set of values and principles, and set out a proposed sequence of measures to be taken.

Great attention inevitably focused on those parts of the document that addressed the role and demands of the FIS. Unsurprisingly, the platform called for a lifting of the ban on the party. More importantly, it endorsed the FIS's essential position on the sequence of events that should proceed talks which would establish transitionary structures to oversee the organisation of fresh elections. In contrast to the regime's established position, the document supported the proposition that release of the FIS's leadership and reunion of the party's scattered cadres should precede the declaration of a formal truce. This endorsement of the FIS's position on the issue that had frustrated the two previous attempts at dialogue between the FIS and the regime was inevitably seized upon by the FIS's independent political opponents inside Algeria. *El Watan* characterised the Platform as "a blank cheque for the FIS" and Said Saadi claimed it was "reinforcing the FIS's power".[94] However, the document contained evidence that the FIS had in fact made several concessions.

The most immediately apparent concession the FIS appeared to have made in the Rome Platform was a clarification of the party's position on violence. The "Values and principles" declared in the document contained a commitment to "the rejection of violence as a means of achieving or maintaining power".[95] Clarifications of the party's position on more fundamental issues were also evident in the document. The Platform was notable for its robust and explicit espousal of various principles that

---

93 The final signatories to the Platform were the FLN, the FFS, the FIS, the MDA, Nahda, the Parti des Travailleurs (PT – a small leftist party) the JMC (an Islamic grouping close to Ahmed Sahnoun) and the Ligue Algérienne de Défense des Droits de l'Homme (LADDH – whose respected leader, Ali Yahia Abdenour acted as a spokesman for the Platform).

94 *El Watan*, 15.1.95; Interview with Said Saadi, *Guardian*, 6.2.95. The RCD had naturally declined to attend the Rome conferences.

95 *Plateforme pour une Solution Politique et Pacifique de la Crise Algérienne*, 13.1.95.

the FIS had been profoundly equivocal about during its legal lifetime. Foremost it proclaimed a respect for "alternation of power through universal suffrage" and for "popular legitimacy", and supported "the guarantee of fundamental liberties, individual and collective, regardless of race, sex, confession or language" as well as "the consecration of multi-partyism". All these were issues that the party had never previously unambiguously backed and had underlain many of the doubts the secular parties, in particular, had had about the nature and implications of the FIS's political programme.

The explicit acceptance of the main tenets of liberal democracy by senior members of the FIS demonstrated by the signatures of Anwar Haddam and Rabah Kebir to the final National Contract was seized upon by supporters of the initiative as a major breakthrough representing the apparent conversion of the FIS to democratic principles. The other signatories of the National Contract were particularly anxious to emphasise this development. A member of the FLN politburo remarked that: "the fact that the FIS has signed the National Contract document represents an acceptance of a full political solution based on accepted principles – democratic and peaceful principles."[96] For the FFS, Hocine Ait Ahmed argued that the initiative had "succeeded in bringing into the political sphere the more moderate elements of the FIS, isolating the advocates of violence."[97]

Scepticism about the genuineness of the FIS's conversion remained, but representatives from the party maintained that the National Contract reflected views that the FIS had held for some time. With regard to the party's support for the principles of alternation of power, pluralism and popular free choice, Abdelkrim Ould Adda, Rabah Kebir's emissary at Rome, remarked:

> I believe that at Rome . . . the other parties were quite surprised to see us holding to this line. In fact they were able to understand when we explained that we remain a political party, even if latterly our struggle has also had an element of armed resistance.[98]

96   Interview with Hocine Sassi, *La Nation*, 25.4.95.
97   *La Nation*, 25.4.95.
98   'L'Après Rome vu par le FIS', interview in *Les Cahiers de l'Orient*, no. 36–7 (1994-95), p. 23.

There were also doubts about the degree to which the Rome Platform had the real backing of the imprisoned leadership of the party, particularly that of Ali Belhadj. Although the letter brought by Abdelhamid Mehri from Algeria supposedly detailed the leadership's position and there were claims that the Rome conference had lines of communication during the proceedings to Ali Belhadj, it seemed incredible to many that the deputy leader of the FIS could really support the document.[99] However, these doubts were substantially dispelled by Belhadj himself, who through publicised letters sent from prison openly backed the outcome of the Rome initiative. He declared that "the beginnings of a peaceful and legitimate solution are contained in the national contract" and supported the FIS's alliance with the other parties.[100] Belhadj endorsed the main proposals of the document, although one observer saw significance in the fact that he omitted any reference to the principal of alternation of power.[101]

It was hoped by the signatories to the National Contract that Ali Belhadj's endorsement of the Rome Platform would add credibility to the initiative and elicit a favourable response from the two elements that were essential to the restoration of civil peace – the regime and the armed groups. Identifying a clear response from the armed groups was complicated not only by the divisions that existed between them, but also by increasing uncertainty about the authenticity of statements and communiqués that appeared to come from the groups. Many statements were contradictory and confusing. Initial communiqués purporting to come from the GIA gave a qualified welcome to the National Contract, but later statements condemned the initiative.[102] Doubt was cast by many

---

99 One of the members of the St Egidio Community affirmed that: "We had a line of communication to Ali Belhadj. Within ten hours we could receive his response to questions put to him by the FIS delegation in Rome. So the signature at the bottom of the document is also Ali Belhadj's signature." *MEED*, 14.4.95.

100 *Jeune Afrique*, 9.3.95; *Financial Times*, 26.1.95.

101 Labat, *Les Islamistes Algériens*, p. 288. A common line taken by supporters of the Rome Platform was that Ali Belhadj had in fact become far more moderate during the period of his imprisonment. Abdelhamid Mehri (who had visited him) argued that "He has become undeniably more political" maintaining that the deputy leader of the FIS had become much more open to Western ideas and had even begun to study French. *Jeune Afrique*, 9.3.95.

102 One communiqué purporting to come from the GIA on 15 January stated: "In order to safeguard the interests of the nation and avoid more wars the (GIA) . . .

observers upon the validity of both stances which suggested that the communiqués were the product of black propaganda on the part of the regime or other elements.[103] Another possible explanation was that they represented different groups within the GIA itself, which had become increasingly factionalised over recent months. There was slightly more clarity on the position adopted by the AIS. It declared its hostility to the Rome Platform's condemnation of violence as a means of achieving power, which it claimed showed "unfairness to the mujahidin", and argued that the agreement had led the FIS to disregard its military role.[104]

No ambiguity surrounded the response of the Algerian regime to the Rome Platform. A government spokesman declared that "We reject it in total and in detail."[105] The officially stated reasons for the rejection were that the initiative constituted inadmissible interference in internal Algerian affairs and, more substantially, represented an endorsement of the FIS's unacceptable position. Algerian national radio stated that the opposition parties appeared content "to endorse the opinions of the FIS" whilst the Prime Minister, Mokdad Sifi argued that " . . . in the Rome 'Platform' terrorism is not condemned. It is those who claim responsibility for the attacks who signed this document."[106] Official sources also attempted to play down the significance of the initiative characterising it as a "non-event".[107]

The regime: military and political initiatives, January–April 1995

The Algerian regime made no official counter-proposal to the challenge of the Rome Platform but continued through the early part of 1995 to

---

is ready to stop the war in the event that the authorities accept the demands expressed in the document drafted by the united opposition parties in Rome." It was accompanied by a demands that Abdelhak Layada and another GIA figure be released and that communist and atheist parties be banned. *Independent*, 16.1.95.

103 Anwar Haddam notably argued that both responses were false and that the GIA had not yet expressed a view on the initiative. *Financial Times*, 2.2.95.

104 *Le Monde*, 24.1.95.

105 *Mideast Mirror*, 19.1.95.

106 *Le Monde*, 15/16.1.95; *Independent*, 8.3.95.

107 *Mideast Mirror*, 19.1.95.

prosecute both its more long-term political plans as well as a vigorous security policy.

The promotion of Mohammed Lamari to the rank of Lieutenant-General in the wake of the collapse of the dialogue initiative of autumn 1994 signalled that the eradicators within the regime were once more in the ascendant. The military campaign against the armed groups was pursued with renewed vigour from the end of 1994 as Lamari publicly promised to "confront the challenge launched by obscurantist and retrograde forces".[108] Evidence of the determination of the military to gain the upper hand in the struggle with the armed groups was provided by three developments that occurred in the opening months of 1995. The first of these occurred in late February when a riot in the Sekardji jail in Algiers resulted in the deaths of large numbers (the official death toll was 96) of predominantly Islamist prisoners, most notably Ikhlef Cherrati and Ahmed El Wed, a founder of the GIA. The authorities portrayed the incident which took place over 21 and 22 February as a necessary response to an attempted breakout. However, there were strong suspicions, not only amongst Islamists, that the affair had been orchestrated by elements within the regime to kill significant numbers of Islamists (FIS sources cited figures as high as 230) in revenge and retaliation for a massive car bomb that had been detonated outside the main police station in Algiers on 30 January, killing 42 people and injuring several hundred. There was also the possible calculation that the liquidation of significant numbers of leading Islamist activists would permanently prevent their re-entry into the armed groups whether through breakouts (as had disastrously occurred at Tazoult a year earlier) or amnesties.

Of more direct impact on the military struggle was the apparent victory the security forces secured at Ain Defla in March. A week-long battle commencing on 18 March resulted in the deaths of several hundred armed Islamists in an area south-west of Algiers. Details of the incident remained uncertain due to official reluctance to reveal information about security operations but the confrontation was reported to have resulted from a planned ambush by the security forces on a large convoy transporting members of the armed groups towards the capital. Reports did emerge suggesting that the fighting was the result of a mutiny at a military barracks, but there was no corroborating evidence for this and it

---

108 *Algérie Actualité*, 1.11.94.

appeared that whether revolt or ambush, the clash had resulted in a significant victory for the security forces.

The third and least dramatic development in the military struggle came with the announcement by the Interior Minister in March that more remote settlements in the country were entitled to form self-defence militias to combat the threat of the armed groups. Such militias had already begun to function, in the rural area of Kabylia, from the middle of 1994 but official sanction for their formation across the country indicated that the regime sought to spread the scope of the anti-terrorist struggle to involve the ordinary population. This heightened fears that the authorities were willing to contemplate real civil war and the break-up of the country into warring militias in order to inflict reverses on the Islamists.

It became clear during the early part of 1995 that the centrepiece of the regime's political policy was the pledge to hold presidential elections before the end of the year. Largely dismissed as a theatrical distraction following the collapse of negotiations with the FIS in October 1994, the government gave every indication that it intended to carry through the commitment. A commission was established in January to draw up plans for the poll and at the end of March, President Zeroual declared that the planned presidential election would be followed by municipal and legislative elections.[109] In April the presidency began to approach the political parties with a view to starting dialogue that would produce candidates for the presidential election.

In spite of the apparent willingness to revive electoral processes, the regime made it very clear from the outset that the FIS would be excluded from participating in any election. On 6 January the Interior Minister explicitly ruled that no candidate representing the party would be permitted to put themselves forward for the presidential election.[110] Evidence that the regime was no longer willing to deal with the party was demonstrated by the official decision at the end of January to separate Abassi Madani and Ali Belhadj in custody and move them to different parts of the country. Occurring in the wake of the Rome Platform the decision reflected the government's conviction that the communication links the two imprisoned leaders had been allowed had firstly produced

---

109 *Le Figaro*, 28.3.95.
110 *Le Monde*, 8/9.1.95.

(at Rome) no acceptable proposals and secondly, could now only serve to undermine the regime's position. The exclusion of the FIS, however, was not absolute. The regime continued to indicate that elements of the party could be allowed back into the political arena. Ahmed Merrani, as a former member of the FIS, was given a significant official platform on which to appeal to members of the party who were willing to denounce violence to support the regime's political initiatives. More directly, government ministers overtly hinted that whilst the party was unquestionably excluded from any planned election, the participation of individual FIS members could prove acceptable. In an interview in May Mokdad Sifi, the Prime Minister, when questioned on FIS participation remarked:

> There is the structure dissolved by law and there are the personalities affiliated to it. Dialogue and the presidential elections are open to all Algerian citizens who respect the Constitution and reject violence.[111]

The apparent equivocation in the official stance on the FIS was reflective not only of a certain pragmatism within the regime but also of the continuing divisions at the head of the regime. Despite the collapse of the dialogue initiative in late 1994, the eradicator faction in the military remained aware that Zeroual and his allies continued to hold out for a negotiated settlement with the Islamists. There were suspicions that the Sekardji prison massacre had been deliberately planned by factions in the regime who were opposed to dialogue and who aimed through the killings to outrage the Islamists and thus sabotage any prospective dialogue.[112] There were also accusations that a slur campaign had been mounted against key allies of Zeroual within the regime.

The armed groups

The failure of the political initiative of autumn 1994 shifted attention once more onto the campaign of the armed groups which continued to be dominated by the GIA and the AIS and their mutual divisions.

---

111 Interview with Mokdad Sifi, *Liberté*, 15.5.95.
112 The FIS had indeed reacted very angrily to the events at Sekardji. Anwar Haddam had been motivated to state that the incident had "smashed the hopes which rested on a peaceful and political solution". *L'Opinion*, 26.2.95.

The GIA

The killing of Cherif Gousmi by the security forces at the end of September 1994 removed the acknowledged head of the GIA for the second time in barely seven months. His death put increasing strains on the integrity of the still fairly loosely linked grouping that had never fully recovered from the loss of Sid Ahmed Mourad and many of its other senior figures in the previous February. Succession to title of "National Emir" of the GIA appeared uncertain and was initially contested. It was reported that a majority of the grouping's Majlis Shura endorsed Tadjine Mahfoud as its new leader defeating, significantly, a rival claim by Mohammed Said who became deputy leader. The position of Said within the GIA continued to attract surprise and comment and there was continued speculation that Said intended to take over the GIA in the name of the Jazara.

The apparent resolution of the leadership struggle, however, did not prevent the emergence in 1995 of increasing dissent and confusion over the identity, stance and unity of the GIA. The various responses to the Rome Platform provided only one example of the array of frequently contradictory communiqués and statements that purported to come from the GIA. Some statements in the name of the grouping argued that impostors were operating under the name of the GIA in Europe. There were the perennial accusations that Algerian Military Security had infiltrated and was now operating several of the armed groups, but although this was almost certainly true in some cases, it appeared that the GIA had become genuinely fractured. Whatever the reality of these divisions, the more tangible fact was that elements claiming to belong to the GIA continued to claim responsibility for acts of violence across the country, most notably a series of car bombs that wreaked considerable havoc throughout Algeria from the autumn of 1994.

The AIS

The Army of Islamic Salvation continued to play an important role in both the armed and, increasingly, the political struggle against the regime. The armed wing of the FIS had expressed significant reservations about the political manoeuvrings of the party both in the autumn of 1994 and at the Rome conferences, but the nomination of a new National Emir to head the group in November 1994 appeared to push it in a new and more politically active direction. Promoted from the command of the

AIS in the east, the new Emir, Madani Merzak, proved himself willing to launch his own political initiatives. Originally a member of Abdallah Djaballah's organisations, Merzak had joined the FIS and had been elected as a deputy for the party at the December 1991 elections. These political and relatively moderate connections and background helped explain Merzak's unprecedented decision to contact publicly all the major political actors in Algeria in an effort to resolve the national crisis. Six separate letters were sent respectively to the President, the political parties, the military, religious scholars, the armed groups and Abassi Madani and Ali Belhadj at the end of March 1995. Each individual letter contained a specific message to each grouping, but the overall message of the letters was an appeal to moderate elements to purge themselves of the constrictions of radical and hardline elements in the search for a solution.[113] Merzak's letter to Liamine Zeroual urged the President to "not offer a political cover to the eradicators" and to "save what can be saved". In the letter to the armed groups, although not referring to the GIA by name, the leader of the AIS argued that greater restraint had to be exercised in the prosecution of the armed struggle and that a "code of conduct" needed to be established. He indicated that although he favoured unification of all the armed groups he saw internecine clashes as inevitable. Similarly, in addressing Abassi and Belhadj, Merzak called for the two historic leaders of the FIS to be firm with "trouble-making elements".[114]

In making these initiatives Merzak was not, however, indicating that the AIS was either abandoning or reducing its military efforts against the regime. In common with the GIA, the armed wing of the FIS had stepped up its operations during Ramadan. Moreover, as well as exhorting Liamine Zeroual to make further efforts to achieve a political solution, the leader of the AIS's letter to the President had warned that if his appeal went unanswered, "We are determined to continue to the end to fight against the heirs and the partisans of France."[115]

Troubled relations
Relations between the GIA and the AIS remained troubled in this period.

---

113 For the fullest treatment of the contents of the letters see *Mideast Mirror*, 5.4.95.
114 *Mideast Mirror*, 5.4.95; *Jeune Afrique*, 6.4.95.
115 *Le Monde*, 11.4.95.

The existing divide between the two factions was further emphasised by the increasing stress the FIS and the AIS put on political initiatives during the early part of 1995. The Rome Platform and the letters sent by Madani Merzak served to create a clearer distinction between those in the Islamist resistance who believed that a political solution was the only feasible end to the conflict and those who saw the armed struggle as the sole and legitimate means of achieving their ends. The announcement of the Rome Platform prompted the defection of over a hundred, predominantly younger, AIS fighters to the GIA in reaction to the document's apparent repudiation of the armed struggle.[116] This did not dissuade those who remained in the FIS and the AIS from taking an increasingly critical line on the excesses of the armed groups. Merzak's letters had underlined this approach, but Rabah Kebir, in particular, spoke out more specifically calling on the GIA in June "to condemn all acts contrary to Islam which are committed in its name, otherwise they will bear the responsibility towards God, the nation and history".[117] Kebir was clearly anxious to distance himself and the FIS from the GIA and their actions and to stress the political priorities of the FIS. He declared in September:

> We don't have any relations with the GIA because this group is only pursuing the military option. They alone are responsible for what they are doing inside Algeria.[118]

For its part, the GIA continued in its efforts to assert its predominance. It portrayed both the defections that had occurred in the wake of the Rome Platform and earlier ones that had occurred following the failure of the autumn peace initiative as evidence that the whole resistance movement was uniting under its own banner.[119] The view that the movement was uniting received the surprising endorsement of Anwar Haddam. Despite having vehemently denied his own adherence to the GIA and having signed the document produced at Rome, Haddam

---

116   It was the defection of AIS units to the GIA that was believed to be behind the dispatching of the convoy of fighters to Algiers which was ambushed by the security forces at Ain Defla in March.

117   *The Times*, 21.6.95.

118   Author's interview with Rabah Kebir, 27.9.95.

119   Following the reported defection of two FIS politicians and four AIS figures to the GIA, Mohammed Said claimed that their defection enjoyed the blessing of Ali Belhadj and Abbassi Madani. *Liberté*, 14.12.94.

continued to assume an ambiguous position towards the GIA. He resisted the move by most FIS leaders to unequivocally condemn the worst aspects of the violence, continuing to blame most of it on the machinations of Military Security and indicated that the FIS should support all aspects of the armed struggle:

> Even if the FIS does not have any organic links with these groups we can do nothing else than support their actions.[120]

Haddam also played down differences between the AIS and the GIA, claiming that both groupings recognised the legitimate authority of the FIS.[121] Later on he began to claim that there was no such entity as the GIA, arguing that it was only a term used by the media and whose use was therefore redundant.[122] His reluctance to distance himself from the GIA attracted the ire of other FIS leaders who were angered by his deviation from the increasingly political line adopted by the party. Hachemi Sahnouni and Kameredine Kherbane declared that he was no longer entitled to speak on behalf of the FIS, with Kherbane going as far as to argue that "the Washington exile is excluded from the FIS".[123]

In addition to failing to prevent the FIS from taking a far more critical line towards the GIA, Anwar Haddam proved similarly powerless to stem reciprocal hostility from the GIA towards the FIS and the AIS. There were increasing numbers of reports concerning clashes between units of the AIS and the GIA. In March 1995 alone, these confrontations resulted in the deaths of an estimated sixty members of both groups. The GIA restated its claim that it was the "sole prosecutor of jihad" in the country and in May warned several FIS and AIS leaders, including Rabah Kebir, Abdelbaki Sahraoui, Abdallah Anas and even Anwar Haddam that they would be killed unless they ceased their pronouncements on the armed struggle within the next month.[124]

---

120   Interview with Anwar Haddam, *Le Figaro*, 10.10.95. In contrast to other FIS leaders who had condemned the huge car bomb detonated in front of a police station in Algiers at the end of January, Haddam had chosen to argue that the police station had been a "torture centre" for the security services. *Financial Times*, 2.2.95.
121   *Le Monde*, 15.5.95.
122   Interview with Anwar Haddam, *Le Figaro*, 10.10.95.
123   *Liberté*, 3.5.95.
124   *Liberté*, 10.10.94; *Le Monde*, 15.5.95.

The third attempt at dialogue, summer 1995

The launching of the Rome Platform in January 1995 had presented a serious political challenge to the Algerian regime, since not only did it appear to have revealed a moderation in the FIS's position on violence but had achieved the backing of the majority of the major opposition parties. Supporters of the National Contract constantly drew attention to the fact that collectively the parties which signed the document had attracted the support of over 80% of the votes that had been cast in December 1991. In the hope that despite its initial rejection of the Platform, the regime might be willing to find some common ground with the contract, the FLN and the FFS accepted the President's invitation to restart dialogue with the legal opposition parties in April 1995. There was considerable disappointment on the part of all the parties supporting the Rome Platform when talks between the government and the parties swiftly broke down over the regime's continued and full rejection of the National Contract.

At the same time as talks between the government and the parties were taking place, however, the beginnings of another attempt at dialogue between the FIS and the authorities were discreetly occurring. On this occasion the initiative was again taken by the imprisoned leadership of the FIS. A letter sent by Abassi Madani to President Zeroual on 9 April condemned acts of violence and stated his readiness once again to search for a political solution. Separated from the other imprisoned FIS leaders, the historic leader of the FIS seemed to offer a far more pragmatic and moderate approach than that previously taken by the party. It even appeared that Abassi might be willing to make the key concession of calling for a ceasefire before he and the other FIS leaders still in detention (notably Ali Belhadj and Abdelkader Hachani) were released. In the event of this concession, the authorities indicated that they would give the armed groups a month to disarm before a general pardon was announced, following which the FIS would be fully rehabilitated, with the single qualification that it change its name.

As details of the contacts and negotiations began to leak out in May and June, optimism that some sort of deal was in sight increased. Official confidence was demonstrated by a number of practical and verbal concessions it made to the FIS and its allies. On 9 June the authorities took the unusual step of allowing the Rome parties to hold a rally in the Harcha stadium in Algiers. Although permission to hold the gathering was granted only three days before the event and Ali Djeddi and Abdelkader Boukhamkham were barred from speaking at the rally, the government's tolerance of the event, which attracted nearly 10,000 people, indicated a significant softening of the regime's line. More startling than this was the admission by the Interior Minister in a French newspaper later that month that, "If the people are for the FIS we will respect their decision."[125]

Optimism about the outcome of the talks was to prove premature. Reluctant to take sole responsibility for the negotiating position of the party, Abassi Madani requested that he be allowed to consult with the other six senior FIS figures with whom he had been originally imprisoned. The outcome of this consultation with Belhadj, Djeddi, Boukhamkham and the others was a joint letter signed by the seven on 19 June. It presented a series of demands that were far less compromising than Abassi had been prepared to be. Significantly, the letter reiterated the proposals set out in the Rome Platform which FIS leaders continued to maintain would remain the basis of all political initiatives. Although supporting the Platform's position on violence, the letter restated the old stumbling block condition that a call for a ceasefire could only come *after* the release of the remaining FIS leaders from prison. Once again this crucial sequence proved unacceptable to the regime and despite several further weeks of intense negotiation, President Zeroual formally announced the final failure of the initiative on 11 July.

The presidential elections

The failure of yet another attempt at a negotiated settlement with FIS forced the regime to refocus its political initiatives on the planned presidential elections. Remaining doubts that the authorities would fail to honour their commitment to hold the poll were finally dispelled by an official announcement on 18 August that the first ballot for the presidential election would occur on 16 November with a second round to take place no more than fifteen days later between the two leading candidates should no individual candidate achieve an absolute majority in the first ballot.

---

125 *The Times*, 26.6.95.

Reactions to the announcement from the FIS and the other leading opposition parties were predictably critical and dismissive. The regime's rejection of the FIS's peace proposals in July had restated the official rejection of the Rome Platform in January. Ten days after the announcement of the date of the presidential poll, the signatories of the Platform launched a call for people not to sign support papers for candidates putting themselves forward for the planned poll. A joint communiqué from the group asserted that a peace deal had to come before any elections arguing that "The return of the electoral process necessitates a national consensus resulting from a full political solution."[126] All the Rome parties expressed the view that no genuine election could feasibly take place when the country remained in the grip of a near civil war. Rabah Kebir argued at the end of September:

> At the moment there is no security . . . People are living in fear and there are killings every day. Elections at this time are senseless . . . This (presidential) election is pointless and means nothing. Most of the popular parties, Islamic and non-Islamic, have refused to participate. Therefore the election is meaningless. You can't have an election without an opposition. There is now no opposition in Algeria. This means that the Algerian government is seeking to replace itself with itself.[127]

The candidates

The government's decision to press ahead with its decision to stage a presidential election raised the first serious questions as to who exactly would be willing to put themselves forward as candidates.

It was a common expectation amongst those opposed to the poll that the election would simply be an orchestrated and fraudulent affair designed to give a semblance of legitimacy to the regime whilst electing a symbolic front man for it. There was the inevitable speculation that the poll might follow established Arab world (and indeed, before 1988, Algerian) practice and be contested by a single candidate who would receive an improbably huge popular endorsement through the poll. All

---

126 *Libération*, 29.8.95.
127 Author's interview with Rabah Kebir, 27.9.95.

that remained to be seen was who precisely the regime would choose as their candidate. This understandable cynicism appeared richly rewarded on 20 September when following "spontaneous" popular demonstrations in Algiers calling for his candidature, Liamine Zeroual announced that he would be putting himself forward as a candidate.

In spite of the appearances of manipulation, it emerged that Zeroual's candidature in the election had not been a preplanned certainty. The President had made it known privately from mid-August that he wanted to stand in the election, but he faced opposition from within the regime. The fact that the main opposition to the idea of Zeroual's candidature came from Mohammed Lamari and his allies indicated that despite the failure of the July peace initiative the power struggle between the eradicators and the conciliators continued. Lamari was said to have expressed a preference for a civilian candidate but this was interpreted as a pretext for his opposition to Zeroual's belief in pursuing a negotiating settlement. Lamari was clearly aware that any "victory" for Zeroual in the presidential election would significantly strengthen the latter's hand in internal power struggles. Nevertheless, the strength of Zeroual's existing position was demonstrated by a meeting of senior military officers on 12 September which formally endorsed Zeroual as a future candidate.

The announcement of Zeroual's participation in the presidential election did not, as some anticipated, mean that the poll would not be contested. Three other candidates were judged to have successfully achieved the required criterion of having collected the signatures of 75,000 electors that would allow them to enter the election by the time nominations closed at the beginning of October. Significantly for the credibility of the poll, the three accepted candidates represented the three largest parties (as defined by levels of support received in December 1991) that had declined involvement in the Rome Platform: Said Saadi of the RCD, Nourredine Boukrouh of the PRA and Mahfoud Nahnah of HAMAS. The involvement of the RCD was the least surprising of the three. Said Saadi had frequently been at odds with the regime but his ferocious antipathy towards the FIS and the Rome Platform (he had refused an invitation even to the first conference in November) together with his fervently held vision for Algeria's future had made him a likely candidate. Nourredine Boukrouh's doubts about a national contract had been expressed at the first meeting of the parties at Rome, but he was no more convinced by the outcome of the second, remarking that "The

Rome Contract brings forward nothing new."[128] Despite presenting himself as an intellectual Islamic modernist, the leader of the PRA's participation in the poll served to support long-running rumours and accusations that he and his party were manipulable creations of the regime.[129]

The most noteworthy candidature of all was that of Mahfoud Nahnah. The participation in the regime's plans by one of the leading figures of the Algerian Islamist movement since the 1960s was seen by most Algerians as marking the final stage in the transition of the Sheikh from subversive opponent of the regime in the 1960s and 1970s to reliable ally. Nahnah's many critics in both Islamist and secularist circles accused the Blida-based leader of cynical opportunism. Islamist opponents of Nahnah, including many in the FIS, had long accused him of complicity with the regime for personal ends (see Chapters Three, Four and Five). They believed that by entering the presidential election Nahnah hoped to attract much of the country's Islamist vote, undermining support for the FIS and its boycott call, thus serving the ends of both himself and the regime. For Nahnah's secularist critics, his candidature in the election was simply a Trojan horse for Islamism. Whilst presenting himself as the "acceptable face of Islamism" the leader of HAMAS sought to introduce an agenda, if elected, that was little different to that advocated by the FIS – his manifesto included pledges to make the sharia the basis of the legal system and to make democracy subservient to a High Islamic Council.[130] There was undoubtedly some truth in both sets of accusations, but it was also likely that Nahnah saw himself as a "middle way" between the discredited regime and the excesses of the armed groups. He had never hesitated to strongly condemn Islamist violence, from which his own party had itself frequently suffered, but still held firm to his belief that an Islamic agenda held the key to the solution of Algeria's multiple problems.[131]

---

128 *Le Soir d'Algérie*, 9.5.95.
129 An economist by training, Boukrouh had worked in the Ministry of Finance and had contributed to *El Moudjahid* and *Algérie Actualité*. Despite the accusations of official complicity against him he claimed inspiration from the work of Malek Bennabi. For more details about Boukrouh and the PRA see Al-Ahnaf, Botiveau and Frégosi, *L'Algérie par ses Islamistes*, p. 294 and Lavenue, *Algérie: La Démocratie Interdite*, pp. 97–101 and 221–2.
130 *The Times*, 13.11.95.
131 More than forty members of Nahnah's HAMAS and Al-Irchad wal Islah association

Although representing parties that had collectively attracted less than 10% of the votes cast in the first ballot of December 1991, the participation of high profile figures such as Nahnah and Saadi in the presidential election boosted the credibility of the poll. Also important was the fact that Nahnah, Saadi and Zeroual represented significantly different strands of opinion and interests in Algerian society. One Algerian newspaper adroitly observed that these three leading candidates shadowed the constituencies and interests of the three main signatories of the Rome Platform: the FIS, the FLN and the FFS.[132] Although this was perceived as a deliberate policy on the part of the regime to marginalise what had become known as the three "Fs" or three Fronts, a more significant observation was that it accurately reflected how deeply split all parts of Algerian political society had become.

The issue of security

It was clear to all the actors on the Algerian political stage that security was central to the success or failure of the planned election. The Rome parties had made the fact of continuing violence one of the main planks of their rejection and boycott of the poll, arguing that a political solution to the violence must be sought before any election of any kind could take place. The armed groups and their allies had gone further and indicated that they would actively seek to prevent through violence any voting taking place. In the immediate wake of the announcement of the date of the election in August, Anwar Haddam had stated that "the freedom fighters will not allow an election".[133] The groups themselves made plain this threat as the election approached, tracts attributed to the GIA promising that "the ballot box will be transformed into a coffin".[134] Similarly slogans painted on walls in Islamist strongholds grimly pledged "one vote, one bullet" for anyone planning to vote on 16 November.[135]

---

had been killed since 1992 including, most prominently, Mohammed Bousilimani, kidnapped and killed by the GIA at the end of 1993. At the end of 1994 Nahnah had expressed his horror at the increasing brutality of the armed groups by exclaiming: "What religion, what right, what logic, what sharia justifies this?" *SWB* ME/2165 MED, 29.11.94.

132 *La Nation*, 30.10.95.
133 *The Times*, 19.8.95.
134 *Le Monde*, 15.11.95.
135 *Le Point*, 11.11.95.

The government was clearly aware that such menaces, together with calls for a boycott from the Rome parties, threatened to drastically reduce popular participation in the election. The achievement of a significant turnout on 16 November was absolutely central to the regime's plans. A poor turnout would severely undermine the legitimacy and importance of the poll and destroy official claims that the electoral process had been fully relaunched. The Algerian authorities set themselves the task of securing at least as large a turnout as had occurred in December 1991 in order to deflect unfavourable comparisons with a poll that had so strongly backed the FIS.

The regime consequently exerted considerable efforts to both assure and provide a sufficient level of security in the run-up to and during the election. On 18 September the Interior Minister declared: "Terrorist operations will not delay the presidential elections . . . all the necessary measures have been taken for people to go to the polling stations in conditions of adequate security."[136] As September and October witnessed a gradual increase in killings and bombings as the election date approached, the authorities made plans to provide a blanket of security cover for the poll. Nearly 300,000 security personnel were drafted in to provide security over the period and significant traffic restrictions were imposed in the major cities to guard against the threat of car bombs. Residents of Islamist strongholds such as the Casbah were advised to vote outside their areas to avoid possible reprisals and members of the security forces were instructed to cast their own votes before the election in order to provide full cover on the 16 November.

The measures taken by the regime appeared to have brought results, as violence within Algiers in particular declined dramatically in the period immediately leading up to the poll. However, there remained real fears that what one foreign journalist described as "an eerie calm" over the capital would prove to be a calm before a storm of bombings and killings unleashed by the armed groups on the day of the poll itself.[137] There was therefore great relief and significant surprise when 16 November passed without any major report of violence.

The absence of any concerted campaign of violence by the armed groups during the election prompted an immediate search for explanations

---

136 *Libération*, 20.9.95.
137 *Financial Times*, 15.11.95.

as to why there had been no attempt to turn the "ballot box into the coffin box". The vast security operation mounted by the authorities with the major cities being swamped with police and army was cited by many as a primary reason why the groups had not been able to interrupt the ballot. However even with a ratio of ten security personnel to every ballot box, many Algerians were convinced that other explanations lay behind the armed groups' near total inactivity over the election period. There was growing evidence to indicate that the armed groups had deliberately suspended their activities over the period. Outside Algeria Anwar Haddam claimed operations had been suspended "so as not to hurt civilians".[138] Inside the country AIS sources indicated that official pressures on people to vote led the group in certain areas to let it be known that no action would be taken against those voting.[139]

There emerged in the aftermath of the ballot a far more dramatic explanation for the armed groups' behaviour. It was suggested that not only did many of the armed groups refrain from violence during the poll but actively encouraged people to vote. It was argued that having witnessed the majority of the population registering to vote before the election, both the AIS and the GIA concluded that most people intended to vote despite their efforts at intimidation. It was therefore decided that there should be a shift in tactics to encourage a vote for the least repugnant of the candidates. Consequently, in the days before the election, it was claimed, clandestine representatives of the FIS and the GIA urged supporters to cast their vote for Mahfoud Nahnah.[140]

The results

The threat of large-scale violence from the armed groups was the most prominent of a number of uncertainties that had existed on the eve of polling on 16 November. Both the turnout and the respective vote shares of the candidates could only be speculated over in the lead up to polling day. No reliable opinion polls had been conducted and many suspected that whatever the preferences expressed on 16 November the regime would engineer a huge victory for Liamine Zeroual.

As the first results began to become known following the close of voting it was clear that Zeroual had indeed won a convincing victory.

---

138 *SWB* ME/2469 ME/23, 24.11.95.
139 *Libération*, 28.11.95.
140 *Jeune Afrique*, 14.12.95 and 21.12.95.

Moreover, he had succeeded in attracting an absolute majority of the votes cast, thus ruling out the need for a further second ballot between the two leading candidates. The final tally revealed that the sitting President had achieved 61% of the vote, with Mahfoud Nahnah coming second with just over 25%, Said Saadi with nearly 10% and Nourredine Boukrouh a predictable fourth with less than 4%. Of equal importance was the size of the turnout, which was officially stated at a sizeable 75.7%.[141]

Of clear importance to the whole exercise was the vital question of how genuine the results were. There had been speculation from the outset of the organisation of the election that all the participating candidates were party to a conspiracy to ensure the re-election of Liamine Zeroual. The vigour with which the incumbent President's main rivals, Nahnah and Saadi, campaigned during October and November largely dispelled these suspicions.[142] Nahnah in particular had organised over forty enthusiastically attended meetings and rallies during the campaign, exhorting voters to vote for Islam. The veracity of their campaign was further underlined by the readiness of the camps of both candidates to criticise official bias towards Zeroual in the media and, in the case of HAMAS, to suggest that the regime might try to falsify the results. [143]

The suspicion of ballot rigging once the votes had been cast was clearly a more likely scenario. Some supporters of Nahnah did indeed claim electoral fraud in the immediate aftermath of the announcement of the results, one senior figure speaking of a "certain number of abuses".[144] This claim was, however, not repeated and none of the teams of election observers from the United Nations, the Organisation of African Unity and

---

141 Final results as declared on Algerian television. *SWB* ME/2470 MED/24, 24.11.95.

142 There had, however, been accusations that the regime had blocked the entry of a fifth candidate into the race. Having formed his own political party, the Alliance National pour le République (ANR), the former Prime Minister Redha Malek claimed to have correctly collected the necessary 75,000 signatures to support him as a candidate for the presidential election. He was officially judged, however, to have not met this requirement and was prevented from standing. Whilst it was initially thought that the hardline anti-Islamism of Malek and the ANR most directly threatened the electoral constituency of Said Saadi, Malek's previous involvement in the FLN was seen as presenting a possible challenge to Zeroual's appeal to the 'nationalist' constituency. This could have been the motivation behind attempts to exclude Malek from the poll.

143 *Observer*, 12.11.95.

144 *Le Monde*, 18.11.95.

the Arab League voiced any substantial reservations about the declared results. Several months later a leaked French intelligence report suggested that the leader of HAMAS had in fact performed better than the official results had shown, achieving 34% of the vote to Zeroual's 40%.[145] This report, however, remained unconfirmed. If fraud had occurred it appeared that it had either been relatively selective or alternatively intelligently handled.[146] Zeroual had not received a totally crushing share of the vote, comparable with presidential polls in other Arab countries, which would have destroyed the credibility of the poll. Nevertheless he achieved a comfortable majority of the votes cast, sufficient to claim popular backing as well as to avoid a damaging and unpredictable second ballot.

Whatever the doubts about the size of Zeroual's victory, there was little to suggest that he had not emerged as the most popular of the four candidates – a fact even confirmed in the French intelligence report. It was clear that the sitting President had succeeded in gathering together the support of a large section of the Algerian population. More importantly, he appeared to have drawn this support from a wide variety of sources. Zeroual's most obvious natural constituency was that part of the electorate associated with the machinery of the regime itself. As the incumbent president, a former general and a mujahid in the liberation struggle, Zeroual could also count on the support of the related and still substantial traditional constituency of the old FLN. In the view of one journalist, the absence of the new FLN and the FFS from the presidential election left Zeroual as the natural choice of the "nationalist" constituency.[147] There was evidence also that Zeroual had attracted support from other

---

145 *The European*, 21.3.96.
146 Results recorded in different regions appeared to support the veracity of the poll in being consistent with the pattern of results seen in both the municipal elections of 1990 and the first ballot of the legislative elections of December 1991. This was most strikingly true of the results in Kabylia where candidates from the RCD and the FFS had dominated the results in previous contests. The communes of Bejaia and Tizi Ouzou in Kabylia were the only ones across the country that did not express a preference for Liamine Zeroual. In both Said Saadi headed the poll beating the sitting president by a massive 86.2% to 8.8% in Saadi and the RCD's heartland of Tizi Ouzou. The credibility of the results in Kabylia was further reinforced by the unusually low turnout of just 52% – a clear indication of the impact of the FFS's call to boycott the poll. *MEI*, 1.12.95; *Independent*, 18.11.95; *Guardian*, 18.11.95.
147 *Financial Times*, 15.11.95.

less obvious quarters. Realisation that Mahfoud Nahnah represented the most serious challenge to Zeroual prompted many of those voters who might otherwise have supported Said Saadi to throw their support behind the sitting President to ensure that the Islamist leader of HAMAS was kept out – an observation that was supported by Saadi himself.[148] The declared support of Abdelhak Benhamouda of the UGTA was also important in this context, supplying Zeroual with the significant vote of Algeria's union movement which might also have been expected to have backed the leader of the secularist RCD. More remarkable was the evidence that indicated that Algerians who had voted for the FIS in previous elections, may have voted in favour of Zeroual in 1995. The reason for this unusual shift was explained by a man who had voted for the FIS in 1991: "All I care about is that the violence ends. Maybe if we give legitimacy to Zeroual he might be able to do something about the violence."[149]

It was this concisely expressed sentiment that most fully explained the substantial backing that Zeroual received. The incumbent President was seen as the only man capable of delivering an end to the violence through a negotiated settlement. Zeroual's battle with the eradicators within the regime was an open secret and many Algerians believed that by granting the President an electoral mandate, they could free him to embrace the solution proposed in the Rome Platform. It was clear that none of the other candidates in the presidential election could deliver a similar settlement. Zeroual represented a middle way between the factionalism of Nahnah's Islamism and Saadi's militant secularism. An electoral victory for either of these two diametrically opposed contenders threatened only to intensify the violence still further.

The fundamental popular wish to bring a halt to the violence also gave credence to the official claim that a convincing majority of the population had chosen to vote on 16 November. There were doubts that the turnout figure of over 75%, representing nearly twelve million Algerians, was truly accurate, but there was far less credence given to the claim by the FIS in the immediate wake of the results, that only around a third of those eligible to vote had done so.[150] It was certainly true that

---

148 *Jeune Afrique*, 21.12.95.
149 *Financial Times*, 15.11.95.
150 Figures quoted by Rabah Kebir and Anwar Haddam ranged from 26% to 37%. Significantly, though, there was a recognition that the turnout had been higher

the regime had exerted certain pressures on people to vote, notably the fear of being marked down as pro-FIS if they did not, but it was clear that most Algerians wanted to use the opportunity of the presidential election to express themselves in a way that had not been allowed since the abandonment of the electoral programme nearly four years earlier. The declining threat of violence on the day of the poll persuaded many voters that it was worth involving themselves in an initiative that might possibly lead to a way out of Algeria's long and bloody impasse.

Reactions: the Islamist camp

The prevailing perception that the presidential elections had constituted a significant success for the regime through the size of the turnout, the absence of violence and the victory for Liamine Zeroual, appeared to severely wrongfoot both the FIS and the armed groups. Widespread relief that the election had not been turned into a bloodbath and a certain nationalistic pride that the poll had actually taken place created a tangible optimism amongst the general population. Not all the residents of Algiers participated in the exuberant and clearly genuine celebrations of Zeroual's supporters on the streets following the announcements of the results, but there was a unmistakable feeling that the presidential election had marked a substantial step along the road to peace.

The Kebir initiative

The immediate aftermath of the election had seen the senior representatives of the FIS abroad restating their rejection of the validity of the role. Rabah Kebir greeted the announcement of the result with the judgement that, "General Zeroual has succeeded General Zeroual with the support of more than 400,000 police and soldiers."[151] Anwar Haddam simply stated that "As far as we are concerned nothing has changed. The actual authorities are the same ones."[152] However, the progressive realisation in the days following the poll that there had been a tangible change in the popular mood, one which for a large part accepted the legitimacy of

---

than expected. *Libération*, 17.11.95; *Le Monde*, 18.11.95; *Independent*, 18.11.95
151   *Le Monde*, 19/20.11.95.
152   *SWB* ME/2469 MED/24, 24.11.95.

Zeroual's victory, prompted a reconsideration of the party's best reaction to the election.

Evidence of a significant strategic shift came with the sending of an open letter to Liamine Zeroual by Rabah Kebir on 22 November. The letter was remarkable in its declared acceptance of the new legitimacy enjoyed by Zeroual by addressing him as "Mr President" and stating that:

> We think that this popularity you have gained could be a significant opportunity for both the authorities and the opposition to over-come the obstacles that have robbed the many attempts at national dialogue of their goal of securing a return to peace, liberties and national reconciliation.[153]

The importance of the party's objection to the election and its call for a boycott were explicitly minimised, as Kebir stressed "our constant readiness for dialogue, consultation and co-operation with the authorities". The conciliatory tone of the letter was further underlined by the significant omission of any of the long-standing conditions that the party had insisted on before dialogue could begin.

In interviews following the publication of the letter, Kebir confirmed the central conciliatory thrust of the message, although he admitted that "real dialogue" had to be preceded by releases of detainees and an easing of the security situation. He affirmed that the initiative had been made on the part of all of the FIS and claimed that it had the implicit support of Abassi Madani and Ali Belhadj because of its grounding in previous agreements.[154] This claim, however, was hotly disputed by other sections of the party. Anwar Haddam angrily condemned what he saw as Kebir's individual initiative rejecting his recognition of Zeroual's legitimacy and stating that: "This betrayal will never be forgiven in the collective consciousness of our people. We can only hope that our brother Rabah Kebir will change his mistaken position."[155]

The armed groups

The response of the armed groups to the fallout from the presidential election was similarly characterised by confusion and division. Initial

---

153 *Ibid.*
154 *Mideast Mirror*, 23.11.95.
155 *Ibid.*, 24.11.95.

hopes that the lull in the violence over the period of the election would persist, were crushed by the resumption of attacks and killings within a week of the announcement of Zeroual's victory. However, this recrudescence was accompanied by a significant increase in the number of fighters from the armed groups who began to turn themselves in to the authorities. Responding to Zeroual's offer of a pardon the numbers deserting the armed resistance – already increasing in the weeks before the election – grew to several hundred by the end of the year. Their desertion reflected a clear decline in morale following the evidence of the lack of popular support for the armed struggle that participation in the election had revealed.[156] Significantly, neither the AIS nor the GIA sought to deny this trend, seeking only to suggest that most were either members of the rival faction or alternatively infiltrators or camp-followers.

The initiative made by Rabah Kebir created confusion within the AIS. The AIS commander in the west, Ahmed Ben Aicha, was angered by the failure of Kebir to consult the FIS's armed wing and in December called upon the AIS to step up the armed struggle against the regime. Ben Aicha was joined in his rejection of Kebir's letter by the centre command, although the east, which had traditionally been closest to the Executive Abroad, remained silent. The following month the commander of the east and overall leader of the AIS, Madani Merzak, reiterated his own preference for a negotiated settlement when he offered the authorities a unilateral truce in return for the release of Ali Belhadj.

Divisions in the stance of the AIS were of little significance compared to the internal ructions that shook the GIA in the aftermath of the presidential election. During December it emerged that Mohammed Said, Abderrazak Redjam and twenty supporters had been executed by other members of the GIA shortly after the election. No definitive account of the killings and the reasons behind it appeared, but it was clear that they were the result of a serious breach that had opened up between Said and Djamel Zitouni, another senior member of the GIA. Initial explanations suggested that Said had objected to the continually

---

156 According to one report desertions from the armed groups had risen from a rate of three per day in the two months leading up to the presidential election to five per day in the weeks following the poll. (*Jeune Afrique*, 21.12.95.) Official radio claimed that the total number of those who had 'repented' of their membership of the groups had risen to a thousand by 10 January 1996. *SWB* ME/2056 MED/21, 11.1.96.

indiscriminate nature of the GIA's campaign of violence. This was explicitly denied by elements of the GIA which claimed this reason had been given as an excuse to conceal the real reason for the rupture which concerned a failed attempt by Mohammed Said and his supporters to take over the GIA on behalf of the Jazara.[157]

The failure of this apparent *coup d'état* within the GIA supported the long-running contention that the whole purpose of Mohammed Said's and Abderrazak Redjam's original defection to the GIA had been part of a plan to infiltrate, take over and moderate the grouping. The timing of the killing of defectors – by a hardline faction headed by Zitouni – coming just after the presidential elections suggested that Said and Redjam had attempted to use the impact of the election to make their move and try and bring the GIA into the moderate mainstream. There were even rumours that Mohammed Said had been planning to declare a unilateral ceasefire on the part of the GIA.[158] Evidence that Said and Redjam were not the only figures associated with this plan was provided by the abrupt change of stance by the other alleged major defector from the FIS in 1994, Anwar Haddam, in the wake of the killings. In an interview in December Haddam formally disassociated himself from the GIA describing its leaders as "a gang of fanatical extremists".[159] On the killings he asserted:

> Said and Redjam were treacherously killed with a group of FIS leaders by sinful hands that usurped the leadership of the framework the FIS had thought was a framework for jihad in Algeria, namely the GIA.[160]

The deaths of Said and Redjam and the renunciation of the GIA by the hitherto equivocal Haddam opened the way for a full conflict between the AIS–FIS and the GIA. In the fullest repudiation yet of the militant grouping, FIS representatives in London claimed they had stripped the GIA of its political cover and welcomed the statements of Haddam who urged all the mujahidin to disassociate themselves from the grouping.[161] *Al Ribat*, a FIS journal close to Rabah Kebir, vociferously

---

157 *Le Monde*, 12.1.96; *SWB* ME/2506 MED/21, 11.1.96.
158 *Jeune Afrique*, 7.2.96.
159 *SWB* ME/2491 MED/19, 20.12.95.
160 *Ibid.*
161 *SWB* ME/2490 MED/19, 19.12.95 and 20.12.95.

denounced the grouping condemning it for the killing of innocent people and respected Islamist leaders such as Mohammed Bousilimani and Abdelbaki Sahraoui.[162] Djamel Zitouni responded by damning attempts by the FIS to deal with the regime and branded Madani Merzak an "apostate" for offering a ceasefire to the regime.[163] In return the leader of the AIS restated the accusation that the GIA was suffering from significant desertions:

> Everyone has now confirmed that the extremists and fanatics have never fulfilled a pledge. They have surrendered to and thrown themselves into the arms of those who declared them apostates and unbelievers.[164]

In the maquis pressures also intensified. Azzedine Baa, leader of the AIS in the centre (and one of the last surviving companions of Mustapha Bouyali) was killed in a GIA ambush in December. At the beginning of January a communiqué released by Djamel Zitouni pledged to fight the AIS as an enemy.[165] Tensions mounted between the two groups – particularly in the west where a bitter battle for full supremacy and domination began in early 1996 – and this internecine struggle was attributed with much of the increase in violence witnessed in this period.

Competing initiatives

Islamist divisions on how to best respond to Zeroual's election victory also occurred amongst the political leadership of the movement. Initially in November there had been disagreements between the mainstream (represented by Rabah Kebir) and a hardline faction (represented by Anwar Haddam). By January it appeared that the mainstream position was being challenged by an even more moderate grouping.

An open letter signed by seventeen founding members of the FIS to Liamine Zeroual requested direct negotiations with the President. That the letter made no formal reference to Abassi Madani and Ali Belhadj alarmed the FIS Executive Abroad which condemned the initiative as an officially encouraged effort designed to replace the legitimate leadership

---

162 *SWB* ME/2489 MED/23–24, 18.12.95.
163 *SWB* ME/2506 MED/21, 11.1.96; *Jeune Afrique*, 6.3.96.
164 *SWB* ME/2506 MED/21, 11.1.96.
165 *Le Monde*, 12.1.96.

of the FIS with one that was "more docile".[166] In attracting the support of founding members of the party, though, the letter had significant authority and involved for the first time two senior figures who had hitherto played little or no role in dialogue initiatives – Benazouz Zebda (in exile in Turkey) and Othman Aissani (at liberty in Algeria).

The regime

In contrast to the upheavals within the Islamist camp the Algerian regime witnessed remarkably few significant developments in the aftermath of the presidential election. At his official swearing-in Liamine Zeroual restated his campaign pledges to seek a national consensus and a peaceful solution and to combat "the remnants of terrorist violence".[167] Little, however, was revealed about how the President planned to use his newly boosted legitimacy to achieve his goals.

Expectations that he would grant senior positions in a new government to his rivals in the presidential election proved to be overstated. Representatives of HAMAS and the PRA were appointed to the new administration announced in January, but these were to very junior positions. Some attention was drawn to the presence of Islamist figures within the government – those from HAMAS being joined by Ahmed Merrani who became Religious Affairs Minister – which appeared to be behind the refusal of the RCD to participate in the new administration.[168] However, this ignored the fact that HAMAS had already held a minor portfolio in the government before the election and that Merrani had long been an anti-FIS mouthpiece for the regime. The most senior position in the government, the prime ministership, was given to Ahmed Ouhayia a former career diplomat and spokesman for the presidency.

The regime appeared to ignore the substantial internal debates and power struggles clearly taking place within the Islamist movement in the months following the election. No official response was made to Rabah Kebir's important letter at the end of November and Zeroual made no significant overtures to the movement. The only identifiable gestures

---

166 *Jeune Afrique*, 7.2.96.
167 *SWB* ME/2472 MED/11, 28.11.95.
168 The absence of the RCD from the new government was also due to the official rejection of its proposal that it take charge of a portfolio charged with looking after the Algerian community abroad.

made were the President's promise of clemency to repented members of the armed groups – whom he referred to as "misguided" – and the release of the remaining 700 inmates of the Ain M'Guel prison in the south of Algeria in early December.[169]

Zeroual's inaction prompted speculation that the President had been unable to launch the new and more radical dialogue initiative that had widely been anticipated in the wake of his election victory because of continuing constraints from hardline elements within the regime. A more probable explanation was that Zeroual was aware of the division and confusion his election victory had thrust on the FIS and the armed groups and was content to let internecine struggles within the Islamist camp run their course. There was the hope that such internal conflicts would not only severely weaken the Islamists but would result in them eventually adopting a more acceptable line towards a settlement. The regime was not averse, though, to encouraging these divisions and promoting the emergence of more moderate factions. It was no accident that Othman Aissani had been allowed to publicise the initiative launched by the seventeen leading FIS figures in January. The regime's policy of keeping Abassi Madani and Ali Belhadj separate and incommunicado also helped to foster divisions, as no definitive statements were allowed to emerge from either figure, prompting different factions to take their own initiatives.

The Islamists were not the only group the regime wished to see divided and weakened. The coalition of the main opposition parties through the Rome Platform had posed a serious political challenge to the regime, most importantly through its representation of over 80% of the votes cast in December 1991. It was a challenge that was only successfully, and potentially temporarily, overcome through the perceived success of the presidential election, which undermined the central charge of popular illegitimacy that had been levelled at all the ruling administrations since 1992. All the Rome parties issued a joint statement in the wake of the election on 10 December restating their proposals. However, like the FIS, the other two main signatories, the FFS and the FLN, were experiencing increasingly serious internal tensions. Unlike the FIS, both parties' adherence to the Rome Platform had already come under significant pressure in the period before the election. Elements within both

---

169 *Jeune Afrique*, 14.12.95.

parties had become more and more restive at the alliance with the FIS, particularly as the armed struggle exacted an increasing toll on their own constituencies. The rise in violence in the FFS's native Kabylia during 1995 not only damaged the party's standing there but threatened to boost support for the rival RCD, whose involvement with the establishment of self-defence militias contrasted badly with images such as that of Hocine Ait Ahmed appearing on television in Germany with Rabah Kebir on the eve of the presidential poll. The FLN found itself under even greater pressure. Many party members were unhappy with what they saw as Abdelhamid Mehri's insufficiently vigorous condemnation of the murders of FLN cadres by the armed groups. Zeroual's candidature in the presidential election, which many party members saw as representing the spirit of the historic FLN, prompted a near revolt within the party. This was headed off by Mehri's agreement not to appeal for a boycott of the election (restricting the party's stance to one of not officially endorsing the poll), but this did not prevent at least three members of the FLN's politburo breaking ranks and publicly backing Zeroual.

The aftermath of the poll and the wave of popular optimism that swept Algeria plunged Mehri's leadership of the FLN into considerable question. The leader of the FLN tempered his criticism of the poll with a public acknowledgement that people had voted for "civil peace".[170] This was not enough to save his six-year headship of the party and at a party meeting in January 1996 Mehri was deposed as General Secretary and replaced by Boualem Benhamouda, a former minister under Boumedienne and a unambiguous representative of the party's orthodox past. In the FFS, Ait Ahmed, who had made conciliatory remarks following Zeroual's election, faced a similar challenge to his leadership at the party's congress in March but in this case was able to weather charges of autocracy levelled at him by disillusioned party figures.

These developments, which resulted in a significant hole being punched in the common front of the Rome Platform as Benhamouda moved to disassociate the party from the Platform, clearly served the Algerian regime's interests, which it was widely suggested had assisted in the challenges to the FFS and FLN leaderships. More significantly, it was argued that the developments within specifically the FLN were part

---

170 *MEI*, 1.12.95.

of the regime's longer-term and still undeclared political strategy. The successful accomplishment of presidential elections cleared the way for the honouring of the official pledge to hold municipal and legislative elections. Liamine Zeroual had represented the regime in the presidential elections but unlike the other candidates he lacked the backing of any formal political party which would put up candidates at future elections. It was therefore suggested that the deposition of Abdelhamid Mehri from the FLN was the first step towards the eventual goal of reintegrating the FLN into the regime in order to serve as a "presidential party" for Liamine Zeroual. The President was quick to deny such suggestions, claiming that "My sole party is Algeria", but it was clear that he would need at least some supporters and allies in any future National Assembly. [171]

The one major obstacle to the regime's policy of watching and waiting whilst the opposition divided and weakened was the resumption of violence. The end of the lull in attacks and bombings that had occurred over the period of the presidential election removed one of the main supports of the popular confidence that had surrounded Zeroual's election victory. The President was aware that a full return to the levels of violence that had been experienced before his election – something which looked increasingly likely as 1996 progressed – would soon sap the popular support and expectation he had attracted in November. The announcement of the lifting of the curfew imposed on Algiers since 1992 on 19 February for reasons of the "improvement in the security situation" was intended to be a gesture of self-confidence on the part of the security forces, but it followed a Ramadan that had once again witnessed an increase in overall levels of violence.[172] There was also a realisation that despite the disarray amongst the opposition a political initiative would have to be launched. Consequently, on 30 March President Zeroual once again invited representatives from all the main parties to enter into discussions prior to full dialogue. Once again the FIS did not receive an invitation.[173]

---

171   *Mideast Mirror,* 24.11.95.
172   *Le Monde,* 20.2.96.
173   *Le Figaro,* 1.4.96.

Support for Islamism: 1994–1996

Support for the armed groups from 1994 continued to follow the same patterns that had been established during the initial period of the struggle against the regime.

The youthful profile of the membership of the armed groups remained unchanged. The dramatic upsurge in the level of violence during 1994 had resulted in both the removal through capture or (more usually) death of the older leaders of the groups and an expansion of the groups' recruitment from amongst Algeria's huge pools of discontented youth. The vast majority of armed Islamists caught by the authorities and brought to trial were young, poor and unemployed. Similarly, 80% of those who surrendered to the authorities in the aftermath of the presidential election had no official job.[174] Continuing economic and social deprivation were not the only factors that facilitated recruitment to the armed opposition. The intensifying of the struggle between the armed groups and the security forces during 1994 created a horrific spiral of violence. The bloody and remorseless tactics of the GIA, in particular, increasingly provoked an equally harsh response from the security forces against whom many of the attacks were directed. Young men became the natural targets for police raids on localities thought to have been responsible for a given attack. As the conflict progressed their treatment at the hands of the authorities deteriorated from simple detention without trial, through beatings, systematic torture and eventually arbitrary killings. Collective punishments on neighbourhoods, involving the killings of large numbers of local youths became common. It was thus unsurprising that young men who had either suffered themselves in detention or who had had friends and brothers tortured or murdered by the security services would hasten to the ranks of the GIA as a means of exacting their revenge. As one young Algerian remarked of the increasingly brutal struggle: "This is a war of the young . . . There are no old terrorists. A kid who joins the maquis is dead within six months."[175]

---

174 *SWB* ME/2056 MED/21, 11.1.96. An analysis of these "repented" revealed that 70% of them were between the ages of 20 and 35, with an estimated 19% aged over 35. Although this indicated that only 11% were in their teens (thus contradicting the assertion that the armed groups recruited heavily from the very young) it was acknowledged that younger members of the armed groups were the most radical and therefore the most resistant to the idea of giving themselves up to the authorities.

175 *Le Monde*, 5.9.95.

Geographically, support for the armed groups remained focused on the large urban areas. Operations by the security forces continued to be a determining factor in the varying regional presence of the groups. The effective withdrawal of the security forces from large parts of the country during Ramadan of 1994 (leaving only the three main cities of Algiers, Constantine and Oran under the effective control of the authorities) gave some indication of the regional strength of the armed groups. It was in the towns of the Mitidja plain around Algiers that the Islamists came most quickly to the fore following the pull-back by the forces of the state. The groups exercised, in the view of one observer, "real control" in places such as Baraki, Larbaa and especially Blida.[176] There the Islamists (of uncertain affiliation but most probably allied to the GIA) set about imposing their vision of society upon the residents of these areas. They dictated their own curfews and determined shop opening hours and even the prices of goods in those shops. Private bus companies were ordered to segregate their passengers, men from women (who were now required to wear the hedjab), and smoking and the selling of French-language newspapers were effectively prohibited.

The gravitation of the vast majority of the armed groups into either the GIA or the AIS enabled observations to be made about the relative regional strengths of the two groupings – the AIS tending to predominate in the east and west with the GIA virtually monopolising armed activity in the centre region. The GIA's strong presence in the Algiers region was clearly explained by its base amongst the young unemployed youth in the poor deprived suburbs of the capital. The wider spread of the AIS's operations reflected, in the view of Séverine Labat, the group's alliance with the FIS. The presence of significant numbers of FIS cadres in the AIS provided it with links with the areas of support the party had established across the country during its legal lifetime. It was notable that the main areas of insurrectionist activity in Algeria corresponded strongly with those areas which had voted most decisively for the FIS in 1990 and 1991.[177]

One area that became increasingly involved in the conflict from 1994, having previously been largely spared significant violence, was

---

176 *Libération*, 14.3.94 .The area between the three towns of Baraki, Larbaa and Blida had become known as "the triangle of death".

177 Labat, *Les Islamistes Algériens*, p. 259.

Kabylia. Although the number of incidents within the Berber heartland did not approach the levels found in other parts of Algeria, armed Islamists became more and more active in the region from the latter part of 1994. Attempts by the groups to establish themselves in the region met with frequent resistance from local people who (with official encouragement) set up armed self-defence units to combat the Islamists. Islamist efforts to penetrate the region which had remained impregnable to the FIS during the elections of 1990 and 1991 were the result of a desire to win it over to the anti-regime cause. Leaders of the armed groups were aware of the vital strategic role Kabylia and the Kabyles had played in the liberation struggle against the French. The initiative was prompted by the rise to the leadership of the GIA of several Kabyles including, most notably, Mohammed Said. However despite the presence of Kabyle figures in the armed groups and an attempt by Abderrazak Redjam to set up a specifically Kabyle armed group (Mouvement Islamique Armé Amazigh), the region remained overwhelmingly hostile and resistant to the armed groups.[178]

The intensification of the armed struggle during 1994 naturally implied an increase in the numbers of men becoming involved with the armed groups. According to one calculation made at the beginning of 1995 active membership of the AIS totalled nearly 6,000, whilst the GIA counted on the support of roughly 8,000 activists.[179] Official estimates of the total numbers involved in the armed groups inevitably quoted smaller figures – the Interior Minister suggesting in June 1995 that active *maquisards* numbered 2–3,000.[180]

The horrific increase in violence during 1994, which claimed the lives of possibly as many as 40,000 people in twelve months suggested that Algeria had finally plunged itself into a state of full civil war. However, despite the fact that ordinary Algerians formed a substantial part of the death toll there remained no evidence to suggest that the armed groups were near winning the active support of the general population. This

---

178 Attempts by the Islamists to win over the region were not helped by the kidnap by Islamists of the hugely popular Berber singer and activist Matoub Lounes in September 1994. Designed as an attempt to persuade the Kabyles not to attack the armed groups, the kidnapping provoked a wave of outrage in the region with calls for a general strike and "total war" against the Islamists if Lounes was not released unharmed (which he eventually was).

179 *L'Express*, 5.1.95.

180 *Le Monde*, 4/5.6.95.

was noted by a senior officer in the Algerian military who remarked of the Islamist opposition in late 1994 that:

> If they had brought 500,000 of their supporters onto the streets, at the time, for example, of Zeroual becoming head of state, or the release of Abassi Madani and Ali Belhadj, the army would never have been able to open fire.[181]

He thus concluded that:

> If they have not tried to mass their power on the streets, it is because they do not have the necessary troops behind them.[182]

The truth was that the vast majority of the Algerian population continued to withhold support from both sides in the conflict. Ordinary Algerians had become the daily victims of the brutal excesses of both the armed groups and the security forces, regularly subjected to the punitive actions of both parties which sought to intimidate the population into taking sides in the struggle. However, the unending flow of killings, bombings, collective punishments, arson and torture practised by both Islamists and the Algerian authorities alike served only to forge a consensus amongst most people that the violence must somehow be brought to an end. The unexpected support the population gave to both the presidential elections and Liamine Zeroual – as the man most capable of ending the conflict – provided the most concrete proof of this sentiment. It was instructive that far more people appeared to give their backing to the sitting President than to the representative of Islamism, Mahfoud Nahnah. This indicated that the bulk of the population saw the restoration of civil peace as more important than taking a step towards an Islamic state. It also supported the observation that a large number of people who had voted for the FIS in 1991 had done so out of a desire to see the discredited ruling order ousted rather than out of a wish to see the establishment of an Islamic state. Whereas the popular priority in 1991 had been the punishment and removal of the regime, by 1995 it had clearly become the desire to end four years of bitter and bloody conflict.

---

181 *Le Figaro*, 1.11.94.
182 *Ibid.*

The international dimension

External support

The question of foreign support for the Islamist cause in Algeria continued to revolve around states such as Iran, Sudan and Saudi Arabia. The Algerian regime remained anxious to emphasise this issue as a means of distracting attention from the genuinely domestic support for the movement.

Allegations of Iranian involvement with the armed groups continued to be made. Particular attention was drawn to the various connections Cherif Gousmi, the Emir of the GIA during most of 1994, appeared to enjoy with the Islamic Republic. The fact that Gousmi had spent time in the Iranian city of Qom and had had good relations with the Iranian Ambassador to Algeria – before his expulsion in November 1992 – was used to suggest that Gousmi and the GIA espoused Shi'ism. More tangible evidence of an Iranian link with the GIA came with the discovery of Israeli-made Uzi machine guns on captured and killed GIA members. Serial numbers on these weapons reportedly indicated that they came from a consignment that had been sent to Iran as part of the infamous "weapons for hostages" deal between the USA and Iran in the mid-1980s. Western intelligence agencies maintained that Iran was able to use Sudan as a route for getting weapons into Algeria, with the Sudanese also assisting in the training of militants. In contrast to Iran and Sudan little new evidence concerning official or individual Saudi support for the Islamist cause emerged after 1994. Significantly, an edition of the GIA's *Al Ansar* in early 1996 criticised Muslim states such as Saudi Arabia for no longer backing Islamist movements.[183]

Tensions persisted between Algeria and its closest neighbours – Morocco and Tunisia. The anti-Islamist press in Algeria continued to allege official Moroccan support for the armed groups, arguing that King Hassan sought to use the conflict as a means of strengthening Morocco's grip on the Western Sahara.[184] Reports that Said Mekhloufi had taken refuge in Morocco were used to support this contention, with some papers even suggesting that he was a Moroccan agent.[185] These accusations were

---

183 *Jeune Afrique*, 7.2.96.
184 *Liberté*, 16.6.94.
185 *Le Matin*, 25.9.94.

however contradicted by indications that Morocco was committed to blocking the supply routes across its territory used by the armed groups in Algeria. In January 1996 eight people (Algerians and Moroccans) were convicted by a Moroccan court for arms smuggling. In contrast to the ambiguities of Morocco's position towards the conflict in Algeria, an incident in early 1995 demonstrated that Algeria's eastern neighbour, Tunisia, was far more supportive of the Algerian regime's position. In February 1995 armed Algerian Islamists attacked a border post inside Tunisian territory, killing several border guards. It subsequently emerged that the attack, which had been mounted by the GIA, had been in retaliation for alleged Tunisian assistance with Algeria's anti-terrorist campaign. A GIA statement said that the attack constituted "a message" to the Tunisian government.[186]

Internationalisation of the conflict

A major feature of the Algerian conflict from 1994 was the increasing interest and involvement of foreign, particularly Western, countries in the developments in Algeria, largely at the invitation of one of the Algerian actors themselves. Since winning independence from France in 1962 Algeria had taken a nationalistic pride in conducting its own internal affairs without foreign assistance or interference. Opposing factions within the country, even before 1989, were quick to accuse each other of the cardinal sin of co-operating with foreign powers – particularly the French. The crisis into which the country was plunged in 1992, however, witnessed the steady dilution of this traditional stance. The realisation that the crisis and the ensuing conflict was not likely to be decisively resolved in the shorter term, forced the regime, the Islamist movement and the other opposition forces to begin to contemplate recruiting allies and support from abroad. The Algerian government sought financial support for the country as well as military and technical hardware to aid the anti-terrorist struggle – soliciting particularly the support of France, which was notably sympathetic to the regime's position.

Algeria's Islamists were not as swift to establish links with foreign states beyond those such as Iran and Sudan that were naturally sympathetic to their cause. The placing of Anwar Haddam and Rabah Kebir in influential Western countries was part of a strategy aimed at publicising

---

186 *Le Figaro*, 21.2.95.

the Algerian military's interruption of the democratisation process and its increasing reliance on arbitrary imprisonment, torture and execution to secure its position. However, this strategy was outflanked and increasingly negated by the decision of the emergent GIA to begin to explicitly target foreigners in Algeria in the autumn of 1993. Largely designed to intimidate Western support for the regime, the campaign had the effect of bolstering French support for Algeria's rulers and in complicating the tasks of Haddam and Kebir.

The year 1995 saw decisive moves on the part of both the GIA and the FIS to try and internationalise the conflict. The end of 1994 had witnessed the dramatic hijacking of an Air France airbus by GIA commandos, the plane being flown to Marseilles before being stormed by French security forces. The failure of this attempt – which had the alleged ultimate objective of exploding the aircraft in mid-air over Paris – was followed by a wave of terrorist incidents in Paris during the summer and early autumn of 1995, involving the bombing of both tourist sites and train stations in the French capital. French support for the Algerian regime was not the only target of the campaign. The assassination of Abdelbaki Sahraoui at a Paris mosque on 11 July indicated a new willingness to spread the fight between Algeria's factions beyond the country's borders. Members of the Islamist movement were quick to blame both the murder of Sahraoui and the Paris bombings on elements in Algerian Military Security who wished to destroy attempts at dialogue with the FIS (in which Sahraoui, as a founder of the party, had played a part) and to harden French attitudes towards the Islamists, but most evidence pointed to the attacks being the work of the GIA. Abdelbaki Sahraoui's good relations with his French hosts, his consistent condemnation of GIA atrocities and his willingness to act as a intermediary in the conflict made him a natural target for the group, who had already explicitly threatened him on several occasions.

In common with Sahraoui and in contrast to the GIA, many of the senior figures in the FIS were aware of the need to establish constructive links with Western governments. This was not just in order to gain diplomatic support for their cause, but more importantly to ensure that any future Islamist regime in Algeria would not have to face hostile reactions from Western governments, particularly when seeking assistance to solve the country's massive economic problems. Significant attempts were made by the FIS to get the GIA to halt the killings of foreigners in

Algeria which figures such as Rabah Kebir and Abdelbaki Sahraoui unequivocally condemned. The decision to host the drawing-up of the National Contract in a Western country, Italy (deferred from Britain) was largely prompted by a belief on the part of the FIS as well as the other signatories, of the importance of attracting Western attention and support for the common platform. The qualified support most Western governments gave to the Rome Platform was seen as evidence of the success of this strategy. The similarly cautious welcome given by Western governments to Liamine Zeroual's victory in the presidential elections ten months later, however, signified a setback for this initiative.

The economic dimension

One of the main reasons why courting Western opinion became more important to all sides in the Algerian conflict, was the increasing influence Western states and Western-dominated institutions began to have over the Algerian economy. Belaid Abdessalem's attempt to turn back over a decade of liberalisation in the economic sphere had resulted in Algeria's economy sinking even further into chaos and decline and had led to his dismissal as Prime Minister in August 1993. His replacement, Redha Malek, had spearheaded attempts to restart liberalisation. By early 1994, with the country's colossal debt on the verge of soaking up the entirety of the national foreign currency earnings, the government relented on its long-standing refusal to contemplate rescheduling its debt which would entail the imposition of foreign conditions (hitherto unacceptable for Algeria's nationalist pride). Consequently, in April 1994 Malek's government agreed to a $1 billion standby loan with the International Monetary Fund which cleared the way for a rescheduling of part of its international debt with the "Paris Club" of creditor nations the following month.[187]

The final surrender to the inevitable provided Algeria's creditors with a potential source of leverage over the country's rulers. Hardening attitudes amongst some Western countries towards the Algerian regime's refusal to come to an agreement with the FIS during the two attempts at dialogue during 1994 prompted speculation that pressure would be put on Algiers to compromise. There was even the suggestion that President Zeroual's announcement of presidential elections in the wake of the failure

---

187 See Willis, 'Algeria's troubled road', pp. 211–2.

of the second attempt had been designed to appease these fears. Western wariness towards the prospect of an Islamist government in Algeria together with strong French support for Algiers, however, succeeded in a further IMF agreement and Paris Club rescheduling deal being achieved in May 1995.

Algeria's creditors joined with most Algerians in welcoming Zeroual's election in November 1995 and the civil peace it seemed initially to bring. The gradual return of violence and the lack of any new initiative on the part of the regime to seek a negotiated solution, however, led to renewed suggestions from many European states that any further agreements with Algiers should be tied to the regime's efforts to seek a political solution. The country's failure to meet many of the IMF stipulations was rightly seen as a direct result of the security situation and there was increasing concern that external funds would be used to fund the campaign against the armed groups.[188]

Aside from Algeria's relations with foreign governments and international institutions such as the IMF, the country was also increasingly reliant on foreign commercial companies. Algeria's economic managers had come to the conclusion that the country's only real hope of economic recovery lay in expanded exploitation of its still substantial oil and gas reserves. It had become clear that only foreign involvement in this field could achieve the sort of increases in revenue that could lift Algeria out of its economic abyss. From Mouloud Hamrouche onwards (with the noted exception of Belaid Abdessalem) administrations sought to attract foreign participation and investment in the country's oil and gas fields. Reluctance by foreign companies to invest in other areas of the stricken Algerian economy due to the clear security risks was far less in the area of hydrocarbons, given the potential gains, the remoteness of the southern oil and gas fields from the strife-torn north, and the stated unwillingness of many of the armed groups to attack such a vital national resource. Nevertheless, the possibility of attack remained and was referred to as a policy of last resort by some Islamist elements. In May 1995 the GIA had already attacked a compound at Ghardaia killing five foreign workers and in February 1996 the grouping issued an warning to workers in the oil and gas industry to stop work or face the consequences.[189]

---

188 *Financial Times*, 18.1.96.
189 *Le Monde*, 16.2.96.

Conclusions

The realisation by the second half of 1993 by Algeria's rulers that exclusion of the FIS and repression of armed Islamist opposition had not removed the threat of the Islamist challenge opened the way for a possible re-entry of the party into the legal political arena. This reconsideration of official strategy provoked not only controversy and breaches within the ruling councils of the Algerian regime, but also exposed the manifold divisions amongst the country's Islamists.

The prospect of a negotiated settlement with the regime appeared to make clear once again the fundamental divide that existed between those Islamists – such as the FIS – who viewed peaceful politics as the best method for pursuing the goals of the movement, and those – such as the GIA – who continued to espouse violent insurrection as the sole and legitimate means of achieving political power. This observation, however, was complicated by considerations of strategy and pragmatism. In the same way that many in the Algerian regime concluded that the armed insurrection was unlikely to be defeated by military and security means alone, leading elements in the FIS were aware that the possibility of the regime being overturned by force was negligible. The continued failure of the Islamist cause to attract the active support of the majority of the Algerian population had become a major feature of the conflict and discredited persistent suggestions from abroad that the country might be on the verge of a popular Islamic revolution.

A paradoxical consequence of the persistence and growth of the armed struggle against the regime was that whilst it induced the regime to consider a political deal with the FIS, it made the FIS's task of reaching a credible agreement more difficult. The various leaders of the party were conscious that they must appear able to deliver the main demand of the regime – a truce with the armed groups. The gradual gathering of many of the disparate elements of the armed resistance under the institutional banner of the FIS (through the AIS) during 1993-94 represented a step towards achieving this end. However, the continued domination of the armed struggle by the GIA – which explicitly rejected the authority of the FIS – presented a major obstacle to the leadership of the FIS's claim to be able to arrange an effective ceasefire. Efforts to solicit the involvement of the GIA in any future political agreement initially appeared to centre on efforts to build up the AIS as a rival in the maquis. However, the internal ructions that shook the GIA in the closing weeks of 1995 indicated that the apparent "defections" of Mohammed Said, Abderrazak Redjam and Anwar Haddam to the GIA in mid 1994 had quite possibly been part of an attempt by elements in the FIS to infiltrate and control the more radical grouping.

The possibility of a rehabilitation of the FIS revived interest in the party's political platform and stance. Considerable significance in this context was attached to the party's involvement with the Rome Platform. The FIS's willingness to both co-operate with non-Islamist parties and to agree to put its name to a declaration upholding the main principles of liberal democracy was seen as a major development on the party's previously opaque stance of pluralism and democracy. Ali Belhadj's expression of support for the document was heralded as evidence of a new-found maturity on the part of the former standard-bearer of radical Islamism who had once vigorously and explicitly denounced the core principles contained in the Platform. However, the extent to which the deputy leader of the FIS's "conversion" to the inherent values of liberal democracy was genuine and not simply a recognition of the possible benefits of political and strategic pragmatism, remained to be seen.

Conclusion

The announcement by Liamine Zeroual in May 1996 that legislative elections would be held in the first part of 1997 appeared to indicate that the President was intent on persevering with his attempts at restoring peace to Algeria through the holding of elections – a process that had begun with his own election as head of state the previous November. The involvement, however, of the Islamists of the FIS in any such elections remained improbable. Representatives from the party had not been invited to attend bilateral talks with the government in April. Furthermore, Zeroual's statement on his plans for elections had been accompanie by notification that he wished to make a number of changes to the Constitution including a tightening of the provisions against political parties using Islam for political ends.[1]

The President's reluctance to allow the FIS to participate in his plans to renew Algerian political life was a further demonstration of the conundrum which had haunted Algeria's leaders since as far back as 1990. The core of the conundrum was how to allow a political force to operate in the formal political arena when, firstly, its own popularity and apparent ideology meant it could threaten to bring down this same political arena; and secondly, a significant section of the population, including powerful elements such as the military, were implacably opposed to the FIS's programme and vision.

The Islamist movement remained, as it had done since 1990, the key element in all Algeria's political equations. It had been the electoral success of the FIS which had precipitated the abandonment of the electoral process. Participation of the FIS remained the primary and most divisive issue in any attempt to relaunch the process and armed Islamist opposition to the regime was the cause of the great bloodshed that Algeria had witnessed since 1992. Social and economic decline, crime and official failures and corruption were all part of Algeria's ongoing travails, but it was the country's Islamists who remained at the hub of the whole crisis.

What remained remarkable was the swiftness of the Islamist movement's rise to prominence in Algeria. As has been shown, an Islamist

---

1 *Financial Times*, 13.5.96.

tradition had been present in the country since the early part of the century with the creation of the Association of Algerian Ulama, but the two decades following independence had seen the movement virtually vanish from the Algerian stage. The 1980s had witnessed a noticeable re-emergence of the movement, but had it not been for the events of 1988-89, it would have simply remained a vocal but ultimately peripheral force. The events of this period allowed certain figures in the movement, notably Abassi Madani and Ali Belhadj, to construct a truly mass popular base for the movement through, firstly, the upheaval of October 1988 and secondly through the formation of the Front Islamique du Salut. This project revolutionised Algerian Islamism and transformed it into something quite different from the sort of movement it had been since the 1920s.

It would be true to say that the FIS was essentially an offspring of the Islamist movement rather than an organic part of it. It is highly significant that so many senior Islamist figures (Sahnoun, Nahnah, Djaballah) did *not* participate in the creation of the party. The party was instead headed by the maverick Abassi, who had no organisational base of support and the young, inexperienced Belhadj. Other senior Islamist figures did join the party in 1989, but it was notable that it was these individuals who formed the bulwark of opposition to Abassi and his strategy in the Majlis Shura in early 1991 and who either left or were ejected from the party the following summer. The true, historic Algerian Islamist movement can be seen as surviving in the Rabitat Dawa and in the organisations and parties established by Mahfoud Nahnah and Abdallah Djaballah. Wary of politics and confrontation, and holding as a primary aim the "re-Islamisation" of the Algerian people through education and preaching, these organisations remained closer to the ideals of Abdelhamid Ben Badis than did the FIS.

In contrast the FIS had become simply a populist political movement. This was not to say that Abassi, Belhadj or any of their successors in the party's BEP were not committed to Islamist ideas and ultimate goals, but the FIS became a means for achieving political power and, through that, these goals. The FIS's populism successfully drew to its banner the swelling numbers of Algerians who saw the party as the best means of overthrowing the existing, deeply unpopular ruling order. A large proportion of such people believed in the party's millenialist promises of a FIS-run Algeria, but given that the core of the party's support was the undereducated and unemployed urban young, it is unlikely that there was any widespread understanding of the FIS programme or Islamist ideas generally.

To get an idea of the true extent of real Islamist influence, support and ideas in Algeria in the 1990s, it is necessary to look harder perhaps at the votes that Mahfoud Nahnah was able to attract in the presidential poll of November 1995 rather than those delivered to the FIS in 1990 or 1991. In 1995 Liamine Zeroual was able, through his perceived ability to deliver peace, to peel away a large slice of the populist constituency previously supportive of the FIS. The three million votes Nahnah received in 1995, representing roughly 20% of the adult population of Algeria, were probably a fair illustration of the genuine popular support Islamist aims and goals enjoyed in the country.

The armed struggle that developed from 1992 was a mutation of the populist phenomenon embodied in the FIS. For the vast majority of those in the armed groups, the ultimate stated goal of an "Islamic State" is really only an icon representing other more basic desires – the overthrow of the regime and the end of official repression and economic and social deprivation. The armed struggle has not exerted the same popular appeal as the FIS – which had attracted the support of millions of Algerians – but has attracted only the most militantly disillusioned section of the population. It is significant that the most militant of all the elements of the armed struggle, the GIA, is composed overwhelmingly of young unemployed youths. Consequently, Séverine Labat is right to characterise the GIA, in particular, as a "social movement" in contrast to the FIS and most of its allies who still hold to political means and aims.[2]

The future course of Algeria and its Islamist movement, in both its populist and more traditional forms is impossible to predict accurately. The issue of Islamist and FIS participation will remain a constant feature of the Algerian political scene, irrespective of future shifts in its popular support and ideology, because it had played the predominant role in Algeria's first experiment with political pluralism and electoral democracy. After over four years of bloody conflict it is abundantly clear that a military "solution" to the impasse is highly unlikely, the armed resistance being at the same time insufficiently powerful to defeat the significant

---

2   See Labat, *Les Islamistes Algériens.*

resources of the Algerian military yet remaining too strong and resilient to be decisively crushed by its adversary. Despite the substantial opposition by hardline elements in both the regime and the armed groups to any agreement between the regime and the FIS , such a deal is the only viable way of breaking the impasse.

The sort of deal that might emerge from agreement with the regime is difficult to judge. The consistent sticking point for both the FIS and the regime through the three attempts at dialogue during 1994 and 1995, was the FIS's demand that its leaders be freed and allowed to meet the rest of the leadership of the party before issuing a call for a ceasefire. Whether one side will be forced to compromise in some way or whether a mutually acceptable fudge will be constructed remains to be seen. It seems, in 1996, that Zeroual is confident of securing compromises from the FIS through capitalising on the divisions and ructions the party has experienced since the presidential elections. He clearly hopes that a section of the party will effectively break ranks and negotiate with him in the hope of being allowed to participate in the planned legislative elections. Having been excluded from the presidential elections, many in the FIS fear that the party's absence from future elections will fatally marginalise it. Should the FIS or any successor party be allowed to enter elections, one can only guess how the party might fare in such contests – the events of the past few years having possibly driven away as many supporters as attracted new ones. The presidential elections demonstrated that priorities for many Algerians had changed since 1991. Central to all of these prognostics remains the issue of the armed struggle against the existing regime. Whether or not the regime is able to come to an agreement with all or part of the FIS, it is certain that violence will continue. The GIA has pledged itself to wage war against the regime until absolute victory. It is yet to be shown if a call by Abassi Madani and particularly Ali Belhadj to abandon the struggle will reduce the numbers of those continuing to fight to an essential hard core whose activities can either be curtailed or eradicated by the regime. What is more certain is that the dire economic and social conditions that have existed in Algeria for some time will continue to prevail for the foreseeable future and will similarly continue to act as powerful recruiting sergeants for the armed groups. Despite the dramatic political developments in the closing weeks of 1995 the stark fact remained that nearly a third of the population was unemployed and they along with the rest of the populations continued to be squeezed even further by factors such as an inflation rate of over 25%.[3]

The lessons and implications that the experiences of Algeria and its Islamist movement have had for the rest of North Africa and the Arab and Muslim worlds are also worthy of consideration. Perspectives differ considerably. For most of Algeria's neighbouring governments in North Africa, Algeria's current predicament is testimony to the dire consequences of firstly, excessively fast political liberalisation, and secondly, permitting Islamism to compete in multi-party elections. Egypt, Morocco and Tunisia have all allowed some degree of multi-party participation in elections. All three, though, have ensured that firstly, such participation is controlled to a degree necessary to prevent a challenge to the ruling order, and secondly, that no explicitly Islamist political party is allowed to compete in elections under its own banner. It was notable that as events in Algeria unfolded in the 1990s both the Tunisian and later the Egyptian governments clamped down on even the hitherto tolerated organisational manifestations of Islamism in their countries. Significant coverage of the horrors of the Algerian conflict is given in the media in all the states, in the hope that this will discourage the significant, latent Islamist sympathies that are present across North Africa. In contrast to this view are the lessons drawn from Algeria's experiences by Islamists internationally. For them Algeria has shown that when given open elections Islamism is shown to be a hugely popular political option, even in a country formerly thought of as being peripheral to the international Islamist movement. The armed conflict has demonstrated that even abandonment of elections and repression is not sufficient to stifle Islamist demands and popularity.

The impact Algerian Islamism itself has had on the world beyond its borders is difficult to assess. The achievements of the FIS in the elections of 1990 and 1991 demonstrated the startling success Islamist movements can have in multi-party elections. The stripping through the *coup d'état* of January 1992 of the party's election victory provided Islamists elsewhere with a powerful image of political martyrdom. The subsequent radicalisation of the armed conflict in Algeria created – in the same way as the conflict in Afghanistan in the 1980s – an ideologically and militarily militant image and reputation for Algerian Islamism.

---

3 *Le Monde*, 12.1.96.

Beyond these exemplary factors, however, Algerian Islamism appeared to have very little influence on Islamist movements and ideas internationally. As has been shown, historically the Algerian movement was, ideologically, largely the product of external influences. The founders of the Association of Algerian Ulama were all driven by ideas and experiences they had gained whilst studying outside the country. Imported Arabic teachers from the Eastern Arab world fed Islamist sentiment in Algeria's schools during the Arabisation programmes of the 1970s. Many of the main Islamist organisations that emerged in Algeria borrowed the names of other foreign Islamist groups – HAMAS, Nahda, Takfir wa Hijra. In ideological terms, the radical and violent statements and stance of some of the armed groups, particularly the GIA, were just crude and confused reworkings of the ideas of Sayyid Qutb. For its part the FIS, in its populist bid for political power, preferred vacuous propaganda to anything more precise or innovatory.

Two potentially distinctive features of Algerian Islamism are however apparent and both could well have a significant future impact on the wider Islamist world. Dating back to the time of Abdelhamid Ben Badis and the Association of Algerian Ulama, Algerian Islamism has been confronted with two fundamental issues: its attitude towards political activism and its relationship toward the concept of the nation.

Algeria's experience of French colonial rule and its bitter liberation struggle imbued all of Algerian society, including the country's Islamists, with a sense of national pride and identity. The AUMA, although having its intellectual origins in the pan-Islamic ideas of Islamic reformism, had allowed its essentially religious notions to become intertwined with those of Algerian nationalism. This relationship between nationalism and Islamism had reached its height in the formal alliance forged between the AUMA and the FLN in 1956. Despite the perceived marginalisation of the AUMA and its ideals in the wake of independence, this alliance between Islamism and nationalism persisted in important parts of the FLN. Most significantly of all it saw its renaissance through the creation of the FIS. Abassi Madani's headship of the party meant that the FIS's message contained strong nationalistic as well as traditional Islamist themes – a reflection of the FIS president's heritage as one of the very first members of the FLN plus his populist instincts. The conclusion of the internal convulsions the FIS experienced in mid-1991 led to the nationalist strain within the party becoming strengthened *vis-à-vis* the more traditionalist salafi wing. The rise to prominence of members of the more nationalistic Jazara within the FIS gave a powerful platform to the views of people who espoused the ideas of Algeria's only truly original indigenous Islamic thinker – Malek Bennabi. The annulment and cancellation of elections in January 1992 deprived observers of the chance not just to see the probable formation of an Islamist government, but, more importantly, one led by figures primarily influenced by a thinker not drawn from the ranks of the traditional Islamic thinkers of the Arab East. This opportunity may yet come.

Algerian Islamism's relationship with the notion of political activism has been characterised by the consistent victory of those Islamists favouring involvement in politics over those who reject it in preference for devotion to exclusively religious activities. Tayyib Uqbi was marginalised in the AUMA in the 1930s for his fierce attachment to the principle of apoliticism and those Islamist figures who held doubts about the nature of the FIS's involvement in competitive party politics were either left behind in 1989 or squeezed out of the party two years later. However, the emergence of the FIS prompted another strain of Islamist opinion to challenge the explicitly political orientations of the party. Mustapha Bouyali's campaign of armed resistance during the 1980s had given birth to a faction of the Islamist movement which believed that violent insurrection was the only proper means for the movement to achieve its ends. The perceived collapse of the FIS's political strategy through the *coup d'état* of January 1992 brought these forces to the fore. Nevertheless, there have remained important elements within the FIS which have remained surprisingly attached to the pursuit of an explicitly political strategy – rather than one exclusively devoted to military means. This attachment culminated in senior figures in the FIS endorsing not only political but apparently liberal democratic means and objectives in the Rome Platform. These developments have led to suggestions that Algeria's Islamists have an unparalleled understanding, experience and now acceptance of democratic and pluralistic politics and can therefore be expected to provide an important example to Islamists elsewhere. The truth of this, however, remains to be seen.

There are other wider lessons to be drawn from Algeria. Many observers both in the Muslim world and the West have argued that Algeria represents part of the ongoing reassertion of the Islamic faith worldwide. Some in Europe have seen it as evidence of a coming conflict between the "Christian" northern Mediterranean and the Muslim-dominated southern shore – immigration and trade set to become the flash points. In Algeria's case this can be seen to be only partially true. Islam has played a largely symbolic role in Algerian politics. As has been shown, the real driving force behind both the successes of the FIS and the ongoing armed struggle has not been a desire for an Islamic state, as such, but a wish to escape from the spiral of economic, social and political decline that Algeria has locked itself in since the late 1970s. Should the FIS ever attain political power, it would be the success it had in breaking this spiral of decline, rather than the ardency with which it applied "Islamic values", which would determine its popular legitimacy. Should it fail, as must be likely, there is a potential opening for some other movement or ideology to launch a populist crusade against the ruling order, using the same methods that the FIS had used to such great effect.

Election Results

Local Elections, 12 June 1990

APC Results

Party	Vote	%	Councils	Seats
FIS	4,331,472	54.3	853	5,987
FLN	2,245,798	28.1	487	4,799
RCD	166,104	2.1	87	623
PNSD	131,100	1.6	2	134
Other parties	179,036	2.2	4	143
Independents	931,278	11.7	106	1,189

Turnout: 8,366,760 (65.2%)
Valid Votes: 7,984,788 (62.2%)

APW Results

Party	Vote	%	Councils*	Seats
FIS	4,520,668	57.4	31	1,031
FLN	2,166,887	27.5	6	667
RCD			1	55
PNSD	(1,182,445	15.0**)	0	8
Other parties			0	13
Independents			1	99

Turnout: 8,238,921 (64.2%)
Valid Votes: 7,877,000 (61.3%)

* 9 councils with no overall control
** Approximate total vote for all non-FLN and FIS candidates
(Full results not available)

Sources: Jacques Fontaine, 'Les elections locales Algériennes du 12 Juin 1990: approche statistique et géographique', *Maghreb-Machrek*, no. 129 (Juillet-Septembre 1990); and Keith Sutton, Ahmed Aghrout and Salah Zaimche, 'Political changes in Algeria: an emerging electoral geography', *Maghreb Review*, vol. 17, nos.1 and 2 (1992).

National Assembly Elections
First Ballot, 26 December 1991

Party	Vote	%	Seats
FIS	3,260,359	47.3	188
FLN	1,613,507	23.4	15
FFS	510,661	7.4	25
HAMAS	368,697	5.3	0
RCD	200,267	2.9	0
Nahda	150,093	2.2	0
MDA	135,882	2.0	0
PRA	67,828	1.0	0
PNSD	48,208	0.7	0
PSD	28,638	0.4	0
MAJD	27,623	0.4	0
Other parties	176,332	2.6	0
Independents	309,624	4.5	3

Turnout: 7,822,625 (59%)
Valid votes: 6,897,906 (52%)

Sources: *Algérie Actualité*, 2.1.92; Keith Sutton and Ahmed Aghrout, 'Multiparty elections in Algeria: problems and prospects', *Bulletin of Francophone Africa*, no. 2 (Autumn 1992).

Presidential Election,
16 November 1995

Candidate	Party	Vote	%
Liamine Zeroual	(None)	7,088,616	61.0
Mahfoud Nahnah	HAMAS	2,971,974	25.6
Said Saadi	RCD	1,115,796	9.6
Nourredine Boukrouh	PRA	443,144	3.8

Turnout: 12,087,281 (75.7%)
Valid votes: 11,619,532 (72.5%)

Source: Algerian radio, *Summary of World Broadcasts* ME/2470 MED/16, 25.11.95.

Bibliography

Books and Articles

Abun-Nasr, Jamil M. *A History of the Maghrib in the Islamic Period,* Cambridge, Cambridge University Press, 1987

Addi, Lahouari. 'De la permanence du populisme Algérien' in *Peuples Méditerranéens,* no. 52–3: *Algérie: vers l'état islamique?* (Juillet–Septembre 1990)

Ageron, Charles-Robert. *Histoire de l'Algérie contemporaine,* Paris, Press Universitaires de France, 1979

—*Modern Algeria: A History from 1830 to the Present,* London, C. Hurst & Co., 1991

Al-Ahnaf, M. Bernard Botiveau and Franck Frégosi. *L'Algérie par ses Islamistes,* Paris, Karthala, 1991

Alleg, Henri, Jacques de Bonis, Henri J. Douzon, Jean Freire and Pierre Haudiquet. *La Guerre d'Algérie,* Paris, Temps Actuel, 1981

Arkoun, Mohammed. 'Algeria' in Shireen T. Hunter, *The Politics of Islamic Revivalism,* Indianapolis and Bloomington, Indiana University Press, 1988

Ayubi, Nazih. *Political Islam: Religion and Politics in the Arab World,* London, Routledge, 1993

Bariun, Fawzia. *Malik Bennabi: His Life and Theory of Civilization,* Kuala Lumpur, Budaya Ilmu Sdn, 1993

Barrada, Hamid. 'Le système a assassiné Mohamed Boudiaf' in *Reporters sans frontières: le drame algérien,* Paris, La Découverte, 1994

Bekkar, Rabia. 'Taking up space in Tlemcen: the Islamist occupation of urban Algeria' (Interview), in *Middle East Report* (November–December 1992)

Belhimer, Ammar. 'Les groupes armés de l'opposition islamiques' in *Les Cahiers de l'Orient,* no. 36–7 (1994-95*)*

Belvaude, Catherine. *L'Algérie,* Paris, Karthala, 1991

Benoune, Mahfoud. *The Making of Contemporary Algeria: 1830–1987* Cambridge, Cambridge University Press, 1988

—'Algeria's façade of democracy' in *Middle East Report* (March–April 1990)

Burgat, François. *L'Islamisme au Maghreb: la voix du sud,* Paris, Karthala, 1988

—and Jean Leca. 'La mobilisation islamiste et les elections algériennes du 12 Juin' in *Maghreb-Machrek*, no. 129 (Juillet–Septembre 1990)

—and William Dowell. *The Islamic Movement in North Africa*, Austin, Center for Middle Eastern Studies, University of Texas, 1993

Callies de Salies, Bruno. 'De la crise à la guerre civile', *Les Cahiers de l'Orient*, no. 36–7 (1994-95)

Charef, Abed. *Algérie: Le Grand Dérapage*, Paris, Editions de l'Aube, 1994

Cheriet, Bouthenia. 'Islamism and feminism: Algeria's "rites of passage" to democracy' in John P. Entelis and Phillip C. Naylor, *State and Society in Algeria*, Boulder, Colorado, Westview Press, 1992

Christelow, Allan. 'Algerian Islam in a time of transition: c. 1890–1930', *Maghreb Review*, vol. 8, no. 5–6 (1983)

—'Ritual, culture and politics of Islamic reformism in Algeria', *Middle Eastern Studies*, vol. 23, no. 3 (July 1987)

—'An Islamic humanist in the 20th Century: Malik Bennabi', *Maghreb Review*, vol. 17, no. 1-2 (1992)

Clemenceau, François. 'Interview: l'après Rome vu par le FIS', *Les Cahiers de l'Orient*, no. 36–7 (1994-95)

Collot, Claude and Jean-Robert Henry. *Le Mouvement national algérien: textes 1912–1954*, Paris, L'Harmattan, 1978

Colonna, Fanny. 'Cultural resistance and religious legitimacy in colonial Algeria', *Economy and Society*, no. 3 (1974)

Cubertafond, Bernard. *La République algérienne démocratique et populaire*, Limoges, Presses Universitaires de France, 1979

Danziger, Raphael. *Abd al-Qadir and the Algerians: Resistance to the French and Internal Consolidation*, New York, Holmes & Meier, 1977

Deheuvals, Luc-Willy. *Islam et pensée contemporaine en Algérie: la revue 'Al-Asala' 1971–1981*, Paris, Editions du Centre National de Recherché Scientifique, 1991

Dévoluy, Pierre and Mirielle Duteil. *La Poudrière algérienne: histoire secrète d'une république sous influence*, Paris, Calman-Lévy, 1994

Dillman, Bradford. 'Transition to democracy in Algeria' in John P. Entelis and Phillip C. Naylor, *State and Society in Algeria*, Boulder, Colorado, Westview, 1992

Dissez, Anne. 'Les partis "democrates": l'impossible coalition', *Les Cahiers de l'Orient*, no. 133 (Juillet–Septembre 1991)

Djeghloul, A. 'La multipartisme à l'Algérienne', *Maghreb-Machrek*, no. 127 (Janvier–Mars 1990)

Dunn, Michael Collins. 'Algeria's agony: the drama so far, the prospects for peace', *Middle East Policy*, vol. 3 (1994)

Entelis, John P. *Algeria: The Revolution Institutionalized*, Boulder, Colorado, Westview, 1986

—and Lisa J. Arone. 'Algeria in turmoil: Islam, democracy and the state', *Middle East Policy*, vol. 1 (1992)

—'The crisis of authoritarianism in North Africa: the case of Algeria', *Problems of Communism* (May–June 1992)

—'Introduction: state and society in transition' in John P. Entelis and Phillip C. Naylor, *State and Society in Algeria*, Boulder, Colorado, Westview, 1992

Etienne, Bruno. *L'Islamisme radical*, Paris, Hachette, 1987

Fontaine, Jacques. 'Les élections locales algériennes du 12 Juin 1990: approche statistique et géographique', *Maghreb-Machrek*, no. 129 (Juillet–Septembre 1990)

—'Les élections legislatives algériennes: resultats du premier tour, 26 Decembre 1991', *Maghreb-Machrek*, no. 135 (Janvier–Mars 1992)

—'Quartiers défavorisés et vote Islamiste à Alger' in Pierre Robert Baduel (ed.), *L'Algérie Incertaine*, Paris, Edisud, 1994

Garçon, José. '11 Janvier: le coup d'état' in *Reporters sans frontières: le drame algérien* Paris, La Découverte, 1994

Gellner, Ernest. 'The unknown Apollo of Biskra: the social base of Algerian puritanism' in *Muslim Society*, Cambridge, Cambridge University Press, 1981.

Haddam, Anwar. 'The political experiment of the Algerian Islamic movement and the new world order' in Azzam Tamimi, *Power-Sharing Islam?*, London, Liberty, 1993

Harbi, Mohammed. *L'Islamisme dans tous ses états*, Paris, Arcantère, 1991

Hiro, Dilip. *Islamic Fundamentalism*, London, Paladin, 1988

Horne, Alistair. *A Savage War of Peace: Algeria 1954–62*, London, Papermac, 1987

Humbaraci, Arslan. *Algeria: A Revolution that Failed*, London, Pall Mall, 1966

Jackson, Henry. *The FLN in Algeria: Party Development in a Revolutionary Society*, Westport USA, Greenwood Press, 1977

Joffé, George. 'Algeria: the failure of dialogue' in *The Middle East and North Africa*, London, Europa Publication, 1995

Julien, Charles-André. *History of North Africa*, London, Routledge & Kegan Paul, 1970

Kapil, Arun. 'Algeria's elections show Islamist strength', *Middle East Report* (September–October 1990)

—'Les partis islamistes en Algérie: eléments de présentation', *Maghreb-Machrek*, no. 133 (Juillet–Septembre 1991)

Kepel, Gilles. *The Prophet and Pharaoh: Muslim Extremism in Egypt*, London, Al Saqi, 1985

Khelladi, Aissa. *Algérie: les Islamistes face au pouvoir*, Algiers, Editions Alfa, 1992

—'Une clandestinité organisée' in *Reporters sans frontières: le drame algérien*, Paris, La Découverte, 1994

—'La formation des groupes armés' in *Reporters sans frontières: le drame algérien*, Paris, La Découverte, 1994

—'Les islamistes algériens à l'assaut du pouvoir', *Les temps modernes: Algérie: La guerre des frères*, no. 580 (Janvier–Février 1995)

Knauss, Peter R. *The Persistence of Patriarchy: Class, Gender and Ideology in Twentieth Century Algeria*, New York, Praeger, 1987

Labat, Séverine. 'Islamism and Islamists: the emergence of new types of politico-religious militants' in John Ruedy, *Islamism and Secularism in North Africa*, London, Macmillan, 1994

—'La "Grève Sainte" de Mai–Juin 1991' in *Reporters sans frontières: le drame algérien*, Paris, La Découverte, 1994

—'Abdelkader Hachani, Islamiste et moderniste' in *Reporters sans frontières: le drame algérien*, Paris, La Découverte, 1994

—'Le FIS à l'épreuve de la lutte armée' in Remy Leveau, *L'Algérie dans la guerre*, Brussels, Editions Complexe, 1995

—*Les Islamistes algériens: entre les urnes et le maquis*, Paris, Seuil, 1995

Lamchichi, Abderrahim. *Islam et contestation au Maghreb*, Paris, L'Harmattan, 1989

—*L'Algérie en crise*, Paris, L'Harmattan, 1990

—*L'Islamisme en Algérie*, Paris, L'Harmattan, 1992

Lavenue, Jean-Jacques. *Algérie: la démocratie interdite*, Paris, L'Harmattan, 1992

Layachi, Azzedine and Abdel-kader Haireche. 'National development and political protest in the Maghreb countries', *Arab Studies Quarterly*, vol. 14, nos. 2 and 3 (Spring/Summer 1992)

Leca, Jean and Jean-Claude Vatin. *L'Algérie politique: institutions et régime*,

Paris, Presses de la Foundation Nationale des Sciences Politiques, 1975

Leveau, Remy. 'L'Algérie en état de siège', *Maghreb-Machrek,* no. 133 (Juillet-Septembre 1991)

Liabes, Djillali. 'La démocratie en Algérie: culture et contre-culture', *Peuples Méditerranéens,* no. 52–3: *Algérie: vers l'état islamique?* (Juillet–Septembre 1990)

Martinez, Luis. 'L'enivrement de la violence: "djihad" dans la Banlieue d'Alger' in Remy Leveau, *L'Algérie dans la guerre,* Brussels, Editions Complexe, 1995

Merad, Ali. *Le reformisme musulman en Algérie de 1925 à 1940,* Paris, Moulton & Co., 1967

—*Ibn Badis: Commentateur du Coran,* Paris, Librarie Orientaliste Paul Geuthner, 1971

Mezhoud, Salem. 'Glasnost the Algerian way: the role of Berber nationalists in political reform' in George Joffé, *North Africa: Nation, State and Region,* London, Routledge, 1993

Mohaddessin, Mohammed. *Islamic Fundamentalism: The New Global Threat,* Washington, Seven Locks Press, 1993

Morsy, Magali. *North Africa 1800–1900: A Survey from the Nile to the Atlantic,* London, Longman, 1984

Mortimer, Robert A. 'Islam and multiparty politics in Algeria' in *Middle East Journal,* vol. 45, no. 4 (Autumn 1991)

—'Algerian foreign policy in transition' in John P. Entelis and Phillip C. Naylor, *State and Society in Algeria,* Boulder, Colorado, Westview Press, 1992

Munson, Henry. *Religion and Power in Morocco,* New Haven and London, Yale University Press, 1993

Ottaway, David and Marina. *Algeria: The Politics of a Socialist Revolution,* Berkeley and Los Angeles, University of California Press, 1970

Parker, Richard B. *North Africa: Regional Tensions and Strategic Concerns,* New York, Praeger, 1984

Payne, Rhys. 'Economic crisis and polity reform in the 1980s' in I. William Zartman and William Mark Habeeb, *Polity and Society in Contemporary North Africa,* Boulder, Colorado, Westview, 1993

Pfeifer, Karen. 'Economic liberalization in the 1980s: Algeria in comparative perspective' in John P. Entelis and Phillip C. Naylor, *State and Society in Algeria,* Boulder, Colorado, Westview Press, 1992

Piscatori, James P. *Islamic Fundamentalisms and the Gulf Crisis*, Chicago, The American Academy of Arts and Sciences, 1991

Quandt, William B. *Revolution and Political Leadership: Algeria 1954–1968*, Cambridge, Massachusetts Institute of Technology, 1969

Roberts, Hugh. 'The unforeseen development of the Kabyle question in contemporary Algeria', *Government and Opposition*, vol. 17, no. 3 (Summer 1982)

—'The politics of Algerian socialism' in R. I. Lawless and A. M. Findlay, *North Africa*, London, Croom Helm, 1984

—'Radical Islamism and the dilemma of Algerian nationalism: the embattled Arians of Algiers', *Third World Quarterly*, vol. 10, no. 2 (April 1988)

—'A new face for the FLN', *Africa Report* (March–April 1990)

—'A trial of strength: Algerian Islamism' in James P. Piscatori, *Islamic Fundamentalisms and the Gulf Crisis*, Chicago, The American Academy of Arts and Sciences, 1991

—'From radical mission to equivocal ambition: the expansion and manipulation of Algerian Islamism, 1979–1992' in Martin E. Marty and R. Scott Appleby, *The Fundamentalism Project; Volume 4: Accounting for Fundamentalisms: The Dynamic Character of Movements*, Chicago, University of Chicago Press, 1994

—'Doctrinaire economics and political opportunism in the strategy of Algerian Islamism' in John Ruedy: *Islamism and Secularism in North Africa*, London, Macmillan, 1994

—'Algeria between eradicators and conciliators', *Middle East Report* (July–August 1994)

—'Algeria's ruinous impasse and the honourable way out', *International Affairs*, vol. 71, no. 2 (1995)

Rouadjia, Ahmed. *Les Frères et la mosquée: enquête sur le mouvement islamiste en Algérie*, Paris, Karthala, 1990

—'Doctrine et discours du Cheikh Abbassi', *Peuples Méditerranéens* no. 52–3: *Algérie: vers l'état islamique?* (Juillet–Septembre 1990)

—'Le FIS: à l'épreuve des elections legislatives', *Les Cahiers de l'Orient*, no. 23 (1991)

—'Le FIS: est-il enterré?', *Esprit*, no. 6 (1993)

—'L'armée et les Islamistes: le compromis impossible?', *Esprit* (January 1995)

—'Discourses and strategy of the Algerian Islamist Movement (1986–

1992)' in Laura Guazzone, *The Islamist Dilemma: The Political Role of Islamist Movements in the Contemporary Arab World*, Reading, Ithaca Press, 1995

Rouzeik, Fawzi. 'Algérie 1990–1993: la démocratie confisquée?' in Pierre Robert Baduel, *L'Algérie incertaine*, Paris, Edisud, 1994

Roy, Olivier. *The Failure of Political Islam*, London, I.B. Tauris, 1994

Ruedy, John. *Modern Algeria: The Origins and Development of a Nation*, Indianapolis, Indiana University Press, 1992

Rummel, Lynette. 'Privatization and democratization in Algeria' in John P. Entelis and Phillip C. Naylor, *State and Society in Algeria*, Boulder, Colorado, Westview Press, 1992

Said, Khalifa. 'Le RCD' in *Reporters sans frontières: le drame algérien*, Paris, La Découverte, 1994

Samai-Ouramdane, Ghania. 'Le Front Islamique du Salut à travers son organe de presse (Al Munqid)', *Peuples Méditerranéens*, no. 52–3: *Algérie: vers l'état islamique?* (Juillet–Septembre 1990)

Schemm, Paul. 'Hope for Algeria?', *Middle East Insight* (September–October 1994)

Sivers, Peter von: 'National integration and traditional rural organisation in Algeria 1970–80: background for Islamic traditionalism?' in Said Amir Arjomand, *From Nationalism to Revolutionary Islam*, London, Macmillan, 1984

Stora, Benjamin. 'Le FIS: à la recherche d'une autre nation', *Les Cahiers de l'Orient*, no. 23, 1991

Sutton, Keith, Ahmed Aghrout and Salah Zaimche. 'Political changes in Algeria: an emerging electoral geography', *Maghreb Review*, vol. 17, no. 1 and 2 (1992)

—and Ahmed Aghrout. 'Multiparty elections in Algeria: problems and prospects', *Bulletin of Francophone Africa*, no. 2 (Autumn 1992)

Taheri, Amir. *Holy Terror: The Inside Story of Islamic Terrorism*, London, Hutchinson, 1987

Tessler, Mark. 'Alienation of urban youth' in I. William Zartman and William Mark Habeeb, *Polity and Society in Contemporary North Africa*, Boulder, Colorado, Westview Press, 1993

Tlemcani, Rachid. *State and Revolution in Algeria*, London, Zed, 1986

—'Chadli's Perestroika', *Middle East Report* (March–April 1990)

Tozy, Mohammed. 'Islam and the state' in I. William Zartman and

William Mark Habeeb, *Polity and Society in Contemporary North Africa*, Boulder, Colorado, Westview Press, 1993

Vallin, Raymond. 'Muslim socialism in Algeria' in I. William Zartman, *Man, State and Society in the Contemporary Maghreb*, London, Pall Mall Press, 1973

Vandewalle, Dirk. 'Breaking with socialism: economic liberalization in Algeria' in Iliya Harik and Denis J. Sullivan, *Privatization and Liberalization in the Middle East*, Indianapolis, Indiana University Press, 1992

Vatin, Jean-Claude. 'Religious resistance and state power in Algeria' in Alexander S. Cudsi and Ali E. Hillal Dessouki (eds.), *Islam and Power*, London, Croom Helm, 1981

—'Popular puritanism versus state reformism: Islam in Algeria' in James P. Piscatori, *Islam in the Political Process*, Cambridge, Cambridge University Press, 1983

Waltz, Susan. 'Islamist appeal in Tunisia', *Middle East Journal*, vol. 40, no. 4 (1986)

Willis, Michael: 'Algeria's troubled road to political and economic liberalization' in Gerd Nonneman, *Political and Economic Liberalization: Dynamics and Linkages in Comparative Perspective*, London, Lynne Rienner, 1996

Wright, Robin. *Sacred Rage: The Wrath of Militant Islam*, London, André Deutsch, 1986

Yacine, Rachida. 'The impact of French colonial heritage on language policies in independent North Africa' in George Joffé, *North Africa: Nation, State and Region*, London, Routledge, 1993

Yefsah, Abdelkader. 'Armée et politique depuis les evénements d'Octobre 88: l'armée sans hidjab', *Les temps modernes: Algérie: La guerre des frères*, no. 580 (Janvier–Février 1995)

Zoubir, Yahia: 'The painful transition from authoritarianism in Algeria', *Arab Studies Quarterly*, vol. 15, no. 3 (Summer 1993)

Newspapers and Journals

Algeria

Alger Républicain
Algérie Actualité
Horizons
Le Jeudi d'Algérie

Liberté
Le Matin
El Moudjahid
La Nation

Révolution Africaine
Le Soir d'Algérie
La Tribune
El Watan

Britain

The Daily Telegraph
The Economist
The European
The Financial Times
The Guardian
The Independent

The Middle East
Middle East Economic
Digest MEED
Middle East
International MEI
Mideast Mirror

The Observer
The Sunday Times
The Tablet
The Times
Trade Finance

France

L'Express
Le Figaro
L'Humanité
Jeune Afrique

Libération
Le Monde
Le Monde Diplomatique
Nouvel Obsevateur

Le Point
Le Quotidien de Paris

Others

L'Opinion (Morocco)
La Presse (Tunisia)
Le Temps (Tunisia)
Time (USA)
New York Times (USA)

Documents

Algerian National Charter 1976, Ministry of Culture and Information
(1981 Edition)
Interview with Rabah Kebir, unclassified FCO document
FIS, communiqués and statements
Plate-forme pour une Solution Politique et Pacifique de la Crise Algérienne,
Community of St Egidio, Rome, 13.1.95

Text of Speech by Abdallah Djaballah to Nahda (MNI) Party conference, Sanoba Club, 7–9.9.94 (In Arabic)

Other Sources
Amnesty International Reports
Associated Press Reports
BBC African World Service News
Economist Intelligence Unit (EIU) Quarterly Reports
Liberty (Friends for Democracy in Algeria Campaign): *The Story of Democracy in Algeria*, 11.1.93
Middle East Watch: *Human Rights in Algeria: No One is Spared,* January 1994
Reuters Reports
Summary of World Broadcasts (SWB)

Journals Published by the FIS in Exile
La Cause (Tribune des élus du Front Islamique du Salut)
Echoes of Truth

Index

DATE DUE